BUTCH CASSIDY

A Biography

Richard Patterson

University of Nebraska Press
Lincoln and London

⊗ The paper in this book meets the minimum
requirements of American National Standard
for Information Sciences—Permanence of Paper for Printed Library Materials, ANSI
Z39.48-1984.
Library of Congress Cataloging-in-Publication Data
Patterson, Richard M., 1934–
Butch Cassidy: a biography / Richard
Patterson.
p. cm.
Includes bibliographical references (p.   )
and index.
ISBN 0-9 65-87 868
1. Cassidy, Butch, b. 1866.   2. Outlaws—
West (U.S.)—Biography.   3. West (U.S.)—
Biography.   4. West (U.S.)—History—
1860–1890.   5. West (U.S.)—History—
1890–1945.   I. Title.
F595.C362P38   1999
978'.02'092—dc21
[B]
98-15765   CIP

To Wynonia, with love

CONTENTS

ILLUSTRATIONS

PREFACE

Biographies of outlaws are unlike those of most law-abiding individuals. Outlaws did not keep diaries, and they wrote few letters. Most rode under aliases, kept on the move, and tried not to leave a trail. An outlaw's story is usually a story of what a man did—or, rather, what others believe he did—and not who he really was.

With Robert LeRoy Parker, alias Butch Cassidy, we are fortunate: we have more than just glimpses of his life. While we would like to know more, from what we do know it appears that there was a certain consistency to the man, a thread suggesting that, except for the path he chose, Butch was respected by most who knew him—by some, even admired. An old timer once summed it up this way: "I wouldn't want to have been in the teller's cage when he came through the door of a bank, but if I ever met him in a saloon, I sure would have bought him a drink."

If it were not for his determination to defy the law, it would be difficult to fault Butch Cassidy's way of life. In his own way he had high standards, but he applied them selectively and not to society in general.

Born to a caring Mormon family, Butch was typical of the restless youth of southern Utah in the 1880s. He was fond of anything that could be accomplished from a saddle, yet most everything else in his life bored him. He seemed to have appreciated the church and the Mormon tradition, but he failed to see how they fit into his plans. He loved his family, but yearned to strike out on his own, which he did as soon as he learned what could be achieved with a rope and running iron.

He had a special way with horses; they would become his life: stealing them, raising them, racing them, and selling them—and eventually escaping on them with other people's money.

Quick-witted and good-humored, he was bright but not complex. His tastes were simple and his desires not unreasonable. He enjoyed a good time on the town, including an audacious prank now and then. Also, he probably engaged in a little too much gambling, a vice at which he was not too skilled, but, unlike most of his pals, he seldom drank to excess.

Despite rumors to the contrary, Butch probably never married—at least no records have been found—but he welcomed the company of women and seldom was without their companionship, even when in hiding. But women came and went. He once admitted that he could be foolish when it came to relationships. Some women found him courtly, but he was no prude. When a companion for the night came only at a price, he was a willing buyer.

He was, of course, a criminal, but he was not a killer. While some who rode with him did kill, there are those who believe that Butch intentionally avoided taking a life. This may have been true, except perhaps at the very end. About that we are still not sure.

Early in his career Butch did almost kill a man to avoid capture, but fate allowed him to miss, and, as a result, he went to prison for the price of a stolen horse, not a man's life. He was still in his twenties when he was sentenced to the penitentiary, and he probably was, as the criminal justice experts say, still salvageable at the time. He served his time, and upon his release he could have made a fresh start, but he had little intention of doing so. When a friend needed money and asked for help, Butch came to his aid by robbing a bank. His motive may have been admirable, but his act was not, and he was a reestablished outlaw.

Apologists, including some Wild Bunch writers, theorize that many western outlaws robbed out of grievances against greedy corporations and ruthless money interests. But Butch and his pals robbed banks and express cars for the treasures they held. Prison had made Butch cautious, and he was too careful to let vindication cloud his judgment.

In time Butch and his gang became too good at what they did, and the law began to crowd them. When Butch saw it closing in, he called it quits. He tried to go straight, but it was not in the cards. Eventually more holdups came. Then one day he was gone, and the facts become murky. Did he die, or was he just in hiding again? We're not sure—and that's part of the story.

ACKNOWLEDGMENTS

It does not seem enough to say, as most writers do, that without the help of many people this book would have never been written. But of course it is true.

At the top of the list have to be Dan Buck and Anne Meadows, whose work I have relied upon shamelessly in chronicling Butch's, Longabaugh's, and Etta's days in South America. Over the past decade, Dan and Anne have so graciously shared their research with their fellow Wild Bunch writers that few of us will ever be able to repay them in kind. And special thanks go to Dan, who took valuable time from his busy schedule to critique this manuscript.

Close behind Dan and Anne is Jim Dullenty, the former Spokane, Washington, reporter who unearthed the enigmatic William T. Phillips and the even more puzzling manuscript "The Bandit Invincible." Jim has been seriously researching Butch Cassidy and the Wild Bunch longer than anyone else and is a storehouse of knowledge on Butch (as my phone bills will attest). His Rocky Mountain House Books in Hamilton, Montana, is probably the best source of published material on Wild Bunch history one can find. Jim also deserves a special thanks for his critical review of this work.

Others who have helped me along the way include Carol Barber, Wyoming State Archives, Cheyenne, Wyoming; Chris Beesley, BYU Press, Provo, Utah; Darrel and Janet Blevins, Red Lodge, Montana; Garland Branch, Charlottesville, Virginia; Janell Brimhall, Utah State Historical Society, Salt Lake City, Utah; Doris Karren Burton, The Outlaw Trail History Association and Center, Vernal, Utah; Dan Davis, American Heritage Center, University of Wyoming, Laramie, Wyoming; La Tonya Harris, Editorial Department, *The Elks Magazine*, Chicago, Illinois; Joy Horton, The Outlaw Trail History Association and Center, Vernal, Utah; Elizabeth Hughes, White Plains Public Library, White Plains, New York; Michael R.

Kelsey and Venetta B. Kelsey, Provo, Utah; Ruth Knight, Charlottesville, Virginia; Robin Machado, Wilkinson Public Library, Telluride, Colorado; Candy Moulton, Encampment, Wyoming; Roy O'Dell, Cambridge, England; Kent Powell, Utah State Historical Society, Salt Lake City, Utah; and Bob Rybolt, Little Bat's Trading Post, Crawford, Nebraska.

I would also like to thank members of the staffs at the American Heritage Center, University of Wyoming, Laramie, Wyoming; Bear Lake County Library, Montpelier, Idaho; Beaver County Public Library, Beaver, Utah; Boise Public Library, Boise, Idaho; Carbon County Public Library, Rawlins, Wyoming; College of Eastern Utah, Price, Utah; Daughters of Utah Pioneers, Salt Lake City, Utah; Fremont County Library, Lander, Wyoming; Grand County Library, Moab, Utah; Humboldt County Library, Winnemucca, Nevada; Idaho State Library, Boise, Idaho; *Idaho Statesman*, Boise, Idaho; Indianapolis-Marion County Public Library, Indianapolis, Indiana; I.U.P.U. Library, Indianapolis, Indiana; *Moab Times-Independent*, Moab, Utah; New Mexico State Library, Santa Fe, New Mexico; Phillips County Public Library, Malta, Montana; Purdue University Libraries, Lafayette, Indiana; *Rawlins Daily Times*, Rawlins, Wyoming; San Juan County Library, Monticello, Utah; Rock Springs Public Library, Rock Springs, Wyoming; Sweetwater County Library, Green River, Wyoming; *Telluride Times Journal*, Telluride, Colorado; Utah State Historical Society, Salt Lake City, Utah; Utah State University, Logan, Utah; Uinta County Library, Evanston, Wyoming; Union Pacific Railroad Museum, Omaha, Nebraska; Weber County Library, Odgen, Utah; Wyoming State Archives, Cheyenne, Wyoming; and Wyoming State Law Library, Cheyenne, Wyoming.

Special thanks go to several individuals who spent anywhere from a few moments to a few hours taking extra steps to help make this a better book. One who immediately comes to mind is John Wirth of Dubois, Wyoming, who graciously responded to my search for somebody familiar with the site of Butch's and Al Hainer's cabin on Horse Creek. John didn't know of it himself, but he knew who did—local historian Mary Allison, who so readily shared that information with me and much more.

Another big help was Jordan Austin of Telluride, who documented the true site of Butch's first bank robbery, thereby correcting an error that has circulated among Wild Bunch writers for many years.

Then there is Lois Archuleta, reference librarian of the periodicals department of The Salt Lake City Public Library who tirelessly sorted through back issues of the *Salt Lake City Tribune*. Lois finally resolved, to my satisfaction, that an article cited by Charles Kelly never made the archives and maybe never even saw the light of day. And there is David Lewis of Indianapolis, an old friend who, remembering my interest in Cassidy, took time to track me down and alert me to an article by a Wyoming geologist whose father knew Butch, a source that I would never otherwise have discovered.

Last is my wife, Wynonia, who provides love and encouragement, and who seems to acquire more patience with each book—or at least she lets me think so.

CIRCLE VALLEY

1879–1884

It was something nearly every Mormon mother dreaded, yet knew full well that someday she might have to face. For Bob Parker's mother, it was especially difficult—he was her firstborn and he was leaving home. But he was now eighteen, not yet a man in her eyes but surely old enough to be one.

Bob had not prepared for the trip, that was plain. She could see that he needed something for the trail, a bedroll or something, because the nights could still get cold if he was heading for the high country. She went to the bedroom and returned with the blue woolen blanket. Also, he had not thought about food, so she hurried to the kitchen and found some cheese, some raisins, some fresh bread, and something he really favored: a jar of bullberry preserves.

Bob watched silently as his mother wrapped the provisions in a cloth and put them in the blanket, making a narrow, tight roll that he could tie behind his saddle. As a final thought, she may have slipped in one of the family's worn, leather-bound copies of *The Book of Mormon*. It would have been like her to do so, and to ask her son to promise that every day, if he had time, he would try to read a passage or two.[1]

Outside, Bob's mare, Babe, and his colt, Cornish, waited patiently, perhaps somehow anticipating that this was to be a special day. The family dog, Dash, sniffed and panted, eager to share in whatever was breaking the Parker family's early morning routine. Bob knew that Dash would try to follow and that he would have to put him on a rope until he had gone.

After tying up Dash, there was nothing left to do but leave. Bob swung up and turned Babe toward the road, trailing Cornish behind on a long lead. His mother held Dash's rope and watched as Bob clicked Babe to a trot, kicking up dust as he skirted the four young Lombardy poplars that he and his mother had planted one day when his father was off working at

Silver Reef or Frisco or somewhere. It was a tradition—Mormons planted Lombardy poplars wherever they settled. It made Mormon country something special and distinctive. Lombardys were kind of like her son—they grew boldly and fast without much tending.

Dash lunged, straining at the rope, but she held it tightly, watching her son grow smaller in the distance. He turned once more and waved, and then he was gone.[2]

According to Utah rancher Patrick Ryan, who first hired Robert LeRoy Parker in 1879 as a hand when the boy was only thirteen, the husky lad could already do a man's work around a ranch. Although Ryan thought young Bob was a little impatient with the horses, he was otherwise quiet and inoffensive.[3] He found the boy smart and dependable, but most of all, Bob's family desperately needed the money he could earn at Ryan's. Ryan and Bob got along well, and the rancher regretted to see him leave a little over two years later when Bob found work with ranchers closer to his home.[4]

Bob's parents, Maximillian and Ann Gillies Parker, had moved their brood of then six children from Beaver, Utah, to near Circleville the year Bob turned thirteen. At the time, the town of Circleville was hardly more than a few stores and a schoolhouse, snugly nestled near the confluence of Cottonwood Creek and the Sevier River in what is now southern Piute County. The Parker property, 160 acres, which Maximillian bought from a homesteader named James, lay three miles south of town at the mouth of Circleville Canyon, at the southern edge of Circle Valley, which was then a dale of hardworking Mormons struggling to make a living from crops and cattle on parched Utah land badly in need of irrigation.[5]

The elder Parker had been born in Lancashire, England, where Bob's grandfather was a weaver in a textile mill. When Maximillian was nine, missionaries converted the family to the Church of Jesus Christ of Latter-Day Saints during a Mormon sweep through England and Europe in a search of artisans and craftsmen who would agree to come to America and enrich the Valley of the Great Salt Lake. In 1856, when Maximillian was twelve, his parents agreed to take on the American adventure. After a perilous trek across the plains with one of the first Mormon handcart companies, the Parkers eventually settled in Beaver, Utah, where Maximillian's father was called to work in the local woolen mill.[6]

Ann Gillies's family, who were Scottish, were also converted to the Mormon church in England and, like the Parkers, came to Utah with one of the handcart companies. Maximillian and Ann met sometime in the early

1860s and were married in 1865. Robert LeRoy, their first child, was born on April 13 the following year.[7]

During their early years of marriage, Maximillian carried the mail on horseback from Beaver south to Panguitch along the Sevier River. During those runs, his route took him through Circle Valley. It was rough country and still only sparsely settled, but the few homesteaders there were friendly and honest people. Someday, Maximillian thought, it might be a good place to raise a family. For Maximillian, that day came in the spring of 1879, when he and Ann packed up the children and what little they had accumulated in fourteen years of marriage and headed south.[8]

The Parkers squeezed the children into a two-room log cabin the former owner had built at the base of a small hill. That first year Max, as he soon was to be called by his neighbors, cleared enough brush away to plant a crop of summer wheat. But soon after the planting, ruthless winds destroyed his efforts. Max planted a second crop, and it, too, was blown away by the dry gusts that often roared in from the west over the northern edge of the aptly named Hurricane Cliffs. When Max's second planting was destroyed, only a few days were left before the summer sun would end any chance of a growing season, but this time the winds eased off and the seeds took root.[9]

With the wheat in the ground, Max went off to look for work and left Ann and the children to attend to the Circle Valley ranch. Most of his jobs consisted of temporary employment with mining companies. The 1880s were an erratic period of Utah mining—promising strikes, overnight boom towns, but then precipitous busts.[10] One of Max's first jobs was cutting and hauling wood at the Silver Reef Mine in the Pine Valley Mountains northeast of St. George.[11] The mine was nearly 100 miles from Circle Valley, which permitted Max only an occasional Sunday at home. Also, Silver Reef, a non-Mormon town created by the mining company, was tough and violent, and soon became famous for drunken brawls and killings. But for the most part, the Mormons who came there to work were treated with respect by the gentiles, and the pay was better than average.[12]

When the Silver Reef job played out, Max found similar work in the San Francisco mountains at Frisco, a silver camp sixteen miles west of Milford.[13] New York financier Jay Cooke was building a leg of the Utah Southern Railroad at Frisco to reach a mine at Squaw Springs, which he had recently added to his investments.[14] At Frisco, Max was again a long way from home, but he was not far from Hay Springs where Bob was helping out at Pat Ryan's ranch. For a while Max also worked in Pioche, Nevada, where he hauled wood for charcoal burners.[15]

With Max's income, plus the pay Bob brought home from Ryan's, that fall the Parkers were able to buy a few cattle. But then came the winter of 1879, one of the worst to strike southern Utah in a decade, and all but two head of the Parker herd were wiped out.[16]

The loss of the cattle set the family back, and their luck was slow to improve. Also, there were more mouths to feed: the Parkers now had seven children, four boys and three girls, and there would be more—in all fourteen.[17] Large families were common among the Mormon families, especially in southern Utah. Not only were they important to rural families in drawing a livelihood from the land, church doctrine proclaimed that it was virtuous to bring waiting souls into the world and that a woman's highest glory was to give birth to many children. Furthermore, it was taught that a man's family went with him to the Hereafter, and that his glory in Heaven would be dependent in part on the progeny that he could gather about him there.[18]

In an effort to make ends meet, Max attempted to homestead a second parcel of land, but his claim was challenged by another settler. The dispute ended up in the hands of the local Mormon bishop who, in the absence of the civil law and in accordance with church custom, mediated the matter. The outcome was not favorable to the Parkers. While Ann Parker was a devout member of the Latter-Day Saints and attempted to raise the children according to Mormon precepts, her husband had wavered at times. Moreover, he had a poor attendance record at services. Also, long before then Max Parker had taken up smoking, which was against Mormon teachings and seriously frowned upon by the local congregation. When the bishop decided against him on the homestead claim, Max was furious, convinced that the bishop had punished him for his slackened attitude toward the teachings of the Saints instead of judging the dispute on its merits.[19]

The bishop may have been prejudiced against Max, but it may not have been for the reasons Max believed. In the bishop's opinion, Max may have been becoming too acquisitive. Max already owned 160 acres, which was not a small parcel of land for a Circle Valley family at the time. By Mormon tradition, farming in the early 1880s was still small scale. The bishop may have only been following the dictates of Brigham Young, who had insisted that no man should own more land than he could personally cultivate.[20]

The Parker family struggled on and things got a little better. Ann found work with a neighboring rancher, Jim Marshall, operating his small dairy, and Marshall also offered to take on young Bob as a hand, which worked out better for the boy. The Marshall ranch, located in what is now the northern edge of the Dixie National Forest, was much closer to the Parker home than Pat Ryan's ranch, which was almost a day's ride from Circle Valley. Working at Marshall's meant young Bob could live at home.[21]

Ann Parker probably was eager to have young Bob back within the fold. While working for rancher Patrick Ryan, the boy had run into trouble with the law. One day Bob rode into town to buy a pair of badly needed overalls. Finding the general store closed, he was no doubt irritated. He had taken time off from work and it appeared that he had made the long, dusty ride for nothing. So when he found a way to gain entry to the building, he thoughtlessly let himself in. He searched the shelves and located the pair of overalls he wanted and hastily scratched out a note to the store owner, leaving his name and promising that he would return later and pay up. But when the owner opened the store the following morning and found the note, Bob's ad hoc arrangement did not set well with him and he complained to the town marshal. The matter was eventually settled, but not without embarrassment to Bob and his family.[22]

Then there was another incident. According to Parley P. Christensen, who served thirty years as sheriff of Juab County, Utah, Bob was also arrested for stealing a saddle. The arrest supposedly occurred in what is now Garfield County, probably sometime between 1879 and 1884. No record of the charges made in this matter have been found, but Christensen claimed that while in custody, Bob had been mistreated by the authorities.[23]

Those who put emphasis on such things might suggest that the trousers incident, the mistreatment by the Garfield authorities, and the impact on the family of the Mormon bishop's biased decision in the dispute over Max Parker's homestead claim all left a strong impression on young Bob that justice was not always rendered fairly, and that perhaps these occurrences may have been largely responsible for Bob's decision in later years to formulate his own rules as to what was right and wrong.[24]

Despite young Bob Parker's difficulties with the law, he was not an unruly youngster at home—although he would have been considered headstrong for a Mormon youth, as perhaps were his brothers. While Ann tried to raise the children in the church, according to Lula Parker Betenson, Bob's sister, most of her brothers followed their father's example and sidestepped its strict covenants when possible. Even before moving to Circleville, while living in Beaver, Bob would find endless excuses not to go to services, and eventually his mother gave up trying to force him to go.[25]

At the ranch in Circle Valley, however, the Parkers did observe the traditional Mormon family weekly "home evenings," the purpose of which was to bind the family together by promoting religion, education, and recreation in informal gatherings. The typical home evening usually began with a prayer, preferably having something to do with the sanctity of the home. The family usually sang hymns next, often followed by recitations or songs by the children. In many homes the father would give a short talk on a topic illustrating a point of faith or morals, or on something emphasizing the importance of children accepting responsibility. This lesson would frequently be followed by games (often charades), and then more singing. The evening would usually end around nine or so with more prayers or hymns.[26] Lula Betenson recalled that Bob willingly participated in these gatherings and joined in the musical parts by playing the harmonica.[27]

Ann Parker's work running the dairy at the Marshall ranch kept the family in milk, cheese, and butter, and brought in needed extra income, but the early morning eight-mile ride to Marshall's was a problem. After discussing the matter with Jim Marshall, Ann decided that the practical thing to do was to move to the ranch, at least during the summer months, so she could get an early start on her daily duties. Bob was already working for Marshall as a hand, and Marshall agreed to hire two of Bob's younger brothers to help their mother with the dairy, and let all four Parkers live in a small house on the property. As one would expect, Max Parker was not exactly enthusiastic about this idea, but he finally conceded that his daughters could keep house for him and that the extra money was worth whatever inconvenience the arrangement would create. With Max's reluctant approval, Ann and the three boys moved to the Marshall ranch in the summer of either 1881 or 1882.[28]

Beginning perhaps as early as 1883, Bob Parker again defied the law, but this time it was with the consent of his family.

A unique aspect of social life in early Mormon Utah was the church-sponsored practice of plural marriage, begun secretly by the Mormons before their migration west. In 1852, polygamy was publicly announced and officially defended by the church leaders as a religious principle. The practice, however, was not widespread, and some Mormon men refused to engage in it because of personal feelings or because they could not afford it. Also, the church wisely required that, before seeking additional wives, a man obtain permission from his first wife. Among church leaders, however, the practice was fairly common.[29]

Polygamy, however, was against federal law. In 1882, Congress passed the Edmunds Act, which declared the practice a felony punishable by up to five years' imprisonment and/or a $500 fine. Aimed specifically at Utah, then still a territory, the law also disfranchised polygamists and rendered them ineligible for public office and even jury service. Polygamous Mormons adopted various measures to elude federal officers, including constructing ingenious hiding places in their homes and on their lands. In rural southern Utah they frequently escaped into hideouts in nearby canyons or were harbored by friends and neighbors until the marshals moved on. Polygamists' "underground railroads" also were developed throughout the territory, with highly successful communication systems complete with secret codes and warning devices.[30]

It is believed by some that the Parker family assisted in operating a branch of one of these underground railroads, temporarily concealing fleeing "polygs" and arranging for their eventual escape into Mexico. According to Utah writer Kerry Ross Boren—whose great-grandfather was supposed to have made use of the escape route through Circle Valley—young Bob Parker played an integral part in this operation.[31]

Ann Parker and her sons had been boarding at the Marshall ranch for about two years when owner Jim Marshall hired a new hand by the name of Mike Cassidy. Although only a few years older than Bob Parker, Cassidy probably had been drifting from ranch to ranch for some time and was an experienced horse wrangler and a skilled livestock handler. He and Bob immediately struck up a friendship, much to the dismay of Bob's mother, who saw in Cassidy a hardened cowboy who had been put on his own too early and no doubt had acquired vices that she did not want to see in her son. Bob, on the other hand, saw in Mike the man he wanted to be—unrestrained and free to drift in any direction.[32]

As suspicious as she was, even Ann Parker may have underestimated Mike Cassidy. By the time Cassidy signed on at the Marshall ranch he probably was already well-experienced at stealing livestock.[33] Rustling was an ongoing problem in and around Circle Valley, especially the picking off of mavericks (unbranded calves separated from their mothers) which would be whisked away from the herd as soon as they could feed on their own.[34] Worse still, when ranch owner Jim Marshall was not around, Mike Cassidy and his pals were probably bringing strays back to the ranch and rebranding them right there in Marshall's corral—and young Bob was probably helping in the task.[35] But as Bob's sister later commented, their mother accepted the fact that her responsibility ended at the dairy barn, and she could do little about what occurred on other parts of the Marshall ranch. But it was especially difficult for her when Cassidy went so far as to give her son a six-gun and teach him how to use it.[36]

Ann knew that lecturing Bob would do no good—he was old enough to do what he pleased—but she felt that it might help if she could put some distance between him and Mike Cassidy. In April of 1884 she moved back to the Parker ranch in Circle Valley, in the hope that Bob would follow. But it was not to be.[37] In June, Bob announced that he would be leaving Circle Valley and probably Utah. When Ann asked where he was going, her son said that he was not sure, maybe to Colorado to work in the mines in the mountains above Telluride. His reasons were familiar words to Circle Valley families: "Ma, there's not much here for me. No future. Pay in Utah is low—you know that. Maybe twenty or thirty dollars a month with board—and the board's not much to brag about in most places. There's no excitement around here. I'm not a kid any more. Gotta be thinking about my future."[38]

When Ann reminded Bob that he was only eighteen, he answered that most of his friends of the same age were on their own and that many of them were already married. When she confided that she worried about him going off alone, he told her that he would not be alone. On hearing this, her first thought might have been that he was riding off with the despised Mike Cassidy, but it was rumored that Cassidy had already left Jim Marshall's ranch. No, it would not be Mike Cassidy; Bob said that his friend, Eli Elder, would be going with him.[39]

Mike Cassidy had in fact already left the Marshall ranch. More than likely his skill with a wide loop and running iron had become too well known. It was rumored that he had gone south, probably to Mexico.[40]

On the night Bob announced that he would be leaving Circle Valley, his father was working away from home and was not expected to return until the next evening. It would hurt him deeply that Bob had left without waiting to say good-bye; yet Bob knew that his father would understand his wanting to leave: the feeling of confinement, the need for adventure. In his youth Max Parker had undoubtedly experienced those feelings himself, and had done something about them. When he was no older than Bob, Maximillian Parker had guided Mormon emigration trains from St. Louis through the treacherous Rocky Mountains. When just a few years older than his son, and newly married, he was dodging Ute arrows while carrying the mail along the rugged banks of the Sevier River. And only months after that he was fighting alongside his fellow Mormons in Utah's Black Hawk War, the culmination of an ongoing dispute over the occupation of the Ute's favorite hunting grounds.[41]

Ann Parker pleaded with her son to postpone leaving for just a day, until his father returned. Although for much of his life Max Parker was away from home for weeks at a time, when he could be with his children he was a loving father. He was never ill-tempered with them, and never laid a hand on them in anger. His children had great respect for him, and when he spoke they listened.[42] But Bob was insistent about going, saying that he should have left already, and that he absolutely had to leave first thing in the morning. Though Ann may have wondered about Bob's hurry, she did not press it, nor did she question her son the next morning why he was "traveling light," without a pack animal or even a camp outfit.[43] But if Ann Parker failed to find it unusual that her son could not wait one more day to tell his father that he was leaving his house, possibly never to return, others did not. There has been much speculation, and some fact bears it out, that Bob Parker had good reason for a quick departure.

Bob Parker may have planned to work in the mines in Telluride, Colorado, as he told his mother the night before he left, but he may already have been hired to do another job: to help deliver a bunch of stolen horses to Telluride for the notorious rustler Cap Brown.

Cap Brown is believed to have drifted into southeastern Utah sometime in the 1870s, making his headquarters somewhere in the desolate Robbers' Roost area—eastern Utah's high desert country of twisting canyons that lay between the Henry Mountains to the west and the La Sal Mountains to the east. On a map, the Roost area is roughly the shape of a parallelogram: one border stretches southeastward along a line from the town of Hanksville to the place where the Dirty Devil River enters the Colorado River, another border runs northeasterly up the Colorado to the Green River, a third follows the Green for fifty miles or so northwest to the San Rafael River, and the fourth runs southwest across the San Rafael Desert back to Hanksville.[44]

Brown may not have been the first rustler to operate out of the Roost, but he was one of the most successful. Early on he found it profitable to supply horses to the mining communities of Colorado by raiding herds and capturing strays in southern Utah. At first Brown probably operated alone, but in time he cautiously recruited local wranglers in crews of three or four, mostly young cowboys eager to bolster their meager wages. One cowboy Brown recruited was probably Mike Cassidy and, in time, another was more than likely Bob Parker.[45]

Bob Parker and Cap Brown probably first met some time around 1882, chances are in the company of Mike Cassidy at the Marshall ranch, where Brown often stayed overnight during forays after horses into Circle Valley and around the northern edge of what is now Dixie National Forest.[46] Alternately, they may have met the following year when Bob was working as a cowhand for Charlie Gibbons of Hanksville, on a ranch Gibbons owned near the Henry Mountains in partnership with a local doctor-turned-cattleman, J. K. W. Bracken.[47]

According to old-timers who frequented Robbers' Roost, in the spring of 1884, at Mike Cassidy's recommendation, Bob had been hired to pick up around twenty horses from two of Cap's men in Kingston Canyon (about six miles east of Circleville), and, after a brief instruction on trail-breaking a herd of that size, lead them along the Dirty Devil River to near Hanksville, where Brown had a shack in Bull Valley. From there Brown was to guide Bob and the herd eastward across the cedar ridges and parched swales of Roost country, giving them a start toward the San Rafael Desert. Brown would eventually turn back and leave Bob to take the herd alone across the Green River and on to Moab, where Bob would cross the Colorado River at Taylors' ferry, if the river was up, then skirt the La Sal Mountains to the north and finally head southeast down the Dolores and San Miguel river valleys to Telluride.[48]

Bob Parker may have been in a hurry to leave Circle Valley to avoid being late for his rendezvous with Cap Brown's pals in Kingston Canyon, or there may have been another reason. According to Matt Warner, who later rode with Bob and joined him in robbing the San Miguel Valley Bank at Telluride in 1889, Bob told him that he had fled Circle Valley that day because he himself had stolen some horses from a neighbor, Jim Kittleman.[49]

A version of this incident that has survived the years, and which probably has enjoyed some elaboration, tells of Bob being pursued by two lawmen, probably deputy marshals, who tracked him down and caught him with Kittleman's missing animals. Bob offered no resistance, but to play it safe the officers handcuffed him before placing him in his saddle for the trip back to Circleville, nearly a full day's ride. Around noon the men decided to stop for a rest and a bite to eat. While one deputy built a fire, the other went to a nearby creek for water for coffee. Seeing his chance, Bob sneaked up on the deputy by the fire and grabbed his gun. Catching the other man by surprise when he returned from the creek, Bob also disarmed him, took his keys, and unlocked the handcuffs. In less than a minute Bob was mounted up and on his way, leading the stolen ponies and the lawmen's horses. But after riding only a short distance Bob noticed that the lawmen's canteens were still tied to their saddles: he had left them without water for the long walk back to town. Bob turned around and rode back, tossed them their canteens, and bid them good-bye once more.[50]

Whether or not this story is true, Kittleman did lose some horses, apparently finding them missing shortly after Bob had left Circle Valley, and Bob was a suspect. However, Lula Parker Betenson vehemently denied that her brother would have taken them. According to Lula, "Bob would as soon have stolen from his own father as from Jim Kittleman," a close friend.

Lula never denied that her brother eventually became an outlaw, but she sternly insisted that he would never have stolen from Kittleman, that one of Bob's "most outstanding virtues was his loyalty to friends and family." Lula acknowledged that Bob had ridden west to Kingston Canyon on leaving Circle Valley that day, but she declared it was not to meet with rustlers. She said that, as he had told his mother, he met his friend, Eli Elder, who was to join him and ride to Telluride to look for work.[51]

The Kittleman incident was not the only cloud under which Bob left Circle Valley that June. The day after his departure, Max Parker was in Circleville and heard gossip that two local boys, whom thus far history has identified only as Charley and Fred, were suspected of stealing cattle. When confronted, the boys, both friends of Bob, produced a bill of sale bearing the name Robert LeRoy Parker, thus suggesting that Bob had owned the cattle and had sold them to the two suspects. Furious, Max sought out the town constable, James Wiley, for an explanation. Wiley's response only angered Max further: the constable more or less admitted that Bob had probably signed the bill of sale simply to help his friends. Wiley's answer was that Bob could afford to take the blame since he was already leaving Circle Valley, while Charley and Fred, both of whom were married, were not in a position to leave. Also, since the cattle had been found and returned to the owners, Wiley apparently intended to drop any charges against Bob. When Max argued that even if the charges were dropped his son could no longer hold his head up in the community, Wiley reminded him that if he insisted on making trouble the issue probably would end up with the local LDS bishop, and Max's record with the bishop was not too good, so why didn't he just drop the matter. There was no way to find Bob and have him return and defend himself, so Max accepted Wiley's advice.[52]

Telluride

1884–1889

Good horses were in demand in Telluride that spring. The town was booming: surrounded by generous gold and silver deposits, Telluride was caught up in the fever for ore that was gripping much of western and central Colorado. Although the fever would occasionally spread into southeastern Utah and cause spurts of excitement as far west as Circle Valley, hopes for rich deposits in the canyon country were never realized. On the La Sal and the Blue Mountains and along the San Juan River, wistful prospectors would stake out claims and pick and pan, but they usually came up with little to show for their efforts. A rush of sorts arose when a prospecting recluse, Cass Hite, leaked information that gold was found in the gravel banks of the Colorado River. Newspapers picked up the story and hundreds of gold seekers invaded Glen Canyon and the nearby mountains, but they found little gold.[1]

Though there was always a lot of talk, the search for gold drew only a few ranchers from Circle Valley. Brigham Young had discouraged his followers from prospecting for precious metals and instead urged the development of iron, lead, and coal mining.[2] However, when times were hard and work was scarce, the men of Circle Valley did consider giving Telluride a try; Bob Parker's father and brother would eventually join these ranks.[3] But not everyone headed for Telluride to earn a living—since it was a boom town, Telluride naturally had other attractions. One Utah cowboy, apparently thinking he had wandered into Sodom by mistake, recalled being overwhelmed by the "saloons, gambling dives, dance halls, and board sidewalks, where thousands of strange, crazy people . . . pulled amazing scads of money out of their pockets and tried to gamble it off or throw it away on drinks and dance hall girls as fast as they could, and who tricked, robbed, shot, and stabbed each other to an amazing extent."[4]

Telluride lies in a steep-walled, flat-bottomed gorge called San Miguel

Park. In almost any other state the area would be called a valley, but in Colorado, valleys are known as parks. San Miguel Park is roughly six miles long and the main fork of the gravel-laden San Miguel River winds through its center, from east to west. Telluride lies at the east end of the gorge, below the beginnings of the river, which is formed above by streams that drain Blue Lake and Ajax Peak. Near the western end of the park the land drops off sharply, plunging the San Miguel into a cascade of foam past Keystone Hill and Skunk Creek toward a junction with the river's south fork.

The first mining claims around Telluride were filed in the mid-1870s. Although the most promising lodes were located at 11,000 feet or above (where snow limited operations to five or six months a year), by the 1880s placer-mining companies were sliding enough gravel down chutes to the San Miguel and its tributaries that the area was being touted as one of the most up-and-coming mining districts in the state.[5]

When founded, the town of Telluride was called Columbia, and it carried that name on many official records well into the 1880s. But when application for incorporation was made in 1878, the Post Office Department in Washington DC rejected the name because there was already a Columbia, California. The postal authorities believed that, with the state abbreviations then in use—"Col." and "Cal."—the risk of misdirected mail was too great.[6] A new name was sought, and someone suggested Telluride, a name derived from the ore of tellurium, the half-metallic element related to sulfur and selenium and one of the most important elements found in combination with gold.

At the time the name seemed appropriate, and it was quickly approved. Geologists later discovered that prospectors in the area around Telluride had apparently confused telluride with pyrite (fool's gold), which looks very much like telluride. The experts now say that there has never been much telluride in the mountains surrounding the town.[7]

But there was gold and silver in the mountains, and Telluride grew rapidly. By 1880 the town boasted twenty-six buildings and more on the contractors' waiting lists. On June 21, 1881, the *Solid Muldoon*, a newspaper published in neighboring Ouray, reported that every available lot in Telluride was sold, and the bustling town could proudly claim seven saloons and a dance hall. The following September a toll road between Telluride and Ouray was completed, and telegraph wires soon followed. These wires, in turn, were connected to other mountain lines, which eventually reached all the way to Denver. This connection drew attention to the area, and in early 1883 the state legislature was persuaded to divide Ouray

County into two counties—Ouray and San Miguel—and Telluride became the seat of the new county.[8]

This was the Telluride into which eighteen-year-old Bob Parker rode sometime in late spring or early summer of 1884, a town probably more intent on becoming a solid community than its reputation suggested, but nonetheless enticing to a bucolic Mormon cowboy looking for adventure.[9]

Bob worked out a deal to pasture Babe, his horse, and Cornish, his colt, with a rancher on the San Miguel River bottom west of town. He then found a job packing ore by mule down from the mountains. The work was hard but the money was good, and now and then he was able to send money home to his family, probably with an assuring note that things were going well. In the evening after a long day on the mountain, Bob would join his coworkers at one of the saloons.

Activity slowed in the mines during the winter months, and Bob may have spent the latter part of 1884 and early 1885 elsewhere. According to one source he ventured as far north as Burnt Fork, Wyoming.[10] He also may have drifted over to western Nebraska, where he worked for the Coad Brothers Cattle Ranch on the North Platte River.[11] By early summer 1885, however, he was back in Telluride.

Cornish the colt was now nearly three years old. One evening after work, Bob took him out of the pasture to begin breaking him. Apparently this sparked an argument with the rancher who owned the pasture. Bob's sister passed on the story that the rancher coveted the fine-looking young animal and became out of sorts when Bob refused to sell it to him. There was probably more to the episode than that; Bob may have owed the rancher for board and feed during the winter, and he may have thought Bob was going take the colt without paying. Whatever the reason for the argument, Bob rode off with the colt and the rancher filed a complaint against him.

Apparently knowing that he was in for trouble, Bob left Telluride and headed northwest, probably taking the old road along the San Miguel River (now State Highway 145). He had followed this route when he first rode into Telluride, and he may have been heading back to Utah. He made it only as far as Montrose County, where he was picked up and taken to the county jail in Montrose City. When his friends back in Telluride found out where he was, they sent a wire to his family in Circle Valley.

Although once again in jail, this time Bob was not mistreated—far from it. According to his father, when he arrived at the jailhouse in Montrose he found his son sitting in his cell *with the cell door open*. When asked about it, Bob replied that the authorities knew that he would not try to escape.

"They know I haven't taken anything that wasn't mine," Bob said. "I plan to stay right here until I get my horse."[12]

Bob apparently won the argument, because he was eventually released. When he checked out of jail, his father tried to persuade him to return with him to Utah, but Bob had changed his mind. He did offer Max some hope, however, suggesting that he might come home later when he had saved more money.

Bob's family lost track of him at this point. They later heard that he had drifted up to Wyoming.[13] In 1886, a severe drought in Wyoming forced many of the large ranchers to move their herds further north.[14] Bob likely was involved in this operation. That year he may have spent some time in Miles City, Montana, and for a while he may have worked on a ranch on the Yellowstone River, across from Forsythe, Montana.[15]

Sometime in 1887 Bob returned to Telluride. While he was gone the town had continued to prosper. The county commissioners had decreed the building of a new courthouse—a handsome, two-story structure of red brick that matched the steep red slopes of the northern valley just three blocks away. The new building, trimmed in white, was proudly topped with a pyramidal tower containing a sturdy and reliable fire alarm bell. (The previous courthouse had gone up in smoke in 1886.) The commissioners had also arranged for the old jail—a sturdy stone structure of twenty by twenty feet, with slit windows in walls two feet thick and eleven feet high—to be carefully dismantled and rebuilt beside the new courthouse.[16]

How Bob earned a living during this period is not known, but apparently he could afford to spend an occasional evening enjoying the pleasures offered by the town's better saloons. It was in one of these, probably during the summer, that he made a new acquaintance: Matt Warner, a fellow cowboy from Utah not much older than Bob but with Mormon roots like his. At fourteen, Warner (whose real name was Willard Christianson) had run away from his home in Levan, Utah, after beating up on a rival in a scuffle over a girl. Young Matt was sure he had killed the boy and believed he was wanted for murder.[17] He fled Levan and never looked back. While on the run he got in with a shady bunch of wranglers and was soon making a living rustling cattle and horses.[18] When Bob and Warner met, Matt had temporarily given up stealing horses and was racing them instead.[19]

Racing horses was a Colorado tradition. Communities took great pride in local favorites, and crowds in the hundreds would come to watch the races (usually quarter- or half-mile matches on a straight track).[20] Thousands of dollars would change hands on one race. In the early 1880s, residents of Saguache, a small town in the San Luis Valley west of the Sangre De Cristo Range, got so excited over a match between a legendary flyer named Red Buck and an unknown long shot from New Mexico that they wagered over $12,000, nearly all the cash in town. When Red Buck lost, the town nearly went under.[21]

Matt Warner's horse racing operation was centered in the southwestern corner of the state, where he made the circuit of small towns looking for citizens who thought they owned horses swift enough to beat his prize mare, Betty. It was on his first trip to Telluride that he crossed paths with the future Butch Cassidy. In town to match Betty against a local horse known as the "Mulcahy colt," Matt was celebrating with a whiskey after setting up the match when he spotted a friendly looking cowboy at the bar who seemed as if he wanted to talk. The two hit it off from the start, especially after learning they were both from Utah.[22]

When Warner revealed why he had come to Telluride, Bob told him that he knew about the Mulcahy colt and warned him it was one fast horse and would probably beat his mare. Warner was not impressed, and the two cowboys, both probably well into their cups, ended up betting their entire riding outfits—horses, saddles, bridles, and spurs—on the outcome of the race.

By local custom in Telluride, an entry in a match race was allowed to select one of the judges. After Matt and Bob made their bet, Matt astounded Bob by asking him to be his judge. Warner, virtually a stranger in town, said he felt uneasy picking someone from the Telluride crowd and believed he would get a better call from a Utah cowboy.[23]

The Mulcahy colt was indeed fast, but Warner's mare was faster. After the race, Bob, true to this word, showed up carrying his saddle and tack. Warner, however, refused to accept them. Bob protested that a bet was a bet, but Warner absolutely refused. Impressed with the young man's forthrightness, Warner agreed to accept the outfit, but on one condition: that his new friend agree to join him in the horse racing business and become a full partner in setting up matches throughout Colorado for the rest of the year or until it got too cold to race. Bob liked the idea: for one thing, it certainly beat packing ore-laden mules down from the mines.[24]

In the beginning the venture was clearly a success. Matt and Bob had no trouble getting matches, and Matt's Betty was seldom beaten. Early on the two men nearly doubled their money. Most of their winnings, however, never left the town where the race was held—it was just too tempting to play the big shot after a successful day. In the words of Warner, "We threw our money away or gave it away as fast as we won it. After we had won a race . . . we would trail around to every saloon, gambling dive, and dance hall in the town and treat the whole population till the community just about had all of its money back."25

Later that summer, following a match in Cortez, Colorado, Warner recognized a dapper-looking man in the crowd. He looked to be in his mid-forties, slim and smallish, with a lean face. He apparently knew Matt, and they waved. When he came over, Warner introduced him to Bob as Tom McCarty, another former Utahan, and the husband of Matt's sister, Teenie.26

Tom McCarty's early career is sketchy. He had been a rustler for some years and perhaps much worse.27 Although he and his brother, Bill, who also rode on the wrong side of the law, had come from a well-to-do family, Tom had a special weakness for gambling, which made it easier for him to turn bad. He and Bill operated around Nephi and Manti, Utah, stealing horses, cutting cattle out of herds, and selling both to whoever would overlook doctored brands.28

Tom's favorite method of stealing cattle was to buy a few cows, maybe ten or so, and start trailing them toward a railroad siding where a shipper would be waiting for him. As he drove his little herd toward the rails, he picked up other ranchers' beef along the way. Depending on the distance he had to cover, by the time he reached the railroad his ten cows would have grown to four or five hundred head. Beef was in great demand at the time and often the shipper would not be interested in looking at brands. The shipper would pay Tom, load up promptly, and be on his way with no questions asked.29

Tom McCarty was still wanted by the law when he and Bob Parker met that day in Cortez, although he later claimed that, at the time, he was engaged in the mining business.30

Several writers have suggested that not long after McCarty and Bob Parker crossed paths, McCarty introduced Bob and Matt Warner to the art of robbing express trains. One express car was robbed that fall, but no proof has ever been uncovered that Tom, Matt, and Bob did the job. In the early morning hours of November 3, 1887, an east-bound Denver & Rio Grande passenger train was stopped by a pile of rocks on the tracks about five miles east of Grand Junction, Colorado, along a curve near the Gunnison River at a spot called Unaweep Switch. The D&RG locomotive, which sported a traditional front-end cowcatcher, probably could have plowed through the barrier, but the engineer chose not to take the chance and reached for the brakes. Three men stormed the express car, but, thanks to the stubborn express messenger who stood up to the robbers and insisted that only the stationmasters along the route knew the combination to the safe, the bandits collected only about $150 and a few pieces of registered mail.[31] Five men were in on the robbery; outlaw historian Charles Kelly believed that three of them were McCarty, Parker, and Warner.[32] However, four other men were eventually captured and all four were convicted of the crime.[33]

Tom McCarty would not have been averse to emptying an express car safe that fall, but he nonetheless accepted Matt Warner's invitation to join Matt and Bob's racing enterprise. McCarty was no stranger to racing horses, having himself ridden in matches in Cortez.[34] By now, however, word had spread that Warner's swift mare Betty had beaten nearly every horse in southwestern Colorado, and it was becoming difficult to arrange matches. Before long, after having squandered their funds and virtually run out of opponents, the three men put the venture on hold.[35]

Bob, out of money, picked up work with a rancher, Harry B. Adsit, who owned the Spectator, a huge spread located about forty miles west of Telluride. The ranch's main camp was at the base of Lone Cone Mountain, but the spread covered nearly thirty square miles and stretched from the San Miguel River south to the Dolores River. Lone Cone itself was a towering dome of over 12,000 feet, but around its base below the timber line was some of the best grazing land in the area. Adsit's cattle herds sometimes reached 5,000 head, and, in addition, he grazed range horses, mostly mavericks. He sold beef to the hungry citizens of Telluride and horses to the mining companies.[36]

As Harry Adsit told the story, Bob Parker and another young fellow (probably Matt Warner) rode up to his ranch one day in 1888 looking for work. When he saw how proficient they were at cutting out cattle and breaking broncs he hired them on the spot. Adsit recalled that Bob had "piercing eyes and a rapid-fire way of talking" and that he didn't seem to care much for liquor or cards, although "he occasionally held the candle while the boys played poker on a saddle blanket in the open." Adsit added that one night while they were camped out with the herd, he and Bob got to chatting, and Bob mentioned that someday he "would make his mark in the world." Adsit said Bob and the other fellow (Warner) worked for him for a year, then told him that they were quitting because they wanted to visit their folks back in Utah. Adsit paid them off and, as a bonus for their hard work, gave them each one of the horses they had recently broken. Bob's was a dappled-brown colt.[37]

Sometime during late winter or early spring of 1889, Bob and Warner met with McCarty in Tom's cabin near Cortez to ponder their future, which, to say the least, was rather bleak. As Warner told it, "We had spent our winnings as fast as we had made 'em, and now at McCarty's cabin we didn't have a thing to do but talk about our next move."[38]

It's possible that perhaps, at least at first, the three men contemplated legitimate, or even semilegitimate work of some kind, but their thoughts eventually turned to developing ways for riches to come more quickly. As McCarty described it: "[H]aving been quiet for so long a time, my restlessness began to annoy me. Times being now rather dull and becoming acquainted with men that had no more money than myself, we thought it time to make a raid of some sort."[39]

It's not clear just what kind of raid McCarty had in mind, but it could have been a unique endeavor to extort $21,000 from a Denver bank. On March 30, 1889, a Saturday, David Moffat, president of First National Bank of Denver, welcomed into his private office a well-dressed gentleman he assumed to be a local businessman and maybe a new customer. Moffat could not have been more wrong. In minutes, the shocked banker realized that he was dealing with what appeared to be a totally deranged man. The stranger began babbling that Moffat's bank was going to be robbed; then, to the banker's astonishment, he added "I am the man who is going to rob your bank." With that the stranger drew a revolver from his coat and began waving it about, shouting that he desperately needed money. He then withdrew a bottle from his coat and held it up with a trembling hand. Moffat saw that it contained some kind of clear liquid, but then nearly fainted when the deranged stranger announced that it was nitroglycerin and that he would blow up the place if Moffat did not follow his instructions. Moffat was to write out a check for $21,000, call in his cashier and order him to exchange it for cash. Nearly petrified, Moffat did as he was told. The cashier could see that something was wrong, but when he questioned the request, Moffat insisted; the cashier reluctantly cashed the check and returned to his duties. Moffat gave the money to the stranger who quickly left the banker's office. As he was leaving the lobby, the man is believed to have passed the loot to a confederate standing by the door. Both men then left the building, walking in opposite directions.[40]

Local sources attributed the crime to Tom McCarty and Matt Warner. Two separate old-timer tales that have circulated for years seem to support the idea. According to the first, as the cashier was exchanging cash for Moffat's $21,000 check, he slipped in a ten-thousand dollar bill, perhaps assuming that if a crime was being committed the guilty party would have difficulty disposing of a bill of that size and it might lead to his capture. To make the bill even more easier to trace, he tore a small piece off of one of the corners.[41]

The second tale involves Warner and McCarty later that year. In the fall of 1889, they turned up in Star Valley, Wyoming, using the names Matt Willard and Tom Smith. Apparently having plenty of cash, they purchased a log cabin on the outskirts of Afton, Wyoming, and stocked it with groceries. To make the oncoming winter a bit easier to endure, they built a bar at one end of the cabin, bought a generous supply of liquor, and let it be known to their new friends in the community that one and all were always welcome to stop by for a drink or two. For years the old-timers in the area attested to the fact that tacked up on the wall behind the bar in Matt and Tom's cabin was a $10,000 bill.[42]

Tom McCarty would later deny being in on the Denver bank incident, saying that he had never met the banker Moffat.[43] If true, Warner and Bob Parker may have been the participants. Warner didn't mention the robbery in his memoirs, but his daughter, Joyce, said that, in later years, both her father and Bob Parker admitted to her their involvement in the scheme.[44]

Regardless of who was in on the Denver affair, little question exists that Warner, McCarty, and Parker, perhaps with the help of a few others, pulled off a major holdup that summer: the robbery of Telluride's San Miguel Valley Bank.

Return to Telluride

1889

With Telluride still in the throes of a mining boom, the San Miguel Valley Bank was an enticing target. The bank, a diminutive, wooden false-front typical of its day, was anything but impressive on the outside. But to a wide-eyed Utah cowboy like Matt Warner, the bank's interior, which had been fancied up for would-be investors, demonstrated the kind of prosperity that Matt had only dreamed of. "I didn't know before that there was any place in the world with such rich trimmings and furnishings as the inside of that bank," Warner said later.[1]

The bank was owned by Lucien L. Nunn, a local lawyer-entrepreneur. Nunn, called "L. L." by his acquaintances, was something of character who had prospered despite a decided touch of eccentricity. After acquiring a law degree somewhere in the East, Nunn operated a restaurant for a while in Leadville, Colorado, where he earned extra money by renting out his tin bathtub on Saturday nights to scruffy miners. When the Leadville restaurant folded, Nunn moved to Durango, Colorado, where he scratched out a living doing ordinary carpentry work. Upon his arrival in Telluride and still of modest means, he lived out of a tent, existed on a diet of oatmeal, and supplemented his upstart lawyer's meager income by shingling roofs. It was rough going, but as the town grew Nunn also developed a fairly successful law practice. He saved every penny he could and began building modest tract houses to rent and sell. Nunn finally prospered and was soon investing heavily in commercial buildings on Telluride's main street, Colorado Avenue. In 1888, he purchased control of the San Miguel Valley Bank.[2]

In writing of those days, Matt Warner recalled that young Bob Parker was as eager as he to rob the San Miguel Valley Bank, but that Tom McCarty was hesitant. According to Warner, McCarty pointed out that nearly every able-bodied man in Telluride carried a gun and would probably be shooting at them before they could get saddled up and ride out of town. Warner's answer to the problem was that he had heard that cowboys all over the West were robbing banks, so it must not be that difficult. Eventually, McCarty was won over.[3]

In another version of this scene, Tom McCarty is given credit for coming up with the idea to rob a bank, and it was Bob Parker who suggested the San Miguel Valley Bank in Telluride, because, having worked in Telluride, he was familiar with the bank's routine.[4] Still another source suggests that Bob was dispatched to Telluride for several weeks to learn when the mine's payroll arrived at the bank. Mrs. John Hancock, a Telluride resident who had formerly lived in Torrey, Utah, and knew Bob on sight, said that she remembered seeing Bob in town during the month before the robbery and that he seemed to be passing his spare time training his horse to stand motionless while he ran toward it and vaulted into the saddle.[5]

While Bob was in Telluride, Matt Warner and Tom McCarty rode over to the Carlisle Ranch, about five miles northwest of Monticello, Utah, and about sixteen miles from the Colorado line. The Carlisle foreman recalled seeing the two men making buckskin bags that would have been ideal to carry stolen bank loot. It has been suggested that Warner and McCarty stayed at the ranch while scouting their escape route and perhaps arranged for relays of fresh horses. Also, it was rumored that Dan Parker, Bob's younger brother, was working there at the time.[6]

The Carlisle spread was known for being friendly to outlaws, whom the owners, cattle barons Edmund and Harold Carlisle, allowed to be put on the payroll to discourage rustlers and chase off sheepmen.[7] A story is told that once, after rustlers began stealing some of their cattle, the Carlisles let it be known that their outfit was declaring war on thieves by hanging out a black flag with a skull and crossbones on it. They then sought out and hired the toughest outlaws they could find. A newspaper editor once quipped that to work for the Carlisles "a man had to have robbed at least three trains."[8]

In 1886, the Carlisle cowboys worked over a handful of New Mexico sheep herders so badly the governor of the Territory of New Mexico had to intercede.[9]

The Carlisle crowd pretty much had their way in the area. When the town of Monticello was settled in the mid-eighties, the Carlisle brothers let it be known that they did not like the idea. Worried mainly about water rights, the Carlisles had their ranchhands dam up the stream that flowed to the town and then encouraged them to ride through the streets, giving off yells and firing their revolvers to intimidate the townspeople. The Carlisle bunch even shot up the schoolhouse while the children were attending class.[10] The Monticello settlers were made of stern stuff, however, and they refused to leave.

In the summer of 1889, Matt Warner and Tom McCarty were hanging out at the Carlisle ranch planning the bank robbery. The ranch ramrod, W. E. "Latigo" Gordon, was a rugged, colorful character who kept rein on his crew of hardcases by being tougher than they. Gordon, described as "good-looking, intelligent, and ordinarily kind and peaceable," had a "streak of wildness" that was usually brought out by "a keg of red-eye." Gordon had no fingers on his right hand (having lost them to a rope loop while throwing a steer) and it was rumored that his body also carried the scars of several bullets. According to one acquaintance, Gordon got the bullet holes from a shootout at the Carlisle ranch headquarters, probably in a showdown with one of his hired hands. After the shooting, a doctor told Gordon that he had only a week to live. The gutsy foreman is said to have replied, "God damn you, I'll be riding the range when you are dead." Two years later the doctor was dead, and Gordon was still riding the range.[11]

It was Gordon himself who later said that he had seen Warner and McCarty making buckskin bags at the ranch that June.[12]

The men who would soon place the San Miguel Valley Bank in the annals of outlaw history rode into Telluride on Saturday, June 22, 1889. They put their horses up at Searle's livery stable and probably headed for the saloons. Although Matt Warner claimed that they had only recently become flat broke, they must have scraped together some cash (perhaps $21,000, courtesy of Denver banker David Moffat?), because witnesses later recalled seeing them drinking and freely spending money that weekend— from all appearances they were recently paid cowhands who had shaken off the trail dust and were out for a good time.[13] According to Warner, this was all part of their plan: "We dressed up top-notch, cowboy style, like we was going to a dance instead of a holdup. . . . There was policy and protection in it. . . . [W]e would be just some more cowboys riding into town to see the girls."[14]

Although the bank may have been open for business that Saturday, the boys decided to wait and make their play the following Monday, possibly because they believed more money would be on hand then.

In Matt Warner's account of the holdup he mentions only himself, Bob Parker, and Tom McCarty as participants. However, others suggest that more were involved.[15] It is possible that Warner did not identify other participants for the sake of their families (since these men did not become known outlaws).

According to witnesses, on the morning of the robbery four strangers checked their horses out of the livery and spent the next few hours in one or more of three saloons located near the bank, probably watching the bank customers come and go. Around noon, Charles Painter, the bank cashier and also the San Miguel County Clerk, left to do some collecting, leaving only a single teller in the bank.[16] As Painter rode off, the four men left the saloon and either rode or led their horses over to the front of the bank. Two of the men stayed with the horses while the other two went inside.[17]

The fourth man may have been Bert Madden, the half-brother of Bill Madden, a Mancos, Colorado, saloonkeeper.[18] Bill Madden eventually rode with the Wild Bunch after Bob Parker became Butch Cassidy. According to one account, Warner, Parker, and McCarty offered Bert—apparently an adventurous lad always looking for excitement—the job of holding their horses.[19]

Another possibility is that the fourth man was Harry Longabaugh, the Sundance Kid, a theory advanced by Donna Ernst, wife of Longabaugh's great nephew, Paul Ernst. To support her claim, Ernst cites interviews and correspondence with members of the Longabaugh family.[20] Harry Longabaugh did live in the area during the late 1880s and could have been acquainted with Warner, Parker, and McCarty.[21] However, Warner does not mention Longabaugh being involved, and, as far as anyone knows, he had no reason to hide this fact if it were true. Harry Longabaugh was well known as the Sundance Kid and a famous outlaw when Warner told his story in 1937.

It is also possible that the fourth man at Telluride was Dan Parker, Bob's brother. For years it was thought that Dan may have been one of several horse-holders at relay points along the escape route.[22] Recently, however, researchers have learned that a lawman involved in the chase after the robbery had definitely identified Dan as one of the four men he had pursued.[23]

The robbers may not have worn masks during the holdup, which seems ill-advised. Warner claimed that they could not wear a mask in a daylight robbery in the middle of the town, but this does not explain why they could not have pulled their bandannas over their faces as they entered the front door of the bank, which is what bank robbers usually did.[24] In Pearl Baker's version of the robbery, probably picked up from tales told by old-timers around campfires in Southern Utah, the Telluride robbers did do just that.[25]

According to the teller in the bank that day, one robber came in and asked him to cash a check. As the teller bent over to examine it, he said the man grabbed him around the neck and pulled his face down to the desk, telling him to keep quiet or he would suffer the "pain of instant death." This robber then called to his partners on the sidewalk outside, saying, "Come on boys, it's all right." The men then went through the room, picking up all available cash as they went. When the others were finished and left the building, the robber holding the teller released him and he "fell in a heap on the floor." The robber looked down at him and said something to the effect that he should shoot him for being such a coward, but the robber just turned and walked away, joining his comrades outside. Then, said the teller, they just saddled up and "rode leisurely away."[26] The bank officials reported to the newspapers that the amount taken was between $20,000 and $21,000.[27]

The above account was gathered from eyewitnesses, including the teller. Matt Warner gives a slightly different version. He says that on reaching the front door of the bank, he and Bob Parker dismounted "casual-like as we could," leaving McCarty with the horses. Inside, when they reached the teller's cage, they saw "a lot of money . . . stacked up in piles in front of him." The teller smiled and asked what he could do for them. Warner said he answered by putting his gun under the teller's nose.[28] As Bob filled a sack with the money, Warner noticed that the vault was open and he told Bob to head there next. Within minutes Bob came out with what appeared to Warner to be "bales of greenbacks and a lotta gold."

Warner says that he and Bob then herded the teller out of the bank ahead of them "with his hands sticking up in the air."[29] (If they really did march the teller out the front door with his hands up they were incredibly stupid. One can imagine the reaction of bystanders on seeing the bank teller standing on the sidewalk in front of the bank with his hands raised.) McCarty, in his account, says nothing about taking the teller outside. According to McCarty, the teller was warned to "stay inside and keep quiet or his life would pay the penalty."[30]

Warner also says that once they were outside he expected to see the town "explode in our faces any minute with everybody in creation shooting at us," but the onlookers did nothing—in fact, they seemed paralyzed.[31]

One witness later said that as the robbers were leaving the bank, one of them shot at the feet of the teller to make him stand still (maybe he was outside after all); the shot frightened the robber's horse, causing the rider to lose his hat and nearly be bucked off.[32] According to other witnesses, the robbers rode a few blocks then suddenly spurred their horses, gave a yell, and fired off their revolvers again.[33] One shot almost hit a youngster named Edward Weller who was standing on the sidewalk.[34] This version of events corresponds with McCarty's account, who said they fired their pistols "in different directions to intimidate the people we would meet."[35]

Although Matt Warner denied it, other sources say that the robbers probably had established a relay of horses along their escape route.[36] Several years after the robbery, a local character, who for obvious reasons chose to remain anonymous, claimed that Tom McCarty had hired him to set up the relay in return for a payment of $1,600. This character, who, in telling his story, used the name "Rambler," said that he and McCarty had met the previous fall in Cortez at a dance hall called French's. Rambler said that he and McCarty had developed a "warm friendship," and that he had spent part of the winter at McCarty's Bar-X ranch at Aztec Springs, south of Cortez, where McCarty was wintering a considerable number of horses that he had picked up in Utah during the previous summer and fall of 1888. Sometime the following spring, Rambler claimed that McCarty asked him if he would "like to go in cahoots" with him and "open up a bank." Rambler thought McCarty was joking, but he indicated a willingness and when he discovered that McCarty was serious, he decided to join in.[37]

Rambler said that he was not actually paid out of the proceeds of the holdup, but rather through a complex arrangement he had made with McCarty prior to the robbery. McCarty wrote out a note resembling a bill of sale under which Rambler was supposed to have sold sixty head of horses to McCarty for $1,600, but for which he had not been paid. If the robbery was a success, Rambler was to present the bill to the sheriff at Cortez, obtain a legal "attachment," and proceed to McCarty's Aztec Springs ranch and "repossess" the horses. Rambler said the scheme worked as McCarty had planned, although local county officials took rather generous fees for assisting him in the process.

According to Rambler, to earn his $1,600 worth of horses he was to set up the robbers' relay stations along their escape route. He said that McCarty wanted fresh horses posted at Keystone Hill, Hot Spring, West Fork, Johnston's Horse Camp, and Mud Springs. This set of locations means that their route of escape likely was west out of Telluride past San Miguel City to the south fork of the San Miguel River, down the south fork to Ames at Wilson Creek, and then south along a trail that is now State Highway 145 past Trout Lake and through Lizard Head Pass to the Dolores River.[38] Somewhere along the Dolores (which eventually leads to the town of Rico) they turned west and followed a trail to Hot Spring near the west fork of the Dolores. From that point they probably followed the west fork back to the main fork of the Dolores, then took various trails west of the river that eventually led them to Cortez.

Rambler implied that he may have actually participated in the robbery, or, at the least, he waited with the first relay of horses at Keystone Hill. By his account, after descending the hill the robbers were apparently confident that they had made a clean getaway up to that point. Although by horseback they were probably no more than four miles from the scene of the robbery, Rambler said they stopped long enough to divide up the money and have a quick lunch.[39]

While the robbers were eating, Rambler said that rancher Harry Adsit, the owner of the Spectator ranch for whom Bob and Matt had worked only weeks before, came riding up. The boys invited Adsit to join them for lunch, but he declined. Another version of the story says that Adsit passed the men on the road near San Miguel City, about halfway between Telluride and Keystone Hill. When Adsit later met the posse that had just been formed in Telluride and told them what he had seen, he apparently was asked to lead the way. In doing so, he got well out ahead of the others and came upon Tom McCarty hiding beside the trail. According to this version of the story, McCarty relieved Adsit of his revolver and warned him not to get close again or he would be killed. Questioned later, Adsit denied this, saying that he did not get that far ahead of the posse. However, he did admit that he had led the posse at a fairly slow pace.[40]

Years later, Harry Adsit discussed the incident in more detail. He said that, on riding into Telluride that day, he did pass the four men on the road coming from town and recognized Bob Parker and the other young man as the boys who had been working for him only a few weeks earlier. He said that he remembered wondering why they had not gone home to Utah as they had planned. Only later did he learn that they had just robbed the San Miguel Valley Bank.[41]

Matt Warner describes a similar incident, but does not mention Adsit by name. He said that on leaving Telluride after the robbery, as he and his companions came out of a clearing to cross a road, they encountered not one but two men. Warner said that one of the men (apparently Adsit) knew both him and Bob Parker and could later identify them. In Warner's words, "Just that little accident made all the difference in the world to us the rest of our lives. It give [sic] 'em a clue so they could trace us for thousands of miles and for years. Right at that point is where we broke with our half-outlaw past, became real outlaws, burned our bridges behind us, and had no way to live except by robbing and stealing." Warner added that, after they rode on, McCarty remarked that he should have shot the two men.[42]

McCarty, in his account of the escape, does not mention encountering these two men nor Harry Adsit, but he did recall that when they were about five miles out of town, one of the robbers' horses pulled up lame. McCarty said they waited near the road until a wagon came along. They stopped the wagon and informed the driver that they were trading their lame horse for one of his. When the driver protested, McCarty said they gave him some money for his horse. Apparently the money satisfied him, McCarty said, because by the time they had the animal unhitched and saddled, the man was smiling. As they rode off the man even tipped his hat and wished them good luck.[43]

The robbers apparently reached their second relay station at Hot Spring without further trouble. Hot Spring lay well west of the Dolores River and required them to leave the main road. Why they chose this route is not known, except that the main road, which followed the river, may have been too well traveled. It was a wise decision: authorities at Rico and Durango had been notified of the robbery and were organizing posses to head them off.[44] The robbers probably left the main road at Cool Creek and reached the west fork of the Dolores by way of Morrison Creek. Here they may have divided up some of the loot, because the posse later found several money wrappers on the ground there.[45]

After Hot Spring, the next relay point, at what Rambler called West Fork, was probably where the Dolores River forked just south of the Dolores County–Montezuma County line. Here, according to Rambler, the robbers came across two strangers with Winchesters, whom they managed to disarm without difficulty.

Around dark, the robbers stopped at their next-to-last relay point at Johnston's Horse Camp, a few miles north of Haycamp Mesa. There they were served supper by the camp proprietor, a Mrs. Olren. After leaving Johnston's they backtracked along an old Indian trail that led to Italian Springs, where Rambler said they thought they had spotted three of their pursuers. However, they eluded them and proceeded on to the last relay stop, Mud Springs, where they arrived at ten o'clock. According to Rambler, at this point they had covered about eighty miles.[46]

Rambler said that he left the group at Mud Springs and headed for Cortez, while Tom McCarty rode for Mancos where he had "friends." Rambler probably meant friends of Matt Warner rather than of McCarty. According to Warner, for some time prior to the robbery he had been maintaining a horse camp near Mancos, which he had left in the hands of two wranglers who had worked for him during racing season, Neils Olson and George Brown, and his jockey, Johnny Nicholson.[47] Warner, convinced that he had been recognized on the trail, said that he told his wranglers what had happened and that he was now an outlaw on the run. He was certain that once he was established as a suspect in the robbery, the authorities would confiscate any property he owned. He gave a bill of sale for all of his horses and equipment to the startled wranglers, telling them that everything he had owned was now theirs free and clear.[48] This may or may not have been the whole truth. It is more likely that Olson, Brown, and Nicholson were given the horses and equipment in payment for their help in carrying out the robbery, an arrangement similar to the one between Rambler and Tom McCarty.

As Warner told the story, he, McCarty, and Bob Parker made a fireless camp in a nearby woods that night, and the next morning hit the trail early. According to Matt, they broke camp just in time, perhaps only minutes ahead of a posse that had apparently ridden most of the night and had picked up their tracks in the morning light.[49]

The posse that had formed at Telluride, headed up by San Miguel County Sheriff James A. Beattie, was later joined by Montezuma County Sheriff J. C. Love. It is not known how many citizens volunteered, but it may have been a sizeable group: San Miguel County records show that nearly $900 was spent on the men and horses involved in the chase.[50]

Tom McCarty also recalled that "quite a large posse was in hot pursuit," but he gives the impression that they lost these pursuers early on, possibly even during the second day's ride, after descending a steep mountain at a spot where such a descent was not thought possible.[51]

Both Warner and McCarty tell of throwing off their pursuers for a while, apparently during the second night, with a trick that later found its way into dozens of Hollywood westerns. As darkness was nearing, the outlaws found an abandoned Indian pony in a basin near the summit of one of the small mountain ranges they had to cross. They threw a lasso on the animal, tied branches and brush to its tail, and sent it back down the mountain toward the posse. As Warner described it, the frightened pony "shot back on the dead run in the direction he came from . . . [making] as much noise as our whole outfit would make bolting for safety."[52] McCarty added: "The noise caused by the breaking and snapping of dry timber . . . made it sound as though we had an army of men and were all making a charge at the posse."[53] The posse, surprised and confused, guessed that the outlaws were making a break back toward the way from where they had come; the pursuers went riding off into the darkness after the sound of the terrified horse.

Somewhere around this point it seems the posse gave up and returned to

Telluride, where it was reported that the robbers' trail had been lost in the brushy hills between the Dolores and Mancos Rivers.[54]

Here the stories vary. Warner gives the impression that he, Bob Parker, and Tom McCarty immediately struck out for Utah, while Rambler said that McCarty "and his little band" remained in the high country near Mancos until the area was thoroughly searched by the authorities with the help of Navajo trackers.[55]

Back at Telluride, Sheriff Beattie and his men began searching for witnesses and asking questions, hoping to identify the robbers. Somebody (presumably Mrs. Hancock) remembered seeing Bob Parker hanging around town the month before the robbery, practicing fast getaways with his horse.[56] Also, when Bert Madden's name came up as a suspect, the local authorities began keeping an eye on his half-brother, Bill. On the sixth day after the robbery, the authorities spotted Bill Madden leaving town with a loaded pack horse. One lawman named Wasson and perhaps others followed him. Madden apparently turned south, probably taking the same road taken earlier by the robbers, the road leading to the Dolores River. The report of this incident does not say how long Madden was trailed, but Wasson eventually saw him turning the pack horse over to another rider who had come from the opposite direction. Wasson moved in and arrested both men. Madden was searched and Wasson found a letter from Madden's half-brother, Bert. In the letter Bert asked Bill to send some supplies and gave instructions as to how to reach him and the others.[57]

Another posse was formed and struck out for the Mancos Mountains, but when it reached the location mentioned in the letter, the robbers had gone. The posse followed the outlaws' tracks for several days, but eventually lost them. Before the tracks petered out, the lawmen found a note from the robbers, warning them not to follow or somebody would get shot. At this point the posse gave up and went home. On returning to Telluride, the story the authorities gave to the newspapers was that the robbers had once more eluded them because they had "padded their horses' feet with gunny sacks and rode across slick rock."[58]

Other posses were still out looking, however. On July 1, more than a week after the robbery, it was reported that twelve or fifteen men were still in pursuit, although it was admitted that hopes for capturing the robbers were diminishing.[59]

Bill Madden was eventually released by the San Miguel sheriff; it appears that no evidence could be found connecting him to planning or carrying out the robbery.[60] Likewise, no record has been found that Matt Warner's wranglers, Neils Olson and George Brown, or his jockey, Johnny

Nicholson, were ever arrested for whatever role they may have played in the crime. However, the local citizenry may have taken it upon themselves to seek justice here. According to Warner, his three former employees lost everything he had given them within two years, presumably to neighbors who "didn't feel bound to respect property that had come from a bank robber."[61]

The robbers may have had other help, too. An interesting story has persisted through the years that the outlaws were assisted by Telluride's own town marshal, a man named Jim Clark. Clark, a shady character with a questionable past who claimed to have been one of Quantrell's guerrillas during the Civil War, was said to have received $2,200 of the stolen loot in return for being "conveniently out of town" on the morning of the robbery. Clark was supposed to have admitted this years later to Colorado's legendary lawman Gunnison County Sheriff Doc Shores; Clark told Shores that the robbers left his share of the loot under a log along the trail they had taken during their escape.[62]

Additionally, Marshal Clark ended up with one of the horses used by the robbers that day. A large, black gelding with a "CT" brand on its thigh was found at the top of Keystone Hill, apparently too winded for Rambler or Bert Madden, or whoever, to drive down the hill with the others. Clark took the horse home, named him "Keystone" and kept him for several years, until one night he disappeared, or was stolen, from Clark's corral.[63]

Another of the robbers' horses was brought back by the posse: the dappled-brown colt that Harry Adsit had given Bob Parker two weeks before the robbery. San Miguel County Sheriff Jim Beattie latched onto this one, claiming he was entitled to it because the county had not reimbursed him for money he had paid out of his own pocket in organizing the manhunt. Adsit said that about ten days or so after the robbery he received a letter from Bob Parker that went something like this: "Dear Harry: I understand the sheriff of San Miguel county is riding the dapple brown colt you gave me. I want you to tell Mr. Sheriff that this horse packed me one hundred and ten miles in ten hours across that broken country and declared a dividend of $22,580.00 and this will be your order for the horse. Please send him over to me at Moab, Utah, at the first opportunity."[64] Adsit said that when he showed the sheriff the letter and pointed out that the animal carried the Adsit brand, the sheriff reminded him that he had given the horse to Parker, so legally it was no longer his. Whether Adsit had received such a letter is questionable, but it is known that in their escape from Telluride the robbers did pass through Moab.[65]

Flight

1889

Outlaw historian Pearl Baker agrees with Rambler that the Telluride bank robbers probably remained in southwestern Colorado for a while before fleeing to Utah, and that they more than likely hid out for a week or so somewhere in the mountains near Dolores. Baker cites an eyewitness, Roy Dickerson, an old cowboy who worked for Baker's family. Dickerson, who had been raised in Dolores, claimed to have seen the robbers on July 4, 1889, ten days after the robbery. Not only that, but Dickerson said he and another boy had watched while the outlaws held up a train at Stoney Creek, a few miles west of Dolores.[1]

Dickerson, then in his early teens, at the time was working for a local rancher who had sent him down to help brand calves that had been turned out near some loading pens at one of the railroad sidings. Dickerson said that on the afternoon of the fourth, a man rode up to the siding and asked when the next train was due. Dickerson told him that it was scheduled to pass at 1:00 PM. The man left and joined two others who had been waiting a short distance away; the three rode over and tied their horses near the right-of-way. Dickerson said that, when the train came, perhaps slowing to take on water at the siding, the men fired shots at the locomotive and the engineer braked to a stop. The men boarded the coaches and ushered off the passengers. With near military precision the robbers lined up their victims by the side of the tracks and quickly relieved them of their cash and valuables. Dickerson described the robber he had talked to as clean-shaven and wearing a battered hat with "the brim tucked up under each side so as it wouldn't lop down and cut off his seeing." He said also that one of the other robbers had a red beard.[2]

Dickerson's story probably should be taken lightly. While it cannot be disputed that he and his pal may have witnessed a train robbery that day, his recollections fail to verify that the outlaws he saw were the same ones who robbed the San Miguel Valley Bank. In planning their escape route from Telluride, the robbers' goal probably was to cross into Utah and reach the ferry on the Colorado River at Moab, which could have meant that they intended to hide out for a while somewhere in the barrens of Robbers' Roost country. Their first destination, as Warner said, would have been the nearest point on the Utah-Colorado line.[3] If so, they would have followed the trails in and out of McElmo Canyon west past Cannon Ball Mesa and on into Utah. According to Rambler, the authorities had guessed that the robbers were heading for Utah, most likely Moab, where, in Rambler's words, there were "pretty Mormon girls and wine from the native grape."[4] However, Matt Warner, Bob Parker, and Tom McCarty were probably hoping that once they crossed into Utah, the posse, which they assumed would be largely made up of Telluride citizens, would give up the chase, turn back, and let the Utah authorities take up the pursuit.

On entering Utah the robbers headed northwest toward the Blue Mountains and the Carlisle Ranch near Monticello, where they probably had fresh horses waiting for them. Matt Warner does not mention the Carlisle Ranch in his account of their flight, but he does mention the Blue Mountains, where he said a posse tried to lay a trap for them, which they avoided by taking a lesser-known trail.[5] According to local legend, a cave in the Blue Mountains allowed men on the run to hide out in relative safety while they rested their horses.[6]

From the Carlisle Ranch the robbers probably rode due north through Peters Canyon into Dry Valley—a course that roughly follows what is now U.S. Highway 191—where they eventually picked up a branch of the old Spanish Trail north of La Sal Junction that led them directly to the ferry across the Colorado River at Moab. Warner says they took what he called an "unfrequented trail" so they wouldn't run into any deputies that might be ahead of them.[7] Although Warner does not mention it, they may have stopped to pick up additional provisions and spend at least one night at Tom McCarty's brother's ranch on the southern slope of the La Sal Mountains.[8] Apparently they were able to avoid the deputies (if there were any), but they didn't ride in unnoticed. Mrs. Lydia Taylor Skewes, daughter of the ferry owners whose home was on the road the robbers took, said later that she and other members of the family saw them ride by, "racing toward the river."[9]

According to Warner it was still early morning when they arrived at the ferry. They carefully scouted the area for signs of deputies by crawling around on their bellies "like night-prowling animals," but they could find no sign of life except the ferrymen themselves, who had abandoned the ferry house because of the heat and were sleeping out in the open down near the river bank.

Warner crawled up to one of the sleeping men and whispered in his ear to stand up and put up his hands. This order brought the other men around, and as each awoke and sat up, to his delight Warner realized that he knew them all: Lester Taylor, whose family operated the ferry, and four of his employees.[10] Warner asked if any deputies were around, and the men answered that they had not seen any. Lester Taylor's son, Jick, who was there that night, told the story years later that Warner said he and his pals wanted to be taken across the river. One of Taylor's men replied that they would have to wait until daylight, that it was too dangerous to cross at night because the river was still high from the late spring run-off. According to Jick, Warner answered: "Our business lies rolling. We've got to get across the river." On hearing this, Lester Taylor stepped in and said, "Come on, we'll put them across."[11]

Lydia Taylor Skewes said that at the time, her grandfather didn't tell her who the early morning ferry customers were, but he did say that they paid with a ten-dollar gold piece instead of the regular charge for three riders and three horses (normally a total of $1.50).[12]

From the ferry landing the outlaws rode north, taking one of the several trails that twisted lazily into the southern edge of Salt Valley and through a maze of bluffs, canyons, and windowed columns called the "Arches."

Above Moab and the river, the land rises gently from the desert on both the east and west. Approaching from the south a rider finds the land cresting more abruptly, over what was once an ancient bulge in the earth that has long since eroded away to form a sort of broad trough that separates a pair of ridges dominated by towering monoliths, slickrock slabs, brush-clad flats, and serpentine canyons. Entering the trough, the rider is met with a cheerless landscape of rock and sand dotted with coarse shrubs and stunted, weather-worn trees—mostly gnarled piñon and juniper—struggling to survive in the unyielding desert sun.

The three outlaws had not encountered any pursuers since leaving Colorado, but that afternoon, as the pillars of the Salt Valley began throwing long shadows across their path, they grew uneasy and began watching their back trail a little more carefully. The Arches had many hiding places, but it was not a place one wanted to get trapped, mainly because there were few dependable water sources. One stream, the Salt Wash, was perennial, but like the lesser washes it was too brackish for drinking.

Warner had brought along a pair of field glasses, and every few minutes he turned and scoured the horizon. As he probably expected, he eventually spotted six men on horseback about three miles behind them. It was just the beginning: other posses had joined the hunt. As Warner described it: "From then on it was hell proper. It wasn't a case of just one outfit of deputies trailing us, but posses was out scouring the whole country, and we was running into fresh outfits every little while and had to suddenly change our direction, or dodge into a rock or timber hide-out, or backtrack, or follow long strips of bare sandstone where we wouldn't leave tracks or wade up or down streams long distances so they would lose our tracks."[13]

Their closest call came in Whipsaw Flat, just south of Thompson Springs. With lawmen nagging their heels, the trio noticed that the trail they were on was gradually taking them closer to a line of cliffs on their right. The riders in pursuit were behind and to the left, apparently gaining on them, and, because of the encroaching cliffs, Matt, Bob, and Tom were being angled toward them. They had just about decided to turn and make a stand when they spotted an opening in the cliffs. Fully aware that it could be a box canyon, which could mean their end, they nevertheless gambled and rode in. Sure enough, they were soon staring up at nothing but straight canyon walls on both sides. They were boxed!

The three fugitives pulled out their Winchesters and turned, ready to fight it out. They waited, fingers on the triggers, but the lawmen were nowhere in sight. They calmed their sweating horses and, after a while, cautiously began guiding them back toward the opening of the canyon. At any second they expected to hear the whine of rifle shots, but none came. They reached the point where they had entered the canyon, and still no sign of the posse. Apparently the possemen had passed up the opening and continued north. The outlaws searched the parched ground but could find no lawmen's tracks. They worked their way toward higher ground until they were high enough to see the lay of the land and figured out what had happened. Further down the line of cliffs was a pass out into open country. The lawmen apparently knew this and knew that Warner, Parker, and McCarty had ridden into a canyon, but did not know that the canyon was a box; they apparently thought it had an opening at the other end, so they had raced around the cliffs to ambush them when they came out.[14]

After encountering the last posse, the three outlaws decided to bypass Thompson Springs.[15] Although it meant passing up fresh water and supplies, Thompson, to which the name was eventually shortened, was a regular stop on the tracks of the Denver & Rio Grande, which at the time connected Denver with Salt Lake City. It didn't take much speculating to figure that as soon as the lawmen who chased them into Utah saw that they were heading north, they would telegraph Colorado authorities and other posses would be dispatched west on the D&RG to be waiting for them at Thompson or, for that matter, at any one of several stops along the line (which in those days would have been Cisco, Whitehouse, Sagers, Crescent, Little Grande, or Solitude).[16]

Just below Thompson the three fugitives likely veered east and crossed the tracks near what is now Vista Station, then headed up Sagers Canyon. From there they probably either continued to angle east through the Grand Valley past the Book Cliffs, or more likely struck out due north toward the rangeland of the Webster City Cattle Company, eventually picking up Willow Creek as it wanders through the Roan Cliffs along the eastern edge of what is now the Hill Creek Extension of the Uintah and Ouray Indian Reservation. The Willow Creek route would have been the safest, since it put more distance between them and the railroad, which at the Colorado River just beyond Cisco turned to the northeast.

If they had wanted to chance it, they could have picked up water and supplies at Webster City. Webster City, not a real city but rather the headquarters of the huge Webster City Cattle Company, could easily have been mistaken for a city: it was comprised of boarding houses for the ranch's employees and their families, a school for the children, a general store, and a saloon. East of the ranch, twisting through the Webster rangeland, were the Owlhoots, a network of trails stretching southwest to northeast through the Roan Cliffs and eventually connecting the Robbers' Roost area of southern Utah to the town of Vernal and Brown's Park in the north.[17] Both Warner and McCarty would have known about these trails, so this is probably the route they took.

Most of the time, if the three outlaws stopped to rest they dared not build a fire in the hope that their constant criss-crossing of the hard rock and slabs would hide their tracks and prevent their pursuers from knowing for sure which of the several trails they had taken. On those few occasions when they believed they could risk a fire, they hurriedly cooked enough bacon and beans to last several days, often to be eaten cold and soggy beside the trail later. McCarty recalled that their longest stops hardly ever exceeded two hours. On one stretch they ran completely out of food. But later that day, just when they figured their luck had run out, they came across hoofprints of a single rider. They backtracked his trail for a short distance and found a prospector's cabin. While two of them stood guard, the third searched the shack and confiscated enough provisions for a good meal.[18]

When they did make camp at night they made it well off the trail. They would stake their horses on long ropes tied near their bedrolls, usually leaving the animals saddled. When they risked building a fire, they never slept beside it, but only at a safe distance, usually in the nearby brush or rocks or behind some kind of protective cover.[19]

Even their stolen loot became a problem. Unwilling to become separated from the cash and coins for which they were risking their lives, they kept the booty in money belts strapped to their bodies. Tying the belts to their saddles would have been unwise because their horses could be shot out from under them. But after several days on the trail under the blistering sun, the continual rubbing of the belts on their skin became nearly unbearable. As Warner recalled, "The sweat would roll down our bellies and backs, and the hard, heavy money belts would gall a raw ring clear around our bodies, and the money got heavier and heavier and the sore rawer and rawer every mile we rode, till we thought we couldn't stand it any longer. More than once one or the other of us let loose and acted like a crazy man, swore like a trooper, pawed at his belt, and threatened to tear the damned thing off and throw it away."[20]

Assuming the robbers came out above the Roan Cliffs, they must have then headed due north just west of the Utah-Colorado line. According to Warner, their next stop was near the White River, where, probably after crossing into Colorado, they encountered a friendly band of White River Indians who traded them fresh horses for their spent mounts plus some of the stolen bank loot. However, before they could get used to their new horses another posse picked up their trail. The robbers swung back into Utah, probably somewhere south of Coyote Basin, then raced north, apparently leaving the lawmen well behind. After working their way around Cliff Ridge they found a place to cross the Green River, then headed northeast toward what they assumed would be a safe haven, the rugged wilderness of Brown's Park.[21]

In 1889, Brown's Park was thirty-five miles of valley wilderness that curved across the Utah-Colorado border a few miles below the Wyoming line. The valley floor, made of layered terraces of woods and pastures, once offered lush grazing for deer, antelope, and mountain sheep. But by the late 1880s, settlers had moved in and were fencing and tilling the bottom land along the Green River, which enters from the west through a deep, jagged canyon that twists between Diamond Mountain, the southern boundary of the Park, and Cold Springs Mountain, the northern boundary. At Diamond Mountain the river then turns south, skirting the mountain's eastern base then joining alkali-laden Vermillion Creek, which drains the eastern slope of Cold Springs Mountain and the wilderness north of Vermillion Bluffs. Bolstered by the Vermillion, the river rushes due south past Zenobia

Peak and Douglas Mountain, then plunges through the sandstone walls of Lodore Canyon, exiting the Park in a western sweep back across the Utah line at Whirlpool Canyon.

The Park was probably named after a French Canadian trapper, Baptiste Brown, one of the first white men to inhabit the area, sometime around 1827. Word soon spread that the rugged valley was a trapper's paradise, especially in the winter because the mountain walls offered protection from the freezing wind. In 1837 a trading post was built near the Green River in a large grove of cottonwoods two miles north of the entrance to Lodore Canyon. The post operated until the early 1840s, when beaver became scarce in the area. A few trappers stayed in the area, but the Park was virtually abandoned until settlers arrived in the 1870s, shortly after track was laid for the transcontinental railroad sixty-five miles to the south.[22]

Although the Park became occupied by a few honest cattlemen, its isolation made it a popular hiding place for stolen stock, much of which was sneaked into the valley by Texas cowboys going north on drives to Wyoming; they usually hung around to prey on other herds that got into trouble in the desert or were scattered by winter storms. From this beginning, the area became a general hangout for rustlers and eventually outlaws of all kinds.[23]

Matt Warner was familiar with the area, having once raised horses on Diamond Mountain.[24] Also, he had a good friend there, a rancher named Charlie Crouse. Bob Parker also may have known Crouse, and may have worked for him breaking and racing horses during the summer of 1886.[25] Crouse, originally from Virginia, had come west sometime in the 1870s. He first worked as a freighter and then settled in Green River, Wyoming, where he learned the cattle business from a local rancher. Later he drifted to the Park and built a rock-walled cabin on Diamond Mountain. In 1880, after an Indian scare on the mountain, Crouse purchased a squatter's claim on the south side of the Green River at the mouth of a small stream about three miles west of the Utah-Colorado line. The land was ideally suited for raising stock, and Crouse expanded his holdings into a sizable horse ranch.[26]

Charley Crouse had grown to manhood in the hard-drinking and rough world of bull whackers and railroad construction crews, and he tended to associate with those types of men. Although not a full-fledged outlaw himself, he used a gun when he thought it necessary and welcomed the companionship of outlaws, especially at his Green River ranch, which, during the 1880s and early 1890s, was as remote and inaccessible as any location in the Brown's Park area.[27] Word around Brown's Park was that Crouse could be counted on to warn his outlaw guests if the law was nearby, and the outlaws paid him well for his service.[28]

Crouse warmly welcomed his old friend Matt Warner and Matt's two trail-weary companions. He gave them food and fresh horses, and suggested they rest up in a cabin he had tucked away in a canyon up toward Diamond Mountain. The cabin, heavily secluded near a spring in a thick grove of pines and cedars, made an excellent hideout. There was no road to the place, just a makeshift trail that was nearly impassable due to the towering cottonwoods and box elders and heavy growth of willows and alders.[29]

At Crouse's cabin the three fugitives relaxed for the first time in days and enjoyed sound sleep at night in the cool breezes that drifted down from the mountain. During the days they probably dozed when they felt like it and, when tired of that, played endless hands of poker. Warner recalled one round of "showdown" when both he and Bob each tossed their entire shares of the loot onto the table. Warner won with four jacks to Bob's three queens, but he refused to take the pot, joking that the extra gold coins were too heavy to carry.[30]

But the bandit trio's respite was short-lived. On the third or fourth day one of Charlie Crouse's hands came riding up with news that right at that moment a posse was at Charlie's ranch looking for the Telluride bank robbers. As hidden as they believed they were, the three outlaws no doubt realized that the cabin was probably well known in the area, and, despite the poor trail that led there, they knew that if they could reach it so could a determined posse. Wasting no time they saddled up, tied on their loot and all the provisions they could carry, and headed further up the mountain—the only possible way to go.[31] Today a road leads from the cabin southeast over part of the mountain and down the other side, eventually coming out on what is now called Brown's Park Road. Whether there was much of a trail there in the summer of 1889 we don't know. But somehow the trio made their escape and turned their horses back in the direction they had come from the previous week, toward what at that point may have been the only safe haven left within riding distance: Robbers' Roost country of southern Utah.[32]

Neither Tom McCarty nor Matt Warner chronicled the next leg of their flight. McCarty says nothing about it, and Warner simply mentioned that they "beat it down there [to Robbers' Roost] in record time, riding by night and hiding by day."[33]

In choosing a place to hide out after the Telluride robbery, one wonders why the trio did not head for Robbers' Roost first. It was much closer to Telluride than Brown's Park, and in Matt Warner's opinion it was the "greatest natural rock fortress" in America, maybe even the world.[34] Maybe Warner and his pals chose Brown's Park first because they knew that the authorities would guess they would head to the Roost and cut them off before they could get there. Or maybe they chose not to hide in the Roost because of its heat—only a desperate man would try to live off the Roost in July and August.

With sufficient water and provisions, it could be done. Although much of the area in the 1880s was, as it is today, barren and desolate, enough natural springs dotted the winding, straight-walled canyons and narrow gorges to make even ranching in some spots worthwhile in most years. What made the area ideal for outlaws, mainly rustlers, was its remoteness and defensibility. Local history suggests that more than one posse rode confidently into the Roost only to ride out exhausted and empty-handed. The Roost protected its own.

Just where the trio of robbers made their hideout in the summer of 1889 we don't know. The Roost has thousands of cliffs and buttes, each made of rising and falling layers of rock strikingly different from the layers above and below, yet each extending as far as the eye can see. According to Matt Warner, they found a place that did have water (presumably a spring) and even grass and some shade. He described it as being "on top of a high mesa at the end of a steep, crooked trail." It was, in Matt's opinion, a spot where they could hold out against a whole army of law officers or at least until their provisions gave out.[35] Most likely their resting place was somewhere in the northwestern corner of the Roost area, either due south of the town of Green River or somewhere along a line between Green River and Hanksville, probably a little south of the San Rafael River.[36]

Despite their hasty departure from Brown's Park, the three outlaws may have had enough provisions to last a month or so. Warner says they remained tucked away on their lonesome mesa "from sometime in the summer to fall."[37]

While at the Roost, Bob may have made a quick trip west in hopes of visiting his family.[38] His sister claimed that he wanted to return to Circle Valley to put his mistakes behind him and start all over again, but he knew that returning home would only cause his family further disgrace.[39] According to Lula, Bob did make an effort. He rode west as far as Beaver County, but at a fork in the road "his heart failed him."[40] He kept well north of Circle Valley, avoiding all roads that led either to Circleville or to Beaver, where he was also known. Several times he considered slipping down to the ranch, but "the closer he got to home, the weaker he felt" about taking the chance. Instead, he rode on, finally stopping at the town of Milford. There, perhaps by prearrangement, he met his younger brother, Dan.[41] Lula did not tell what was said between the brothers, only that the two spent several hours together over a long meal. She did say that afterward Bob was more convinced than ever that he must "steer clear of home for the time being." It is possible Dan had warned him that word had spread through Circle Valley that he was wanted for the Telluride robbery. Lula gives the impression that Bob left Milford soon after meeting with Dan. She also suggests that it was at this time that Bob decided to change his name from Robert LeRoy Parker to George Cassidy (the "Butch" would come later).[42]

Back at the mesa in Roost country, provisions were beginning to run low and it was decided that somebody had to go into the nearest town and stock up. Since Warner and McCarty were both known in the area, Bob was elected for the job. It was definitely a gamble: the nearest town, Green River, was on the Denver & Rio Grande Railroad line, and, like all railroad towns in Utah at the time, it enjoyed a steady flow of travelers. Since strangers came and went daily, Bob might have been able to blend in with the crowd and go unnoticed; however, a busy town also increased his chances of being spotted by someone who knew him (which is exactly what happened). Bob was spotted by an old acquaintance from Circleville, Dan Gillis.[43]

Bob rode quickly back to the mesa to warn the others. Worried that the authorities would follow Bob's tracks into the Roost hideout, from that night on the men took turns standing guard. Also, every day one of them would ride out and carefully check for any new hoofprints along the route Bob had taken from Green River. Sure enough, one day Warner found fresh tracks of shod horses. He alerted the others and the three rode back along the trail and hid in rocks at the rim of a canyon. Before long they spotted three men coming along the trail. According Matt Warner, the following took place.[44]

Instead of continuing on the trail that Bob had taken into camp, the three unfamiliar riders veered off at a fork and headed in another direction, a direction that led straight into the desert. In Warner's words, the riders, one of whom he recognized as a local lawman named Tom Fares, were heading toward "rough, broken country where a bird would get lost and there wasn't a drop of water." Overcome with compassion for any man destined for a slow death on a Utah desert, Matt and his companions decided to warn the riders of the danger, even if it meant risking their own capture. Warner fired his Winchester in the air. When the riders turned and spotted Warner, he waved his hat and motioned for them to come back. He then rode down to the trail, quickly scribbled a note on a piece of paper, attached the note to a stick and stuck it in the ground. The note said that the men were headed for death if they went south, and that they should follow him if they needed water.

Warner quickly rode to a nearby rise and waited while the men read the note. When they looked up he signaled for them to follow. They did and he led them to a spring, where, from a hiding place not far away (actually so close he claimed he could hear their conversation), he watched them "drink like desert men drink when they are choking to death." He let them get their fill, eat some grub they had brought with them, and then he yelled out to them to raise their hands and throw down their guns.

Bob Parker and Tom McCarty, who had been watching all of these events transpire, rode down and joined the group. Apparently swayed by the ease with which Warner had captured the lawmen, the three fugitives decided to have some fun with them. They unsaddled Fares's horse, ordered him to remove his trousers, and then told him to climb back on. They then turned him and his companions loose and pointed them in the general direction of Hanksville. Warner said that he later heard that after a few miles, Fares had become so sore between the legs that he had to dismount and lead his horse into town.[45]

If Warner's story is true, the three outlaws realized that it was time to move on. They had made a fool of a tough lawman who would likely return with a sizable posse. It was probably Butch's idea to head for Wyoming. All three men were too well known in Utah to be safe there, and they could not return to Colorado. Bob remembered a friend, a fellow rustler, who owned a ranch on the eastern slope of the Wyoming Rockies not far from Lander. Bob figured they might be welcome there for the winter. Apparently, Warner and McCarty could not come up with a better suggestion.

On Upper Wind River

1889–1890

The first two trips the three outlaws had taken across Utah's rugged canyon country had been harrowing, but this third journey was uneventful. Aware now that he was wanted for the Telluride robbery and conscious of the dishonor he had brought to his family back home in Circle Valley, it was probably sometime during this trip that Bob Parker decided to abandon his rightful name and become George Cassidy.[1] Why Cassidy? A simple explanation would be that it was a name that sounded good to him. His early mentor, Mike Cassidy, was the man he most wanted to emulate. Why he chose "George" is not clear. Butch's sister, Lula, offers one explanation. About the time Butch began to get in trouble with the law, another George Parker was living in Rock Springs, Wyoming, who, in Lula's words, also was "frequently stirring up some devilment." She believed that Butch might have thought it would be to his advantage to be confused with this George Parker, especially since George Parker's brother was a lawmen.[2] The nickname "Butch" came later.[3]

According to Matt Warner, shortly before the trio reached Lander, Butch struck out on his own, telling his companions that he wanted to look for his friend's ranch. Warner and McCarty, apparently having gone too long without experiencing the taste of good whiskey, favored riding on into Lander. Butch considered this move foolhardy and warned his friends that it was still too dangerous to show themselves in public. Warner and McCarty thought otherwise, or at least believed the pleasure was worth the risk.[4]

As Matt and Tom rode in, Lander looked peaceful enough. To be on the safe side, however, when they came to the first saloon they rode around to the back of the building and tied up near the rear door. As it turned out, their precaution was a smart move: they had only begun their first round when a local cowboy whispered to them that lawmen were in town looking for strangers. They gulped their drinks, paid up, and quickly headed for the back door.

Faced with unfamiliar surroundings to the north and east of town, Warner and McCarty probably backtracked toward South Pass City, returning the way they had come in, and then headed west, hoping to lose any pursuers in the mountains. Their quick departure did not go unnoticed, and the lawmen they had stirred up were soon at their heels. The pair lost them only after they reached a point along the trail that was blocked by an early high country snowfall.[5]

The route they took most likely was the Lander Cutoff, a trail first used by Indians and trappers during the fur period and later by western-bound emigrants. Built in 1859 by Mormon laborers and bridge builders from Maine, the cutoff became a northern shortcut to the Snake River in Idaho and eventually part of the Oregon Trail. It roughly parallels what is now State Highway 351, crossing it near Marbleton then running north of Highway 350 over the Salt Range and exiting Wyoming from Star Valley, which at that point in time was a narrow corridor of Mormon settlements on the western slope of the Salt River Range.[6] During the winter months, when the trails were covered by snow, Star Valley was nearly inaccessible from the east. Warner and McCarty could not have asked for a better place to hide.

According to Warner, Butch told him that the friend who had a ranch near Lander was named Brown. This may have been Cap Brown, the rustler who roamed Robbers' Roost country when Butch was still a lad living in Circle Valley.[7] Cap Brown was much older than Butch, probably in his fifties when they first met, but the two may have shared enough hours on the trail to have become friends. Brown had been pushing his luck for many years in southern Utah, and the law may have been closing in on him. It is conceivable that sometime between 1884 and 1889 he headed north for a safer life in the mountains of Wyoming.

Another possibility is that Butch was looking for William "Bill" Brown, a former Texan in his early thirties. Although no evidence has been found that Butch knew Bill Brown, it is possible that he did: Brown was known to hang around Charley Crouse's place.[8] Also, Bill Brown was acquainted with Butch's brother, Dan Parker. Later that same year, just before Christmas, Bill Brown and Dan Parker robbed a mail stage on a road five miles north of Muddy Station between Rawlins and Dixon, Wyoming.[9]

It is also possible that Butch never found his friend Brown. Sometime that fall Butch rode south to Brown's Park, perhaps to Charley Crouse's ranch. Since Crouse had a reputation for entertaining outlaws (which may

have accounted for Butch's and his companions' close call there in July),
Butch probably felt that it was not safe to hide out there, but he may have
paid Charley a brief visit for advice on where he could lay low for a while.
Charley may have suggested the Bassett Ranch.

Herb and Elizabeth Bassett had come to Brown's Park from Arkansas in
1878. Herb had been clerk of court in Hot Springs, but he lost his job when
the local political party was thrown out of office. He and Elizabeth had
boarded the train, intending to go to California and look for work there,
but they stopped off at Green River, Wyoming, to visit Herb's brother,
Sam, a homesteader in Brown's Park. Sam had already tried his luck in California, did not like what he had seen, and talked Herb into staying in Wyoming for a while. Herb, a fairly well-educated man who had been a
schoolteacher in his youth, got a job in Green River as a bookkeeper for a
mercantile company. He later taught school there for a while. Eventually,
however, he and Elizabeth probably concluded that in that part of the West
real success lay in ranching, and they moved to Brown's Park to homestead.[10]

Though as a boy Herb had lived on a farm, he was not cut out for ranching. Also, he was not in good health, having an asthma condition and perhaps malaria as well. Thus the actual operation of the ranch, located on the
north side of Vermillion Creek just west of where the Vermillion joined the
Green River, was mostly left up to Elizabeth, who seemed well-suited for
it.[11]

The Bassetts were known for playing host to any traveler who needed a
place to sleep, and they did it without asking many questions. To Herb and
Elizabeth, where a stranger came from and what he did for a living was his
own business.[12] Butch may have come just when the Bassetts were needing
help around the place, and, being a good-natured and polite young man,
he was probably hired right away.

Although taken on as a ranch hand, Butch apparently had the run of the
Bassett home. Herb was the local postmaster, and when Butch was not
needed in the barn or corral, he spent much of his time reading the newspapers and magazines that accumulated in Herb's office. Also, Butch took
advantage of the Bassett family's extensive library. On Sundays, Butch
would sometimes join in when neighbors gathered at the Bassett home for
church services, and he was always welcome at social gatherings hosted by
the family. Occasionally he attended local dances, probably escorting the
Bassetts' daughter Josie, then fifteen. Some say that Butch may have even
courted Josie briefly. In later years, when Josie was asked about this, she
would neither confirm nor deny it but would merely say that she and

Butch, whom she referred to as "a big dumb kid who liked to joke," were just "good friends."[13] On the other hand, on at least one occasion she was heard to refer to Butch as her "Brown's Park beau."[14] Josie's younger sister, Ann, then eleven, evidently adored Butch and would tag after him when he was working.[15]

It is not clear how long Butch stayed with the Bassetts. While there, it is possible that he made several trips north to Lander, because sometime that fall he and fellow cowboy Al Hainer purchased a piece of property on Horse Creek in northern Fremont County, just north of where the town of Dubois stands today.[16] Apparently the two men intended to go into the horse business together.[17]

Little is known about Al Hainer. Like Butch, he may have been from southern Utah and was possibly acquainted with Butch's brother, Dan Parker.[18] The property Hainer and Butch purchased was believed to have included a two-room cabin recently built by the previous owners.[19] However, one neighbor, William L. (Will) Simpson, did not remember it that way. According to Simpson, Butch and Hainer built the cabin themselves.[20]

Dubois lies about seventy-five miles northwest of Lander, in what is called the Upper Wind River area, a region largely known for its sagebrush flats, rolling hills, and red-flanked mountains.[21] Also, it didn't rain much. A rancher who grew up in the area in the late 1800s was fond of saying, "When there was rain in the Wind River Basin—an event that happened about as often as a birthday—wagons were stopped in their tracks."[22]

In 1889 the area was still sparsely populated: within a hundred miles each way from the Cassidy-Hainer cabin there were probably less than twenty-five inhabitants, mostly cattle ranchers and a few trappers.[23] Next to raising cattle the biggest industry was probably cutting railroad ties, which began in the late 1860s with the laying of track for the Union Pacific Railroad. "Tie hacks" using broad axes with deep, wide blades felled trees and roughly squared them into the shape and size of railroad ties. Much of the cutting was done in the winter, when the timber could be taken from the forests covered in deep snow by horse-drawn sleds. The hacks would haul the ties to landings near streams, and when the ice melted in the spring they would float them down to collection points.[24]

Using the name George Cassidy, Butch, good natured and friendly, mixed well with the other ranchers in the area. The two neighbors who got to know him best were probably John and Margaret Simpson, the parents of Will Simpson who was a local rancher and lawyer and the grandfather of Wyoming's former U.S. Senator Alan Simpson. The John Simpson ranch on the Wind River was near Jakey's Fork Creek, about four miles southeast of Horse Creek.[25] For a while Margaret Simpson operated the local post office, and Butch and Al Hainer often rode over to send and receive mail.[26] According to Ida Simpson Redmond, John and Margaret's daughter, her mother enjoyed having Butch around because he was so cheerful and also helpful, always keeping the water buckets and woodbox full.[27]

Another neighbor was Eugene Amoretti Jr., whose father owned a bank in Lander. Amoretti worked for his father at the bank and raised cattle on the EA Ranch, a 240-acre spread also on Horse Creek. According to the younger Amoretti, he was in his office at the bank the day Butch first rode into Lander and deposited $17,500 with the Amorettis for safekeeping (part of which may have been Butch's share of the Telluride robbery).[28] At times Butch also worked on Amoretti's ranch, which was adjacent to the Cassidy-Hainer property.[29] It was on this ranch that Butch probably first met Al Hainer, who also worked for Amoretti.[30] Butch and Eugene Amoretti became good friends, and in later years, when Butch ran short of cash, he could usually count on Eugene to tide him over with a bank or personal loan.[31]

Butch and Hainer had another neighbor, Andrew Manseau, a French Canadian who owned a ranch south of their property. According to Manseau, who sold hay to Butch and Hainer for their horses, Butch also spent a lot of time at the ranch of a family named Meeks and became acquainted with Henry Wilbur "Bub" Meeks, a young man of about the same age as Butch. Bub Meeks later rode with Butch during a brief career as an outlaw.[32]

Will Simpson's wife, who arrived in the area before her mother-in-law, was the first pioneer woman in the Upper Wind River area, and she took it upon herself to try to bring a semblance of refinement to the rough, male-dominated area.[33] During Butch's first winter on Horse Creek, in the midst of a bitter snowstorm Mrs. Simpson sent word to her Wind River neighbors that she would welcome their presence for a Christmas dinner.

The party went well and gave Butch an opportunity to get to know most of the other residents of the area. According to A. F. C. Greene, believed to be an acquaintance of the Simpsons', Al Hainer was quiet that day and generally kept to himself, but Butch was congenial and something of the life of the party.[34] He got along especially well with the youngsters. "Cassidy had the spirit of frolic with him," Greene said. "Before dinner was on the table, those who had grinned in silence were beginning to laugh out loud. The children hovered close about him. In the afternoon there was an eggnog, and then they had games. There are old-timers who tell to this day how the cowboys of Wind River roared with laughter, and the children shrieked with mirth, and how Butch Cassidy set the pace, with his tow-colored hair in wild disorder and his puckered blue eyes blazing."[35]

Will Simpson's son, Jim, then sixteen, was clearly taken with the outgoing Cassidy. Also present at the party was Will's younger sister, Ida, who recalled that Butch, on receiving his invitation to the affair, had ridden down to Lander and bought presents for the children, including material for a new dress for her.[36]

It seems Butch also got along well with the older girls. Lander was a cowboy-friendly town, and when the boys rode in from the ranches for a good time they usually found the "Dance Tonight" sign out.[37] Ada Calvert Piper, a local girl who was interviewed years later, recalled that Butch enjoyed squiring the girls, many of whom thought of him as "a good catch." But he was no angel, Mrs. Piper said. He was actually full of devilment, she recalled, often playing practical jokes on his friends.[38]

Dora Lamorreaux Robertson, who also lived in Lander at the time, was said to be Butch's special girlfriend for a while, and the two would go horseback riding and dancing together. According to Mrs. Robertson, Butch was always a gentleman.[39] Another possible girlfriend was Mary Boyd, the daughter of a Missouri freighter, Bill Boyd. This relationship may have been serious. According to Cassidy biographer Larry Pointer, descendants of several local pioneers say that Butch may have considered settling down and making a home for Mary.[40]

Another neighbor who spoke well of Butch was C. E. Baker, an easterner close to Butch's age who claimed that Butch was largely responsible for teaching him about homesteading in the West. Baker later became a highly successful rancher in northwestern Colorado.[41]

Although Cassidy is frequently referred to as "Butch" in stories passed on by residents of the Upper Wind River and Lander, as of 1889 he had not yet picked up that nickname and still called himself George Cassidy. While some of his neighbors may have suspected that he was a Mormon with roots in Utah, Butch told the Simpsons that he had originally come from New York City.[42] He would repeat this story later when he got in trouble with the law.[43]

A. F. C. Greene told of a severe influenza epidemic that spread through the Upper Wind River area, and recalled that Butch, one of the few to escape the illness, made weekly rides to the Simpson ranch to pick up home remedies prepared by the Simpson women, and distributed them to his sick neighbors, sometimes making a round trip of fifty miles.[44] Will Simpson, on the other hand, did not remember this incident and implied that in those days there were not enough neighbors in the Upper Wind River area to have an "epidemic."[45] However, Will's sister did recall the epidemic, mentioning that her mother was adept at preparing medicines and herbs, and that Butch did cheerfully deliver them to the flu sufferers.[46]

The winter of 1889–90 in Wyoming was long and bitter. In a letter from Butch to his brother, Dan Parker, the following spring Butch apologized for writing in pencil, which he claimed was necessary because "the ink froze" during the winter.[47] In his letter Butch said that he was living "in a good house about 18 miles from Lander" and that he was "raising horses which I think suits this country just fine."[48] He mentioned that he had "thrown in lots" with "H" and that together they had thirty-eight horses between them, and would have had more except for the severe winter. He added: "Business here is very dull and money hard but you know I am well . . . [and] I should be in perfect health if I did not have such a good appetite and eat so much 3 times each day." He admitted that he was homesick, especially for his mother, and that in the summer he was going to try to go home to Utah to see the family.[49]

Butch joined his Upper Wind River neighbors in the first spring roundup of the year, accompanied by Will Simpson's son Jim, whom Butch probably coached on the skills of wrangling and branding.[50] Once they returned to Horse Creek, Butch and Al Hainer sold off their horses to other stockmen in the area, closed up the ranch, and rode off without telling anyone where they were going.[51] Butch may have kept his promise to visit to his family, although if he did it is doubtful that he stayed at the Circle Valley ranch. Instead, he may have bunked with his old employer, rancher Pat Ryan, at Hay Springs, where between visits to his family he worked as an ordinary cowhand.[52]

Blue Creek and Afterward

1890–1892

Instead of restocking his ranch on Horse Creek when he returned from Utah, Butch headed for Johnson County, Wyoming. During the late 1880s Johnson County had become a hotbed of rustling—both horses and cattle—and reports had spread throughout Wyoming that the law was doing very little about the problem. The large ranches (the livestock barons) usually had a difficult time prosecuting rustlers in nearly all areas of the West, but the problem was seldom more severe than in the Powder River country of northeastern Wyoming. Despite the thousands of head of livestock stolen in Johnson County from 1886 through 1889, there had been only nineteen indictments for rustling and one conviction (which brought a fine of only $100).[1]

For a rustler of Butch's talents, Johnson County was the place to be, and apparently he planned to stay a while. Sometime that spring or summer he purchased a piece of land on Blue Creek, a small stream that wanders through the valley behind the famous outlaw hideout the Hole-in-the-Wall. According to local history, the land that Butch bought had been homesteaded by Tom F. Barnum, a transplanted Vermonter who had been attracted to the site when he passed through the area while serving as a scout for the Army. Barnum filed his homestead claim with the intention of starting a ranch, and built two attached cabins on the property. When he tried ranching, however, he found that he wasn't very good at it so he opened a post office in one of the cabins. Later he was joined by his brother, Guy, and his brother's wife. Guy's wife took over the post office while the brothers picked up any work they could on nearby ranches. When Butch purchased the property in 1890 it was known as the Barnum post office.[2]

Butch soon made friends with Shorty Wheelwright, a former army scout and one of the first squatters along Blue Creek. According to Shorty, who had a placer claim in the hills above Butch's place, times were not too good for Butch that first year, but he recalled that when Butch got a few dollars ahead, he always shared them with his friends.[3]

It is possible that Butch's venture on Blue Creek was not a one-man undertaking but actually part of a larger operation, one that spread far beyond Johnson County and even well beyond Wyoming. It has been suggested that by 1890 a network of horse thieves operated as far west as Washington state and perhaps as far east as Illinois, a network that grew out of the realization that to make stealing horses profitable (and profitable it could be), the animals had to be disposed of somewhere far from where they were stolen. In the 1870s horses could be stolen and safely sold no more than a few hundred miles from their owners, but by the late 1880s, with a larger population and better cooperation among ranchers and law enforcement agencies, rustlers had to transport stolen animals far greater distances before they could safely dispose of them.[4]

Butch's neighbor on Horse Creek, Andrew Manseau, recalled that Butch would steal horses in the Dakotas, trail them to Utah by way of Jackson Hole, sell them there, and then steal horses in Utah and take them back to the Dakotas. He added that Butch often stayed overnight at his (Manseau's) ranch during these cross-country trips.[5]

It is doubtful that this network of horse thieves ever reached the level where it could be called a "syndicate." While apparently effective it never became completely organized. At most it was a loose arrangement in which one band of horse thieves would hustle away a bunch of animals as quickly as possible, and drive them three hundred miles or so to a relay point at an isolated ranch or a box canyon and pick up their money from a go-between. Shortly thereafter four or five riders would arrive, gather up the animals, and, after paying off the go-between, drive the horses off to another relay point. Sometimes the gangs would meet at a relay point and simply switch herds of comparable value. Using this method, horses stolen from ranches in eastern Washington may have ended up in Idaho or even Wyoming, while Wyoming animals were likely driven to Montana, Utah, Colorado, or the Dakotas.[6] It is quite possible that Butch's ranch on isolated Blue Creek behind the Hole-in-the-Wall was one of these relay points.

As a buzzard flies, Butch's ranch on Blue Creek was about ten miles northwest of the Hole-in-the-Wall, which in turn is nearly sixteen miles southwest of Kaycee. Today, the nearest public road to both the ranch and the Hole-in-the-Wall is County Road 190, which follows the Powder River's Middle Fork upstream from Kaycee toward the Big Horn Mountains that straddle the Johnson County–Washakie County line. About twelve miles from Kaycee the road begins to wind in a more westerly direction, then slightly north, and finally leaves the river to follow along Beaver Creek. To reach the site of Butch's ranch, a traveler must follow 190 along Beaver Creek until it joins Blue Creek.

To reach the Hole-in-the-Wall today one must leave County Road 190 (preferably on horseback) where it splits from the Powder River's Middle Fork and follow the river south to where it joins Buffalo Creek, which in Butch Cassidy's day was also called the South Fork of the Powder.[7] Following Buffalo Creek the land gradually gets lonelier and rougher. Eventually, far to the east an ominous, red sandstone cliff rises from the horizon, to which the creek seems somehow drawn in wide swaths.

On reaching this cliff the creek twists and turns, as if unsure of its path, but finally begins to edge further east. Darting and seeking an outlet, the creek leaves the cliff, returns to it, leaves again, and then begins a long, sweeping arc back west toward the Big Horns. At the beginning of this bend, a look hard to the left with a careful scan of the wall reveals the Hole.

The Hole-in-the-Wall itself is unremarkable. In fact, it is not even a hole but more of a roughly V-shaped notch near the rim of a steep vermillion-colored cliff. Tales about the Hole are innumerable; one of the most popular, which at times has been fused into Hollywood westerns, is that behind the Hole once lay a classic outlaw town, complete with false-front buildings and houses with picket fences, all securely protected by towering cliffs through which there was but the one, narrow entrance that was guarded day and night by sharpshooters with Winchesters.

True, there is a valley behind the wall, and once there were even a few rough-hewn cabins here and there, but nothing resembling a town and nothing so impregnable ever existed. In fact, few persons familiar with the area during its outlaw days could even agree on how valuable the place was as a hideout, except that a posse approaching directly from the east could be held off fairly easily at the Hole. But the ability to defend the valley at the Hole itself meant little, because anybody familiar with the valley would not invade it from that direction. To the north, west, and south it was surrounded by great rolling foothills, all of which contained ancient Indian trails that led in and out of the valley.

Butch's layout on Blue Creek would have been well-suited for holding stolen horses, and yet would have still given the appearance of a normal spread. To his original claim of 160 acres he added 420 acres of surrounding land. In addition to various outbuildings Butch planted trees (Mormon poplars?) and dug irrigation ditches, traces of which could still be seen as late as the early 1980s.[8]

Despite being a little short on cash, as Shorty Wheelwright said, Butch may have enjoyed an exciting summer and fall on Blue Creek though he may have arrived on the scene a little too late: the heyday for rustlers in Johnson County was nearing an end. Just before Christmas Butch got word that law officers were closing in. Whether it was the law or stock detectives hired by the cattle owners is unclear. In any event, Butch no doubt saw the disadvantage of somebody in his line of work being too immobile. He quickly unloaded his Blue Creek property to another rancher, Jim Stubbs, and left the area, promising Stubbs that he would send him the deed the following spring.[9]

On Butch's return from Blue Creek he may have picked up work at the Pitchfork Ranch, a large spread on the Greybull River northwest of Thermopolis.[10] The Pitchfork probably need extra help. Practically no snow had fallen in the Big Horn Basin that winter, and the cattle were drying out. The Pitchfork ranch hands were kept busy keeping water holes open.[11]

Butch and Al Hainer may have returned to their Horse Creek ranch off and on during 1891. They also may have spent some time at Tom Osborne's Quien Sabe Ranch, an operation previously owned by a group of Englishmen who had abandoned it several years earlier following a severe winter. The Quien Sabe, in northeastern Fremont County, lies just south of Copper Mountain on upper Hoodoo Creek, about five miles south of the Hot Springs County line.[12] More than likely Butch and Hainer divided their time between the two operations, though. As they were seen less and less at Horse Creek, neighbors began to assume they had abandoned the ranch.[13]

According to Cassidy's old bank-robbing pal Matt Warner, Butch made at least one trip west to Star Valley, near where Warner and Tom McCarty had settled. When Warner heard that Butch was in the area, he and McCarty looked him up. It had been three years since the trio had parted after the Telluride robbery. Warner recalled that Butch seemed just like his old self, except that maybe he looked a little "older, tougher, and harder."[14]

Butch may have regretted his hasty departure from Johnson County— he had let the sound of hoof beats scare him away. A proud man, he probably felt that he had overreacted. He wanted to return, Warner said, and he invited Matt and McCarty to go along. According to Warner, Butch was angry over the big cattle owners waging war against hungry cowboys just because they killed a beef now and then, and against struggling homesteaders who added to their modest herds by plucking off strays.[15]

The battle was heating up in Johnson County. Angry that the law was permitting small ranchers to homestead the best public lands—the areas along creek bottoms—the big cattle companies were fighting back any way they could, including creating illegal "straw man" homesteads, a device by which a large livestock company would hire a cowboy to enter a homestead claim under an agreement that he would later sell it to the company.[16]

Warner claimed that all this troubled Butch considerably. Matt, however, always had a tendency to justify criminal conduct by reciting lofty purposes. More than likely Butch and Warner, and Tom McCarty even more so, were just hankering to do some more serious rustling.

The summer of 1891 was what old-timers called a "weather breeder": mostly dry, cloudless days and nights with just enough rain to keep the prairie green.[17] It was good weather for rustling, since steers could find grass on the run and wouldn't lose much weight.

Once again the trio of Cassidy, Warner, and McCarty struck out across open country, this time with pack horses loaded with a rustler's essentials: bedroll, grub, cooking gear, extra lariats, and branding irons. They made a large circle, probably sweeping as far north as Ten Sleep and as far east as the west bank of the Powder River, picking up strays and mavericks as they went.[18] It was clearly a risky venture. Word had spread throughout the area that some of the large livestock owners were no longer going to wait on the law to solve their problems: they were going to hire men who could deal with rustlers on the spot without relying on the law. The rumors were true. During the first week of July, Major Frank Wolcott, manager of the Tolland Cattle Company's VR Ranch, revealed to a few insiders a plan to take a large body of armed men and comb northern Wyoming, exterminating all who were thought to be rustlers.[19]

By the time Butch, Warner, and McCarty were ready for their return trip, they had gathered nearly fifty head of cattle—enough for a small profit but not so many that they couldn't handle them conveniently, unless of course they ran into serious trouble. Using field glasses they watched the trail behind them all morning, and, believing they were fairly safe, stopped for a noon meal. At this point they were more than likely somewhere east of Thermopolis and north of Lost Cabin, probably just north of the Washakie County line. It was fairly open country, mostly grass in long, narrow valleys formed by dried-up streams that left as their only trace an occasional winding row of brush and timber. The three had just removed their saddles and gear to rest their horses when Butch spotted riders on the horizon: maybe ten of them, all carrying Winchesters and pushing their horses hard as if they knew exactly where they were heading. Butch shouted to the others, and they tossed their gear aside and quickly slapped their saddles back on. The cattle and pack horses were forgotten—the outlaws would soon be racing for their lives.[20]

Within minutes the riders were close enough to fire, and bullets began to whistle past. It was no use to try to make a stand: there was nothing to hide behind, and, worse still, the trio had not brought their rifles. By the time they could do any damage with their six-guns the Winchesters would have finished them off. It was simply a matter of whose horses would carry them faster and farther.

Butch and his companions were well mounted, and the chase continued throughout the afternoon. Around sundown, as they reached the top of a hill, the trio spotted the first real timber they had seen for hours: a curling strip of trees, mostly willows, about two miles ahead. The way the strip curled, and with so many willows, they knew it had to be the Wind River. They decided that their best chance was to split up. Butch veered off to the right, McCarty to the left, and Warner, kicking his horse hard, raced straight ahead.

Warner could hear the distant crack of the Winchesters. Ducking his head he leaned forward and hugged his horse's neck, trying to make as small a target as possible. When he reached the trees he saw that the spot he had picked was not as heavily timbered as it had looked from a distance. The river itself offered a possibility, but it was running high and swift and he was on a steep bank. For just a moment he was sure that he was done for, but when he glanced back he saw that the riders had slowed down, perhaps thinking that he was going to turn and fight. This gave him a chance. He spurred his horse forward and plunged down the bank and into the water, letting the swift current take them both under. In seconds they were being swept downstream. His followers, apparently unsure whether he had actually entered the water or was waiting just below the edge of the river bank to pick them off, approached cautiously. By the time they realized what had happened, darkness had set in and Warner had drifted out of sight.[21]

How Butch and McCarty escaped is not known. McCarty does not include a description of this little foray in his memoirs but both probably reached the line of timber. If the pursuers split up to follow them, they too would have approached the trees cautiously, thus giving Butch and McCarty time to enter the river and escape the same way as Warner had.

Following this misadventure Butch made another mistake, one that cost him dearly. In August of 1891, while Butch was hanging out at a spot called Mail Camp in northern Fremont County near the southern fork of Owl Creek, a young cowboy rode into camp trailing three fine-looking saddle horses. Butch liked the looks of the animals and the two men soon made a deal. It was a simple sale, the kind that Butch probably had made dozens of times. The horses, of course, were stolen. Maybe Butch was aware of this or maybe he wasn't, but it is unlikely that he gave it much thought. He should have.

It isn't known whether Butch was engaged in any serious outlawry during this period, that is, other than stealing livestock. He and Al Hainer may still have been part of the ubiquitous network of horse thieves. It was said that by now Butch had developed quite a reputation as a rustler—so much so that ranchers wanted him on their payroll as a hand because it was generally known that he would not steal from an employer.[22] Although the dates are nearly impossible to verify, various sources suggest that during this period Butch worked for Charlie Ayers, who owned a spread near the Colorado line just south of Dixon, Wyoming; for Tom Beason, whose ranch was east of Opal, Wyoming; and for the huge Two-Bar Cattle Company, which had headquarters near Casper.[23]

Butch spent at least one winter at Rock Springs, Wyoming. Rock Springs was a coal mining town, and many cowboys would ride in during late fall to work for the coal companies. According to several writers, Butch found an easier job: cutting and selling meat for a butcher, William Gottsche.[24] Although most cowboys would have considered butcher shop work degrading for a man born to straddle a horse, Butch adjusted well to the job. His sister proudly said that it was not long before Butch made friends with most of the housewives in town and that they could count on him to always give them "good measure with the meat."[25]

Not all Wild Bunch historians accept the butcher shop story. Jim Dullenty doubts that with so many lawmen about Butch would have taken a job in a place as public as a butcher shop. As to Butch's giving customers good measure with the meat, Dullenty, no fan of Lula Bentenson's stories about her brother, says that it "sounds like another of Lula's many inventions."[26]

On the other hand, some writers believe that the butcher shop job gave George Cassidy, formerly Bob Parker, his nickname "Butch."[27] However, several other versions of this story exist. Matt Warner claims that he and Tom McCarty gave Butch his nickname after Cassidy had difficulty operating a favorite rifle of Warner's, one that Matt had previously named "Butch." Warner said that when Butch fired the gun, it knocked him on his back.[28] Another version is supplied by Larry Pointer, citing the enigmatic William Phillips manuscript *Bandit Invincible*, in which Phillips, who may have known and even ridden with Butch, claims that Butch acquired the nickname from a camp cook on a roundup when Butch was designated to furnish meat for the outfit.[29]

Outlaw writer Kerry Ross Boren also contributes a version. Boren claims that his grandfather, Willard Schofield, whose family knew the Parker family, once asked Butch himself how he came by the name. The answer Butch supposedly gave fell short of resolving the matter. According to Grandpa Schofield, Butch gave Matt Warner the credit, but not for the reason Warner claimed. Boren says that Butch's answer was that he got the nickname "a long time ago when I first came to this area. I took a job in Rock Springs in the butcher shop when I needed to lay low for a while. Matt Warner nicknamed me Butch; he thought it was a big joke."[30]

While praising her brother's talents as Rock Springs's friendly butcher, Lula Parker Betenson failed to mention that he probably acquired his meat-cutting skills as a rustler. It was not unusual for rustlers to steal calves, butcher them out, and, often through the help of a friendly rancher, sell the meat to retailers in town. This practice was especially popular in and around Rock Springs.[31] In a variation of this custom, in some towns the butchers themselves were tied in with the rustlers. The rustlers would steal the cattle and drive them to slaughterhouses operated by the butchers; the meat would be available for sale at local shops the following day.[32]

According to regional historian John Rolfe Burroughs, Butch had a good time that winter in Rock Springs, where he "walked pretty much on the wild side of life, spending his spare time and money drinking and gambling in Rock Springs's numerous saloons and paying far more attention to the ladies than was his custom."[33] Sources generally agree that Butch was not a heavy drinker, but he was known at times to enjoy himself to the fullest.

Old-timers tell of an incident in Lander when Cassidy and a few friends startled the town with one of their frequent pranks. As a contemporary source described the incident, "Cassidy and several exuberant fellow spirits hitched four unbroken horses to the old overland stage coach, filled the inside with rouged women and, having disposed themselves on top of the conveyance wherever there was room to hang on, let her go reeling down the main street to the banging of their six-shooters and the shrieking of the female passengers."[34]

On another occasion, Harry Logue, a Fremont County deputy sheriff, recalled that Butch, Al Hainer, and a man named Whitney had rented rooms at the Cottage Home Hotel at Fourth and Main Streets in Lander.

Probably well-liquored, the three men talked a friend, John Lee, into letting them take a ride in his buckboard. According to Logue:

> They went on up the street to the old livery stable which stood on the
> bank of Dick Creek where Walt Ferry's feed store now stands. Well,
> they got the horses hooked up O.K., and Whitney and Butch got in.
> The team started to run down Main Street until they ran afoul of a
> hitching rack in front of Coalter's Saloon, just about where the
> Thomas Pool Hall is located. Butch didn't stop when the team did
> and he landed on the sidewalk. Whitney [landed] in the middle of the
> street. The buckboard was a total wreck. Butch called to John Lee,
> who was standing out in front of the Noble & Lane Store, now
> Lander Furniture and Hardware, "John, come and get your buck-
> board."[35]

In addition to practical jokes, Butch may have had a weakness for the
gambling tables, and there is some evidence that he might have been an
easy mark. According to Will Simpson, during one winter in Lander Butch
lost a considerable amount of money at faro.[36] Apparently it was not unusual for both Butch and Al Hainer to be frequently taken at the faro and
monte tables.[37]

Butch also had an unlucky night in Rock Springs. A story is told that one
evening Butch was seen drinking with a fellow customer who later complained to the authorities that he had been robbed. Butch was arrested and
thrown in the Rock Springs jail, but he was eventually released when no
evidence could be produced to convict him.[38] No arrest record of this incident has been found, but according to one account, as related by Harry
George Parker, son of Rock Springs town marshal Harry S. Parker, the
guilty party was the bartender, who had scooped the money off the bar
while the victim was in a drunken stupor.[39]

Another story passed down by the Parkers tells how Butch eventually
became a long-term client of noted Wyoming attorney Douglas A. Preston,
one of the state's foremost criminal lawyers. According to the tale, one
night Butch interceded after Preston became involved in a brawl while
drinking in one of Rock Springs's barrooms, possibly saving the lawyer's
hide. As the story goes, Preston felt indebted to the young cowboy and
thereafter was at Butch's side whenever he or his renegade friends ran afoul
of the law.[40] Before long, attorney Preston was needed.

A Five-Dollar Horse

1892–1894

The young cowboy who sold the three horses to Butch at Mail Camp was twenty-year-old Joseph "Billy" Nutcher, a Lander fellow who at the time was riding with a gang of rustlers and horse thieves operating in and around the Owl Creek Mountains.[1] Butch later argued that Nutcher told him that he had picked up the animals in Johnson County, that he had traded cattle for them, and that their "title was all right." This information was, of course, questionable. Witnesses later claimed that Nutcher had stolen the horses from the Grey Bull Cattle Company in northern Wyoming, an outfit owned by absentee British rancher Richard Ashworth.[2] Butch and Hainer were named suspects when a witness, David "Arapaho Dave" Blanchard, and possibly several others saw the horses in Cassidy's possession.[3]

When Cassidy and Al Hainer could not be found at Mail Camp, one Big Horn Basin rancher, John Chapman, volunteered to track them down. The large ranch owners in the area had been concerned about Butch and Hainer for some time, especially after a rumor circulated that the two had disappeared from their Horse Creek ranch only to turn up later in Lander flashing a wad of cash. Butch claimed they had made the money in Colorado, but apparently few listeners bought the story.[4]

While searching for Butch and Hainer in the Owl Creek Mountains, John Chapman interviewed an acquaintance of Butch's, James Thomas, who said that Butch had been planning a trip to southwestern Wyoming to somewhere near Evanston. When a clerk at the Shoshone agency at Fort Washakie verified this story, Chapman headed for Evanston. He met with the local authorities there, told them of his mission, and, with the help of Uinta County Deputy Sheriff Bob Calverly, checked most of the ranches in the area. However, they could find no trace of either Cassidy or Hainer, and since winter was approaching Chapman gave up and returned home.[5]

The following April, as Chapman was putting together another team of ranchers to go rustler hunting, he received word that Cassidy and Hainer had been seen in Lincoln County, Wyoming, the first county north of Uinta County, at a ranch near the town of Auburn.[6] The tip sounded reliable. Furthermore, rumors had been drifting in and out of Big Horn country that somewhere in the Teton Basin nearly a thousand stolen horses were hidden away, some of them highly valuable animals imported from Belgium.[7]

Chapman saddled up and headed southwest once more, and once again sought the services of deputy sheriff Bob Calverly. Officially, Auburn was outside of Calverly's jurisdiction, but Uinta County Sheriff John Ward, who had a more-than-average dislike of rustlers, did not mind bending the rules when it seemed worthwhile. Also, Calverly was one of his most able deputies and had an excellent record of breaking up gangs of cowpunchers who helped themselves to other people's cattle.[8]

Chapman and his neighbors desperately wanted to nail Butch Cassidy and Al Hainer. He and his fellow Big Horn ranchers had dedicated that spring to clearing their range of horse thieves. And they were not the only ones. The spring of 1892 saw the beginning of an enormous effort by ranchers in the West to tackle the very serious problem of horse stealing. A major sweep began in the Badlands of South Dakota and spread across Wyoming to Star Valley on the Idaho border. This effort was soon followed by a similar purge in the state of Washington. Come summer it was Idaho ranchers' turn, followed shortly thereafter by a second sweep across Wyoming's Big Horn Basin.[9]

Little has been written about these purges. Unlike the battles between the Wyoming Stock Growers Association and the rustlers in Johnson County, Wyoming, which were covered extensively by the press, in other areas of the West horse thieves were hunted down and shot or hanged on the spot with little being said.[10]

Several versions of what happened when deputy sheriff Bob Calverly and stockman John Chapman arrived at Auburn looking for Butch and Al Hainer survive. According to one story they learned that Butch and Hainer were hiding out southeast of town in the rugged area that is now Bridger-Teton National Forest. The lawmen also heard that the two rustlers had hired a young girl named Kate Davis to run errands for them into town. Calverly and Chapman waited around town until Kate showed up and convinced her that it would be to her advantage to take them out to the ranch where the two men were supposed to be holed up.[11] Another version of this incident is that Kate Davis was the daughter of a rancher near

Afton, Wyoming, and that she was picking up mail for Cassidy and Hainer at the Afton post office (rather than at Auburn). Afton is about eight miles southeast of Auburn. According to this version, the local postmaster pointed the girl out and Calverly and Chapman simply followed her out to the ranch where Butch and Hainer were hiding.[12]

In yet another account the site of the ranch where the two fugitives were holed up was actually at Ham's Fork, which, depending upon the route taken, in those days was from forty to sixty miles southeast of Auburn.[13]

Regardless of which version is correct, John Chapman and deputy Calverly, accompanied by local law officers, arrived at the ranch on April 11, a Monday. They found Hainer working at a small sawmill on the property, some distance away from the ranch house. The lawmen easily got the drop on Al, put him under arrest, and tied him to a tree.[14]

Butch was up at the bunkhouse, unaware that Hainer had been captured. In one version of the events, Butch was said to be lying on a bunk near the door with his gunbelt hung over a nearby chair, expecting the arrival of Kate Davis with the mail. When he heard unfamiliar footsteps, he went for his gun.[15] According to Deputy Calverly, he shouted through the door to Butch that he had a warrant for his arrest. Calverly said that Butch shouted back, "Well get to shooting!" With that, Calverly charged into the bunkhouse, pointed his revolver at Butch's stomach, and pulled the trigger. The gun, however, misfired. By then Butch had grabbed his gun, though one of the men with Calverly had also rushed in and somehow got caught between Butch and the deputy, preventing Butch from getting a clear shot at the deputy.[16] In the meantime, Calverly, struggling with his misfiring gun, kept snapping the trigger. Finally, on the fourth snap the weapon fired, and the bullet struck Butch a glancing blow on the forehead. It wasn't a serious wound, but it stunned Butch enough that Calverly and the others were able to subdue him.[17]

Butch and Hainer were taken to the Uinta County jail at Evanston and then transported back to Lander. Word was sent from Lander to Rock Springs lawyer Douglas A. Preston that his client was in trouble. A local lawyer, C. F. Rathbone, was hired to represent Hainer. Their case was scheduled for arraignment on July 16. Apparently neither Butch nor Hainer could make bail, set at $400 each, and they sweated out the next two months in the Fremont County jail.[18]

In the typical awkward and redundant legalese of the day, the charges against Butch and Hainer stated that they "unlawfully, knowingly, and feloniously did steal, take and carry away, lead away, drive away and ride away . . . one horse of the value of Forty Dollars of the goods, chattels and personal property of The Grey Bull Cattle Company, a corporation duly organized and existing under, and, by virtue of the laws of the State of New Jersey, and doing business within the said County of Fremont, State of Wyoming."[19]

The prosecuting attorney for Fremont County was James S. Vidal; Otto Franc, the primary prosecuting witness who filed the original complaint and later testified against Cassidy and Hainer, was owner of the Pitchfork Ranch, a large spread in the Big Horn Basin that bordered the rangeland of the Grey Bull Cattle Company, the supposed owner of the stolen horses.[20] Other witnesses listed by the prosecutor as having been interviewed and upon whose testimony the charges were based were Arapaho Dave Blanchard, John Chapman, James Thomas, David Stewart, Speed Stagner, and the young rustler who had sold the horses to Butch, Joseph "Billy" Nutcher.[21]

Butch and Hainer remained in jail until July 30 when their lawyers, with the help of four local citizens, finally arranged bail. Court records show that two Lander businessmen, Fred Whitney and Leonard Short, signed a surety bond for Cassidy, and that Bill and Edward Lannigan, sons of a local saloonkeeper, did the same for Al Hainer.[22]

The judge set to hear the case was Jesse Knight. Under the law, Butch and Hainer were entitled to a speedy trial though they apparently waived this right and agreed to prosecutor James Vidal's request for a continuance because two of the prosecution's witnesses, John Chapman and James Thomas, were absent. It is unusual that lawyers Preston and Rathbone would agree to do this unless they believed that the evidence was strong to convict their clients even without the missing witnesses. It can only be assumed that the lawyers had good reason: possibly in return for the prosecutor's agreement not to insist on higher bail, or perhaps to allow Butch and Hainer time to find defense witnesses, or, as is sometimes the case, to allow time for the defendants to obtain money to pay their lawyers' fees.

The court's granting of a continuance and the defendants' release from jail meant that Butch and Hainer were free for at least a year.[23] Butch settled for a while in a cabin on Owl Creek, around thirty miles west of Thermopolis and sixty to seventy miles north of Lander.[24] While there he became friends with Christian Heiden, a lad of about fifteen whose parents had homesteaded near the huge M-Bar Ranch on the north fork of Owl Creek.[25] Heiden's uncle ran a saloon near the ranch, a spot where Butch and Al Hainer occasionally washed away the taste of trail dust. Christian Heiden, despite his youth, drove a stage on the Grey Bull River road, and sometimes Butch would tie his horse on back and ride shotgun. According to young Chris, Butch made a good companion on a lonely run, as did his "wicked looking Colt .45 with a big wooden handle." Also, Heiden found Butch fun to have along. He remembered him as quick-witted, almost always full of entertainment, and usually packing a bottle on his hip.[26]

Heiden also recalled that one of Cassidy's pals in those days was Jacob "Jakie" Snyder. Snyder, who was four years younger than Butch, came from Helena, Montana, and, like Butch, apparently specialized in the "horse business." Four years later Snyder was sentenced to the Territorial Penitentiary at Laramie for stealing Indian ponies.[27]

It is not known why Butch relocated from Horse Creek to Owl Creek. Possibly to get money for his legal fees, and if so, it was an ironic twist since Butch may have acquired the money by stealing livestock from the very ranchers who were trying to send him to prison. The big stock owners of the Big Horn Basin seldom saw all of their cattle. They usually estimated the size of their herds from a "book count," they trusted their cowboys to brand all new calves and watch over them, and, to account for the effects of disease and predators (both animal and human), they routinely wrote off a two percent loss each year. This loose arrangement left a rather wide opening for ranch hands to start their own herds or to work out a deal with somebody like Butch to let a few head intentionally slip away.[28]

During the latter half of 1892, Butch may have traveled to Texas. A story is told that once while Butch was visiting Fannie Porter's bordello in San Antonio (which eventually became a favorite hangout for the Wild Bunch), he took a fancy to one of Fannie's young girls, a sixteen-year-old named Laura. Believing that she was too young and too pretty for Fannie's stable of prostitutes, Butch took her with him on his way back to Wyoming and placed her with a Mormon family in Wellington, Utah.[29]

Butch returned to Lander on June 20, 1893, ready to stand trial before Judge Jesse Knight. This time, however, Butch and Al Hainer's lawyers asked for a continuance, claiming that the defendants had found two witnesses whose testimony was vital to their case but who could not be present to testify until a later date. According to Preston and Rathbone, the two witnesses—J. S. Green and C. F. Willis—had stopped off at Mail Camp while on a trip from Johnson County, Wyoming, to Uinta County, and were present when Nutcher sold Butch the horses. Preston and Rathbone claimed that subpoenas had been issued ordering the two men to appear in court on the trial date, but that the subpoenas had not been returned. However, in their motion for the continuance, Cassidy and Hainer stated that they had been in contact with Green and Willis and that both men had promised to attend the trial if it were postponed until July. Unpersuaded, Judge Knight denied the request and ordered the case to go to trial. His reason does not appear in the court records.

Court was convened and a jury was selected and seated. Prosecutor James Vidal, who had brought the charges against Cassidy and Hainer the previous term, had been replaced during the fall election by Butch's old friend and neighbor Will Simpson, who had given up ranching long enough to study law. Perhaps because of this friendship or perhaps because he had just recently been admitted to the bar and was without trial experience, Simpson chose not to try the case himself.[30] Instead a special prosecutor, former judge M. C. Brown, was hired to represent the state.

The prosecution presented its evidence and rested. The defense, apparently without witnesses and believing the prosecution did not make its case, did not offer any evidence. The jury apparently agreed that the prosecution had come up short—it deliberated for two hours and acquitted both defendants.[31]

The weak spot in the prosecution's case may have involved positive identification of the horse that Butch was supposed to have purchased, or it may have involved insufficient proof of the true original owner of the animal, both of which would have been necessary for conviction. Either way, the prosecution had apparently anticipated losing: three days earlier a new complaint had been sworn out by the original prosecuting witness, Otto Franc. In this second complaint a different horse was claimed stolen, and the owner was identified as Richard Ashworth rather than the Grey Bull Cattle Company.

When presented with the new complaint Preston and Rathbone probably briefly argued that their clients were victims of "double jeopardy"—being subjected to a second trial for the same crime—but as experienced lawyers they would have known this was a futile argument. By alleging the theft of a different horse (one that had not been named in the first complaint), the prosecution was bringing an entirely new charge. Under the law Butch and Hainer were being charged with a separate crime.[32]

The defendants were again placed under arrest. But neither their lawyers nor the prosecution were prepared to go through another trial immediately. Also, the court's schedule was probably full for the current term. Judge Knight set a new trial date, for probably sometime the following November. Butch and Hainer would have another five months to wait before they knew their fate. Surety bonds were again obtained for both men and they were released from custody.

When November arrived the trial was postponed again, this time until June 1894. No doubt disgusted at this most recent turn of events, Butch saddled up and left town. Just where he went no one knows. He may have spent part of the winter in Billings and Miles City, Montana.[33] By late June 1894 he was back in Lander, ready once more to stand trial.

Sometime between November and June, Butch and Hainer may have had a falling out. There is some evidence, albeit weak, that Butch may have begun to suspect that his partner had double-crossed him. To save his own skin Hainer may have quietly worked a deal with the authorities. If so, Hainer was probably worried that Butch might come looking for him.[34]

Will Simpson was still prosecutor for Fremont County, and this time he decided to try the case himself. The prosecution was much better prepared for this second trial. Englishman Richard Ashworth, absentee owner of the Grey Bull Cattle Company, was present to testify.[35] However, missing from the prosecution's witness list this time was Billy Nutcher, the young rustler who had sold Butch the horse. Nutcher's absence was not explained, but he may no longer have been a willing witness: at the time he was a guest of the state of Wyoming at the penitentiary in Laramie, having been convicted of horse stealing the previous July.[36]

Assuming Will Simpson followed the usual procedures, he opened the prosecution's case with a brief statement to the jury, which was then followed by opening statements from Douglas Preston and C. F. Rathbone. Simpson then presented his witnesses, through which he established the identity of the horse and its value: the identity of the horse's rightful owner, Richard Ashworth; the fact that the horse disappeared from the owner's property; and the fact that the horse was later seen in Butch and Hainer's possession.

Even without the mysterious defense witnesses J. S. Green and C. F. Willis—if they did in fact exist—Douglas Preston believed that, in view of Billy Nutcher's absence, he had a chance to challenge the prosecution's evidence by raising a question in the minds of the jury as to just how the horse actually came into Butch's possession. Preston was ready to introduce into evidence an authentic-looking note that purported to be a bill of sale signed by a known horse dealer from Nebraska. The bill supposedly contained a description of several horses, including a description that matched perfectly the horse that the prosecution claimed was stolen and later found in Butch's possession.

The instrument was obviously a forgery, and it never left the counsel table. Just as Preston was about to introduce it into evidence a man edged his way up to Preston and whispered something in his ear. Those sitting nearby may have noticed that the attorney suddenly looked a little pale. The messenger said to Preston: "See that big man in the middle of the fourth row? He's the fellow whose name is signed to your bill of sale. The prosecution brought him here."[37] Disheartened, Douglas Preston probably took a deep breath, carefully folded the document, and returned it to his briefcase.

The bill of sale could have raised a reasonable doubt as to Butch's guilt, all that would have been needed for an acquittal, but without it the defense had little chance of winning. Preston did the best he could, probably arguing that Butch had no knowledge that the horse was stolen. Al Hainer's lawyer, C. F. Rathbone, undoubtedly based his client's defense on the fact that it was Butch, not Hainer, who had bought the horse. The lawyers gave their respective closing arguments and the case was given to the jury.

The jury reached its decision on Saturday, probably late in the day. Rather than reconvene the court on a weekend, Judge Knight announced that the verdict would be sealed until the following Monday, when it would be read in open court.[38]

Early the next morning as prosecutor Will Simpson rode down the main street of Lander he was approached by Al Hainer, still out on bail, and two other men, a Mexican named Armento (who was also a defendant in a case being prosecuted by Simpson that term) and a man named Lamareaux. The three men had been drinking all night and were in a nasty mood. As Simpson passed the livery stable the men rushed him and attempted to pull him off of his horse, apparently intending to drag him inside the stable and give him a good going-over. Simpson, however, grabbed his horse's bridle and hung on, causing the horse, frightened by the scuffle, to kick out, slamming Lamareaux against the stable wall. The other two men backed off instantly, giving Simpson a chance to reach his pistol. Seeing the gun, all three attackers made a hasty retreat.[39]

Fremont County Sheriff Charley Stough heard the commotion and came rushing over. Simpson told him what had happened, and he and Stough rode down to the Fremont Hotel where Judge Jesse Knight was staying. The town was already nervous: during the night somebody had horse-whipped Arapaho Dave Blanchard, apparently for testifying against Butch and Hainer. Also, it was rumored that some of Butch's friends, among them Matt Warner, assumed Butch would be convicted and were coming to cause trouble. A report then came that maybe as many as ten strangers were seen camped about a mile outside of town. Judge Knight immediately authorized Stough to arrest Hainer, Armento, and Lamareaux, and, for good measure, he told the sheriff to find Butch and lock him up, too.[40]

Later in the day word was sent to Lander's concerned citizens that a meeting was to be held that night at F. G. Burnett's jewelry store to discuss how to handle a possible raid by Butch's outlaw friends. At the meeting some suggested that a posse should ride out and deal with them head-on. Will Simpson, however, did not think this was a good idea. He urged everybody to simmer down—to be on their guard, yes, but not start the trouble. Apparently, they accepted his advice.[41]

When court convened the following morning the town was, indeed, on guard. By order of Judge Knight no strangers were to be allowed in the courtroom until after the verdict was announced. The courtroom, however, was full. Ready to assist Sheriff Stough and his deputies were the mayor, town councilmen, and a sizable number of Lander citizens, all armed and prepared for a confrontation. Armed as well were the attorneys in the case and most of the court personnel—even Judge Knight, who had a pistol hidden under his robe.[42]

The courtroom was called to order and the crowd hushed as the written verdict, signed by the foreman George S. Russell, was unsealed and read. The verdict stated: "We the jury find the above named defendant George Cassidy guilty of horse stealing, as charged in the information, and we find the value of the property stolen to be $5.00. And we find the above named defendant Al Hainer not guilty. And the jury recommend the said Cassidy to the mercy of the court."[43]

Judge Knight did show some mercy. He sentenced Butch to two years in the Wyoming State Penitentiary at Laramie. Under the statute, he could have given him ten.

It had been a productive week for Otto Franc, the rancher who had signed the complaint against Butch. Chosen by his fellow Big Horn Basin cattlemen as one of the leaders in the war against rustlers, Franc, also the local Justice of the Peace, had managed to get two of them off the range the same week—the other was a neighbor of Franc's, a homesteader named Isaac Winkle, who had slipped over to Franc's Pitchfork Ranch and slaughtered one of his bulls. On his return to the Pitchfork on July 9, Franc, pleased with his accomplishments, made this entry in his diary: "I return from Lander; the Wind Mill is up and pumping water into the tank near the house; At Lander I had Winkle convicted of killing one Pitchfork Bull and Cassidy for horse stealing."[44]

Douglas Preston filed a motion for a new trial, but Judge Knight turned it down. The grounds Preston specified in the motion were not noted in the court records, but he could have raised several technicalities. One was that Butch was not actually convicted of the crime for which he was accused. Originally Butch had been charged with "grand larceny," at the time a vio-

lation of the Wyoming criminal statutes, which read: "Whoever feloniously steals, takes and carries, leads, or drives away the personal goods of
another of the value of twenty-five dollars or upwards, is guilty of grand
larceny, and shall be imprisoned in the penitentiary not more than ten
years."[45] Actually, Butch could not have been legally convicted under this
section because the jury, in the written verdict, specifically found that the
stolen horse Butch had purchased had a value of only $5.00, not $25.00.
Furthermore, this section of the Wyoming statute states that it applies to a
person who "steals, takes and carries, leads, or drives away" property of
another, which, in Butch's case, the state did not prove. The state only offered evidence that Butch *purchased* the horse that was claimed to be
stolen and that, at the time he purchased it, Butch knew it to be stolen.

Under the common law at the time, any person who purchased or received property known to be stolen was guilty of "compounding a felony,"
which constituted a misdemeanor and carried a lesser sentence than a felony like grand larceny.[46] However, by 1894 many states had enacted criminal statutes that took precedence over the common law and that provided
punishment for receiving stolen property as a separate offense.[47] Wyoming
had such a statute, and it applied specifically to stealing livestock. The statute read: "Whoever steals any horse, mule or neat cattle, of the value of five
dollars or upwards; or receives, buys or conceals any such horse, mule or
neat cattle which shall have been stolen, knowing the same to have been
stolen, shall be imprisoned in the penitentiary not more than five years, or
may be imprisoned in the county jail not more than six months."[48] It is possible that Butch was actually convicted under this section of the statutes,
but it is not likely. The written verdict stated that the jury found Butch
guilty "as charged," which meant grand larceny, not stealing livestock. If
the charge was unclear, that in itself was probably grounds for reversal.

Under the law at the time, unless otherwise instructed by the judge the
jury could simply have stated that Butch was "guilty as charged" and
stopped there. The jury would not have had to make a finding as to the
value of the horse unless specifically told to do so by Judge Knight. However, if the jury found Butch guilty as charged—that is, guilty of grand larceny of a horse worth $25.00 or more—and the evidence failed to establish
the value of the horse at $25.00 (which apparently did happen, since the
jury found the horse worth only $5.00), the conviction could have been
overturned on the grounds that it was not supported by the evidence.

To make things more confusing, it is possible that Judge Knight considered the crime under Section 4988 simply a "lesser offense" to the crime of
grand larceny under Section 4984, so he may have instructed the jury to de-

termine the value of the horse which, in turn, would determine the sentence that Butch should serve. The penalty for grand larceny was "not more than ten years" in the penitentiary, while stealing livestock (or receiving stolen livestock), drew a sentence of "not more than five years" in the penitentiary or "not more than six months" in the county jail.

This speculation raises still another and separate legal technicality. Assuming that Butch was convicted of grand larceny as the written verdict proclaimed, if Section 4988 was considered a lesser offense to Section 4984 and the judge *had not instructed the jury that it could have found Butch guilty of the lesser offense*, the conviction for grand larceny would have been in error and would have been reversible on appeal. This was clearly the law at the time of Butch's trial.[49] From what little is left of the court record it is not clear whether such a jury instruction was given; however, the fact that the jury returned a verdict containing a specific finding as to the value of the horse suggests that the judge did give such an instruction.

If Judge Knight did not give the required instruction, or if the other errors in the law existed, Douglas Preston probably should have appealed Butch's conviction. But what would that have meant? If the appeal was successful, the case would be tried again, probably sometime the following year. Assuming the witnesses were still available to testify for the prosecution, the procedural mistakes in the earlier trial would have been avoided and Butch probably would have been convicted again. It is possible that, after already waiting two years and faced with a probable conviction anyway, Butch would have wanted to serve his time and get it over with. More likely, however, attorney Douglas Preston cut a deal with prosecutor Will Simpson and Judge Knight: accept the verdict and take a light sentence. After all, in the end Butch was sentenced to only two years, when he could have received five years just for the lesser offense of stealing (i.e., receiving stolen) livestock. And for grand larceny he could have received a ten-year sentence. Also, Butch may have exhausted his funds: he may have had no money to pay Preston for an appeal, let alone another trial. Butch and Hainer had probably spent all of their cash, and more than likely had already mortgaged the Horse Creek property to Butch's friend and neighbor, banker Eugene Amoretti Jr.[50]

Despite the trouble he had caused, Butch may still have had friends among Fremont County officials. A story is told that the evening before he was to be transported to Laramie to begin serving his sentence, Butch persuaded the jail deputy to ask the clerk of the court, Ben Sheldon, to allow him to be released long enough to take care of some unfinished business. Sheriff Stough was out of town that evening and, as the story goes, the

jailer walked over to Sheldon's house where Sheldon was watering his garden. "Butch Cassidy wants me to let him loose tonight," the deputy told
Sheldon. "He says there's something he wants to tend to, and that nobody
in town will see him. He promises he'll show up by daybreak." Sheldon
supposedly told the deputy to let him go, adding, "If Cassidy said so, he'll
keep his word."[51]

According to Will Simpson's daughter Ida, Butch spent that night at
Will Simpson's home in Lander, and, even though Simpson had just been
instrumental in sending Butch to prison, it was a friendly visit. In the morning, Butch kept his promise to the deputy: he was back at the jail by
dawn.[52]

Will Simpson's wife and mother were both particularly fond of Butch,
and persons who visited the Simpsons in later years say that the rest of the
family never completely forgave Will for Butch's conviction. Just how
Butch felt about Will Simpson is not known, but Simpson's wife said that,
years later, after Butch was released her husband spotted Butch in town
one day and he "stayed under cover, fearing reprisal."[53]

The Big Stone House

1894–1896

On July 15, 1894, after a long, dreary ride by wagon from Lander to Rawlins, and then hours on the train from Rawlins to Laramie, Butch and five fellow prisoners, all recently convicted of various felonies in Judge Jesse Knight's court, entered the gates of the Wyoming State Penitentiary.[1]

The penitentiary, built in 1872, was an impressive fortress-like structure with exterior walls of hand-quarried limestone and sandstone two-feet thick surrounded by a high, wooden stockade. By 1894 the facility, which had been expanded several times, consisted of a central area, which housed the warden's office, guards' quarters, and dining hall and cellblocks in two wings, each containing forty-two cells. In the original north wing the cells had brick walls and measured six by eight feet. In the south wing, added in 1889, the cells were steel and measured five by seven feet. Each of the men's cells was designed to house two prisoners who slept on canvas hammocks.[2] Over the years the complex would also include a broom factory, blacksmith's shop, barns and livestock pens, boiler houses, icehouses, and a bakery.[3]

In the women's area, which was appropriately isolated from the men's, the female inmates enjoyed a washroom with hot running water and a sewing room.[4]

The prison was located on the west side of Laramie, separated from the town by the Big Laramie River. Not long after the facility was built it was indulgently labeled by the townspeople as the "big stone house across the river."[5] The year Butch became a guest of the State of Wyoming, the average daily prison population was 115 inmates.[6]

On the trip down from Lander to Laramie, Butch and five fellow prisoners were accompanied by Fremont County Sheriff Charley Stough, Deputy Sheriff Harry Logue, and Lander Town Constable Henry Boedeker. As the six sweaty, soot-covered convicts stepped down out of the prison wagon that brought them from Laramie's Union Pacific station, standing nearby was Warden W. H. Adams, a former prison official from Nebraska who had taken the job as warden only the previous November.[7] Adams, a stickler for protocol, was stunned to see that one of the prisoners was not wearing leg shackles. It was George Cassidy, soon to become Convict No. 187. When Adams demanded to know why this prisoner was not shackled, before Sheriff Stough could answer, Butch, with his sense of humor apparently undiminished, muttered to the warden, "Honor among thieves, I guess."[8]

The prison was impressive, but it was hardly escape-proof. In the first two years of operation, before the wooden stockade was built, eleven of the forty-four inmates being housed there had managed to escape.[9] The stockade helped reduce the problem some, and by 1894 the escape rate had dropped considerably. But while Butch was confined there at least four successful breakouts occurred. On October 3, 1894, Kinch McKinney, a rustler from Laramie County, scaled the stockade and was gone for over two months. The following month John Tregoning, a Fremont County cowboy serving life at hard labor for second-degree murder, slipped away during a snowstorm while working in one of the prison fields. He was never recaptured. On May 15, 1895, Tom Morrison, a Carbon County roughneck also in for second-degree murder, and Butch's acquaintance, Charley Brown, a young cowboy from Texas by way of Fremont County, serving three years for grand larceny, dug through the wall of their cell into the cellar below and then under the foundation of the building to the outside. Brown was captured two days later, but Morrison was free for over eight months.[10]

If Butch had thoughts about joining in on these breakouts, he never acted upon them; he apparently served his time without incident. At least the Prison Record Book officially credits him with good conduct.[11] His sister Lula believed that he was a model prisoner throughout his sentence, even though all the while he was deeply bitter over the conviction.[12]

At the time, Butch's family may not have known that he was in prison.[13] He was convicted as George Cassidy and served his sentence under that name. Had the family known they may have attempted to gain him a pardon, as they had done for his brother Dan, who in July 1894 was in his fourth year of a life sentence at the Detroit House of Corrections for robbing the United States mails. During most of Butch's confinement the Parker family was engaged in an all-out effort to obtain Dan's release. Arguing that Dan's sentence was totally out of proportion to his crime, in 1895 the Parkers began writing a series of letters to Joseph Rawlins, U.S. Senator from Wyoming, and Frank Cannon, U.S. Senator from Utah, pleading Dan's case. They followed up with direct pleas to President Grover Cleveland. When that failed the family hired a lawyer to point out possible procedural errors in Dan's conviction, and they also prevailed upon the U.S. district attorney who prosecuted Dan to write on his behalf, pointing out that Dan had been sufficiently punished under a statute that was clearly too severe.[14]

The family's dogged efforts finally paid off. While President Cleveland saw no reason to interfere with the court's decision, his successor, William McKinley, did. In December 1897, over two and one-half years after the family began their campaign, President McKinley granted Dan a pardon.[15]

If the Parker family did know about Butch's confinement in Wyoming at the time, one may wonder why they chose to intervene on Dan's behalf but not his. Butch, however, had been sentenced to only two years. In view of the many months it took to obtain Dan's release, the family may have felt that it would have been a waste of time to plead Butch's case.

Lula later said that she was convinced that it was Butch's imprisonment that really made an outlaw out of her brother.[16] She may have been right. Up to the day he entered the gates at Laramie it was quite possible that he still might have chosen to straighten out his life. Of course, this has been said of many lawbreakers, that their criminal ways were instilled in prison. But in Butch's case it may have been true. From the day Bob Calverly arrested him at Ham's Fork, and except for the few months he sat in jail, Butch was out on bail—free to thumb his nose at the law, ride off, and avoid the risk of prison. Unless Douglas Preston offered him false hopes about an acquittal (something lawyers seldom do), Butch must have known that he faced a good chance of being convicted. Yet he stayed around and faced trial, which suggests that maybe he still gave some thought to serving a sentence if he had to and eventually returning to society as a useful citizen.

But if he had those thoughts he left them behind the prison walls. In prison an inmate joins a brotherhood that is capable of conveying a powerful influence. The experts say that prison seldom makes a man a criminal—typically the criminal has already established a lawbreaking pattern—but it does offer a school for crime. They say that some men, especially the younger ones, actually look forward to the criminal environment that prison offers.[17]

Whether Butch took advantage of this environment isn't known; we don't even know who all became his pals at Laramie. In the prison yard a newcomer initially tends to hang out with other newcomers. In Butch's case, on the trip from Fremont County he had spent almost two days in the company of five other prisoners. One was twenty-one-year-old Harry Gilchrist, originally from Harrisburg, Illinois. Like Butch he had been convicted of stealing horses. He would serve two years and seven months of a three-year sentence. Another, Isaac Winkle, age thirty-nine, was from Embar, Wyoming. While mean-looking, Winkle wasn't much of a criminal: his crime was killing Otto Franc's bull. He had been a laborer before being arrested, and had a wife waiting for him at home. He would be released after serving a little more than one year of a two-year sentence. Bill Nichol, a horse thief from Missouri, was also in Butch's group. He was only eighteen and would serve two years and seven months of a three-year sentence.[18]

The youngest of the group was Charley Brown, age sixteen, the cowboy who briefly escaped by digging through the wall of his cell.[19]

Another inmate who arrived in the same prison wagon with Butch was Bill Wheaton. At twenty-three he was the nearest to Butch in age. He was also a cowboy and, like Butch, from Utah. A tougher customer than the others, Wheaton was in for eight years for manslaughter. He would become a problem prisoner. In March 1899 he and another inmate, Charley Dow, started a fire in the prison broom shop. As a result of this and other bad behavior, he would serve nearly seven years.[20]

Another relative newcomer was John Worley, who entered the penitentiary about a month before Butch. Worley, who was originally from Kansas City, had been a locomotive fireman before he was arrested in Albany County, Wyoming, for grand larceny.[21] There is no evidence that he and Butch became close associates while confined, but Butch, who eventually acquired a greater-than-average knowledge of trains—especially express cars—might have found some of Worley's railroad stories informative.

Butch may have developed a close friendship with an older inmate, Abraham "Rocky" Stoner, a fifty-one-year-old sheep rancher from Cokeville, Wyoming, who was serving a four-year term for larceny.[22] The two apparently hit it off well and would later rekindle their relationship after their release. It was rumored around Cokeville that, in later years, when Butch was leading the Wild Bunch, he used Rocky's ranch as a depository for stolen loot, occasionally even dropping by immediately after a robbery and leaving the proceeds for safe keeping.[23]

Another inmate with whom some say Butch may have kept in touch after prison was a horse thief named Richard Carr—or at least Carr was the name carried on the Prison Record Book.[24] Some believe the man was actually James Bliss, alias C. L. "Gunplay Maxwell," a wannabe outlaw who tried but failed to make it into the Wild Bunch. According to writer Frank

Adams, after being released from the penitentiary Bliss maintained contact of sorts with Butch for a couple of years.[25]

Another prison pal was Tom Osborne, whom Butch knew before entering prison. Osborne owned the Quien Sabe Ranch near Copper Mountain in northeastern Fremont County where Butch often stayed when "dealing" in horses. Butch and Tom had been fairly close until Tom got into a little trouble in 1893. It seems Osborne had befriended a drifter named Thorn while on a trip to Casper. The man fancied one of Tom's horses and asked to buy it, offering to work off the price as a hand on Tom's ranch.

Tom agreed and took Thorn back to the Quien Sabe. While there, Thorn discovered that Osborne had never learned to read. Seeing a rare opportunity, Thorn suggested that, when he had worked off the price of the horse, he should have a bill of sale. Tom said that certainly seemed reasonable and told Thorn when the time came to draw one up. But when Thorn had worked off the price of the horse, instead of preparing a bill of sale he drafted a deed to Tom's ranch and all of his livestock. As soon as Tom signed it, Thorn took off for Lander and had it recorded. When Tom found out what had happened, he went to Lander looking for Thorn, found him at Lanigan's Saloon and shot him dead. Tom was convicted of manslaughter and sentenced to fifteen years. He began his term in December 1893, seven months before Butch entered prison.[26]

Butch was acquainted with at least one other inmate: Joseph "Billy" Nutcher, the young rustler whom Butch claimed sold him the stolen horses. Nutcher was convicted of horse stealing in July 1893 and received a sentence of four years. He would serve three years and five months.[27]

By prison standards in the 1890s, the big stone house was probably average. Built in 1873 as a territorial penitentiary, at first it mainly housed miscreants who preyed upon settlers and homesteaders as they migrated into the area. Later, the discovery of gold in the Black Hills brought a tougher criminal element to the territory and the cells began to fill. In 1880 the prison officially became a federal institution, and a decade later, when Wyoming became a state, it was made the state penitentiary. By then, with the cattle industry flourishing, most new inmates were cattle rustlers and horse thieves.[28]

When Butch entered the gates, there were around a hundred inmates.[29] Butch had been sentenced to hard labor, which for the most part meant working on construction jobs for the improvement of the buildings and grounds, making brooms in the prison workshop, cleaning out the barns and outbuildings that housed the prison's horses, cows, pigs, and chickens, and being detailed to the arduous jobs required in making a success of the prison farm, which included grain fields and fifty acres of potatoes. During July of 1895 Butch also probably worked on the erection of an additional four feet to the stockade that encompassed the enclosed portion of the penitentiary buildings, as well as the addition of three watchtowers at the front of the facility.[30]

For a nineteenth century prison, the Wyoming penitentiary was in some ways progressive. For example, holidays were considered special occasions. During 1894, July 4th was celebrated by bringing an opera company to perform, after which the inmates were given extra free time in the yard. On Labor Day the prisoners were treated to a rodeo, a baseball game, and sack races. There were, however, the same problems that plagued most prisons: diarrhea and stomach complaints were common, especially in the summer months, which led to charges that the water supply was contaminated. Prisoners were supposed to receive a reasonable amount of fresh fruit, but there was seldom enough to go around and the inmates often grumbled. Punishment for misbehavior could be severe: for major infractions inmates were confined in the prison "dungeon" on a diet of bread and water, often handcuffed to chains suspended from the ceiling.[31] For less serious infractions, such as talking without permission or using profanity, prisoners were often relegated to a windowless cell for several days, sometimes handcuffed to the door.[32]

While Butch was learning to adjust to his daily routine in prison, the rest of the country was trying to adjust to hard times of its own. The nationwide business Panic of 1893 was followed by five years of severe economic depression. In Wyoming the livestock industry was hit hard. This nearly brought down the Union Pacific Railroad, which had filed bankruptcy in October 1893. By 1894 Wyoming wool was bringing in little more than half as much revenue as it had from 1890 to 1893, and the cattle industry was doing even worse. In August 1894 the Warren Livestock Company, Wyoming's largest, went into receivership with debts in excess of $200,000, a substantial amount in those days. A related company, the Warren Mercantile Company, which was also the largest concern of its kind in Wyoming, avoided bankruptcy but suffered under a great financial strain for several years. By 1895 four of Wyoming's seventeen banks had failed.[33]

The state also had problems the rest of the country did not face. When Wyoming achieved statehood in 1890, its leaders had great expectations of an influx of enterprising companies and individuals eager to develop the state's sixty-two million acres of rich, virtually untapped resources. When this progress did not happen, property values remained virtually flat. In

1890 the state's total property valuation for tax purposes had been $30.6 million; by 1898 it had increased by only $100,000.[34]

Times were also difficult in Utah. Overall production in the state had declined considerably: many businesses and mines had failed, cash had become scarce, and unemployment was soaring.[35] The cattle industry was hit especially hard. Sales were down generally because of overseas competition and a demand for better breeds of cattle that could provide more palatable cuts of beef than those offered by range stock. In Utah, thanks to a decade of drought plus overstocking and overgrazing, the price of beef had plunged from between $30 to $75 a head down to $8. In the southeastern part of the state, the giant Carlisle ranch began abandoning its ranges in 1892, and by 1896 huge ranches like the Lacy Cattle (LC) Company and Pittsburgh Cattle Company were nearly finished.[36]

The news was more personal from the Big Horn Range. In February 1895 an attempt was made on the life of stockman Richard Ashworth, the British cattle baron who had owned the horse that sent Butch to prison. The attack occurred at Ashworth's ranch house. Shortly after dark a shot was fired through the front room window. Ashworth was standing only a few feet away and should have been killed, but the bullet missed and instead struck a painting of "The Great Stag" that was hanging on the opposite wall. It was later assumed that the bullet had been deflected slightly by the thick glass in the window. There was no evidence that Butch or his friends had anything to do with the incident. The authorities concluded that the shot had been fired by Wilfred Jevons, also an Englishman and a foreman at Ashworth's ranch. Jevons, who committed suicide later that evening, was known to have been infatuated with a young lady who was staying with Ashworth.[37]

Such was the news from the outside when, shortly after Christmas of 1895, Butch, whose sentence would not be up until the following July, learned that he had a chance of being released early. Few inmates served their full sentences unless they were guilty of bad behavior, so Butch had applied to Wyoming Governor William A. Richards for a pardon. His record as an inmate had been good, but the timing was bad: Richards, who had been in office only a year, was already being criticized by his political opponents because of the number of pardons he had issued.[38]

A story has persisted over the years regarding Butch's application for early release. Attempts to determine its source have been unsuccessful.[39] The most popular version is that Butch, after requesting a pardon at the end of a year and a half, was personally interviewed by the governor himself. Butch was supposed to have told Richards that he wanted the pardon because he had some property in Colorado that needed attending to. Richards then asked, "If it is your intention to go straight after you get out, perhaps it could be arranged. You're still young, and smart enough to make a success in almost any line. Will you give me your word that you'll quit rustling?" Butch supposedly replied, "Can't do that, governor, because if I gave you my word I'd only have to break it. I'm in too deep now to quit the game. But I'll promise you one thing: if you give me a pardon, I'll keep out of Wyoming." Richards was said to be so impressed by Butch's frankness that he granted the pardon.[40]

That Butch actually told the governor that he could not quit rustling is difficult to accept and cannot be verified. It smacks of pure myth, rivaling the hokey Robin Hood type of tales that are forever told about Butch. Yet the story persists. At least one writer has suggested that it might be true because Butch was never caught rustling again in Wyoming.[41] But that seems pretty weak reasoning. Why would Butch jeopardize his chance for an early release with such a statement? Butch's rustling days were mostly behind him by then anyway; he would soon became a major outlaw. However, whatever Butch told the governor—if he did in fact even meet with the governor—on January 19, 1896, Butch did walk out of the gates of the big stone house a free man.[42]

If Governor Richards's pardons were being scrutinized, it was quite possible that he did interview Butch personally. The Prison Record Book shows that the governor was at the penitentiary on January 19, the day Butch was released. He had come to Laramie for a meeting with the warden about arranging for the return of an escaped prisoner who had been captured in Idaho. However, the governor had already signed Butch's pardon, two weeks earlier on January 6.[43] If Governor Richards did meet with Butch and did ask him the perfunctory question about going straight, unless Butch was a complete fool, which of course he was not, he told the governor exactly what he wanted to hear and with no conditions.

Free Again

1896

On leaving prison, Butch headed for Brown's Park where his old pal Matt Warner had refurbished a cabin on a ranch on Diamond Mountain. During the time Butch was a guest of the state, Matt had married, having fallen in love with an eighteen-year-old Mormon lass from Star Valley named Rose Morgan. Matt had experienced several brief, unhappy relationships and was just about to swear off women when he met Rose, whom he described as blonde, mighty good looking, middle-sized, jolly, and good company, and having "eyes that plumb got me from the first."[1]

When Matt and Rose married, his bride was unaware that Matt was wanted by the law, but it was a secret that he could not keep for long. When Rose learned the truth she agreed to stay with him, but when Matt refused to give up the outlaw life, even after their little girl, Hayda, was born, Rose had second thoughts. When Matt's luck ran out and he was eventually captured, Rose took Hayda and disappeared. Matt managed to avoid prison by finding a pair of lawyers who, according to Matt, specialized in black-mailing prosecuting witnesses, but it cost Matt every cent he had. After this near miss, and weary from a decade of running, Matt went straight and returned to Brown's Park, hoping that the authorities would forget about him.[2]

But Matt desperately missed Rose and his daughter, and when he finally located them he wrote to Rose, explaining how he had given up the outlaw life and fervently hoped that she and Hayda would return to him. Rose finally gave in and agreed to come and live on Diamond Mountain. Matt was overjoyed: the ranch was beginning to take shape and things looked bright for the Warners. But their happiness was short-lived. For years Rose had been having a problem with a sore on her knee, and when she finally saw a doctor the diagnosis was cancer. The malignancy had advanced to the point where amputation was the only choice.[3] She was taken to the

Fort Duchesne Hospital, where surgeons removed her leg.[4] After the amputation complications set in, and she and Hayda had to move into Vernal, where a doctor could see her regularly. Matt stayed at the ranch, trying to make a go of it.[5] This was Matt's situation when Butch was released from prison. He found his friend living alone, and Butch readily accepted Matt's invitation to move in with him on Diamond Mountain.[6]

Butch had always earned his keep and he no doubt helped his host with his ranching chores, but he likely had other things on his mind. Matt had given up the outlaw life, and he probably suggested to Butch that he do the same. But Butch was probably already plotting his future, and it is doubtful that his plans included ranching in Brown's Park.

Upon his release from prison Butch would have received the usual cheap suit of clothes and maybe a few dollars in cash, but the State of Wyoming did not provide released convicts with the tools that Butch needed for what he had in mind. Although Matt was reformed—or at least said he was reformed—he no doubt had a number of guns lying around the cabin. Apparently none of these suited Butch so he rode into Vernal where he bought a new .45 caliber, single-action Colt revolver at the Ashley Valley Co-op store.[7]

While staying with Warner, Butch renewed another Brown's Park acquaintance: Elzy Lay, a cowboy of Butch's age who had been working at the Bassett ranch when Butch had stayed there in the fall of 1889.[8] Elzy was tall and dark-complected, often described as handsome, although some of his photos do not always bear this out. He was, however, a ladies man: according to his daughter, a woman who knew Elzy in those days once told her that she thought he had "striking dark eyes that radiated charm."[9] Some said that Elzy was also a flashy dresser, and when he dressed up he liked to wear jewelry, especially a diamond stickpin.[10]

For many years Lay's origins were a mystery. Some writers believe he came from Boston.[11] Others said Iowa was his original home.[12] Still others suggested that, like Butch, he hailed from Utah, and that his real name was William McGinnis.[13] In fact, Elzy was born William Ellsworth Lay in McArthur, Ohio, on November 25, 1868.[14] William McGinnis, whose name Lay would use in later years as an alias, was actually Lay's boyhood friend.[15]

Lay's family left Ohio in the late 1860s or early 1870s, migrating first to Illinois, then to Iowa, and finally to northeastern Colorado, settling on a farm between the towns of Laird and Wray.[16] Bored with farm life, as soon as Elzy turned eighteen he and his friend William (Bill) McGinnis struck out on their own. McGinnis, however, got homesick and returned home.

Having lost his wanderlust, Bill settled down, went into business and politics, and eventually served as both Colorado state auditor and state treasurer. Some have speculated that Elzy, when he later became a full-fledged outlaw, used his highly successful and respectable friend's name as a joke.[17]

A story is told that, after splitting up with McGinnis, Elzy's first stop was Denver, where he got a job driving a horse-drawn streetcar. One day while Lay was on the job a drunk attempted to molest a woman passenger, and Elzy threw him off the car. The man landed with such force on the hard pavement that Lay thought he had killed him. Elzy panicked and left town, figuring the law was on his heels. He headed for what appeared to be the nearest place to safely disappear, the rugged wilderness of the nearby Rocky Mountains. Ranging north and west, he picked up work with haying crews that were sweeping through the grassy valleys in the area and eventually found his way to Brown's Park and the Bassett ranch.[18]

Josie Bassett thought a great deal of Elzy and once referred to him as "the finest gentleman I have ever known." Elzy spent much more time in Brown's Park than Butch did, probably several years during the early 1890s when Josie was in her late teens. Josie and Lay went to dances together and apparently saw a lot of each other. In talking to Josie in later years, Elzy's grandson got the impression that she may indeed have been in love with Elzy.[19] However, Josie was also taken with Butch, as was her sister, Ann. In fact, this conflict may have caused problems between the two women. According to a neighbor, a man named Meacham, one day he watched the sisters actually get into a "knock-down-drag-out" fight over Butch.[20]

Elzy Lay was an unusually intelligent lad, and he apparently realized the value of an education.[21] Although in his early twenties by then, Elzy spent at least one winter attending school with Josie and her friends.[22] Some suggest that he continued to improve his mind, even after he became a member of the Wild Bunch, apparently taking books along in his saddlebags.[23]

While Josie was clearly fond of Lay, she was aware that he, like Butch, was involved in things that he did not discuss when she was around. She recalled that both Elzy and Butch were careful never to get liquored up and become too talkative, that for some reason they needed to keep certain things to themselves.[24] Ann Bassett, on the other hand, may have eventually become Elzy's confidante. In later years she reportedly made a very important promise to him: that if anything should ever happen to him, she would dig up a cache of stolen loot he had buried and send it to his mother.[25]

Butch, of course, still under the name Bob Parker, was already wanted for the Telluride bank robbery when he first arrived at the Bassett ranch in

1889. Just when Elzy crossed the line between law abiding and law breaking is unknown. Like Butch, Elzy may have been mixed up in some of Matt Warner's wrongdoings in the late 1880s, including the robbing of a peddler near Brown's Park and maybe some rustling.[26] Also, at some point in time Lay and several partners operated a saloon on the Duchesne Strip, a scattering of shanties about fifteen miles southwest of Vernal, Utah, that served the pleasures of the soldiers at nearby Fort Duchesne as well as anyone else willing to risk being mugged or fleeced for a night of entertainment. The word was that Lay's place, nicknamed the "Gambling-Hell Saloon," was one of the worst spots for Saturday night shootings. It also was rumored that in their spare time, Elzy and his pals counterfeited money.[27]

Debauchery could be endured, even in Utah, but counterfeiting was another matter. It was a serious crime that the federal government did not take lightly. When knowledge of Lay's operation reached the U.S. district attorney's office, he assigned Uintah County Sheriff John T. Pope to ride out and close down Elzy's operation. When Pope took inventory of the saloon's stock, he found $2,000 in phony bills that Lay had failed to dispose of.[28] Even so, there was not enough evidence to convict Lay, or at least no record of a conviction has ever been found.

Lay was probably up to mischief well before the counterfeiting episode. Back in 1893, while Butch was awaiting trial over the stolen horses he had purchased from Billy Nutcher, Elzy got into trouble with a merchant in Lander. Lay and a fellow named Frankie Wilson, who had once been a jeweler in Ohio, talked a local merchant, F. G. Burnett, into trading a new Winchester for a rifle they had. Their rifle was defective and Burnett complained to the sheriff, Charley Stough, claiming that he had been conned and defrauded. Stough picked up Lay and Wilson, but they were able to talk their way out of the predicament. Wilson's luck didn't hold, however: later that year he was convicted of burglary and sentenced to nine years at the state penitentiary in Laramie.[29]

By 1896 Lay was back in Brown's Park, but Josie Bassett was no longer on his mind. Elzy had fallen for twenty-two-year-old Maude Davis, whose father had a ranch on Ashley Fork near Maeser, Utah, which is now a part of Vernal.[30] Lay was working with Maude's brother, Albert Davis, putting up hay. One day Lay came to the Davis home and Albert introduced him to his sister, Maude. Maude later said that she took one look at Elzy and knew that he was the man for her.[31]

While Elzy was courting Maude he stayed with Butch at Matt Warner's cabin on Diamond Mountain, helping to keep an eye on things while Matt was in Vernal with Rosa, whose cancer was rapidly worsening.[32] Matt may have paid Butch and Elzy a little something for tending Matt's livestock, and more than likely they picked up additional spending money plucking off neighboring ranchers' mavericks when they wandered too far from the herd.[33]

Later on, Butch and Lay moved into a former trapper's cabin at what was then called Little Hole, a tiny valley that bordered the Green River north of Vernal. At the time a loosely knit bunch of rowdies called the Bender gang were bringing in counterfeit money from Canada. It didn't take much persuading to talk Butch and Elzy into becoming the outfit's "front runners." The pair would buy the phony money at a discount and take it out to a road ranch at Halfway Hollow west of Vernal, where the owner, Henry Lee, would ride out and unload it at the Uintah and Ouray reservation. Lee would split the proceeds with Butch and Elzy, and they would return to the gang and buy more money. The venture was believed to be fairly short-lived. It seems some of the counterfeit found its way to a store in Vernal, which no doubt upset the local authorities, and the operation had to shut down.[34]

Butch may have renewed yet another acquaintance while at Brown's Park: Tom McCarty. Following their near-disastrous rustling adventure in 1891, when Butch, Matt Warner, and Tom McCarty had to swim the Wind River to escape a posse of cattle owners, McCarty drifted into the shadows. In September 1893, he briefly reappeared at Delta, Colorado. On the morning of September 7, two men entered Delta's Farmers and Merchants Bank, walked up to the cashier's window and drew their revolvers. The cashier, Andrew Blachly, was busy typing. One of the men leaped over the counter and pointed his gun at Blachly and the assistant cashier, H. H. Wolbert. Startled, Blachly shouted for help. The man with the gun told Blachly to shut up, which he did for a few minutes, but as the robbers were gathering up the money Blachly yelled again. The robber turned and fired twice, putting one bullet into Blachly's head, killing him instantly. The robbers grabbed what cash they could and ran through the rear door of the bank and out into an alley, where they joined a third robber who had been waiting with their horses.[35]

Ray Simpson, the younger partner of the W. G. Simpson & Son Hardware store across the street from the bank, was sitting near the front of the store cleaning his rifle, a Sharps 44. When he heard the shots he quickly dropped a shell into the chamber, grabbed several more, and ran outside. The three robbers had just emerged from the alley and were crossing the street. Simpson quickly raised and fired at the last rider. His aim was perfect: the bullet struck the man in the left temple. The shot should have killed the rider instantly, but according to one eyewitness, somehow he remained upright in his saddle for almost a block before he fell.[36]

According to another witness, the second of the three fleeing bandits reigned up and turned, as if he were going to return and help his comrade, but changed his mind and continued on. As he did, Simpson took aim again. His second bullet entered at the base of the man's skull and blew away his forehead.[37]

The remaining robber was Tom McCarty. The two dead men on the street were his brother, Bill, and his nephew, Fred. Tom later said: "As we passed the first street I heard the sharp crack of a rifle, and looking for my partners, I saw one of them fall from his horse; my other companion being a little ahead, then partly turned his horse as though he wanted to see where the shot had come from. I told him quickly to go on, but as I spoke another shot come which struck his horse, and before he could get his animal in motion again another shot came which struck him and he fell dead."[38]

Tom spurred his horse and was almost out of range when a bullet caught one of his horse's hind legs. The animal began to falter, but luck was with Tom that day. He and his companions had planned to change horses just beyond the outskirts of town, and he managed to reach the spot where they had the next relay hidden. He quickly slipped off his injured horse, mounted the fastest looking of the three waiting animals, and was gone.[39]

McCarty rode west along the Gunnison River toward Dominguez Canyon. Somewhere along the way, probably in the wilderness of Mesa County, he found friends who took him in and were willing to hide him. While there he learned that the Delta County authorities had identified him as one of the robbers, but had mistakenly reported that he was one of those killed. Figuring they would no longer be searching for him until they discovered their mistake, he joined a couple of trappers and headed north toward Wyoming. Following a winter of trapping in northwestern Wyoming, which netted him about $1,400, he moved on to the Black Hills. There at a mining camp somebody recognized him, and he had to move on again. He headed further north, probably into Montana, where he settled down and used his $1,400 to go into the cattle business. In early 1896, once he became bored with ranching, he drifted back south to what he would later describe as an "out of the way place."[40]

This place may have been in Rio Blanco County, Colorado, on Texas Creek, about twenty miles southwest of the town of Rangely, where he may have taken the name Charlie Stevens. According to Henry Lee, who operated the road ranch west of Vernal during Butch and Elzy Lay's brief career as front-runners in the counterfeit currency business, Charlie Stevens and Tom McCarty were indeed one and the same. Lee claimed that McCarty, who spent his summers in and around Vernal and the Brown's Park area, admitted this fact to him in June 1897, while he and Lee were planning a robbery of their own.[41] Ralph Chew, another Brown's Park resident, whose father, Jack Chew, lived with the McCartys for a while in Utah as a teenager when he ran away from home, said that this was probably true.[42]

If Henry Lee can be believed (since he was well acquainted with Butch), Tom McCarty and Butch may have crossed paths while Butch was in Brown's Park. On the other hand, Avvon Chew, Ralph's sister, weakens Lee's story. She also knew McCarty but recalled that her father was still receiving letters from Tom well beyond the year Charlie Stevens was supposed to have died. Furthermore, according to Avvon, McCarty did not spend his last years in the Brown's Park area, but rather in Montana, where he gave up the cattle business to herd sheep.[43]

By 1896, Matt Warner's friend Charley Crouse had sold his ranch in Brown's Park and, with a partner, Aaron Overholt, had opened a saloon in Vernal.[44] When Matt was not visiting Rosa or his daughter Hayda, he could be found at the Overholt, a popular watering hole for Crouse's old buddies who used to drop by his ranch.[45] One day in early May, as Matt was drinking with his pal, Bill Wall, a gambler and drifter whom Matt and Butch had known back in Telluride, Colorado, they struck up a conversation with a local prospector and mining promoter, E. B. Coleman.[46] Coleman had a gold campsite near Dry Fork in the Uintah Mountains north of Vernal that he wanted to close down, and he was looking for someone to help him pack up and remove his equipment. Matt later claimed that Coleman offered him one hundred dollars to go with him to the camp, pack up the equipment, and store it at Matt's ranch on Diamond Mountain until Coleman needed it again. According to Matt that was all there was to the arrangement.[47] As it turned out, there was much more.

In reality Coleman and a partner, Bob Swift, had spotted what looked like a good deposit of ore high up in the Uintahs, and he and Swift were trying to find its source. They had a problem, however. Three other men— Dave Milton and two brothers, Ike and Dick Staunton—were also prospecting in the area, apparently looking for the same deposit. Coleman and Swift were worried that Milton and the Stauntons would find the source first. Coleman decided to hire somebody with a reputation as a tough customer to accompany him up the mountain, presumably to scare off their competition. Warner and Wall accepted the offer and rode up with Cole-man. Milton and the Stauntons, however, were not about to be scared off, and a gun battle erupted. Dave Milton and Dick Staunton were killed, and Warner, Wall, and Coleman were charged with murder.[48]

The defendants were locked up in the Uintah County jail at Vernal. When word of the killings circulated throughout town, angry citizens formed a vigilance committee and there was serious talk of a lynching, but Sheriff John T. Pope put extra guards at the jail and managed to keep a lid on things.[49] As soon as it could be arranged the prisoners were transported to Ogden to stand trial there.[50]

Coleman reportedly had some money with which to defend himself.[51] However, Warner and Wall were without funds, and Matt turned to his old pal, Butch Cassidy.

Two versions of what happened next have survived. In one version, as reported by Charles Kelly, several weeks after Warner's arrest Butch visited him in his cell and told him that he would be sending attorney Douglas Preston over from Rock Springs to take his case. When Matt told him that he didn't have the money to pay Preston, Butch told him not to worry, that he would be back in a few days with the money.[52]

Matt Warner remembered it differently. Having been taken to Ogden and not having heard from Butch in three months, Matt said that he smug-gled two notes out of jail by giving them to a prisoner who was being re-leased. The prisoner was to take the notes to Charley Crouse at the Over-holt Saloon in Vernal. In one note Matt asked Charley to pay the messenger $50.00 for his trouble and to send the second note to Butch. In the note to Butch, Matt wrote "we're goners if we don't get some money quick to hire lawyers." Warner said that about a month later Douglas Pres-ton showed up, introduced himself as his lawyer, and told him that he had been paid.[53] Most sources agree that the money came from Butch, with ad-ditional help from Elzy Lay and Henry "Bub" Meeks.

Bub Meeks was from Fremont County, Wyoming. He probably first met Butch when Butch and Al Hainer had their ranch on Horse Creek. Bub's father, Henry Sr., owned property nearby.[54] The Meekses, like Butch's family, were Mormons. In fact, Henry Meeks Sr. was one of the first midwestern Mormon converts to follow Brigham Young to Utah, where he worked as a freighter out of Wallsburg in Wasatch County before moving to Wyoming.[55]

The Meeks's family had been part of a large colony of Utah Mormons that began migrating to Wyoming in the 1880s, first to the southwestern part of the territory, then later up the Old Lander Road and eventually into the Big Horn Basin. As a colony the venture was unsuccessful at first. Plans for ambitious irrigation projects in the Basin failed to work out. Little help came from the Church in Salt Lake City, which had never officially approved of the undertaking. Over half of the Mormons who came with the early groups had left by 1894, but another influx began the following year, and the irrigation ditches were finally completed.[56] For young Bub Meeks, however, bringing life to the parched grasslands by channeling mountain streams did not offer enough excitement. But helping Butch and Elzy Lay rob a bank did.

Montpelier

1896

Montpelier, Idaho, located in the southeastern corner of the state, is nestled snugly in the mountains between what today are the Cache and Caribou National Forests. Founded in 1865 by Mormons at the direction of Brigham Young and named by his followers after what was mistakenly thought to be Young's Vermont birthplace (Young was actually born in Whittingham, Vermont), the town of Montpelier remained isolated and for the most part undefiled until rails were laid nearby for the Oregon Short Line. With the railroad came federal marshals and bounty hunters seeking polygamists, and later a steady flow of travelers. A second business district in Montpelier grew up along the track's right-of-way, the tawdry kind of businesses routinely spawned by the railroads and frowned upon by the Mormons. The town became divided between the old and the new, and a gate was built to separate the two districts—to remind both residents and visitors where they were going and where they had been.[1]

The town grew rapidly and soon had its own bank: a modest single-story structure with log walls faced with the usual false front plus a huge awning to keep out the summer sun that blistered the south side of Washington Street, the town's main thoroughfare.[2]

It was on just such a hot afternoon—Thursday, August 13, 1896—that Butch, Elzy Lay, and Bub Meeks rode into Montpelier trailing a small sorrel pack mare. Their first stop was the general store. From their appearance the storekeeper assumed they were sheepherders, although later witnesses remembered that they were a little too well-mounted and their tack was a little too fancy for average sheepmen, who seldom were seen around Montpelier sporting expensive outfits.[3]

Business was slow in Montpelier that afternoon, and the town was unusually quiet. It was haying time, and the ranchers were busy with the second cutting. In fact, Butch, Elzy, and Meeks had spent the previous two weeks putting up hay just east of town at a ranch eight miles north of Cokeville, Wyoming, near a little town called Border.[4] It had been a hot, tiresome job, hardly fit labor for cowboys used to working from a saddle, but Butch apparently thought it was necessary. The plan was to become familiar with the town of Montpelier and the area around it, especially the best escape routes and the best places to stash relays of fresh horses.

The ranch where the boys had worked was owned by a Montpelier jeweler, S. P. Emelle. During the week Emelle operated a small shop in town while his wife supervised the operation of the ranch. Butch, Elzy, and Meeks had ridden in looking for work and the Emelles immediately hired them. They told Mrs. Emelle that their names were George Ingerfield, Willie McGuiness, and Marty Makensie. She later said that they were excellent workers, although she did notice that they were heavily armed, and when they had time off they went for long rides around the countryside.[5]

Having finished with their business in the general store, Butch, Elzy, and Meeks saddled up and headed east down Washington Street, keeping their horses at a slow walk. As they neared the bank they probably checked the time: a little after 3:00 PM. The bank's normal closing time was 3:30. When the three reached the hitching posts in front of the bank they dismounted. With their backs to the bank, two of them, probably Butch and Elzy, pulled their bandannas up over the lower part of their faces. Several men were standing on the board sidewalk just outside the bank. They may have watched the three men ride up, but probably paid little attention to them. Now, suddenly, they were staring at drawn revolvers and being ordered to step quickly into the bank.[6]

On duty inside that day were Cashier E. C. Gray, his assistant, A. N. "Bud" McIntosh, and a stenographer. Gray was probably at his desk and McIntosh behind the teller's window. Although the bank was fully insured against a daylight robbery, near McIntosh's feet and resting against the wall was a loaded Winchester. Among the customers still in the bank were two of Montpelier's town councilmen, William Perkins and Ed Hoover. They and the others inside the bank later testified to the events that took place that day.

Once inside the masked men ordered everybody to put their hands up and line up with their faces against the wall. One of the robbers, the one witnesses later described as blond and stocky and apparently the leader, remained by the door and covered the crowd with his pistol, while the other man, the taller and darker-complected of the two, went behind the counter and demanded that McIntosh give him all the bills he had. According to the witnesses, when McIntosh answered that there were no bills, the gunman called him a "God damn liar" and cuffed him on the forehead with his revolver. This angered the robber standing guard by the door, who shouted at his partner not to hit him again.[7]

McIntosh dug the bills out of his cage drawer and reluctantly handed them to the masked man, who then quickly stuffed them into a sack he had brought with him.[8] But while the gunman was busy gathering money, McIntosh glanced out the window and got a good look at the third robber who was holding the horses. He was not masked, and McIntosh memorized his features.[9] When the tall robber had cleaned out McIntosh's cage, he headed for the still-open vault and found more bills. As he came out of the vault he noticed a stack of gold coins neatly piled on a table behind the counter, and threw those into a cloth bank money bag as well. As an afterthought he gathered up what loose silver coins he could find in McIntosh's cage and stuffed them into the bag. Last he reached down and picked up McIntosh's Winchester.[10]

The tall gunman calmly carried the money and the rifle out to the horses, where he tied the sack of bills to his saddle and fastened the heavier sacks to the pack on the little sorrel. The blond man remained in the bank until his partner was ready to ride, then ordered everyone to keep quiet and not to leave the bank for ten minutes. He joined his comrades, and they rode off at an easy pace. When they had reached the edge of town they spurred their horses and turned northeast, up Montpelier Canyon on Thomas Fork Road toward the Wyoming line, fifteen miles away.[11]

Cashier Gray waited until he could no longer hear the robbers' hoofbeats, then ran from the bank and gave the alarm. Fred Cruickshank, a part-time Bear Lake County deputy sheriff, was working at his full-time job as a clerk at Brennan and Davis Merchandise Store (located about two blocks west of the bank), when someone ran in and told him about the robbery. According to Cruickshank's grandson, Richard D. Sweet, to whom his grandfather related the story, although Cruickshank was deputized by Bear Lake County he was no professional lawman. Until that day the town of Montpelier, still mostly inhabited by peaceful Mormons, had not needed one. Of course there was the rowdy district down by the tracks, but Montpelier had a town marshal who handled any mischief that went on down there; deputy Cruickshank had very little law enforcement work to keep him busy. His work, for which he was paid $10.00 a month, consisted mainly in serving process papers. He didn't carry a gun and didn't even have a horse. So when he received word that the bank had been robbed he raced out the door of the merchandise store and grabbed the first thing in sight: a bicycle, the old-fashioned kind with a huge front wheel.[12]

Cruickshank shakily peddled down the street as fast as he could go. He had no chance of overtaking the robbers, but at least he could see which way they were headed in making their escape. When he saw that they had taken the road toward the Wyoming line, he gave up and returned to town.[13] He later learned that somewhere about three miles out of Montpelier they had stopped at the ranch of John Jewett, where Jewett was harvesting a field of oats. On Jewett's wagon, which was sitting just off the road, was a pile of oat sacks. Jewett later said that the robbers rode over to the wagon, and one of them took one of the sacks, stuffed something into it and tied it to his saddle. Jewett assumed that it was the money taken from the bank. Satisfied, they spurred their horses and rode on.[14]

Before long Bear Lake County Sheriff M. Jeff Davis and his deputy, Mike Malone, arrived from Paris, then the county seat. They quickly rounded up as many volunteers as they could find and rode off in pursuit. But when the posse reached Montpelier Canyon, they began to have second thoughts. Most were peaceful townsmen; few were used to carrying firearms and even fewer were experienced in using them. When they began thinking that they could be riding into a trap they began to slow down. Instead of waiting for them, Sheriff Davis and Deputy Malone raced on ahead and were soon out of sight. A few minutes later the possemen heard gunfire echoing down the canyon walls. Convinced that the sheriff and his deputy had been ambushed, the shaken volunteers turned and rode back to town.[15]

When the posse returned to Montpelier without Davis and Malone, word quickly spread that the two lawmen had been killed. This fact was reported to the editor of the local newspaper, the Montpelier *Examiner*, who was already preparing the next edition. However, it was not the case. When the sheriff and his deputy discovered that the robbers had stashed away a fresh relay of horses, they realized they were chasing a gang that had planned their flight well and they might be on the heels of hardened professionals. The two lawmen carefully weighed their chances of success and decided to return to town and organize a real posse. (The gunfire the townsmen heard was never explained.) When Davis and Malone returned to Montpelier, however, apparently nobody informed the editor of the newspaper. As a result, when the Saturday edition came out the two lawmen were amused to read about their own deaths.[16]

No sooner had Davis and Malone returned to Montpelier than rumors began circulating that the leader of the gang was Tom McCarty, especially when it was learned that the robbers had crossed the Wyoming state line and were heading north toward Star Valley, where McCarty had once operated.[17] If Star Valley was their destination, Sheriff Davis came up with a plan that he believed would cut them off. He would send deputy Malone with a well-armed posse up Thomas Fork Road, the route the outlaws had taken, while he would take a second posse up Crow Creek Road, a shorter route to Star Valley. He believed that by riding hard he might be able to reach the Valley first and lay a trap for the outlaws. Deputy Cruickshank remained in Montpelier to take messages from out-of-town newspaper reporters and law enforcement officers seeking a description of the bandits. In doing so he learned that it was unlikely that Tom McCarty was involved. According to the Salt Lake City police, McCarty was in his fifties, which, in the opinions of the witnesses at the bank, would have been nearly twice the age of any of the robbers.[18]

Although the outlaws' trail was now twelve hours old, Deputy Mike Malone was able to determine that the trio did not continue northward toward Star Valley but instead turned east at Smith's Fork toward Sublette Flat. Malone found their trail surprisingly easy to follow and sent word back to Deputy Cruickshank that his posse was making progress, but then added that the robbers' obvious familiarity with the terrain gave them a distinct advantage.[19]

Bolstered by another relay of fresh horses, and confident that their hard riding had given them a safe lead, Butch and his companions made a cold camp and gambled on a few hours' sleep. When they saddled up again they left the main trail and took to the rocky ridges. Then, before they returned again to soft turf, they slipped homemade leather moccasins over their horses' hooves—an old Indian trick—which made it difficult for their pursuers to know which way they were heading. This brought an end to the chase. Disheartened, Deputy Malone realized that he had been overly optimistic. Ahead of him lay Commissary Ridge and beyond that, South Fork Mountain. He had absolutely no idea which direction his quarry had gone. Reluctantly, he sent word back to Cruickshank that they had lost the robbers' trail.[20]

Back at the bank an audit should have shown how much the robbers got away with, but several conflicting figures were given. The day after the crime the estimate released to the newspapers was $5,000, but later the amount grew to $7,165, and eventually to over $16,500.[21] Whatever the true amount, Bankers Mutual Casualty Insurance Company covered at least part of the loss. To take advantage of the favorable publicity, Bankers Mutual president, J. C. Rounds, made a special trip to Montpelier to deliver the check. The bank announced that a reward of $500 would be paid for the capture and successful prosecution of the robbers. This amount was later raised to $2,000.[22]

Despite the payment from the insurance company, Assistant Cashier Bud McIntosh was upset over the loss. A superstitious man, McIntosh blamed the loss on bad luck, telling anyone who would listen that fate had dealt the hand that day. The robbery occurred on the 13th day of the month at 13 minutes after 3:00 PM, just after he had made the 13th deposit of the day, which was in the amount of $13.00.[23]

When a week went by and no further trace of the robbers could be found, the editor of the *Examiner*, after noting that the offer of a reward had produced no results, chided Sheriff Davis that the robbers were off somewhere gloating, probably "playing stallion poker or feeding the tiger in some city" with the bank's money.[24] It was more likely, however, that once Butch and his pals eluded Deputy Mike Malone's posse, they rode directly to Rock Springs and deposited the money with attorney Douglas Preston for Matt Warner's and Bill Wall's defense.[25]

With Butch Cassidy's own lawyer and undoubtedly one of the best criminal attorneys in southwestern Wyoming heading up their cause, Matt Warner figured that he and Wall had a fighting chance in court. Douglas Preston, however, informed them that he would not be trying the case himself. He was a Wyoming lawyer, and while he could take part in the trial, Matt and Wall would officially be defended by two Utah criminal defense lawyers, D. N. Straupp and Orlando W. Powers, whose fees had also been paid by Butch.[26] That was how things were done. A lawyer from one state did not go into another state and take business away from lawyers in that state. The local lawyers did not like it, and the judges did not like it. After all, the judges were themselves practicing lawyers before they became judges, and most of them returned to practice after they left the bench.[27] Also, it was wise to have local counsel in on a case. In those days as well as today, court procedure and even substantive law can differ from state to state. A Utah criminal case needed Utah lawyers. Preston assured Matt, however, that Powers and Straupp were as good as they come.[28]

As the opening day of the trial neared, a rumor began to spread throughout Ogden that Butch Cassidy had heard that Douglas Preston was not sure that Warner and Wall would be acquitted. As Charles Kelly told the story, Butch had arranged for Bob Swift, E. B. Coleman's partner at the time of the shooting at Dry Fork, to visit Matt in jail and slip him a note. The note supposedly said: "Dear Matt: The boys are here. If you say the word we'll come and take you out." However, the authorities suspected something like that might be attempted, so they searched Swift and found the note. After reading it they told Swift to deliver the note but act as if nothing had happened. To make sure that Swift complied, the Ogden chief of police stood close by Matt's cell and listened.

Warner read the note and wrote a reply for Swift to give to Butch. It read, "Dear Butch: Don't do it. The boys here have been mighty good to us, and I wouldn't want them to get hurt. Preston says they can't convict us. If they do, we'll be out in a couple of years. Don't take the chance. Thanks anyway."As the story goes, one more note passed between the men, in which Butch wrote: "Matt: If they keep you more than two years we'll come and take the place apart sure as hell. Good luck."[29]

The trial began on September 8. The following day the *Salt Lake City Herald* ran a front-page story reporting that there had been allegations made that the fees for the attorneys for Matt Warner and Bill Wall were being paid out of the proceeds of the Montpelier Bank robbery. The article went on to say that Cassidy and his gang were camped outside Ogden, waiting for an opportunity to rescue Warner and Wall.[30] According to the *Herald*, "A bold plot to set him [Warner] free at the point of pistols has been discovered. Cassady [sic], at the head of a gang of desperadoes, has planned to be present at Warner's trial. When the opportunity should present itself, Sheriff Wright and his deputies were to be overpowered—shot down like so many dogs, if necessary, and the prisoners liberated."[31]

When interviewed by a reporter from the *Standard*, an Ogden newspaper, Preston vehemently denied the accusation, calling it a malicious falsehood and claiming that he had not been engaged by Cassidy to defend Warner and Wall, and that he had received his fee before the Montpelier robbery when he was hired by friends of Bill Wall, which was well before the Montpelier robbery. He added that the allegation that Cassidy and his gang were camped outside Ogden was also false. He insisted that Cassidy was in Vernal and had been there for some time. He also denied that there was any truth to the rumor that Cassidy had committed the Montpelier robbery.[32]

It had been alleged that Cassidy was wanted by the authorities and that there was a reward for his capture. Preston said that this also was untrue, that Cassidy could produce reliable proof that he was not in Montpelier at the time of the robbery. And as for the reward, Preston said that if any party will deposit $1,000 in any bank payable to the sheriff of Weber County upon the delivery of Cassidy, he, Cassidy, will surrender to any officer who says he wants him.[33]

Preston blamed the reward story on a detective from Iowa who had fabricated the whole tale. In his interview with the reporter from the Ogden *Standard*, Preston stated: "Cassidy can prove by reliable testimony that he was not nor could he have been at Montpelier at the time of the robbery. The truth is that Cassidy is not wanted anywhere by the authorities, and the same is true of Warner. In face of all the charges in the *Herald*, upon investigation it has been found that he is not wanted on a single criminal charge. All this sensational stuff given for publication at this time, in my opinion, emanates from the overdrawn imagination of a would-be detective who is looking for notoriety and for the purpose of stiffening up a weak case."[34] Attorney Orlando Powers issued a similar denial, claiming that the story in the *Herald* was "infernal rot." He said that he was employed to defend Warner, Wall, and Coleman not later than ten days after Milton and Staunton were killed. He said that he was hired by Coleman's wife, and that his fee, part of which was paid in advance, was guaranteed by Coleman's brother, who lived in Iowa.[35]

Prompted by the denials by attorneys Preston and Powers, the editor of the *Ogden Standard* jumped on his rival newspaper, the *Salt Lake City Herald*, calling the article about the Cassidy involvement in the trial "the fake of the century," a "gigantic lie," and an "outrageous piece of work." A reporter from the *Standard* sought out Weber County Sheriff Heber Wright, who stated that the story about Bob Swift sneaking notes back and forth between Butch Cassidy and Matt Warner was not true, that no notes had passed between the two men, and that it was no indication that Butch Cassidy and his gang were about to attempt to rescue the defendants.[36]

But according to Charles Kelly, the question of the notes cannot be dismissed so lightly. Kelly says that during the trial, a *third* newspaper, the *Salt Lake City Tribune*, entered the fray with an article claiming that Butch Cassidy had admitted to two witnesses that he had, indeed, written the notes to Matt Warner. Citing the article in the *Tribune*, Kelly said that two salesmen, Joe Decker and W. C. A. Smoot, told a *Tribune* reporter that during the trial they had stopped at a hotel in Loa, Utah, in Wayne County about ninety miles west of Robber's Roost.[37] Also staying at the hotel, they said, were Butch Cassidy and Henry "Bub" Meeks. Decker and Smoot said Cassidy and Meeks, who made no attempt to hide their identities, were carrying large rolls of money and claimed that they were in town to buy cattle.[38]

Decker and Smoot said that one day they met Cassidy and Bub Meeks in the stable, and Cassidy had asked them if they had any news of the trial that was going on up in Ogden. The salesmen showed Butch a newspaper containing the story published in the *Salt Lake City Herald* about him passing the notes to Matt Warner and threatening to rescue Matt from jail. Decker and Smoot said that Butch admitted to them that he had sent the notes, but he added that he had not intended take Warner and Wall out of jail by force—he would rescue them only "if money could do it."[39]

According to Decker and Smoot, Butch told them that the information contained in the article had been given to the *Herald* by Matt Warner's wife, Rose, whom the salesmen said Cassidy described as a "loose woman" who wanted her husband to go to jail so that she could carry on with other men. They said Butch told them that Rose had written to him, promising him that he could have "anything he wanted" from her or her sister if he would come and see her. Cassidy said that he believed it was a trap.[40]

The information for the *Herald* article may have indeed come from Rose Warner. It seems that the *Herald* reporter who wrote the article had been shown a letter Butch had written to Rose the previous month, apparently in response to her request that he come see her.[41]

> Vernal, Utah Aug. 25, 1896.
> Mrs. Rosa Warner, Salt Lake;
>
> My Dear friend. Through the kindness of Mrs. Rummel, I received your letter last night. I am sorry that I can't comply with your request, but at present it is impossible for me to go to see you, and I can't tell just when I can get there. If you have got anything to tell me that will help your Matt, write and tell me what it is and I will be there on time. I can't understand what it can be, for I have heard from reliable partys that you did not want Matt to get out, and I can't see what benefit it could be to you unless it was in his behalf. I may be misinformed, but I got it so straight that I would have to be shown why you made this talk before I could think otherwise. But that is neither here nor there, you are a lady, and I would do all I could for you or any of the sex that was in trouble, of course. I am foolish (Which you have found out), but it is my nature and I can't change it. I may be wrong in this, but if so, I hope you will look over it and prove to me that you are all right, and I will ask forgiveness for writing you as I have. I understand you and Matt named your boy Rex Leroy after me, thank you. I hope I will be able to meet you all before long if everything is satisfactory. I [am] sorry to hear about your leg. If I can do anything to help you out let me know and I will do it. Lay and I have got a good man to defend Matt and Wall, and put up plenty of money, too, for Matt and Wall to defend themselves. Write me here in care of John Bluford, and believe me to be a true friend to my kind of people.
> George Cassidy

Douglas Preston was probably "technically" correct when he told the reporter for the *Ogden Standard* that there were no authorities looking for Butch. It was likely that, by 1896, seven years after the robbery of the San Miguel Valley Bank in Telluride, Colorado, peace officers had given up their search for the "Bob Parker" who had allegedly been involved in the crime. And there is no evidence that Butch was officially wanted for any crimes since his release from the Wyoming State Penitentiary. (Butch may have been suspected of robbing the Montpelier, Idaho, bank, but no arrest warrants were issued for that crime.)

Meanwhile, the trial of Matt Warner and his fellow defendants continued. In the beginning it appeared that the prosecution, led by Ogden attorney David Evans and assisted by Uintah County prosecutor J. P. Evans, had a fairly strong case. But Ike Staunton, after suggesting in his pretrial statement that Warner fired the first shots, wavered on this issue on the witness stand. Instead of convicting Warner and Wall of first-degree murder, which they could have done, the jury settled on voluntary manslaughter and the judge sentenced each of them to five years in the Utah State Penitentiary. E. B. Coleman was acquitted.[42]

Castle Gate

1896–1897

According to an alleged first-hand account, following Matt Warner's trial in Ogden, Butch and Elzy rented a cabin from rancher Jim Jones near Maeser, a rural area north of Vernal, Utah, not far from the home of the parents of Maude Davis, Elzy's girlfriend.[1] Sometime that fall Elzy and Maude were married, or at least they told people they were, and Maude joined Elzy and Butch in the cabin.[2] For privacy, Elzy and Butch divided the room by stretching a wire from one end of the cabin to the other and hung blankets over it. Butch also had a female companion, possibly the young lady who later would be known as Etta Place, but more likely it was Ann Bassett from Brown's Park.[3]

Though he had yet to be charged, by the second week in September the newspapers were mentioning Butch as a suspect in the Montpelier bank robbery.[4] The situation changed, however, in late October, when Uintah County Sheriff John Pope received notice that the sheriff in Bear Lake County, Idaho, had issued an arrest warrant for Butch and Elzy. This was not welcome news for Pope, who knew both men well and considered them friends.[5]

A week or so later Pope got a tip that Butch and Elzy were visiting Maude's parents. With four deputies he rode out to the Davis place with a copy of the warrant. It was evening. Rather than rush the house and try to take Cassidy and Lay by force, Pope sent in his part-time deputy, Pete Dillman, on the pretext that Dillman wanted to hire Maude's brother Albert to work for him for a couple of weeks.[6]

Maude's parents answered the door and told Dillman that Albert was not at home. As Dillman left, Maude's father, who had seen through the ruse, ran out the back door intending to find Butch and Elzy and warn them. But Pope was waiting for him behind the house. Under questioning, a shaken Mr. Davis finally admitted that Butch and Elzy had been at his

house but had left. In the meantime, however, Maude's other brother, sev-
enteen-year-old Frank Davis, had spotted Pope's deputies hiding in the
shadows and had slipped away without Pope noticing. Frank ran to the
cabin at Jones's ranch, where he found Elzy Lay asleep, and told him what
had happened. Lay quickly dressed, saddled up, and rode off.[7]

While all this was going on Butch was in Vernal, having a drink at the
Overholt Saloon. When Sheriff Pope failed to find Butch and Elzy at the
Davis place, he and his deputies returned to town. As they passed the Overholt, Pete Dillman noticed Albert Davis sitting on the steps out front.
When Albert saw the posse he jumped up and ran inside. Dillman passed
the word to Pope, who ordered his men to surround the building, but they
were too late. By the time they closed in Butch was gone.[8]

The nearest place for Butch and Elzy to hide was Brown's Park. But the
Park was familiar territory to Sheriff John Pope, who had prospected there
and had even owned a ranch on Red Creek.[9] Eventually and with enough
manpower Pope probably could have flushed them out. On the other hand,
Pope may not have been that serious about making the arrests—at least
that was the opinion of Ann Bassett, who said later that Pope probably intentionally delayed rushing into the Overholt Saloon at Vernal so that
Butch could escape.[10]

While the natural wilderness of Brown's Park offered refuge to someone
with a little ingenuity, the ranchers and homesteaders who lived there did
not exactly open their arms to strangers. Butch and his friends had always
been welcome because they behaved themselves in the Park, but most of
the outsiders who regularly came and went were simply tolerated. The valleys of the Little Snake and Yampa Rivers provided access to Brown's Park
from the east, and the nearby Two-Bar Ranch, a huge spread on the Little
Snake River owned by Ora Haley, saw more than its share of drifters.[11]
James Sizer, Haley's foreman, recalled that saddle-weary strangers, many
of them obviously dodging the law, usually "arrived on jaded horses sometimes with a pack outfit, or a greasy sack tied behind their saddle." They
would camp where the feed was good and loaf around until their animals
regained enough strength to go on. If they didn't have a camp outfit they
would stop at one of the ranch houses. Usually the rancher would treat
them well; if he didn't, said Sizer, after the drifters left the rancher might
find the drifters' worn-out horses on his range and find his own animals
gone. Since the ranchers could not afford to lose horses, they reluctantly
cooperated and kept their mouths shut. Eventually their reluctant cooperation caused the Park's residents to acquire the reputation that they actually invited and harbored outlaws, which was not the case.[12]

Since he was clearly wanted by the law again, Butch may have decided to pull another job to fatten the larder. Charles Kelly says that Butch and a few others rode up to Rock Springs sometime during the third week in October 1896 to check out the payroll shipments of one of the mining companies owned by the Union Pacific Railroad. The payroll in question, however, was not truly shipped but personally delivered by the mining company manager, Finley P. Gridley. Twice a month Gridley rode in a buckboard to pick up the cash at the bank in Rock Springs, then the driver took him and two guards to the mine with the money tucked away in a leather bag under the front seat.

It was a foolish thing to do, but Gridley had never been bothered by robbers and he must have believed that he never would be. However, as the story goes, on October 18, while having a drink in one of the Rock Springs saloons, Gridley was approached by a stranger who asked if he was going out with the payroll the next day. When Gridley, who must have been incredibly naïve, replied that he was, the stranger said "I wouldn't do it, if I was you."[13]

The stranger wouldn't provide any more information than that, but after thinking it over Gridley decided to take the man's advice. The following morning he ordered the payroll sent out to the mine by a special train car. Gridley, however, was not only naïve but evidently stupid as well. He still had his driver and the two guards pick him up in the buckboard at the regular time and take him to the bank, but this time with an empty leather bag. Sure enough, at the head of a narrow canyon they were ordered to stop by a masked man brandishing a rifle. But instead of stopping the driver whipped the team and tried to escape. Shots rang out from the boulders above, and the horses stumbled and fell, causing the buckboard to pile on top of its riders. Neither Gridley nor the other men were badly injured, and all four quickly crawled away and scurried out of sight. The masked gunman searched the shattered buckboard, found the empty bag and angrily rode off.[14]

Butch and Elzy Lay, still hiding out in Brown's Park, may have felt safe enough to spend Thanksgiving Day, 1896, with the Bassett family and their neighbors. According to Ann Bassett, Butch, Elzy, and some of their friends actually gave the party, apparently in return for the kindness the local residents—especially the Bassetts—had shown them. Years later Ann wrote of that day in detail, even describing the menu and how the guests were dressed.[15]

According to Ann the main course was roast turkey with chestnut dressing, giblet gravy, cranberries, mashed potatoes, sweet potatoes, and creamed peas. Dessert consisted of pumpkin pie and plum pudding. As to the guests, Ann wrote:

Men wore dark suits (vests were always worn) white shirts stiff starched collars, patent low cuts. No man would be seen minus a coat and a bow tie at the party—if it killed them and it almost did I am sure. If a mustache existed that must be waxed and curled. The women wore tight fitted long dress with leg-o-mutton sleeves and boned collars—hair done on top of the head either in a French twist or a bun and bangs curled into a friz. Girls in their teens wore dresses about 3 inches below the knees—spring heeled slippers and their hair in curls or braids tucked up with a big bow of ribbons at nap of neck.

There were at least thirty-five people at the gathering, and it lasted well into the evening—for some, all night. Butch, Elzy, and possibly Harry Longabaugh (Ann Bassett called him Harry Roudenbaugh) served as waiters, and some of the other men helped in the kitchen. According to Ann, Butch was not adept at serving, which gave her an opportunity to poke a little fun at him:

[P]oor Butch he could perform such minor jobs as robbing banks and holding up pay trains without the flicker of an eye lash but serving coffee at a grand party that was something else. The blood curdeling [*sic*] job almost floored him, he became panicky and showed that his nerve was completely shot to bits. He became frustrated and embarrassed over the blunders he had made when some of the other hoasts [*sic*] better informed told him it was not good form to pour coffee from a big black coffee pot and reach from left to right across a guests plate, to grab a cup right under their noses. The boys went into a hudle [*sic*] in the kitchen and instructed Butch in the more formal art of filling coffee cups at the table. This just shows how etiquette can put fear into a brave man's heart.[16]

Reflecting on the attitude of the Brown's Park community toward sharing a holiday with fugitives, McClure suggested that had a posse come looking for Butch and Elzy that day the Bassetts and their neighbors would not have prevented the lawmen from carrying out their civic duty. On the other hand, they probably did not expect to be put to the test. Thus far the authorities had avoided invading the sanctum of the Park, and the residents saw no reason why this should change.[17] However, Butch and Elzy may not have shared their feelings. After the Thanksgiving holiday they packed up and headed south, to the isolated canyons of Robbers' Roost.

Their hideout at the Roost was near the desolate Horseshoe Canyon in northern Wayne County, Utah, about twenty-five miles east of Hanksville.[18] The site was about three miles from several natural springs, later appropriately named "Robbers' Roost Springs," which had been fenced in sometime in the early 1890s and equipped with wooden troughs for watering livestock.[19] The nearest ranch was owned by J. B. Buhr, a former Denver tailor who had moved to Utah canyon country for his health.[20]

Although Hanksville was the town nearest the hideout, newlywed Elzy Lay (probably at the suggestion of the ever-cautious Butch) arranged to have Maude join him by way of Green River.[21] The town of Green River was twice as far from Horseshoe Canyon as Hanksville, but it was clearly a much safer choice, mainly because it was a railroad town. The Denver & Rio Grande Railroad had arrived in Green River in the early 1880s; and though the town was no longer a D&RG division point, the popular Palmer House—an elegant structure with wide verandas and landscaped grounds—was where the rail passengers stopped to dine. (The D&RG had yet to put on dining cars.[22]) With all these comings and goings a young lady traveling alone would not be conspicuous.

Maude's instructions were to go to Green River and wait, probably at the Palmer House, and eventually someone would come and get her. Someone did: a strange-looking desert character with one blue eye and one brown eye who talked with a cockney accent, "Blue John" Griffith. Griffith, who had once worked for the Carlisle Ranch down in San Juan County, was a part-time rustler and full-time runner for Butch and his gang.[23]

Blue John introduced himself to Maude, quickly loaded her baggage onto a wagon (which was already stacked high with supplies), and helped her up on the seat. As he headed the team out of town toward the desert, Maude must have expected the worst. But, as odd as the man appeared, he turned out to be no threat, and eventually she relaxed and began to enjoy the journey. On the second day of the trip, while riding in a long, narrow valley near a small pinnacle called Runt's Knob, she found Elzy and another man waiting with packhorses. They transferred Maude's belongings and the supplies from the wagon to the horses for the last leg of the trip: into Horseshoe Canyon itself and along a slim, winding trail that eventually led up the canyon's eastern wall. The camp was at the top of the wall, in a grove of cedars not far from the rim.[24] Somewhere below along the trail Maude may have noticed that the side of a cliff had been dug out to make a large cave, probably as a secondary hideout or a lookout spot.[25]

The cedar grove made a perfect hideaway, accessible from below by only the one narrow switchback where approaching riders could easily be seen from above. The camp itself, probably well-nestled in the trees to take advantage of the shelter, consisted of three tents: two large and one small. Elzy told Maude that the small one would be theirs.[26]

Several days later another guest arrived, presumably the woman with whom Butch had shared his half of the cabin on the Jones ranch at Maeser. Years later Maude told her daughter, Marvel, that the woman was Etta Place.[27] Other women have been mentioned, however, including Sadie Moran, the daughter of a local cowboy-rancher.[28] Also, it would have been an adventure that Ann Bassett would have enjoyed. She loved excitement and was not put off by outlaws; in fact, in later years she herself was accused of doing a little cattle rustling.[29]

Another small tent was set up for Butch and his young lady. She and Maude ate with the men but spent most of their days chatting in one or the other's tent or taking long walks among the cedars.[30]

Just who all among Butch's male companions were present at the time has never been determined, but it is fairly certain that Butch was beginning to form the nucleus of an outlaw gang. One member was probably Joe Walker, a Texas cowpuncher whose specialty was stealing horses.[31] Another would have been Bub Meeks, veteran of the Montpelier bank robbery. There was also, of course, Elzy Lay and, if Harry Longabaugh was the "Harry Roudenbaugh" mentioned by Ann Bassett as having been at the Thanksgiving Day gathering at Brown's Park, he, too, may have been present at the camp.[32]

The women stayed at the camp through the winter, which in southern Utah would not have been so severe as to make tent living unbearable. In March 1897, Blue John Griffith took the ladies back to civilization.[33] By then Butch and Elzy were probably making plans for their next robbery: the payroll office of the Pleasant Valley Coal Company at Castle Gate, Utah. Castle Gate rests in a long, narrow canyon in northwestern Carbon County, about ten miles south of the county line and almost directly below the north-south border between Utah and Duchesne Counties. The name Castle Gate came from the twin rock towers that hover over what was then the only road that led in and out of the town.[34] In 1897 the Pleasant Valley Coal Company, which virtually owned the town and employed nearly all of its citizens, was one of the largest mining enterprises in the state. It and several other coal mining operations in the area were owned by the Denver & Rio Grande Railroad.[35]

Every two weeks the company payroll was brought in on the D&RG from Salt Lake City.[36] The operators of the coal company were well aware that the payroll was tempting to robbers, so arrangements were made at Salt Lake City to use an irregular schedule for shipping the money. The miners were paid every second week but not on the same day of the week. In fact, the workers would not know which day was payday or which train the money would come in on until they heard a specific blast of the mine whistle, which meant that their pay was waiting for them at the paymaster's office located with other Pleasant Valley offices on the second floor above the company store near the tracks.[37]

Since no one knew the exact day the payroll would be shipped, Butch and his men would have to hang around the town, possibly for several days, waiting for the right train to arrive. According to one version of the story, this delay presented a special problem. Butch and his pals were cowboys and Castle Gate was not a cowboy town; in fact, it was one of the few towns in Utah where a cowpuncher on a horse was not commonly seen. The miners who occupied the town, many of them foreigners, had no need for horses: they had no place to go but work, which was only a few blocks from where they lived. Also the town was squeezed into a crowded, narrow canyon, where space was at a premium. There was barely enough room to provide housing for the miners, let alone for a livery or corral. As Butch commented to the others after scouting the town, "a man on a horse loomed up like a sore thumb."

Another problem was access to the paymaster's office: it could only be reached by an outside stairway at the side of the building. Since the payroll would arrive during the workday, as soon as the whistle sounded there would be workers milling around on the ground below, impatient to receive their money. The stairway to the paymaster's office was unique: A-shaped with two rows of steps leading up the front and a single row at the rear, it suggested that the workers formed a line up one side of the stairs, received and signed for their pay, and exited down the other side. Once the men knew that the paymaster was ready with their money the stairs would be filled with workers.

After several days of pondering the problem that it was a horseless town, someone came up with a possible solution. Though a stranger sitting astride a cowpuncher's saddle—with its familiar roping horn, wide fenders, and range rigging—was an uncommon sight in Castle Gate, another kind of rider was not uncommon. Someone in the gang learned that the locals were used to seeing racing horses in town, that is, horses with single girdles and no saddles. Horse racing was nearly as popular in some parts of Utah as it was in Colorado, and it was not unusual for horse owners to ride in and out of Castle Gate while working out their mounts. A person could ride into town bareback with racing surcingles and nobody would be the wiser.[38]

There were at least four in the party that rode up from the Roost: Butch, Elzy, and probably Bub Meeks and Joe Walker. Since Castle Gate was well over a hundred miles from Horseshoe Canyon, to scout the town in advance the four would have had to have camped somewhere nearby. According to one story, using the names Tom Gillis and Bert Fowler, Butch and Elzy temporarily hired on at a ranch south of town owned by Peter Murning and Joe Meeks (a cousin of Bub Meeks's).[39] Another story has Butch and Elzy (posing as Gillis and Fowler) spending those weeks at the ranch of a man named Jens Nielson on Huntington Creek, about thirty miles southwest of the town of Helper.[40]

Butch probably had a rough idea as to when the next payroll would arrive. During periodic visits to town it would have been easy for him or Elzy to engage one of the miners in casual talk and learn when the man was last paid. Knowing what week the next payroll would arrive, they could ride into town on a Monday morning and wait around for the trains to pull in. If the money did not arrive by the end of the workday they would return the next day.

But hanging around town was risky. James L. Smith, manager of the Pleasant Valley Coal Company, apparently had a premonition of trouble. The first week of April he had petitioned the Carbon County Commissioners to fire the local sheriff, Gus Donant, claiming that Donant was not doing enough to protect the interests of the company from "desperados" whom Smith had heard had infiltrated the county.[41]

Whether Butch was aware that Smith was suddenly worried about the safety of his payroll isn't known, but he and Elzy probably began their daily bareback rides into Castle Gate on Monday, April 19. No one recalled seeing them in town that day, but a witness did see them in one of the saloons on Tuesday. They watched and waited, and listened for the whistle that would tell them which train held the treasure. If a stranger showed interest in their saddleless horse and racing rigging, they would tell him that they were conditioning the horses for match races in Salt Lake City.[42]

The payroll finally arrived on the noon train Wednesday. When the whistle went off Butch had just hitched his horse and was lounging in the front of the company store, around the corner from the stairs that led up to the paymaster's office. Elzy was nearby, sitting astride his horse. There was no mistaking the signal: shortly after hearing it echo off the canyon walls Butch glanced around the corner and saw the Pleasant Valley Coal Company paymaster, E. L. Carpenter, and his clerk, T. W. Lewis, come out of their office and start down the stairs.

Carpenter's routine on payday seldom varied: he and Lewis would walk over to the station and wait for the express car messenger to unload a leather satchel and three sacks of coins. Carpenter would sign for them, and the two men would quickly return to their office. On this day the payroll totaled $9,860. In the leather satchel were currency and checks in the amount of $1,000. One of the sacks contained $7,000 in gold; in the other two were $1,000 in currency and $860 in silver.

Butch watched Carpenter and Lewis enter the door to the station, then seconds later come out with the money. As they came toward him Butch edged over to the bottom of the stairs and leaned back against the side of the building. Elzy was still on his horse; he had untied Butch's horse and was holding the reins, waiting for Butch to make his move.

When Carpenter reached the stairs Butch stepped out, pointed his gun at the paymaster's face and told him to drop the sacks. The stunned paymaster complied, but the clerk, Lewis, who was carrying the sack containing $1,000 in silver, made a dash for the front door of the store. A miner, Frank Caffey, was standing inside. Seeing Lewis rush in Caffey hurried to the door to see what all the trouble was about. Elzy Lay, still on his horse, pointed his revolver at him and said, "Get back in there, you son-of-a-bitch, or I'll fill your belly full of hot lead!"[43]

Meanwhile, Butch had picked up the satchel and two sacks Carpenter had dropped and was running toward Elzy. He tossed the sacks to Elzy, who caught them, but, in doing so, dropped the reins to Butch's horse. The horse, spooked by the excitement, bolted and started down the street. Unperturbed, Butch announced to the crowed, "Don't anybody make a mistake, everything's going to be all right."[44] Elzy spurred his horse and managed to get in front of the animal, slowing him down. This allowed Butch time to catch up and grab the bridle. In seconds Butch was mounted, and he and Elzy raced down the street.

By this time several Pleasant Valley employees in the offices above the store had gathered their wits and had grabbed rifles that were kept on hand in case of trouble. They got off a few shots at the fleeing riders, but failed to hit them.

Carpenter the paymaster ran to the train station to telegraph the sheriff in Price, the county seat. The telegraph line, however, was dead: apparently one of the members of the gang, probably Joe Walker, had shinnied a pole somewhere south of town and cut the wire. The noon train was still standing at the station with its locomotive pointed south toward Price. Carpenter climbed into the cab and shouted for the brakeman to cut the tender loose from the rest of the train, then ordered the engineer to get him to Price as fast as possible.[45]

The robbers had raced south out of Castle Gate on the road that led to Helper. Miner Frank Caffey, after his nerves had steadied some, climbed into a buggy and started to follow. Near the edge of town he pulled to a stop. There on the road was the sack containing the $860 in silver. Nearby was the leather satchel; the checks were still in it, but the currency was gone.

Butch and Elzy had planned their escape route well. They followed the main road until they came to Spring Canyon. There they took a trail that circled west and bypassed Helper and the next two towns, Spring Glen and Price. About ten miles further on this trail, at a spot where it crossed Gordon Creek, they had stashed fresh horses and probably a change of clothes.

In the meantime the locomotive carrying Carpenter the paymaster had reached Price, where Sheriff Gus Donant, alerted by the engineer's screaming whistle that something was wrong, was waiting at the station.[46] Carpenter gave him the bad news and Donant hurriedly put out a call for a posse.

Back on the trail the robbers were making good time. By mid-afternoon they had circled Price and had returned to the main road, which led to Cleveland. At about twenty-five miles south of Price they stopped and cut more telegraph wires, but later discovered this was a waste of time. Sheriff Donant had spread the word, and posses were being formed in Huntington, about six miles west of Cleveland, and at Castle Dale, ten miles further south. According to Charles Kelly, the Huntington posse was led by Joe Meeks, cousin of Bub Meeks, and one of the horses Butch used in the getaway belonged to Joe, who had lent it to Bub.[47]

Around four o'clock Butch and Elzy met a U.S. Mail carrier coming north out of Cleveland who later gave the authorities a description of the two riders he had passed. He said one was wearing a blue coat and a black hat, and had on "goggles," apparently to keep the dust out of his eyes. The other had on a light slouch hat, denim overalls, and a brown coat. He added that both men were sun-browned and looked like cowboys or drifters.

Butch and Elzy passed through Cleveland without trouble. Once beyond the town they took a trail east to Desert Lake, then headed south to Buckhorn Draw, a long, dry wash that winds around near the foot of Cedar Mountain.[48] There they picked up two more fresh horses that probably were being attended to by one of the gang, possibly Bub Meeks.

Meanwhile, back to the north the posses were not faring well. Between Price and Cleveland, Sheriff Donant's men may have been as close as four or five miles behind the two robbers, but after passing through Cleveland and apparently unsure as to which road the outlaws had taken, they lost valuable time. As darkness fell they dropped back even further, not wanting to ride blindly into an ambush. The other two posses, one from Huntington and one from Castle Dale, fared even worse. Along a dark stretch in Buckhorn Draw the Huntington group surprised the boys from Castle Dale and the men began firing at each other. Two horses were killed, and Joe Meeks, Bub's cousin, took a bullet in the leg.

According to Charles Kelly, Butch and Elzy, perhaps joined by Bub Meeks, rode southeast to the foot of Assembly Hall Peak where Buckhorn Draw opens out at the San Rafael River.[49] From there they mostly stayed along the river as it wandered into the San Rafael Desert and eventually turned south, toward Robbers' Roost, where additional relays of horses were waiting along the route. Kelly also claims that at strategic points well off the trail other members of the gang stood watch, guarding their companions' backs.[50]

Pearl Baker's sources provided her with a slightly different version of the boys' escape. Baker says that shortly after Butch and Elzy passed through Cleveland they were joined by Joe Walker. These three (she doesn't mention that Bub Meeks was along) continued down Buckhorn Draw and along the San Rafael River until they reached Mexican Bend, where the river turns east and makes a loop around Mexican Mountain. The trio had left another relay of horses there. After a brief discussion they decided that Walker would take the money, and Butch and Elzy would continue down river as if they were heading to Robbers' Roost. They apparently reasoned that if a posse caught up with Butch and Elzy, at least they would not have the money on them. In the meantime, Walker was to ride east on an unshod horse (taking pains to leave as few tracks as possible) toward what is now Smith's Camp Road, and then northeast to a designated spot in the maze of canyons that surround Florence Creek, east of the Green River on the Uintah and Ouray Indian Reservation. Butch and Elzy would keep riding south toward the Roost until they were sure they had lost the posses, then head back and join Walker at Florence Creek. If they didn't arrive in two days, Walker's instructions were to head for Brown's Park.[51]

At least one posse was still in the hunt, but it had dwindled in number considerably. Most of the volunteers as well as Carbon County Sheriff Gus Donant were tired and hungry, and with other obligations back home they had turned back. Only five men were left: Deputy U.S. Marshal Joe Bush from Salt Lake City; Pleasant Valley Coal Company paymaster E. L. Carpenter, and two hardy souls from Castle Gate, Pete Anderson and a man named Floyd or Lloyd.[52] The fifth man was George Whitmore, a volunteer from Provo who apparently had been passing through when the robbery occurred.

According to Baker, Marshal Bush and his posse didn't see the hoofprints of Joe Walker's shoeless horse that led up a faint deer trail and away from Mexican Bend, so Bush continued to follow the tracks that headed south toward Robbers' Roost. Out on the desert north of Little Flat Top, somewhere near Wildcat Butte, the posse did get within shooting distance of the outlaws and a few shots were exchanged, but this may have caused the pursuers only to rethink their situation. The outlaws were entering territory familiar only to them, and they obviously were willing to fight. Worse still, at any moment the outlaws could be reinforced by their friends from the Roost. Bush and his followers did the only sensible thing: they turned back.[53] There were probably a few more forays out in pursuit of the outlaws, but the search was abandoned completely sometime during the first week of May.[54]

The day after the robbery the Price daily newspaper accurately blamed the crime on the outlaws who were inhabiting the Robbers' Roost area, and reported that it was "reasonably certain" that one of the culprits responsible for the Castle Gate robbery was Butch Cassidy.[55] According to a witness, this fact was more or less confirmed when E. L. Carpenter was shown a picture of Butch.[56]

Summer was now approaching, and on returning to the Roost, Butch and his men moved their headquarters twelve miles east of Horseshoe Canyon to take advantage of a shady spot under the rim of one of the Orange Cliffs. They also bought better tents and brought in three new female companions: Ella Butler, Millie Nelson, and Maggie Blackburn, who, among other things, earned their keep by making periodic trips to Green River for supplies. As summer neared the days at the Roost were mostly spent in friendly competition: seeing who was the best shot or the best rider, or finding out who had the fastest horse. Evenings were usually reserved for drinking and cards. There were all-night poker games, some attended by trusted friends from Hanksville or Green River.[57] Other evenings were spent singing, with Butch often providing tunes on the harmonica.[58]

While the authorities were no doubt aware that Butch and his pals were holed up in the Roost, few officers of the law showed an interest in venturing into its blind canyons.[59] But who could blame them? Even the judiciary was concerned. Seventh District Judge Jacob Johnson from Sanpete County, whose circuit included Emery County, made no attempt to hide the fact that he was troubled about presiding over local trials involving defendants who had friends out at the Roost, which someone with a wild imagination led him to believe numbered somewhere between 225 and 250 outlaws.[60]

Carbon County citizens grumbled over their elected officials' inaction following the Castle Gate robbery. Some of the complainers blamed it on weak livers, while others suggested that the local officials, especially certain members of the County Board of Commissioners, were soft on the outlaws because they themselves had friends or relatives involved in the rustling business.[61]

Livestock rustling was rampant in Carbon County, so much so that officials of the Ireland Cattle Company, one of the heaviest losers up to that date, decided to take matters into their own hands. Deputy U.S. Marshal Joe Bush, a bear of a man with steely eyes, a gruff voice, and a penchant for carrying a sawed-off shotgun, was the only lawman willing to lead a force into the Roost.[62] Summoned from Salt Lake City and outfitted with a posse of eight volunteers, presumably at the expense of the Ireland company, Bush and his contingent embarked on their pursuit sometime the second week of June. Riding west out of Hanksville they spent two days on the trail and failed to find any outlaws. They did, however, stumble across Blue John Griffith, catching him by surprise at dawn at a ranch in the Henry Mountains while he was standing outside the bunkhouse answering the call of nature. Half asleep and startled by the intrusion, without thinking Blue John drew his pistol, which allowed Bush to charge him with resisting arrest. The charge, however, failed to hold up; nothing substantial could be levied against Blue John and a Wayne County jury turned him loose, all of which confirmed a disgruntled Beaver County newspaper editor's observation that a Utah peace officer was a fool to risk running down outlaws in Robbers' Roost because they probably would never be convicted anyway.[63]

Despite the upgrade in accommodations at the Horseshoe Canyon hideout, the desert country of southern Utah was not the ideal place to spend the summer. Butch and his friends broke camp in late spring and headed for Brown's Park. On their way, Elzy Lay, lonesome for Maude, stopped by her parents' home. Maude was now pregnant with their daughter, Marvel, but despite Elzy's pleas she refused to leave with him. While spending a winter at an outlaw hideout may have been something of a lark for Maude, she could not see raising a child among fugitives. She begged Elzy to give up the outlaw life and settle down, but he was not ready for that. There was more talk, but neither would give in.[64]

Longabaugh

It is difficult to know just when Butch Cassidy and Harry Long-abaugh, alias The Sundance Kid, first met. Longabaugh probably was in the area before Butch went to prison and may have played a minor role in the rustling game, but only much later would the two become sidekicks, with their names permanently linked in the annals of outlaw history.

Harry Alonzo Longabaugh was born in 1867 in eastern Pennsylvania, probably in the town of Phoenixville located about ten miles northwest of the outskirts of Philadelphia. His family, devout Baptists, were of modest means. By the age of thirteen Harry was working as a hired servant and boarding with a farm family named Ralston near West Vincent, Pennsylvania, about ten miles from his home. Although his schooling was probably sporadic, young Harry appreciated books and even belonged to a local literary society.[1]

In 1882, Harry left Pennsylvania to live with his cousin, George (who spelled his name Longenbaugh) and his family in Illinois. At the time, George Longenbaugh and his wife, Mary, and their two small children were preparing to join the parade west and look for land to homestead. Harry, who had learned to ride and tend animals on the Ralston farm, was apparently eager to go along.[2]

George Longenbaugh was caught up in the excitement over the new town of Durango being promoted in southwestern Colorado. Durango, founded by Colorado railroad pioneer William J. Palmer in 1880, had grown to a population of over two thousand in its first two years, mainly as a result of advertisements placed in newspapers in the eastern cities proclaiming it as the new "Denver of the Southwest."[3]

The Longenbaugh family first settled on a small ranch north of Durango. For two years George, with Harry's help, homesteaded and raised horses. Then, apparently seeking greener pastures, George sold out and moved the family fifty miles west to Montezuma County, to another small ranch on what was then the outskirts of Cortez.[4]

Beginning around 1885 with the move to Cortez, there were many opportunities for Harry and Butch to cross paths. Cortez was less than eighty miles south of Telluride, where Butch was working for one of the mining companies at the time. Telluride was a bustling community, and the mines were always on the lookout for good horses. Since Harry's cousin was in the business of raising horses, he and Harry may have made trips to Telluride to sell their animals, and Harry and Butch may have met during one of these trips.

Although Harry was only seventeen, soon after the move to Cortez he may have taken a job wrangling cattle near Springer, New Mexico, and that year he may have had his first taste of excitement: dodging bullets in the midst of a cattle war.[5] Later, around 1886, he went to work as a horse wrangler for the Lacy Cattle Company—in local parlance the LC Ranch—a huge spread centered in Utah at the head of Montezuma Canyon south of Monticello.[6] In the summer of 1886 cattle were bringing record prices, and the LC was probably grazing over 15,000 head on the lush canyon and mountain grasses along the Recapture, Cottonwood, Johnson, and South Montezuma Creeks.[7]

After wandering into the range war in New Mexico, Harry probably figured the LC would be a quieter place to work. He may have been mistaken. In addition to its large herd of cattle, the LC also ran fine horse flesh on their range, and that year a gang of thieves rode off a bunch of the outfit's best animals. While chasing the thieves the ranch foreman, William Ball, was shot and killed.[8] Whether Harry was involved in the chase, isn't known, but if so it may have begun to look as though trouble was following him.

To the northwest of the LC spread, about five or six miles north of Monticello, was the Carlisle Ranch.[9] One wrangler working there about that time was Butch Cassidy's younger brother, Dan Parker.[10] It is possible that Longabaugh and Dan Parker became acquainted, and Dan may have introduced Harry to Butch, who occasionally may have ridden down from Telluride to visit his brother.[11]

Besides the LC Ranch, Harry may have worked for another outfit in the area, the giant Pittsburgh Land and Cattle Company, which was running thousands of cattle in the La Sal Mountains and in Dry Valley, a favorite winter range.[12]

A severe drought hit southwestern Colorado in late summer 1886. When ranchers began laying off their hired hands, Longabaugh signed on with the N Bar N outfit and picked up a cattle drive going from Texas to eastern Montana. In Montana, the N Bar N operated a range office in Miles City and ran its cattle on the open range between there and Wolf Point.[13] If Harry stayed with the drive all the way to Miles City (and there is no reason to believe he didn't), it is possible that he and Butch met there. According to a source cited by outlaw historian James Horan, Butch spent a few months working on a ranch near Miles City around that time.[14]

It is also possible that Butch and Longabaugh first met when Butch and Matt Warner were making the rounds of southwestern Colorado towns and ranches matching Matt's speedy mare, Betty, against other racehorses in the area. The racing circuit in southwestern Colorado covered at least four counties: San Miguel, Dolores, Montezuma, and La Plata, and races were being held on a rotating basis at Telluride, Mancos, Durango, Rico, McElmo Gulch, and Cortez.[15] If Longabaugh was in the area during this time it is possible that he and Butch met at one of the races. It depends on when Butch and Warner competed in these races. In telling of their horse racing venture, Warner was not clear on dates.

While wrangling or cow punching for the N Bar N or for one of the other spreads near Miles City in 1886, Longabaugh, along with many other cowboys, was again laid off when work became scarce. He drifted over to the Black Hills for a while, then returned to Wyoming.[16] He may have picked up a temporary job at the Powder River Cattle Company.[17] At the time the company was probably moving its herd north because of the severe drought that had struck the region.[18]

The drought that fall was unrelenting, and, as if that wasn't bad enough, winter came early and struck with unusual vengeance. On November 16 the temperature in the Rockies dropped to zero degrees, and six inches of wind-whipped snow blanketed most of Wyoming and Montana. Three weeks later a second blizzard struck. But that was only the beginning. On the 9th of January a third blizzard began dumping an inch of snow per hour. Then, just when it appeared that the wind was going to stop and the skies would clear, the snow would begin again. By January 15 thermometers were reading forty-six degrees below zero.[19]

Later it would be called the Great Blizzard of 1886–87, the worst winter in Wyoming history.[20] On January 28 the wind and snow returned for seventy-two hours straight. When it finally ended, cattle on the open range were scattered for miles, many of them dead or dying. The storm nearly leveled the landscape, filling gulches and ravines with drifts of snow over a hundred feet deep. Some ranch houses were completely covered by snow.[21] Most of the open-range cattle were already in poor condition because of the drought, and when the ponds and streams froze solid the animals that had not perished from the cold desperately gulped snow to keep from dying from thirst. Later, when the thaw finally came, thousands more cattle broke through the ice and drowned or were swept away by raging streams.[22]

Where Harry Longabaugh rode out the storm isn't known, but February found him looking for work in Crook County, Wyoming. Having sold nearly everything he owned to get money to eat, when he was ready to move on he made a serious mistake, one that would cost him dearly. He stole a horse, saddle, and bridle from a local cowboy, Alonzo Craven, a wrangler employed by Western Ranches, Ltd., better known as the Three-v Ranch. From another Three-v hand, Jim Widner, he filched a revolver.[23]

It was a bad choice of victims: the Three-v was a powerful force in the area. Its manager, John Clay, an influential member of the Wyoming Stock Growers Association, had little patience with thieves and rustlers. Clay respected the honest ranchhand who took life seriously and was a good citizen, but he viewed the cowboy who drifted from one ranch to another as a degenerate and a loser. Longabaugh, of course, fell into the latter group. When the thefts were reported to Crook County Sheriff Jim Ryan, Clay made it clear that Ryan was not to rest until he caught the thief.[24] Ryan apparently had a good description of Longabaugh, who by then, at twenty years of age had attained his full growth.[25]

Ryan sent Longabaugh's description to the neighboring towns with instructions to also look for the stolen horse, a light gray animal with a "J" brand on its left shoulder. Ryan's efforts got results. In April he received word that Longabaugh was spotted in Miles City. Ryan left for Montana to bring Longabaugh back himself. Harry was picked up, apparently offering little if any resistance, and was turned over to the local sheriff for safekeeping in the county jail. On April 12, with the prisoner in shackles and handcuffs, Ryan and Longabaugh boarded a Northern Pacific train. The train, however, was not bound for Wyoming, but for St. Paul, Minnesota, where Ryan apparently had other business to manage. On the way, somewhere near Duluth, Minnesota, while Ryan was using the latrine at the back of the coach, Harry slipped out of his cuffs and shackles and escaped, possibly, as some have suggested, with the help of a confederate.[26] The train was stopped and a search was conducted along the tracks, but the railroad had a schedule to make and a disheartened Sheriff Ryan had to give up and return to Wyoming empty-handed.

Longabaugh, perhaps thinking that neither Sheriff Ryan nor the Custer

County authorities would ever think that he would risk returning to the Miles City area, did just that. It was not a smart move. In June he was recaptured, this time by Custer County Deputy Sheriff E. K. "Eph" Davis and a stock inspector named Smith. The capture took place near the Powder River in the southeastern part of the county. It was too late in the day to start back to town, so Davis and Smith put Harry in handcuffs and shackles and locked him in a cabin. During the night, when Harry thought his captors were asleep, he managed to free himself but Davis caught him trying to climb out a window.[27]

During the month following Longabaugh's escape from the train in Minnesota, there had been a series of robberies at ranches in the Miles City area, mostly horses and saddles and a few guns. Since it was presumed that Harry was in the area at the time, he was the prime suspect. On his recapture, the *Daily Yellowstone Journal* ran an article suggesting that Longabaugh was a major outlaw wanted in various parts of the West. Sitting in his cell and having nothing better to do, Longabaugh responded with a letter to the editor of the newspaper proclaiming his innocence. The editor published the letter. Thinking, perhaps, that the letter might now make it difficult to get a jury conviction, or more likely hoping to collect the $250 reward being offered for Harry by the Territory of Wyoming, the sheriff in Miles City wired Sheriff Ryan that, if he still wanted this man, he could come and get him.[28]

By June 22 Longabaugh was back in Crook County, Wyoming, in the jail in Sundance, the county seat, awaiting trial for stealing from Three-v ranchhands Alonzo Craven and Jim Widner. Harry was still bent on escaping and made several attempts to do so, but the jail was brand new—only three months old—and Sheriff Ryan made sure that his slippery prisoner was locked up tight and guarded well. The fall judicial term of the U.S. District for the Territory of Wyoming began on August 2, and a local attorney, Joseph Stotts, was appointed to defend Harry.[29] A grand jury brought three indictments: one for stealing the horse from Cravens, a second for stealing his saddle, bridle, chaps, and spurs, and a third for stealing the revolver from Widner.[30]

At first Harry claimed he was innocent, but Stotts advised him not to risk a jury trial and instead to plead guilty to the theft of the horse and see if the prosecutor would agree to drop the remaining charges. They could then approach the judge with the agreement and try to get a reduced sentence. Despite Longabaugh's troubles in Miles City and his daring escape from Sheriff Ryan on the train to St. Paul, as far as anyone else knew it would have been Harry's first conviction. The judge accepted the plea bargain and sentenced Harry to eighteen months at hard labor.[31]

Following his sentencing, Harry was placed under the authority of the Wyoming Territorial Board of Penitentiary Commissioners, which oversaw the operation of the Territorial Penitentiary at Laramie. Had Harry been sentenced prior to March 8, 1887, he would have been sent to Joliet, Illinois, under an agreement with the State of Illinois to accept Wyoming prisoners with terms of six months or more.[32] However, on March 8 the contract between the Territory of Wyoming and the State of Illinois expired, and because of political disagreement in Illinois the agreement had not yet been renewed. Rather than overcrowd the penitentiary at Laramie, the Wyoming Board of Penitentiary Commissioners designated several Wyoming county jails as official "Territorial Penitentiaries," and the local sheriffs were made "wardens." The new jail at Sundance, having been built in April, was one of the jails so designated.[33] As a result, Harry Longabaugh remained there for his term of confinement, as did a fellow prisoner, Bill McArthur, who had also been convicted of stealing a horse.[34] (Had it not been for this lapse in the agreement between the Territory of Wyoming and the State of Illinois, Harry Longabaugh might have been known as the "Joliet Kid."[35])

Longabaugh was considered a slippery prisoner, and Sheriff Jim Ryan no doubt ordered his men to keep a close eye on him. At first they probably did, but they may have become lax. On May 1, 1888, as the jailor, whose name was Daley, was delivering the evening meals to the prisoners, Harry and another inmate, Jim O'Connor, jumped him. But Daley was no pushover and he managed to overpower Harry. O'Connor, however, escaped and was free for several hours.[36]

Were it not for this incident and perhaps a couple of other unsuccessful escape attempts, Longabaugh probably could have applied for a pardon and received an early release. His fellow prisoner Bill McArthur, who also had been sentenced to eighteen months, was released after serving only fourteen months, but Harry served his full sentence.[37]

Harry's term ended on February 5, 1889. In January a petition was filed for a full pardon. Even though it would not mean an early release, a full pardon would restore his civil rights. Despite Harry's assault on jailer Daley the previous year, Sheriff Jim Ryan endorsed the request and attested to the fact that Longabaugh's behavior while confined had been good. The governor granted the request, but the pardon did not arrive before Harry was released, and some question still remains as to whether he ever received the document itself.[38]

To receive a full pardon a prisoner needed to have shown an earnest desire to reform. If Longabaugh had such a desire it was short-lived. On being released he boarded a stage for Deadwood, Dakota Territory, the nearest town that offered the pleasures a man would miss most after eighteen months in jail. Afterward he returned to Crook County and immediately got into trouble again. While hanging out with a trio of unsavory characters—one of whom was the outlaw Bob Minor, also known as Buck Hanby—Harry was a witness to a killing. Peace officers surprised the trio hiding in a dugout about thirty-five miles outside of Sundance, and Minor went for his gun. A deputy sheriff, Jim Swisher, fired first, killing Minor. Though Harry was not directly involved he apparently said something threatening to Swisher, and when the deputy returned to Sundance he swore out a complaint against Harry. Although a warrant was issued for Harry's arrest, at the time the charge of threatening an officer of the law was an offense that seldom resulted in a conviction in Wyoming Territory, and the matter was apparently dismissed.[39]

Donna Ernst, wife of the great-nephew of Harry Longabaugh, believes that Harry returned to his cousin George's ranch in southwestern Colorado following the trouble in Miles City with Deputy Sheriff Jim Swisher, and that he may have joined Butch Cassidy, Matt Warner, and Tom McCarty in robbing the San Miguel Valley Bank in Telluride the following month.[40]

While it is possible that Harry was in on the Telluride holdup, Edward Kirby, who, like Ernst, has spent many hours chronicling Harry Longabaugh's career, believes that after the Swisher affair in Miles City Harry rode north to near Lavina, Montana, about fifty miles northwest of Billings, where he found work with the John T. Murphy Cattle Company.[41] Kirby thinks that the following spring Harry headed even further north, to near Malta in Valley County, Montana, where he broke broncs for an R. H. McNeil and a Henry Ester.[42]

Later that year Harry rode up to Alberta, Canada, where he got a job breaking broncs on the Bar U Ranch near High River, about thirty-five miles south of Calgary. The Bar U had a contract to supply beef to the Blackfeet Indians. The foreman at the ranch was Everett Johnson, whom Harry had known back in Wyoming, possibly when the two men both rode herd for the Powder River Cattle Company. When things slowed on the Bar U, Harry picked up extra work with railroad construction contractors out of Edmonton who were building a right-of-way from Calgary south to Fort Macleod, about forty miles north of the United States–Canadian border.[43]

The cowboys who worked with Harry may or may not have known that he had a criminal record in the United States. He likely kept the fact quiet, since Canadian cowboys were generally more law-abiding than their counterparts south of the border. However, one of Harry's fellow bronc-busters, Canadian Herb Millar, may have guessed that Harry had a shady past when he spotted a hacksaw blade that Harry kept hidden under his saddle. While Millar probably had never stepped foot in a jail cell himself, he later said that he was well aware why a cowboy like Harry Longabaugh would be carrying a saw blade.[44]

Even in Canada Harry could not stay completely out of trouble. Court records in Calgary reveal that in August 1891 he was charged with "cruelty to animals." Perhaps somebody thought that he was too hard on one of the broncs he was hired to break.[45] No other information was given and the matter was dismissed without a trial. Otherwise Harry apparently behaved himself in Canada. One acquaintance, Fred Ings, later wrote in his memoirs that even if Harry had been dodging the law in the United States, while in Canada "no one could have been better behaved or more decent." Ings considered Harry a "thoroughly likeable fellow" and "a favorite with everyone."[46] Everett Johnson also must have thought Harry was OK. In November 1891 Harry served as best man in Johnson's marriage to a young lady from High River.[47]

Fred Ings worked on the Midway Ranch in nearby Nanton, about twenty miles south of High River. He tells of once being out on a late roundup with Harry and the Bar U outfit one fall day when Harry probably saved his life. A surprise blizzard blew up that blinded the cattle and men. Ings was at the rear of the herd and was hopelessly lost. Harry rode back and found him, and suggested they give their horses their heads and let them take them back to camp. It took them all night, but they made it.[48]

In early 1892 Longabaugh bought part interest in a saloon at the Grand Central Hotel in Calgary. His partner was a man named Frank Hamilton who also owned Calgary's Pacific Livery Stables. However, the two did not get along and the partnership was soon dissolved.[49]

Following the aborted saloon venture, Longabaugh probably drifted back to Montana looking for work. He likely spent the summer on one of the ranches near Miles City, doing what he did best: breaking broncs. Sometime that summer, or perhaps in the fall, he ran across Bill Madden, the former bartender from Mancos, Colorado, who, with his half-brother Bert, may have assisted Butch, Matt Warner, and Tom McCarty in the June 1889 robbery of the San Miguel Valley Bank of Telluride.[50]

Whether Harry and Bill Madden had been acquainted back in Colorado isn't known. If so, when they crossed paths in Montana they probably spent much of their free time in one of the Miles City saloons lamenting about better days gone by. In Miles City in those days, as in most of Montana in the early 1890s, cowboys without roots often spent the fall of the year worrying about a job for the winter. On the northern plains those jobs usually went to the older, more stable cowhands and not to drifters like Harry and Bill. Chances are, Longabaugh's and Madden's prospects for that winter were as gloomy as the approaching weather. They both had experience tending bar, but so had dozens of other out-of-work cowboys. And probably by late November even the least desirable of the so-called town jobs—washing dishes, swamping saloons, and shoveling out the livery stable—were already taken. Talk likely turned to dishonest work: in Harry's and Bill's case, what it would be like to rob a train.

By 1892 probably few would-be outlaws had not given some thought to robbing a train. The newspapers seemed filled with reports of express car robberies, and it appeared that those who were bold enough to try usually got away with it. The first train robbery west of the Rockies occurred in 1870, on the Central Pacific line near Verdi, Nevada. Four or five men wearing masks jumped aboard between the express car and the locomotive tender as the train was leaving town. At a deserted stretch in Truckee Canyon they crawled forward and pointed guns at the ribs of the engineer and fireman. The train was stopped and the coaches behind the express were cut loose. The engineer was ordered to pull ahead and stop again. The masked men then forced their way into the express car and took more than $40,000 from the express company safe.[51]

Word spread throughout the West that express cars were easy targets, and for the next decade robbers ran roughshod over the railroads and express companies, with the James–Younger Gang and Sam Bass leading the way. Although the reports of losses were seldom accurate, the hauls averaged nearly $30,000, with Sam Bass taking the prize—$60,000—at Big Springs, Nebraska, in 1877.[52]

The methods used by most rail bandits of the seventies were crude but effective. The trains were usually halted by loosening a rail, stacking ties or logs on the tracks, or signaling the engineer with a fake emergency. Sometimes the robbers would get the drop on the locomotive crew while the train was stopped at a water tank or a desolate station. The more agile robbers might swing aboard as the train was pulling away from a stop and then work their way forward to the cab. Once a train was halted, usually on a deserted stretch of track, the crew and the passengers would be kept at bay by several of the gang members while the others would attack the express car.[53]

The express companies seemed to move slowly against the problem. As late as 1875 some companies were still requiring their messengers to supply their own guns and ammunition, and the simple expedient of locking express car doors was not always enforced. But even when locked the wooden cars seldom kept out determined bandits. A favorite device to gain entry was to drill out the door locks with a brace and bit. The safes did not present much of a problem either. If the messengers could not be convinced to open them, they could be blown open with the dangerous but effective black powder.

It was the early 1880s before the express companies put up much of a defense. Express car doors were finally strengthened (many with boiler iron), and bigger and meaner messengers were hired for the train runs. The messengers were given better arms and encouraged to use them, sometimes with the promise of a reward if they thwarted a holdup attempt. The number of robberies declined for awhile, but then picked up again in the late eighties.[54] When they did occur some of the losses were huge. In 1886, a westbound St. Louis & San Francisco express was struck for $59,000. Shortly thereafter the same line was hit for $67,000. The following year robbers got $50,000 from an express car on the International and Great Northern, and later a messenger on a Southern Pacific run had to fork over $40,000 in cash and $200,000 in negotiable bonds.[55]

In 1889, a new dimension was added—dynamite—which gave a decided advantage over unpredictable black powder. By 1892 robbers were becoming adept at its use, both in entering the express cars and in blowing open the safes.[56]

As to how much of all this activity was known to Harry Longabaugh and Bill Madden in the fall of 1892, we can only guess. They were probably aware that to make a train robbery work one usually needed at least three men. So somewhere along the way they picked up a third man: a drifter named Harry Bass. Maybe the name impressed them. After all, Sam Bass had done all right emptying express car safes.

They chose Malta, Montana, as their point of attack, a small stop on the Great Northern Railroad about sixty-five miles west of Glasgow and about fifty miles south of the Canadian border. For several days, they scouted the town and station and probably studied the train schedule. Looking for a train that could be expected to carry a generous amount of cash and valuables in the express and mail cars, they finally chose Great

Northern No. 23, a passenger run from St. Paul, Minnesota, to Butte, Montana.[57]

Sometime before daylight on November 29, 1892, they pulled handkerchiefs over their faces and slipped aboard the "blind baggage" as No. 23 was leaving Malta.[58] As the train gathered speed one of the men crawled over the tender and, about a mile out of town, ordered the engineer to apply the brakes. While this robber held the engineer and firemen at gunpoint, the other two climbed off the train and headed back toward the side door of the express car. On their way they met the conductor and brakeman who were coming forward to see why the train had stopped. They were ordered to raise their hands, and the conductor was instructed to tell the mail clerk to open the mail car. Finding nothing of value in the registered mail, the robbers then told the conductor to order the express car messenger to open up. He complied, and when the robbers were satisfied that the messenger was alone, one of them stayed with the conductor and brakeman and the other, who appeared to be the leader, climbed into the express car.

This bandit, whom a witness later described as about five feet ten inches tall and wearing a fur overcoat and blue overalls, ordered the messenger to open the "through safe."[59] The messenger, Jacob "Jerry" Hauert, told them that he was unable to do so because he did not have the combination. He was then ordered to open the local safe. This he did, but the safe contained only three small packages and less than twenty dollars in cash. The robber stuffed the money and one of the packages in his pocket and tossed the other two packages away. Then he turned to Hauert and again ordered him to open the through safe. When Hauert repeated that he did not have the combination, that it was known only to the express company's division agents, the masked man replied, "You open that safe or you die!"

The shaken messenger gulped and answered, "Very well, then, I suppose I've got to die."[60] This may have taken the robber by surprise. The messenger, who probably earned no more than $70.00 a month, if that much, was either telling the truth or laying his life on the line to protect his employer's shipment.[61]

The robber thought for a moment, then began backing toward the door. When he reached it he bid the messenger "Good bye" and jumped down, calling to his companions that they were leaving. Hauert grabbed his Winchester off the wall rack and ran to the door hoping to get a shot, but the three men had disappeared.

Later, on being interviewed at Helena, a general agent for the express company reported that the package taken by the robber was probably worth no more than $50.00. This would have brought the robbers' total haul to less than $70.00. Had they chosen to rob the passengers, who did not know why the train had been stopped until the robbery was over, they would have fared much better. One passenger, Edward Goodkind of Helena, was carrying $2,000 in cash, which he had planned to place in the express car safe on boarding the train but failed to do so because he had arrived late.[62]

The robbery was hardly profitable, but, worse than that, the robbers had difficulty keeping their handkerchiefs in place, which gave the train crew a peek at their faces. After the robbery Madden and Bass, having nowhere better to go, foolishly returned to Malta, where they had spent several days before the robbery hanging around town. Unaware that the local authorities had their descriptions, on December 1 Madden and Bass dropped by Alex Black's saloon, which they had frequented in the days before the robbery. Later that night they were arrested and under questioning named Longabaugh as the third man they had been seen with while hanging around town.[63] According to one report Harry was picked up trying to board a train at the Malta station, but he escaped shortly thereafter.[64]

Madden and Bass were tried and convicted on the testimony of the train crew and sent to the Montana State Prison at Deer Lodge. Longabaugh is believed to have returned to Wyoming, where he hid out for a while somewhere west of the Hole-in-the-Wall, then fled to safer surroundings at Brown's Park.[65]

The Wild Bunch

1896–1897

Brown's Park offered Butch and his pals a respite from the brutal heat of Robbers' Roost, but hiding was still hiding. The payday visit to the Pleasant Valley Coal Company at Castle Gate provided Butch and his companions with plenty of money, but there was no place to spend it in Brown's Park on just plain fun. Finding a drink of passable whiskey was possible at John Jarvie's store on the Green River near Indian Crossing.[1] However, Jarvie's place was in Sheriff John Pope's county and Butch was no longer sure where Pope's loyalties lay. Also, Jarvie's was on the stage line between Vernal and Rock Springs, and Butch was pretty well known in both places.

Butch may have had an "early warning" system of sorts at Jarvie's. Albert "Speck" Williams, who at times operated the ferry there, considered Butch a good friend and would have gladly sent word to him immediately if any strangers with badges came looking for him. Williams, an African American, later claimed that he never actually rode with Butch's gang, but he did admit that he ran errands for them and had the pleasure of drinking and gambling with them. When a friend asked Williams one day if he was ever abused by whites in Brown's Park, Williams answered something to the effect that they had better not, because if Butch Cassidy was around "he'd get after them."[2]

Cassidy's pack of followers, soon to be known as the Wild Bunch, had grown to eight or nine in number and were approaching their first anniversary as a loosely knit gang.[3]

The title "Wild Bunch" was probably derived from the gang's antics in riding into towns for a little fun and excitement. It has been suggested that saloonkeepers in and around Vernal, Utah, and southwestern Wyoming began calling them "that wild bunch from Brown's Park" in the late 1890s, although it was probably several years before they were known by this label among the public in general.[4] By November 1902, however, the American Bankers' Association used the name Wild Bunch to describe the gang in their annual report.[5] According to frontier historian Chuck Parsons, the first newspaper account that he could find mentioning the gang by the name "Wild Bunch" appeared in the *Omaha World Herald* on July II, 1904.[6] Pearl Baker believed that Butch originally wanted to call the gang the "Train Robbers' Syndicate," but it didn't catch on.[7]

Harry Longabaugh, alias the Sundance Kid, probably joined the group sometime during 1896 or 1897, and the members by this time also included Harvey Logan and "Flat Nose" George Currie.[8]

Harvey Logan, also called "Kid Curry," had turned up in the Hole-in-the-Wall region of Wyoming sometime in 1895 after killing a man in a brawl in Landusky, Montana.[9] Logan was no stranger to Johnson County. He has rustled cattle there for several years with enough success to put together a herd and try honest ranching in Montana with his brothers Lonny and John. But two days after Christmas, 1894, during a holiday party Logan got into a fist fight with Pike Landusky, a tough Missourian who had founded the town that bore his name.[10]

Landusky and the Logan brothers had been feuding over one thing or another for several years. Although Landusky had quite a reputation as a bare-knuckle fighter, and Logan was the smaller of the two, Logan was wiry and younger and was clearly winning the battle. Fearing that Logan would beat him to death, Pike went for his pistol, but it misfired. Logan drew his gun and shot Pike dead. Although the act appeared to be self-defense, Logan had started the fight and knew that Landusky had many friends who would want to even the score. He decided it would be best to leave town.[11]

George Currie got his nickname "Flat Nose" for a good reason: He resembled a prize fighter who has had the cartilage removed from his nose. Prior to joining the Wild Bunch, Currie also roamed the Hole-in-the-Wall area. He and Butch probably met sometime in 1890, when Butch had his Blue Creek Ranch in western Johnson County. Currie may have even helped Butch improve the property and outfit it for his rustling operation.[12]

One of the charter members of the Wild Bunch not around for the gang's first anniversary was Bub Meeks. About a week after the Castle Gate robbery Meeks left Brown's Park and went wandering about on his own. Sometime during the first week of June 1897 he rode into Fort Bridger, Wyoming (a small town east of Evanston in Uinta County), possibly to visit his brother who had a ranch nearby.[13]

While in Fort Bridger, Meeks spent most of his time at Charley Guild's place, a combination general store, post office, and saloon. On June 15, a Tuesday night, few cowboys were in town and business at Charley's was slow. Around nine, when everybody had left except Meeks, Bub told Guild that he had to take care of some matters but would return shortly. A few minutes later, two masked men barged through the front door and robbed Guild of $123.00. Minutes after they left Meeks returned. This seemed too much of a coincidence to Guild, and he accused Bub of being in on the job, claiming that he had given the robbers the signal when to charge in.[14]

Meeks was taken to Evanston, the county seat. It was doubtful that the county prosecutor had enough evidence to make Charley Guild's accusations stick, but, on a hunch, Uinta County Sheriff John Ward sent for Bud McIntosh, the assistant cashier at the Montpelier bank who claimed that he had gotten a good look at the man who held the horses while the bank was being robbed. McIntosh positively identified Meeks as that man.[15]

Since Meeks was believed to be riding with the Wild Bunch, Ward put his deputies on alert for a possible rescue attempt by Butch and the gang, but nothing developed.[16]

Butch may not have known about Meeks's arrest. About that time Butch may have been busy with other matters: one of the most widely publicized robberies involving the Wild Bunch, the assault on the Butte County Bank in Belle Fourche, South Dakota, in June 1897.

The town of Belle Fourche lies just across the South Dakota–Wyoming line at the confluence of two streams, which no doubt accounts for the town's name, meaning "beautiful fork" in French. From June 24 through June 26, 1897, the town hosted a reunion of Civil War veterans, a three-day period when a greater-than-usual amount of outside revenue flowed into the community. By June 28, much of that money had been deposited by local retailers in the vault of the Butte County Bank.

The bank, a formidable two-story limestone structure, was located at the corner of what is now State and Sixth Streets. Shortly before 10:00 AM on the 28th, six strangers came riding down State Street and stopped at the corner near the building. Four of the riders dismounted and tied their horses at the side entrance. The other two stationed themselves across the street. It is doubtful that anyone paid much attention to them: although the festivities were officially over, a few veterans had stayed in town to have one more drink and swap one more story before heading home.[17]

Three of the four strangers who had tied up at the bank entrance—believed to be Harry Longabaugh, Harvey Logan, and George Currie—glanced up and down the street, then quickly entered the lobby. The fourth man stayed with the horses.[18]

Inside the bank were the head cashier, Arthur R. Marble, his assistant, Harry Ticknor, and four customers. As the strangers entered one of them shouted to those inside to hold up their hands. They all complied. Cashier Marble, however, was not to be so easily subdued, at least as he later told the story. Marble said that he waited for just the right moment—when the robbers seemed to glance away—to reach for a pistol he kept under the counter. In one swift move he pulled the gun out, pointed it at Harvey Logan, and pulled the trigger. But the gun only snapped: it was a misfire. Logan swung around ready to shoot, but stopped himself when Marble sheepishly laid down the weapon and raised his hands.[19]

George Currie had brought a sack. When he saw that the four customers had money in their hands, ready to make deposits, he ordered them to put their deposits in the sack instead. One of the customers, a shopkeeper named Sam Arnold, promptly stepped forward and dropped in $97.00 in cash: his receipts from the previous day's business.[20]

At this moment, Alanson Giles looked out the window of his hardware store directly across the street and saw the customers in the bank with their hands raised. He hurried outside for a better look. When he realized what was happening he turned and ran back to his store, shouting, "They're robbing the bank!" When George Currie heard Giles's shout, he fired a shot through the glass of the bank door. Giles probably thought the bullet was meant for him, but it was a signal to the two men across the street to pull out their guns and begin firing toward the sky, hoping to convince bystanders that the ruckus was merely a couple of cowboys who had yet to sleep off a long night of hard drinking.

The shooting called for a fast exit. The gunfire was frightening the horses: they were prancing around with their ears back, straining at their reins. It took several seconds to calm them enough to mount, but five of the six bandits eventually managed to swing into their saddles. The sixth, Tom O'Day, was not so lucky. His horse was thoroughly spooked, and with one last lunge it broke loose and raced off, chasing the other horses as they headed down Sixth Street toward the railroad tracks. O'Day, on foot and desperate, tried to commandeer a mule but could not get it to move, so he ran to the nearest saloon, hoping to get lost in the crowd and play the part of an innocent bystander.[21]

The rest of the gang rode hard down Sixth Street with O'Day's horse trailing behind. When they saw that O'Day was missing they rode up a small hill at the end of the street, apparently to get a better view. According to R. I. Martin, an eyewitness of the events, John McClure (one of the old Civil War veterans) had found an ancient .44 caliber rifle and was kneeling on the walk near the bank trying to get the robbers in his sights. He finally got off a few rounds but they fell far short of the mark. Another townsman, blacksmith Joe Miller, grabbed his rifle, jumped on a horse, and raced toward the hill where the robbers waited. Half the way up the hill, however, his horse was brought down by a shot from the rifle of Frank Bennett, who was firing from the second-story window of Teall & Bennett's flour mill. Unable to spot Tom O'Day, the robbers could wait no longer and raced away. After the loss of their comrade and their own narrow escape, all they had to show for the day was a sack containing shopkeeper Sam Arnold's $97.00.[22]

Back in town, O'Day was in trouble. A witness told the sheriff that he had seen Tom toss his gun and gunbelt down the hole of a privy located near the saloon to which he had fled. As it was being fished out, other witnesses came forward and confirmed that they had seen Tom ride into town with the robbers.[23]

The five escaping riders headed southwest toward Wyoming where, somewhere across the state line, they split up. Butte County Sheriff George Fuller quickly formed a posse and rode off after them. According to an unconfirmed report, at one point Fuller got close enough for somebody to shoot Harry Longabaugh's horse, but Harry still got away.[24]

A story is told that Longabaugh made it as far as Newcastle, Wyoming, about ten miles west of the South Dakota line. He may have been on foot and he probably had been without sleep for many hours. He needed to keep going but he also needed rest and food. Without money he couldn't go in somewhere and buy a meal, and it was too dangerous to curl up in a doorway or at the livery stable. Newcastle was a county seat, which meant it had a sheriff's office and deputies that made rounds at night. With news of the jailbreak circulating throughout the area, the authorities would be checking closely for vagrants. Stealing a horse was also out of the question, at least until he got some sleep. It was about then that Longabaugh spotted a light in the office of Ben F. Hilton, publisher of Newcastle's local newspaper.[25]

Hilton was just about ready to lock up the office when the door swung open and Longabaugh entered with his gun drawn. Harry got right to the point: he needed a place to stay. Hilton did have an attic above the print shop, which at times he rented out for sleeping. There was even a mattress that had been left by the previous tenant.[26] The arrangement Harry offered was probably very simple: if Hilton let him sleep up there a while and brought him food, he would then go about his business and Hilton would be none the worse. But if Hilton ran for the sheriff, Harry's friends would come and kill him and his family. Whatever the actual terms were, Hilton agreed to them.

Longabaugh was Hilton's guest for at least two days. Only one person discovered that he was harboring the famous Sundance Kid: Hilton's eight-year-old daughter, Edith. While helping her father in the print shop the next day, she heard Harry walking about overhead and guessed what was going on. Hilton asked her to not tell anyone, and she didn't.[27]

There is no evidence that Butch Cassidy took an active part in the Belle Fourche robbery, but there is some evidence that he was in northeastern Wyoming—about 175 miles west of the scene—when it occurred, which suggests that he may have been involved in planning the affair. According to Fred Hilman, the son of a rancher who owned a spread a few miles south of Sheridan in Little Goose Canyon, Butch spent the summer of 1897 working for his father, Daniel Hilman. Fred, then a boy of thirteen, said that his father hired Butch (who told the Hilmans that his name was Parker) in late April, and that he worked on the ranch until "one morning towards fall."[28]

Fred remembered Butch as likable and a hard-working hand, although he recalled that regardless of where Butch was working, he always seemed to keep a saddled horse picketed nearby. Also, whenever he was in the ranch house Butch seemed nervous, and he usually sat so that he could keep an eye on the door and windows. Fred further recalled that Butch had a friend, a tall, dark-complected fellow, who would come to visit him now and then. Occasionally Butch would ask for time off and the two men would ride away and be gone for several days. The Hilmans believed that Butch had called his friend Elzy.[29]

On the morning Butch left the Hilman ranch, Fred was sent to the bunkhouse to see why he didn't show up for breakfast. Fastened to the bunkhouse door was a note: "Sorry to be leaving you. The authorities are getting on to us. Best home I've ever had. LeRoy Parker (Butch Cassidy)."[30]

Whether it was really Butch at the Hilman ranch that summer may never be established. Henry Lee, the small-time Brown's Park outlaw who, with Butch and Elzy had papered the Uintah and Ouray reservation with counterfeit money the previous year, claimed that he saw Butch in Baggs, Wyoming, on July 4, 1897, eight days after the Belle Fourche robbery. Lee said he met Butch that day in Jack Ryan's saloon. According to Lee, Butch was in Baggs looking for Bub Meeks. Lee said that he told Butch that Meeks had been picked up by the Idaho authorities for the Montpelier robbery.[31] Lee apparently did not say how Butch had reacted to the news of Meeks's arrest.

On learning of Meeks's predicament, Butch may have considered trying to free him. It would have been fun to ride in and snatch Bub from under deputy Bob Calverly's nose, a feat that would have come mighty close to settling the score for Calverly's capture of Butch at Ham's Fork. But the risk would have been great. Also, Butch may have decided that Bub Meeks had foolishly brought his misfortune on himself. Foolish or not, Butch probably missed Bub. They had been good friends and had shared some exciting moments together. When Bub's trial came up that fall, Henry and his brother, Ike Lee, risked a perjury charge and appeared as alibi witnesses for Bub, but their effort didn't help. Meeks was convicted and sentenced to the Idaho penitentiary.[32] Lee had a special reason to try to help Meeks: he was one of the two men who had robbed Charley Guild's store at Fort Bridger, which resulted in Bub's arrest.[33]

Charles Kelly believes that Butch did plan to get revenge for Meeks's capture, but the plot never materialized. According to Kelly, Butch decided to rob the Beckwith Bank in Evanston. In an unguarded moment word of the plan leaked out and somebody notified Deputy Sheriff Bob Calverly, who in turn warned Ashael C. Beckwith, owner of the bank. Beckwith's first move was to transfer most of his cash to a bank in Salt Lake City. Next he hired a sharpshooter and stationed him in a vacant building across the street from the bank. His third move was to arm two tellers with Winchester and pistols. Beckwith supposedly sweated out a week waiting for something to happen, but, as Kelly tells the story, the man who tipped off Bob Calverly of Butch's intentions must have had second thoughts because he tipped off Butch that a trap had been laid for him.[34]

If Butch was grieving for his friend, he put such thoughts aside for a while during the last week of July while the Wild Bunch gathered for a little celebration. The gang began their frolic in the usually peaceful town of Dixon on the Little Snake River just north of the Wyoming–Colorado line. They rode in whooping and hollering in Saturday night style, firing their guns toward the sky and clearing the street of startled bystanders. When they were fully liquored and at the peak of their mischief they climbed back on their saddles and rode west toward Baggs, about eight miles down river. As the story is told, somebody had tipped off the residents of Baggs that trouble was heading their way, and the town was deserted when the gang rode in. But at least one establishment—Jack Ryan's Bulldog Saloon—was open and the celebrators quickly decorated the bar with twenty-five bullet holes, for which, as the story goes, they compensated Ryan at the rate of one silver dollar per hole.[35] Ryan would later boast to customers that he applied the money toward a stake to buy a better saloon in Rawlins.[36]

Later that summer Walt Punteney and two other Wild Bunch members, possibly Harry Longabaugh and Harvey Logan, rode north to Montana. On September 19 they showed up in Red Lodge, looking for the town marshal, Byron St. Clair. They hoped that St. Clair, whom they knew from Fremont County, might want to work out a little deal. They suggested that it would be advantageous for St. Clair to make himself scarce while they paid a visit to the Red Lodge bank. Apparently it was a fairly good offer, and many peace officers would have jumped at the chance. But they had misjudged Marshal St. Clair: he wanted no part of the arrangement and he instead informed Sheriff John Dunn what the outlaws had in mind. Perhaps suspicious that St. Clair was not going to cooperate, the trio left town before a trap could be set. Sheriff Dunn organized a posse and was soon on their trail northwest out of Billings toward Lavina, Montana.[37]

The posse caught up with the trio just as they were setting up camp on the Musselshell River near Lavina. Dunn ordered them to surrender but they chose to put up a fight. One of them, believed to be Harvey Logan, made a dash for his horse, and both he and the animal were hit. The horse, although badly wounded, struggled for a mile before it stumbled and fell. Logan fared better, having received only a wound in the wrist, and he surrendered. The other two outlaws gave up at the scene. Dunn was certain that his prisoners were three of those involved in the bank robbery at Belle Fourche. The outlaws were taken to Billings, and Butte County Bank assistant cashier Harry Ticknor was summoned from Belle Fourche to look them over. He identified two of them as part of the gang that had entered the bank that day, and all three were transported to Deadwood to await arraignment.[38]

At the arraignment Walt Punteney gave his true name but the other two told the court they were Thomas Jones and Frank Jones. On October 15, the three, together with Tom O'Day (who had been sitting in jail since June), were indicted by a Butte County grand jury for the robbery. However, on the night of October 31 they overpowered their jailor and escaped. It was rumored that they had had horses saddled and waiting for them outside of town. O'Day and Punteney were recaptured near Spearfish, but the other two were never caught. Despite their escape, a crime in itself, O'Day and Punteney were not convicted. With the assistance of good counsel, possibly financed by Butch, the case against Punteney was dropped for insufficient evidence, and O'Day was acquitted.[39]

It was rumored that in addition to financing Punteney's and O'Day's defense, Butch had also engineered the foursome's escape from jail, but no proof of this has ever been found.[40]

Busy Times

1897–1898

During 1897 the large cattle ranches in the tristate area of Colorado, Utah, and Wyoming suffered increasingly heavy losses at the hands of rustlers. Smaller ranchers, too, as well as farmers, freight haulers, and even ordinary travelers were routinely falling victim to robbers. For the most part the blame was laid on organized packs of thieves, which the newspapers frequently labeled the "Robbers' Roost gang" or the "Hole-in-the-Wall gang," or sometimes the "Powder Springs gang."[1] While rustlers in and around Brown's Park left their friends' livestock alone, many cattlemen watched as their herds were steadily depleted. Much of the beef stolen in the northwestern corner of Moffat County, Colorado, found its way out of Brown's Park and down to central and southern Utah. This puzzled the livestock owners because they could not see how rustlers were able to gather up their stock and drive it out of the Park without being seen. According to some old-timers it was accomplished by way of "The Shelf Trail."[2]

At the southernmost bend of the Green River, about two miles east of the Utah-Colorado line, a trail leading south from Wild Mountain appears to end abruptly in a canyon on the north bank of the river. From a distance the canyon seems to end at the edge of a cliff that has a drop of at least several hundred feet to the water and rocks below. However, by carefully peering over the edge an observer could see a fairly wide shelf not far below that gently slants downward. From the top this shelf also appears to end in an abrupt drop to the river. However, the lower end of the shelf, out of view from the top, actually terminates just a few feet above another shelf that slants in the opposite direction. From this point on, also hidden by overhanging rock from above, is a steep trail that descends directly to the river.

For years rustlers had somehow kept this hidden trail a secret. It may have been spotted by a few ranchers, but it was unlikely that any of them believed that a skittish herd of cattle could be driven down it. But according to the old-timers, the rustlers figured out how to do it. Once at the bottom of the canyon they swam the beef across the river and were on their way to market.

As would be expected, not every cow made it safely to the bottom. Many years later, when hearty souls began running the Green River with rafts and boats, remnants of the Shelf Trail's boneyard were detected among the rocks and eddies. By then the trail had been discovered by the ranchers and rendered virtually worthless with a few sticks of dynamite.[3]

This trail is sometimes confused with Brown's Park "Outlaw Trail" that paralleled the east rim of Lodore Canyon and terminated at the Yampa River just before it joins the Green River north of Steamboat Rock. Outlaws used the Outlaw Trail as an exit from the east end of the Park, but it was unfit for driving livestock until 1910 when a local rancher, Jack Chew, and his sons used black powder, dynamite, and picks and crowbars to smooth it out enough to get their cattle off Douglas Mountain and onto a virtually unlimited range near Pool Creek.[4]

As in 1892, when law enforcement agencies in northeastern Wyoming seemed unable or unwilling to cope with the problem of rustlers, the cattlemen of the tristate area banded together and demanded stricter measures. In early March 1898, representatives of the cattle industry met in Denver with the governors of Colorado and Wyoming and a state official from Utah to discuss the situation. Secretly, the cattlemen longed for total extermination of the outlaws—legal or otherwise—but cooler heads suggested asking help from the military, possibly a detachment of troopers from Fort Duchesne with, if it could be obtained, a declaration of martial law.[5]

But even as the meeting was being held, news came from Brown's Park that made it evident that something had to be done about the reckless element that controlled that region. On February 17, 1898, at the ranch of Valentine Hoy near Pine Mountain and just north of the Wyoming-Colorado line, a hard-drinking cowpuncher and part-time rustler named Patrick Johnson shot and killed a sixteen-year-old boy, Willie Strang. The boy's only offense was that he playfully spilled water down the front of Johnson's shirt. Johnson claimed that he was only trying to scare young Willie, but he did not wait around to square things: he saddled up one of Hoy's horses and, accompanied by fellow rustler John (Jack) Bennett, fled to nearby Powder Springs where the two had been maintaining a camp.[6]

Powder Springs, located just below the Wyoming line in Moffat County, Colorado, about midway between Baggs, Wyoming, and Brown's Park, was a favorite stopping place for outlaws and drifters traveling between the Park and the Hole-in-the-Wall in northern Wyoming. There were actually two Powder Springs: upper and lower. The upper springs, about a mile south of the Wyoming-Colorado line, lay nestled among rocks and crevices in a bowl-shaped valley along Powder Wash, slightly west of Powder Mountain. The lower springs, about two miles further south, lay in flatter, more rolling terrain, a tiny oasis in a bleak, sage-covered wasteland.[7]

Sharing Johnson and Bennett's camp at Powder Springs were a pair of even worse characters, Harry Tracy and Dave Lant, both of whom had escaped the previous October from the Utah State Penitentiary. Tracy and Lant had been hiding out in Uintah County, southeast of Vernal near Naples. Lant was familiar with the Vernal area, having once worked for the McCoy Sheep Company. The two outlaws had stolen a couple of horses in Ashley Valley, and when Uintah County Sheriff William Preece gathered up a posse and went looking for them, they fled east through Brown's Park to the springs.[8] At first the rugged wilderness of the springs area seemed a fairly safe place to hide, but when Tracy and Lant learned about the death of the Strang boy they began to worry that the law would be coming after Johnson. Also, they faced another month of bitter weather, and camping outdoors in northern Colorado is not the best way to spend late winter. After thinking it over the four men decided it would be best to pack up and head for the warmer canyons of Robbers' Roost country in southern Utah.[9]

Before leaving for the Roost they had to gather more supplies, so Jack Bennett (the only one of the four not wanted by the law) was elected to go. Before he left it was decided that while Bennett was gone, Johnson, Tracy, and Lant would move the camp from Powder Springs down into the Park at a spot near Lodore Canyon. The move turned out to be a mistake. Before long a posse led by Sheriff Charles Neiman of Routt County, Colorado, spotted the camp and quickly closed in. Valentine Hoy, a member of the posse out in front of the others, got too close and Harry Tracy shot and killed him. Shaken by Hoy's death, the posse retreated to regroup, which allowed the three fugitives to escape. However, Neiman's men later captured Jack Bennett as he rode in with the supplies.[10]

Hoy's death seemed to confirm the general opinion that Brown's Park was an outlaw sanctuary and could not be invaded, but the residents of Brown's Park were not willing to turn their heads this time. Willie Strang was barely more than a child, and Valentine Hoy was a respected member of the ranching community. The tragic deaths of these two could not be dismissed lightly.

Jack Bennett was the first to feel the community's anger. He was taken to the Bassett ranch for safekeeping, but safe he was not. The next day a handful of masked men rode to the ranch, overpowered the deputy who had been placed as guard, and hanged Bennett from the crossbar of one of Bassett's gates.[11]

The original posse led by Sheriff Neiman consisted of nine volunteers, probably reluctant ones at that, but when word spread of Valentine Hoy's death over sixty citizens showed up at the Park, ready to hunt down Hoy's murderers. It did not take long to find the killers. On March 5, at a site about five or six miles south of Powder Springs, Tracy, Lant, and Johnson, nearly frozen and with their clothes in rags, surrendered without a fight.[12]

When the trio was brought to the Bassett ranch, few bystanders would have wagered that the three would live to see another sunrise; however, throughout the night Sheriff Neiman mingled with the crowd that had gathered at the ranch and kept a lid on everyone's tempers. The next day Patrick Johnson was turned over to federal marshals who took him back to Wyoming to stand trial. Neiman and one of his deputies then bundled up Tracy and Lant and hurried them off to the Routt County jail in Hahn's Peak. The pair briefly escaped twelve days later by overpowering Neiman at the jail, but they were recaptured near Steamboat Springs. They were returned to Hahn's Peak and later transferred to Aspen, Colorado, which was supposed to have a stronger jail, but in late April they escaped again.[13]

Although Butch Cassidy played no role in the story of fugitives Tracy and Lant—which has come to be known as the "Battle of Brown's Park"—when Harry Tracy later became famous as a desperado a few writers erroneously connected him with Butch and the Wild Bunch. With one exception, nothing suggesting such a connection has ever been uncovered. Kerry Ross Boren, the lone exception, says that his grandfather, who was supposed to have known Butch, claimed that Butch personally ordered Tracy to leave Brown's Park.[14] Tracy's contact with outlaws in the Park area probably was limited to knowing Patrick Johnson and Jack Bennett.[15] And while Johnson and Bennett themselves may have been acquainted with Butch, more than likely they were never more than on the fringe of the Wild Bunch.[16]

Although not involved in the series of events, Butch and the Wild Bunch would feel the effects of the killings of Willie Strang and Valentine Hoy. The uproar over the deaths brought about the beginning of a gradual decline of Brown's Park as an outlaw sanctuary.

In mid-March 1898, the governors of Colorado and Wyoming met with the Governor of Utah at Salt Lake City and announced that a concerted action would be made to break up the outlaw gangs that were terrorizing the tristate area. Several plans were considered. One was to dispatch a novel multistate force: officers with special powers to pursue and make arrests in all three states.[17] Another was to place a large reward on the head of each outlaw and encourage bounty hunters who were familiar with the area to work alone or in pairs. J. S. Hoy, brother of slain rancher Valentine Hoy, favored this approach. He believed that one or two highly trained men who would stick to the trail of an outlaw would succeed where a hundred men would fail.[18]

Before any plan could be fully launched, however, attention was diverted to a greater problem: on April 24 the United States declared war on Spain. Even before the declaration, war fever had taken hold of Wyoming. Shortly after the sinking of the battleship *Maine*, lawyer and former Big Horn Basin rancher Jay L. Torrey, who once held the rank of general in the National Guard, proposed organizing a volunteer cavalry regiment made of Wyoming cowboys. U.S. Senator Francis E. Warren of Wyoming thought it was a great idea and introduced a bill in Congress authorizing such a unit. Within weeks the War Department allocated Torrey nearly $250,000 to raise and train troops.[19]

The press praised the idea, urging Wyoming cowboys to volunteer and share in an opportunity "to make the earth tremble and win glory in some of the greatest cavalry charges of modern times."[20]

These patriotic pleas must have reached Butch and the Wild Bunch. What effect they had is not known. It has been suggested that the gang did give some thought to joining the cause. As the story was told, Butch, Harry Longabaugh, Harvey and Lonny Logan, and possibly Elzy Lay, gathered with perhaps a half-dozen other outlaws near Steamboat Springs, Colorado, to discuss signing up en masse. Although some writers have suggested that the meeting was called because of an outpouring of patriotism, it is more likely that the outlaws were more interested in pursuing an exchange of military service for amnesty. Whatever the reason for the gathering, if there was one, nothing came of it.[21]

Some outlaws probably did volunteer on their own. According to two separate accounts given by officers who served in the Philippines, several members of the Wild Bunch ended up in a detachment of muleskinners, whose job was to get supplies through an area infested with Moros, the fierce tribesmen causing trouble for American occupation forces. As the officers told the story, soon after the arrival of the Wild Bunchers and after several disastrous encounters, the Moros backed off, finding the raids too costly.[22]

It is not known whether any of the Wild Bunch joined Colonel Jay Torrey's Second U.S. Volunteer Cavalry. A few may have slipped in under aliases. If they did they were probably disappointed in the outcome. The regiment, which eventually reached a force of 1,100 men, failed to see action against the enemy, though it did suffer casualties. On June 26, at Tupelo, Mississippi, a train carrying the regiment to Jacksonville, Florida, was involved in a serious accident. Five members of the outfit were killed and fifteen were seriously injured, including Colonel Torrey, who suffered badly crushed feet.[23]

Where there is little evidence as to how many western outlaws joined the war effort, the war did take some of the most experienced outlaw hunters, particularly from the ranks of deputy United States marshals.[24]

Whether Butch considered volunteering for military service isn't known, but it has been hinted that he may have displayed at least one patriotic gesture. In early 1898 it was rumored that the railroads and express companies were considering extreme measures to ward off train robbers, including a demand that the states served by the railroads provide them with militia to guard their shipments, militia that were clearly needed elsewhere. According to Wyoming frontier historian A. F. C. Greene, during the governors' conference at Salt Lake City in mid-March 1898, Butch sent word to Wyoming Governor W. A. Richards that the railroads and express companies need not worry, that he was giving his word that they did not have to put extra armed guards on the trains.[25]

If the story is true, few bought it. Later that month Colorado Governor Alva Adams informed Governor Richards that he had hired a noted bounty hunter, James Catton, to go one-on-one after Butch, and that there was a good chance that Catton would get him. But less than two weeks later Adams was forced to admit to Richards that the plan was abandoned, that Catton was not the man for the job after all.[26]

Following the lead of the railroads and express companies, several Wyoming banks began putting pressure on Governor Richards to do more about the outlaws. The first week in May 1898, the president of the First National Bank in Buffalo, concerned over the release of Wild Bunch bank robbers Tom O'Day and Walt Punteney, urged the governor to form a Wyoming strike force similar to the Texas Rangers to capture or drive the outlaws out of the state.[27]

A week later the Butch Cassidy problem appeared to be solved. On May 13, 1898, Governor Heber Wells of Utah received the following telegram from Joe Bush, a U.S. deputy marshal on assignment in Carbon County, Utah. The telegram was sent from Thompson Springs: "Came up with out-

laws five this morning. Killed Joe Walker and Cassiday [sic], captured Lay
and one man. Have prisoners and dead men here. Send message to my
house please. Sheriff Allred and posse did nobly. J. R. Bush"[28]

The week before, a posse led by Carbon County's newly appointed sheriff, C. W. Allred, rode out of Price, the county seat. Riding with Allred were
Pete Anderson, J. W. Warf, J. M. Whitmore, George Whitmore, Jack Gen-
fry, Jim Inglefild, Billy McGuire, and Jack Watson. Although well-armed
and probably packing enough provisions for at least two weeks, the posse
was not bent on invading Butch Cassidy's hideout in Robbers' Roost but
simply wanted to find a bunch of horses and cattle that had been stolen
from the Whitmores.[29]

The nine men rode southwest along the winding Price River, the route
the thieves were believed to have taken. At a spot on the river west of the
Book Cliffs called Lower Crossing, they picked up what they believed to be
the rustlers' trail. Probably much to the posse's relief the hoofprints did not
lead south toward the Roost, but back north and slightly west, toward the
cliffs and Range Valley. Before long they knew they were on the right track
when they came across several strays from the Whitmore herd. Also,
nearby was a horse, apparently abandoned by the rustlers. Allred sent several of the men back to the Whitmore ranch with the strays with instructions to catch up with the posse later in Range Valley.[30]

In Range Valley the trail led past a ranch. Allred called out the owner,
Jim McPherson, and questioned him, but McPherson said that he had not
seen the rustlers. Allred didn't believe him, however, and suggested rather
forcefully that he ride along with them and serve as a guide.[31]

The tracks turned southwest, toward the Green River. Once across the
river Allred saw that they would have to enter a series of long, narrow canyons with craggy walls that offered dozens of hiding places—a perfect spot
for an ambush. But this was the new sheriff's first major manhunt and it
would not look good if he turned back. He decided to wait until near night-
fall, when he and his men would not make such good targets for the
rustlers' Winchesters.[32]

Under the cover of darkness the possemen carefully advanced about another fifteen miles. At best guess they were still somewhere on McPherson's land, probably about fifty miles north of Thompson Springs. It was
now well past midnight and they were approaching the end of the canyon.
Assuming the outlaws would have to stop to sleep, Allred figured that they
might be getting close to their camp. He passed the word to his men to dismount; they would get out their blankets and wait until early light.

About an hour before dawn the posse remounted. They had ridden only a few minutes when Allred saw that he had guessed right: ahead, not far off the trail, was the outlaws' camp. The sheriff signaled to dismount and advance on foot.

Allred could see only four men, all asleep, wrapped in their blankets on a shelf of rock protected on one side by a deep ravine. After making sure that his men were set and their guns were ready, Allred called out to the rustlers, "Come out and surrender!" Pete Anderson and J. M. Whitmore, nearly in unison, added, "You're surrounded by a hundred men!"[33]

Two of the outlaws threw up their hands immediately, pleading not to be shot. The other two grabbed their guns and began firing. When they had emptied their weapons they tried to run. The first man ran about sixty feet before he was brought down; the second man made it not quite as far. Both were dead where they lay. The first man was identified immediately: it was Joe Walker, a member of Butch Cassidy's gang. When the second man was turned over, Sheriff Allred could not believe his eyes: it was Butch himself. Jubilant, Allred and his men handcuffed the two captured outlaws, tied Walker and Cassidy to their saddles, and started off for Thompson Springs, the nearest town with a Western Union office. At Thompson, Marshal Joe Bush telegraphed Utah Governor Heber Wells that the notorious Butch Cassidy was dead.[34]

The following day, a Saturday, the posse returned to Price. As townsmen filed in to take a look at the dead men, some agreed with Allred that the man laid out beside Joe Walker was most definitely Butch Cassidy; others, however, had some doubt. A makeshift inquest was quickly held, and the "jury," relying mainly upon the testimony of Allred and that of Emery County Sheriff Ebenezer Tuttle, decided that it was indeed Butch. As soon as the decision was announced the bodies were prepared for burial. That night they were placed in two wooden coffins, and the next day they were buried.[35]

Even as the remains were being lowered in the graves, a controversy was arising over whether the second outlaw was really Cassidy. The two captured rustlers, who gave their names as Thompson and Schulz, said that it was not Cassidy, that it was a Wyoming cowboy named John Herring (or Herron). Someone suggested that Allred should get in touch with officials in Wyoming who had actually known Cassidy. A wire was sent to Sheriff John Ward at Evanston. Ward knew what Butch looked like from having briefly held him in jail following his arrest in 1892. Also summoned was former Gunnison County (Colorado) Sheriff Cyrus "Doc" Shores, who was then working for the Denver & Rio Grande Railroad. On Monday, the body thought to be Cassidy's was exhumed, and, much to Sheriff Allred and his posse's dismay, both Ward and Shores stated that the man definitely was not Butch.[36] Hearts sank: rumors had been circulating that there might be as much as $15,000 in outstanding rewards on Butch.[37]

To add to Allred's woes, Thompson and Schultz, the two men who had surrendered during the shootout, had to be turned loose for lack of evidence connecting them to the theft of the Whitmore cattle.[38] There was a small reward for Joe Walker, and apparently it was eventually paid, but Sheriff Allred and his posse had to share it with Emery County Sheriff Tuttle and his posse.[39]

A story has persisted through the years, passed on by Charles Kelly and confirmed by Butch's sister in 1975, that Butch actually paid a visit to Price while his "dead body" was laid out for public viewing. According to the story, Butch was on his way between Robbers' Roost and Brown's Park when he learned of his own demise. He rode over to the cabin of a friend, Jim Sprouse, who lived just outside Price. As the tale is told, Butch, thinking that it would be a great story to tell his pals, talked Sprouse into driving a wagon down the main street of Price with Butch hidden under a layer of straw. Through a crack in the sideboards Butch was able to see the crowd that milled around the entrance of the building where he was supposed to have been laid out.[40] According to Butch's sister, he later told her that he thought "it would be a good idea to attend his own funeral just once during his lifetime." He added that he was touched when he saw a number of women wiping their eyes.[41]

Charles Kelly provides a footnote to the story, which, if true, places Butch's Wyoming attorney, Douglas Preston, in a bad light. Kelly says that a mining entrepreneur named Finley P. Gridley happened to run into Preston sometime shortly after the report hit the newspapers that Cassidy had been killed. According to Gridley, when he mentioned Butch's death Preston threw back his head and laughed. When Gridley asked him what was so funny, he said that Preston replied, "Nothing much, except that I talked to Butch just before I left Brown's Hole this morning."[42]

If the story is true, Preston had met and conferred with a suspected criminal who was wanted by the law. Such conduct by an attorney, an officer of the court, though common in the West during the 1890s, was officially frowned upon by the legal profession and, under some circumstances, was considered a criminal act in itself. This didn't seem to bother Preston, however, and in later years he would brag about his meetings with Butch between holdups.[43]

Sheriff Allred's excursion into Robbers' Roost country and the killing of Walker and Herring may have led Butch to reconsider whether the Wild

Bunch was as safe in the Roost as they had believed.[44] This incident, plus the threat of an all-out effort by the governors of Utah, Wyoming, and Colorado to rid their states of the Wild Bunch once and for all, may have persuaded Butch to abandon his favorite hideouts and head for distant places. It was probably a difficult decision. Robbers' Roost and Brown's Park had been ideal sanctuaries. In both places Butch had an assortment of friends and acquaintances where he and his pals, even if on the run, could usually stop for a meal or put up for the night. Foremost among these were Ford DeJournette, a transplanted North Carolinian who had a sheep camp in southern Wyoming between Brown's Park and Rock Springs; Jack Edwards, who operated a spread near Powder Wash in Moffat County, Colorado; and John Sampson Hacking Jr., a large sheep rancher who ran his herd on Diamond Mountain in Uintah County, Utah.[45]

Although Butch may have regretted leaving the gang's favorite haunts, he did leave. It isn't known exactly when, but he eventually turned up in the Southwest, on a ranch near Alma, New Mexico, where he would spend a brief but relatively peaceful period as an ordinary trail boss.

Alias Jim Lowe

1898–1900

Those who probe the criminal mind suggest that some criminals return now and then to stretches of honest work, even when they do not have
to, possibly because they tire of being outcasts and long for the decency
that steady work characterizes.[1]

When Butch headed south, his first stop may have been Cochise County,
Arizona, at the Erie Cattle Company ranch about twenty miles northeast
of Bisbee—one of seven or eight ranches on the so-called Outlaw Trail that
stretched from Montana to Mexico, ranches where a cowboy could ride in
and sign on without answering too many questions about his past. The
Erie, which ran about 20,000 head of cattle, was owned by easterners who
seldom visited their operation and probably cared little who drew wages if
the work got done.[2] If Butch did stop at the Erie, his hitch there was short-
lived, for a few months later he showed up at the ws Ranch, about a hundred miles north of the Erie and just across the line in southwestern New
Mexico.

The ws Ranch lay in a flat valley that ran along the San Francisco River.
The spread was founded in the early 1880s by an Englishman, Harold C.
Wilson, and managed until 1887 by James H. Cook, who had been Wilson's
guide on several trips to the West. On Cook's departure the operation was
taken over by William French, also an Englishman and a former professional soldier who gave up his commission to try raising cattle in America.[3]

To the south of the ranch was a sleepy pueblo called Alma, then little
more than a store, a saloon, and a pair of dry-rotting hitching posts.[4]

Why Butch, accompanied by Elzy Lay, ended up at the ws is unclear, except that perhaps William French was not too particular whether a cowboy signed on under his own name. More important was whether a newcomer was willing to work hard, and if he was trustworthy: loyalty to the
ranch and the ws brand was what French looked for in a cowboy.[5] Also,

that part of the Territory of New Mexico was virtually free of lawmen. According to the locals, the sheriff over in Socorro, then the county seat, had difficulty finding a deputy who would take the western part of the county, which was thought to be too dangerous a place to try to maintain order.[6]

According to French, the two men he later learned were the outlaws Butch Cassidy and Elzy Lay, showed up at the WS in the company of a ranch ramrod named Perry Tucker, who was also looking for a job. Butch was using the name Jim Lowe, and Elzy called himself William McGinnis. French needed a new foreman and Perry Tucker had been recommended. French liked what he saw in Tucker and offered him the position. Tucker agreed to take the job and suggested that Jim Lowe be taken on as his assistant. He also recommended McGinnis, supposedly a first-rate hand at breaking broncs.

French liked what he saw in Lowe. He was solidly built and probably could handle himself if things got tough. Also, he liked the way Lowe had of grinning at you when he spoke. The man who called himself McGinnis seemed several years younger than Lowe and was taller. Both were clearly a cut above ordinary cowboys and seemed to be better educated than most.[7] French had hired a lot worse than these two.

Perry Tucker and Jim Lowe worked well together. Dead weight that had accumulated at the WS over the previous months under the prior foreman was soon eliminated, and new hands seemed to show up looking for work just when they were needed. More important, the number of stray cattle being lost to rustlers decreased almost at once.

At the ranch and on the range Perry Tucker was boss, but when cattle were to be driven to the railroad Jim Lowe was in charge. French marveled at Lowe's skill. He later remarked, "The way he handled those poor cattle over that long and dusty trail of nearly two hundred miles was a revelation. Frequently they had to go as much as seventy-five miles without water, but he never dropped a hoof, and there was no tail to his herd when he arrived at the road." Elzy, whom they called "Mac," usually accompanied Jim Lowe on the drives as wrangler, and on the way he often broke broncs for the hands back at the ranch, returning them "nice and gentle," French recalled.[8]

To French, Jim Lowe and Mac McGinnis were near perfect as trail boss and wrangler–bronc buster; they even bypassed the age-old tradition of getting drunk and shooting up a town at the end of a drive. Jim had his men so well-disciplined that the merchants in Magdalena went out of their way to congratulate French on what a well-behaved outfit he had. The only problem, as French remembered, was a high turnover rate on the drives.

After almost every drive a few of the men quit. But since this didn't seem to bother Jim Lowe, and since he always seemed able to replace them with hands just as capable, French didn't let it bother him either.

Although French would later claim that he had no idea that Jim Lowe was the outlaw Butch Cassidy, he did notice something unusual. When Lowe found new men for Perry Tucker to take on, they almost always appeared to be strangers to Lowe and McGinnis, at least when they were around French, but when they were off together they often acted as if they were all old friends.[9]

Although French failed to mention it in his recollections, Lowe and McGinnis may have taken a week or two off in late May.

About an hour after dawn on June 2, 1899, the telegraph center at the general offices of the Union Pacific Railroad in Omaha received an urgent message from Medicine Bow, Wyoming, a stop about six miles east of the Carbon-Albany County line. It was from the engineer of the first of two sections of the UP's westbound No. 1 Overland Limited, which had left Omaha the previous morning: "First section No. 1 held up a mile west of Wilcox. Express car blown up, contents gone. We were ordered to pull over a bridge just west of Wilcox, and after we passed the bridge the explosion occurred. Can't tell how bad the bridge was damaged. No one hurt except Jones—scalp wound and cut on hand. Jones, engineer."[10] Later in the day additional details came in from the scene of the holdup. The dispatches, parts of which the UP summarized and released to the newspapers, said that the masked robbers, believed to be four in number, boarded the train at Wilcox, about fifteen miles southeast of Medicine Bow. One of them crawled forward over the locomotive tender, pointed a gun at W. R. Jones, the engineer, and ordered him to pull up just on the other side of a bridge a few miles out of Wilcox near Como Ridge. Conflicting reports from the site said the train was stopped by a man waiving a red lantern or an emergency flare, and one dispatch gave the number of robbers as six.[11]

The robbers forced the engineer and fireman out of their cab and made them walk back to one of the two railway mail cars where a pair of postal clerks had been sorting mail. They shouted for the men inside to open up. Burt Bruce, the clerk in charge, refused to open the door and told his fellow clerk, Robert Lawson, to put out all the lights and wait. Outside, the robbers, growing angry, shouted threats that they were going to blow the car up if the door wasn't opened. After about fifteen minutes Bruce and Lawson heard shots. Two balls ripped into the car, one striking the tank that held drinking water. A few minutes later an explosion nearly rocked the car off the tracks. When the dust settled, the robbers shouted to the clerks that the next charge would blow up the whole car. Bruce and Lawson opened the door and jumped down.[12]

As the robbers were lining up their captives along the side of the car, they saw the headlight from the second section of the train. They asked what was on that train and somebody answered that there were two cars of soldiers. Lawson said that on hearing this the robbers hurried the crew and the clerks back to the locomotive and ordered them to climb up. They then told the engineer to pull ahead. As the fireman was closing the boiler door he brushed against one of the robbers, apparently trying to dislodge his mask to get a look at his face. The robber grabbed his mask and angrily warned the fireman not to try that again or he would shoot him.

The engineer was ordered to drive ahead a short distance and stop. Several of the robbers ran back and placed either blasting powder or dynamite on the timbers of the bridge. The blast lit up the sky but it failed to bring the structure down. Next, the robbers uncoupled the train behind the mail car, leaving the locomotive with only the tender car, baggage car, express car, and the two mail cars. The engineer was ordered to pull ahead again, this time for about two miles.[13]

Apparently deciding that it would take too long to search through the mail for money and valuables, the robbers turned to the express car and ordered the messenger, E. C. Woodcock, to open up. He refused, and the robbers placed a charge under the door and blew out the side of the car. Woodcock was stunned but otherwise uninjured. The robbers climbed aboard the express car and used the rest of their explosives to open the two express company safes. After scooping up the contents—mostly unsigned bank notes—they left the scene on foot, heading in a northerly direction to where their horses were waiting.[14]

There is an interesting sidebar to the robbery. On the train that morning was Finley P. Gridley, manager of one of the Union Pacific Railroad's coal mines near Rock Springs, Wyoming. When the train was halted, Gridley went forward to see what was causing the trouble. After the robbers had left, while the wreckage of the express car was being cleared from the track, Gridley nosed around the area, examining the spot where the robbers' horses had been tied and where they had camped while they had waited for the train. When the train was finally ready to roll again, Gridley boarded and started back to his Pullman. On the way he bumped into Douglas Preston, Butch Cassidy's lawyer-in-waiting. Apparently Preston had not come forward to see what all the excitement was about, and before

Gridley could tell him what had happened Preston threw up his hands and said, "Don't shoot, Grid! Don't shoot! I can prove an alibi!" Gridley said that he had the feeling that Preston knew that the train would be robbed that morning.[15]

Around Rock Springs it was common knowledge that Preston was the Cassidy gang's lawyer, and Gridley, who considered Preston a friend, was openly critical of him for maintaining such a close relationship with the outlaws, warning him that some people even suspected him of being a tip-off man for the Wild Bunch and that he was getting a share of the proceeds of the gang's robberies.[16]

Preston was probably well-paid for his services, and he apparently had some influence over Butch, which on at least one occasion turned out to work to Finley Gridley's advantage. According to Gridley, one day he told Preston that he would quit harping about Preston's connection with the Wild Bunch if Preston would talk to Butch and get him to promise to not bother Gridley's own company payroll. Later, Preston told Gridley that he had met with Butch and that Butch had given him his word that he would not bother Gridley's company.[17]

Years later, Douglas Preston admitted to close friends that he often had meetings with Butch after the gang's holdups, presumably to advise his client on "legal matters." Preston said that these meetings took place in the desert between Rock Springs and Brown's Park.[18]

There are conflicting reports as to the route the robbers took in making their escape after the Wilcox robbery. They split up soon after leaving the scene, and a hard rain made their trail difficult to follow. One group took a northerly course, which suggested that they might be headed for Natrona County, and the authorities in that area were alerted. By Saturday afternoon, June 3, a sizable force of law officers and Union Pacific detectives had gathered in Casper, the county seat.[19]

On Sunday a report came in that three strangers were occupying a cabin on Casper Creek about six miles northwest of town. When a neighbor rode up to check them out, two men with rifles came out of the cabin and told him to "hit the road and hit it quick." The neighbor rode directly to Casper and reported the incident. A posse consisting of Converse County Sheriff Josiah Hazen, Natrona County Sheriff Oscar Hiestand, and nine others was quickly formed.[20]

By the time the posse reached the cabin the strangers were gone, but the rain had slacked off and their tracks were easy to follow. The posse caught up with them near a ranch on the Salt Creek Road about five miles west of Casper Creek. The outlaws chose to make a stand and began firing. One of the lawmen's horses was hit and another was chased off. The possemen dismounted and attempted to close in. More shots were fired, and Sheriff Hazen was hit in the abdomen. One of the members of the posse was a doctor and he attended to the sheriff's wound the best he could. Somebody found a wagon, and Hazen was rushed back to Casper. From there he was taken by special train to Douglas, his hometown, but he had lost much blood and he died the next day.[21]

Despite an all-out manhunt—said to be one of the largest ever organized in Wyoming for the killing of a peace officer—the three outlaws managed to escape and were not seen again, at least by a posse.[22] Word had it that after the shooting they headed north into Johnson County by way of Castle Creek, where they picked up supplies and fresh horses before riding west toward Thermopolis.[23] They may have camped for a while in southwestern Johnson County near Mayoworth near a ranch owned by Albert Brock.[24] From there they disappeared, leaving hundreds of pursuers with hardly a clue. Fred M. Hans, a professional manhunter brought in on the chase, called their escape "the most remarkable flight in the criminal history of the West."[25]

There is still disagreement among Wild Bunch historians as to just who all were at the scene at Wilcox. According to a Natrona County sheepherder, John C. DeVore, the men who shot it out with Sheriff Joe Hazen and his posse were Flat Nose George Currie, Harvey Logan, and Logan's brother, Lonny.[26] DeVore, who knew the Logans locally as the Roberts brothers, told the authorities that the three men had stopped by a sheep camp at Sullivan's Springs where he was working, and he had fixed them a meal, but, of course, at the time he had no idea they were wanted by the law.[27]

Most newspapers gave George Currie, the "Roberts brothers," and the "Hole-in-the-Wall" gang credit for the assault at Wilcox. The holdup and successful escape drew national attention to the gang, which stimulated a flowery New York newspaperman to pontificate that they were "lawless men who have lived long in the crags and become like eagles, shunning mankind, except when they swooped down upon some country bank to rob it at the point of pistol, or rode out on the range to gather in the cattle or horses of other men."[28]

No one has produced solid evidence that Butch was at the scene at Wilcox, but, except for George Currie, the Logans, and Bob Lee (a cousin of the Logans), the participants were never positively identified.[29] The members of the gang who split off from Currie and the Logan brothers headed west from the tracks and the authorities did not pick up their trail until much later. It is not clear whether this bunch detoured north again to rejoin the others, but eventually—possibly after reuniting with the northern trio—they headed for Brown's Park.[30] One source thinks that the robbers who headed directly west hid out for almost a week in a grove of aspens not more than three miles from the scene of the robbery where a friendly rancher kept them supplied with food and water. When they finally came out of hiding their faces were scrubbed, their hair was combed, and they were wearing dignified, well-cut business suits. Posing as important-looking land speculators they headed for Brown's Park in two buckboards loaded with valises and carpetbags.[31]

As fanciful as this story seems, there may have been something to it. A second source recalls that on a "Saturday night in the late summer 1899," Butch and Longabaugh, together with other Wild Bunch members, were seen at Linwood, Utah, a tiny town on the Utah-Wyoming border north of Vernal, presumably celebrating the success of the Wilcox robbery. The witness said Longabaugh was wearing "a magnificent gold-braided vest with shiny brass buttons" and one of the other members of the gang wore a "somber gray suit with [a] conservative vest of brown."[32]

There is no proof that Elzy Lay was one of the robbers at Wilcox, but according to Ann Bassett, about that time Lay rode to the Bassett ranch in Brown's Park and gave a map of the Powder Springs area to Ann that showed where he had buried a cache of stolen money. He made Ann promise that, should something happen to him, she would dig up the money and see that it was sent to his mother.[33]

Donna Ernst believes that Harry Longabaugh was at Wilcox.[34] This may have been so. About a week after the robbery, Harry was spotted near the Snake River in Colorado just south of the Wyoming border, presumably heading for Brown's Park. He had stopped at a store in Battle Creek and traded a worn-out horse plus $20.00 for a fresh one.[35]

In the files of the Union Pacific Railroad, Harvey Logan was listed as the leader of the gang at Wilcox. What proof the UP officials had of this fact isn't known, though it may have been because they considered him the most callous and dangerous of the Wild Bunch.[36]

If the Wilcox robbers reunited before going their separate ways, it could have been near the Emery Burnaugh ranch on Muddy Creek Road northeast of Lander. According to the Burnaughs, about that time Butch and five of his pals met in a cave behind the ranch that was sometimes used as a hideout.[37] Attorney Will Simpson would later claim that Butch told him that he, himself, took no part in the robbery at Wilcox, though Simpson supposedly admitted to writer Frederick Bechdolt that Butch was present at the gathering when the loot from Wilcox was split up.[38] According to Simpson, Butch attended the rendezvous at Burnaugh's only to confer with Harvey Logan about possibly leaving the United States, but Bechdolt claimed that Simpson admitted that Butch had received a share of the loot.[39] Simpson may have known what he was talking about: he himself may have been at Burnaugh's Muddy Creek Road ranch when the money was split up.[40]

A legend has circulated around the Lander area for years that, following one of the Wild Bunch's train robberies—possibly the Wilcox raid—Butch buried his share of the loot somewhere near South Pass, Wyoming. As the story is told, Butch placed the money in an iron pot, covered it with a lid, and buried at a spot near four trees. The spot he chose was exactly in the center of the four trees, an equal distance from each one. To mark the location he nailed a muleshoe to each tree. Luck, however, was not with him. A fire later swept through the area and destroyed the trees, and he could never find his cache.[41]

With the Wilcox holdup and Sheriff Joe Hazen's killing, Butch, while not specifically named as a participant, suddenly became a national figure. His picture, a likeness based upon his prison photo taken at the Wyoming State Penitentiary at Laramie, appeared in a June 25, 1899, article in the *New York Herald* about the Hole-in-the-Wall bandits. In the article, George Currie and the "Roberts" brothers were identified as leaders of the gang, but Butch was mentioned as standing by, ready to take over as leader should something happen to the others.[42]

Several weeks after the Wilcox robbery a report was circulated among the law enforcement agencies that two of the robbers had been seen in southwestern Wyoming driving thirteen head of saddle horses toward Brown's Park. A week or so later the same two, still leading the horses, were reported to have passed through Hanksville, Utah, heading south. One of these riders may have been Butch.[43] Two Pinkerton detectives, Charles Siringo and W. O. Sayles, were dispatched to pick up their trail.[44]

Siringo and Sayles were two of Pinkerton's most experienced operatives. Siringo, especially, who fancied himself as the original "cowboy detective," was a skilled tracker who often operated undercover, sometimes joining an outlaw gang and riding with them for weeks to get a lead on the man or men he was after.

Siringo was originally from Texas, and later spent some time in New Mexico, where he claimed to be a pal of both Billy the Kid and Pat Garrett. In fact, according to the Pinkertons he used Garrett as a reference when he joined the agency. His first major assignment was the Pinkertons' Chicago office, but he was not happy there. He was not cut out for "city duty," and he also had trouble accepting some of the shady practices that were going on in the Chicago office at the time.[45]

On being transferred to Denver in the late 1880s, Siringo found conditions more to his liking but he still didn't get along well with his fellow operatives. He was, however, a good detective, especially at undercover work. In 1892, during the labor trouble in the mines of northern Idaho, he infiltrated the union and even became one of its leaders. Later, with great risk to his life, Siringo testified at a trial that resulted in eighteen union officials going to jail. Throughout the nineties he continued to compile an excellent record with the agency and eventually became one of William Pinkerton's personal favorites.[46]

At Hanksville, Siringo and Sayles learned that the men they were after, still driving the bunch horses, had ridden south into Garfield County, Utah, and had crossed the Colorado River on Johnny Hite's ferry near the mouth of Dirty Devil River. When Siringo and Sayles inquired at the ferry they were told that another man, a single rider who was leading five horses and apparently was a friend of the first two, had crossed the river five days later. Hite said that the man mentioned that he was going to go "where the grass was good and camp until he heard from his friends." This man's description matched that of Harvey Logan, and the detectives assumed that the outlaws had a camp somewhere on the south side of the river where they had arranged to meet.[47]

Siringo and Sayles crossed the river and soon picked up the man's trail, which appeared to lead up White's Canyon. However, it was getting late in the day and the detectives' horses needed feed. It was decided that Sayles would return to the ferry to buy some grain and in the meantime Siringo would follow the tracks until dark.

Siringo followed the trail up a steep bluff and onto a mesa, but soon lost the tracks in a rocky arroyo. He searched the arroyo for another two miles and finally gave up. (About a year later, Siringo learned from a prospector, a man named John Duckett who was working a claim on a ridge above the canyon, that he had come within a half-mile of the outlaw's camp. Duckett told him that he had watched him and the man he was trailing from his vantage point and had seen Siringo give up and leave. He added that the outlaw had camped there for about two weeks before moving on.[48])

Although Siringo failed to spot the lone outlaw's camp on the mesa above White Canyon, when he and Sayles returned to the canyon they managed to again pick up the trail of the two riders who were leading the saddle horses.

From White Canyon the robbers' trail led southeast to Bluff, Utah, on the San Juan River, about twenty miles north of the Arizona line. At Bluff, Siringo and Sayles learned that two other Pinkerton operatives had preceded them and were already on the trail of the outlaws, who had headed east out of town after loading up with supplies. By then Siringo had little doubt that the two men they were following were the Wilcox robbers: a report had arrived that a bill from the express car safe had been traced to Hanksville and another one had been passed earlier at Thompson's Springs, which also had been on the robbers' path.[49]

From the direction the outlaws had taken out of Bluff they could be heading either for Colorado or New Mexico. Rather than simply follow the other two Pinkertons, Siringo and Sayles rode directly to Mancos, Colorado, and there boarded a train for Durango.

Siringo had been hunting outlaws for over twelve years, and in addition to the Pinkerton network of operatives at his disposal he had cultivated many useful contacts throughout the West. Telegrams to acquaintances in Colorado and New Mexico brought him a much-welcomed reply. A friend, J. M. Archuleta, sent word that the two men he was chasing had been seen near Lumberton, New Mexico. There was little doubt that they were the same men: two of the thirteen horses the outlaws had with them, one a bright cream color and the other a large, dapple-iron gray, were easy to spot. Siringo and Sayles rushed to Lumberton.[50]

The two suspects and their horses were gone by the time the detectives arrived at Lumberton. After asking around Siringo found someone who believed that they had headed south, toward Santa Fe. It was the best lead they had, so Siringo and Sayles rode in that direction until they were just outside of Santa Fe before they concluded that they probably had been misled. At this point the detectives, possibly in disagreement over where to go next, decided to split up. Siringo picked up what appeared to be some promising leads that sent him on a useless chase throughout the southern states. Sayles, on the other hand, had better luck. Deciding to stick to the trail of bills stolen at Wilcox, he eventually traced them to Montana and to Harvey Logan and his brother, Lonny. This evidence, coupled with the positive identification of the Logans by sheepherder John DeVore at Sullivan Springs, Wyoming, firmly established the Logans as two of the Wilcox robbers.[51]

In the meantime the men the detectives had been following, probably Butch and Elzy Lay, continued south toward Alma, New Mexico, where they again became Jim Lowe and Mac McGinnis at the ws Ranch.

Once Lowe and McGinnis returned, things at the ws began operating as smoothly as owner William French had ever seen. But then one day in late June 1899, Lowe went to French with the unwelcome news that McGinnis was thinking of leaving. Mac's reason, according to Lowe, was that all the broncs had been broken and he just wasn't interested in doing other work around the ranch.

During the second week in July, not long after McGinnis had left, William French was in northern New Mexico on business, on his way from Springer to Cimarron in a buggy, when he spotted a man on foot coming across the prairie toward the road. He was in rather bad shape, and French helped him climb aboard. The man said that he was a special officer for the Colorado Southern Railroad and that he had been part of a posse that had been chasing train robbers. French had heard about the robbery; three or four men had held up an express car on the Colorado & Southern near Folsom, and a posse was looking for them somewhere south of Cimarron.[52]

The stranger, whose name was William H. Reno, had been with the posse which was formed at Trinidad, Colorado, by Huerfano County Sheriff Edward Farr.[53] They had gotten to Raton by rail, where they picked up horses and went looking for the robbers' trail.[54] They found the outlaws' camp in Turkey Canyon (also called Turkey Creek Canyon), just southwest of the road he and French were now on, and there was a terrible gunfight. Reno was sure that one of the robbers was killed, and was pretty sure that Sheriff Farr had also been shot. He said that Farr had fallen from his horse and the frightened animal had run off with the sheriff's Winchester, which he (Reno) thought they needed, so he had gone after it. He said the horse had eluded him and he soon became lost in the canyon and only just recently had found his way out. French doubted the man's story, figuring that he simply became frightened and ran away from the fight. He agreed to take him back to Springer so that he could send a telegram to his employers and let them know what had happened.[55]

The incident had certainly livened up what otherwise would have been a routine business trip for French, but Reno had said something that bothered him: before he had fled the scene he had heard one of the possemen say that the robber who had been shot was an outlaw named McGinnis.

Before French left Cimarron he learned that one of the train robbers had been captured and identified: a local outlaw named Sam Ketchum. French had heard of Ketchum; in fact, Ketchum had stolen two horses from the ws shortly before Jim Lowe and Mac McGinnis had hired on at the ranch. The other two robbers, yet to be found, had not been positively identified. However, if French had any doubts that the man he knew as McGinnis was one of these other two, those doubts were removed when he returned to the ws. The place was buzzing with excitement, and the men were eager to know if he had learned whether the other two robbers had been taken by the law.[56]

As French suspected, the details of the shootout in Turkey Canyon were not exactly as Special Agent William Reno described them. According to the story, which was eventually pieced together from accounts given by individuals at the scene, the robbers had foolishly built a campfire and the posse had spotted the smoke. As the possemen were sneaking into position, the robber who called himself Mac McGinnis (Elzy Lay) had started for the creek with his canteen to get water. The other two outlaws were standing near the campfire. Someone may have shouted for the outlaws to surrender—there was disagreement on this point—but if they had the possemen did not wait for an answer. McGinnis was hit immediately, first in the shoulder and then in the back.

As the outlaws returned the lawmen's fire, Sheriff Farr and another member of the posse, F. H. Smith, ducked behind the same tree. The tree was not large enough to protect them both: Farr was hit in the arm near the wrist, and Smith took a bullet in the calf of his leg. As Farr was trying to wrap his wound either McGinnis, who may have recovered enough from his injuries enough to use his rifle, or one of the other outlaws put a bullet into Farr's chest, killing him almost instantly.[57]

A second outlaw, later identified as Sam Ketchum, took a bullet in the arm just below the shoulder which broke the bone, and a third member of the posse, Henry Love, was hit in the thigh. The rest of the posse, seeing their members begin to fall, promptly retreated which allowed the outlaws to escape.[58]

McGinnis's and Ketchum's wounds made it difficult to travel, and they and the third robber, later identified as Will Carver, stopped to rest at a cabin near the junction of Cimarron and Ute creeks. The cabin was owned by a man named Ed McBride, whom the outlaws knew. Once rested, McGinnis was able to go on, but Ketchum was too weak and remained at the cabin. When McBride and his family returned they bandaged his wound, but the following day they turned him in to the authorities.[59]

Several days later Jim Lowe went to French and told him that their friend Mac McGinnis had been arrested as one of the suspects in the Folsom robbery. Lowe was with a former ws hand whom French knew as Tom Capehart.[60] Lowe said that Capehart had just ridden in with the news about McGinnis from Lincoln County. By now, French was suspicious of anything he was told. As to Tom Capehart, he was fairly certain that he, too, was one of the outlaw gang and probably had been involved in the robbery.

Jim Lowe then made a request that must have surprised French, at least a little. Would he put up security for McGinnis's bail until he and the others could get enough money for a bond? French thought about it for a second, probably wondering just how many members of the famous Wild Bunch he had in his employ and where this trouble might eventually lead. He did like McGinnis, and despite what the man had done he felt sorry for him. French told Lowe that he would put up the security for McGinnis if it was possible, but that he doubted he would be given the opportunity since the Territory of New Mexico had made train robbery a capital offense and usually not bailable. French did say, however, that if he was given the chance he would testify to McGinnis's apparent good character during the period that he had worked at the ws.[61]

French then turned to Tom Capehart and asked how McGinnis had been captured. Without admitting in so many words that he himself had taken part in the robbery, Capehart replied that he had been helping McGinnis hide out in Lincoln County until his wounds healed, but that McGinnis had been accidentally discovered by a posse looking for horse thieves. He said that McGinnis had put up a brief fight but was eventually subdued.[62]

Elzy Lay, still claiming that his name was William McGinnis, was taken to Santa Fe where he was bound over on a charge of interfering with the U.S. Mail. Later, after statements of the posse members were gathered up, he was charged with the murder of Sheriff Farr.

The case against William McGinnis was set for trial at Raton, seat of Colfax County, during the first week of October 1899. His attorneys had tried to get a continuance, claiming their client's fellow cowboys back at the ws Ranch were having trouble scraping up a defense fund for him because ranch owner William French, who owed them wages, was out of town. This move fell flat when the prosecution introduced affidavits that McGinnis's friends were not paid by French himself but by the ranch foreman, Perry Tucker.[63]

The trial began on October 2. The evidence proving that McGinnis had fired the shot that killed Sheriff Farr was weak, but the Territory of New Mexico, just then seeking statehood, was eager to prove that murder would not be tolerated there. Just how much of this feeling was shared by the trial judge is not known, but many procedural rulings went against the defense. McGinnis's lawyers put only two witnesses on the stand, one of them the defendant himself. McGinnis appeared convincing when he de-

nied killing Farr, but his credibility was weakened when, on cross-exam-
ination, he refused to answer any questions regarding his past or his true
identity. The jury found him guilty of murder in the second degree, which,
under the law of the territory at the time, called for imprisonment of "any
period of time not less than three years." The judge sentenced him to life.[64]

Back at the ws Butch, still calling himself Jim Lowe, was probably dev-
astated at Elzy's sentence. At the time Lay was probably much closer to
Butch than any of the others, including Longabaugh.[65] But Butch no doubt
realized that the jury could have found Elzy guilty of first-degree murder
and recommended death.

After the trial things calmed down at the ws and operations again became routine, which allowed William French time to pursue plans for ex-
pansion of the spread and other business matters. French, however, had
grown uneasy. He could no longer ignore the fact that he had members of
the Wild Bunch in his employ, and he could not help thinking that the law
could come knocking at his door at any time. Indeed, about a month after
McGinnis's conviction a stranger came calling on French. When he identified himself as an operative of Pinkerton's National Detective Agency,
French assumed that he was looking for Tom Capehart in connection with
the Folsom train robbery. However, the detective said that he was investi-
gating a different train robbery, one that occurred in Wyoming; he was in
New Mexico following a trail of bank notes that had been taken in that
robbery. The bills had shown up at a bank in Silver City and had been
traced to the store at Alma. He added that these particular bills had been
easy to trace because, when the robbers dynamited the express car safe, the
explosion had blown off the tip of one corner of the packet in which the
bills were contained.[66]

The detective claimed that a storekeeper in Alma had told him that he
had received the bills from an employee of the ws Ranch who called himself Johnny Ward. There were in fact two Johnny Wards working at the
ranch at the time: the other men called them "Big" Johnny and "Little"
Johnny. French figured Big Johnny was the guilty party (since he was a
newcomer), so he decided to find Little Johnny for the detective. Much to
French's surprise, Little Johnny Ward admitted spending the bills in Alma
and indicated that he still had some in his possession. He had gotten the
bills from another ws hand who had since left, a man named McGonigal
who had worked for Jim Lowe a week or so on a trail drive. Just before
McGonigal had left, Ward had sold him a horse, and McGonigal had paid
him with the bills in question. This seemed to satisfy the detective, who

Photographs

The Parker family home in Circle Valley, Utah. The date of the photo is unknown, but the poplars at the left are believed to have been planted by Butch and his mother before he left home in 1884. (By permission, Utah State Historical Society, all rights reserved.)

The ferry across the Colorado River at Moab, Utah, used by Cassidy and his companions in their escape following the robbery at Telluride. (By permission, Utah State Historical Society, all rights reserved.)

The Hole-in-the-Wall area, Johnson County, Wyoming. Butch had a ranch and probably a rustling operation on Blue Creek, northwest of the Hole, in the early 1890s. (Caroline Lockhart Collection, No. 177, American Heritage Center, University of Wyoming.)

Butch's double cabins on his Blue Creek ranch behind the Hole-in-the-Wall. (Rocky Mountain House, Hamilton, Montana.)

Family home of Maud Davis near Vernal, Utah, where Butch narrowly escaped capture in 1897. Maud was the wife of Butch's pal, Elzy Lay. (Rocky Mountain House, Hamilton, Montana.)

Upper Horseshoe Canyon, Wayne County, Utah, looking north from Wildcat Spring. Butch and the Wild Bunch used these rugged cliffs for their hideout in the late 1890s. (Kelsey Publishing, Provo, Utah.)

Robbers' Roost Spring, Wayne County, Utah, looking east and up the South Fork of Roost Canyon. Another hideout area used by the Wild Bunch. (Kelsey Publishing, Provo, Utah.)

Aftermath of the Wild Bunch's assault on a Union Pacific express car at Tipton, Wyoming, in August 1900. (Union Pacific Railroad, Union Pacific Museum Collection.)

A Union Pacific "Horse Car" and posse, ready to pursue train robbers. The Union Pacific Railroad's aggressive response to attacks on its line in the late 1890s was partially responsible for the demise of the Wild Bunch. (Union Pacific Railroad, Union Pacific Museum Collection.)

Pinkerton detective Charlie Siringo, who tracked Cassidy and the Wild Bunch across much of the West and was sued by the Pinkertons for publishing his memoirs. (Union Pacific Railroad, Union Pacific Museum Collection.)

The "Fort Worth Five." From left to right: Harry Longabaugh (the Sundance Kid), Will Carver, Ben Kilpatrick, Harvey Logan (Kid Curry), and Butch Cassidy. This photo, apparently taken in 1900 as a lark at a photography studio in Fort Worth, Texas, led to the identification of the inner circle of the Wild Bunch. (Union Pacific Railroad, Union Pacific Museum Collection.)

Harry Longabaugh and Etta Place. This photo was taken in New York City in 1901 while the couple was waiting to embark for South America. (Rocky Mountain House, Hamilton, Montana.)

Cabin occupied by Cassidy, Longabaugh, and Place on their ranch in Cholila Valley, Argentina. (Rocky Mountain House, Hamilton, Montana.)

William T. Phillips. Spokane, Washington, machine shop owner who claimed to be Butch Cassidy and posed as the outlaw during trips to Wyoming in the 1930s. (Rocky Mountain House, Hamilton, Montana.)

copied down the numbers from the bills Little Johnny still had but let him keep them.[67]

After Ward left, the detective showed French a picture of a group of men and asked him if he recognized any of them. He did: one of them was his trail boss, Jim Lowe. The detective said that the Pinkertons knew the man as Butch Cassidy, that he was believed to be the leader of one of the best organized outlaw gangs that had ever existed in the West, and that there was hardly a state or territory south of the Canadian line that didn't want him. He added that Cassidy's gang of outlaws was causing the authorities no end of worry because it seemed that time after time they were able to gain inside information as to when large express shipments were to be made by rail. He said that the Pinkertons had lost track of Cassidy, but that he himself had spotted him that very morning in Alma. French asked if he had come to arrest this Cassidy, and the detective assured him that he had not, certainly not here at the ranch, that he would be a fool to try such a thing without a regiment of cavalry to back him up. He said that he was there only to follow up on the report of the stolen bank notes, that his job now was to look for the man who called himself McGonigal.[68]

The man French knew as Jim Lowe was away from the ranch when the detective came calling. On his return French told him about his visit, probably adding that the masquerade, at least between the two of them, was no longer necessary. French said that the outlaw Butch Cassidy didn't seem the least bit worried. He just grinned that familiar grin and said that he knew the detective was in the area snooping around; in fact, he said, the evening after the man's visit with French at the ranch he and Tom Capehart had bought him a drink in Alma. Butch didn't say what was discussed that evening, only that it was likely that someday he, Cassidy, would have to leave the ws, but he had no plans to pull out right away.

The Pinkerton who had called at the ws was Frank Murray, who eventually became assistant superintendent of the agency's Denver office. Sometime later he would reveal that the drink he had at the saloon at Alma that evening was almost his last on earth. He reported that he could have easily been killed that night had it not been for the man known as Jim Lowe, who had intervened and saved his life.[69]

One can only guess what kind of deal Butch may have worked out with Murray. To be allowed to leave Alma unharmed Murray must have convinced Butch that he would keep his mouth shut. Also he must have promised Butch that if he learned that the Pinkertons were sending any other detectives to Alma, he would warn Butch in advance. His narrow escape may have been enough incentive for him to keep his word or, more likely, Butch or Tom Capehart convinced him that if he did not keep his word the Wild Bunch would see that he was made to pay. Murray apparently kept his word: he reported the incident to his superiors but failed to mention that Jim Lowe was Butch Cassidy. In his report he said that Jim Lowe was the saloonkeeper at Alma.[70]

According to William French, when Butch did finally leave the ws it was at his own choosing. Just before the ranch was to drive its last herd of the year to the railroad, Perry Tucker informed French that he was going to be leaving, that he had interests in Arizona that he needed to look after. When French asked him to stay until he found somebody to replace him, Tucker suggested that Butch be put in charge of the outfit. French, however, was hesitant; after the visit by the Pinkerton detective he figured that Butch's days at the ws were probably numbered. He talked this over with Butch, who still did not seem uneasy about the Pinkertons knowing where he could be found. As to Tucker's job, Butch said that he would take it if it was offered, but he added that he understood how French felt about the situation, meaning, presumably, how he felt about having a well-known fugitive running his outfit. French said that he would be glad to keep him on for the last drive, but Butch decided that it was probably time to go.[71]

Before leaving Butch asked French for a favor: Could he have a pair of the custom-made kyacks that were lying unused in the stable?[72] French, of course, gladly let him have a pair.

When Butch left, one of the ws hands, Red Weaver, went with him. According to French, before they left the area they made a stop at the ranch of a neighbor named Ashby. Apparently Butch and the men at the ws had been having trouble with Ashby. They suspected him of building his herd at the expense of his neighbors' strays, and when they approached him about the problem he had assumed a virtuous attitude that Butch found particularly annoying. Rather than start trouble between Ashby and French, who at the time wanted to work out a deal to buy Ashby out, Butch did nothing about it. But on taking their leave from the ws, Butch decided to settle the score. He and Weaver dropped by Ashby's ranch and took every one of his saddle horses with them. The exasperated Ashby was forced to walk several miles to borrow a horse to ride into town and report the loss.[73]

French said later that he believed that Butch's devilment turned out to be a favor to the ws: he was pretty sure that the loss of all of his horses had finally induced Ashby to sell out.

The stunt almost backfired, however. On leaving Ashby's ranch Butch and Weaver, trailing the stolen horses, rode northwest into Arizona. At St.

Johns, in Apache County, they stopped to buy provisions. The local sheriff became suspicious, and when their explanation as to where they got the horses didn't satisfy him he marched them off to jail. Butch told the sheriff that his name was Jim Lowe and that he should get in touch with William French at the ws, that he, French, would vouch for him and Weaver. The sheriff sent a telegraph to French by way of Magdalena, asking if he knew them. French replied that he did.[74] The two men appeared in court in Socorro on April 28, 1900, and pled not guilty to the charge of larceny of horses. A trial was scheduled for Weaver on May 4, but was continued to the next term of court and he was released on $1,000 bail.[75] The local newspaper gave no further details of the case, suggesting that the charges were eventually dismissed.

French heard nothing more from Butch, but about a year later, during another business trip to Cimarron, he did hear about two men who had been seen in the mountains in Colfax County not far from the scene of the Folsom train robbery. They had come upon the camp of a survey party in the process of surveying a tract of land being sold by the Maxwell Grant Company. There was nothing special about the pair, and the surveyors would probably have never mentioned them when they got back to town except that one of the two travelers had a very unusual kyack on his pack horse: a box-like affair made of rawhide and wood.[76]

Tipton and Winnemucca

1900

While Butch may have been indirectly involved in the Wild Bunch's activities while at the WS Ranch, and may have participated in at least one robbery, the months spent at the WS were relatively quiet ones. Butch was in hiding but he was not on the run. Life was near normal and most likely pleasurable.

Less than ten miles east of Alma was Mogollon, a place where WS cowhands who behaved themselves could enjoy a social life of sorts, one that even included community dances. For Butch there may also have been a romance: a local lass named Agnes Meader Snider, who it was said had a definite crush on him.[1]

The days at the WS Ranch were probably as routine as they could get for an outlaw wanted in at least four states. This taste of normalcy may have given Butch a different outlook on the course he had taken and may explain why he began to think about reforming. On the other hand, Butch may have been more concerned that the Wild Bunch's luck was beginning to run out. Elzy Lay, after nearly being killed at Turkey Canyon, was serving a life sentence in Santa Fe, and Bub Meeks was doing his third year of thirty-five at the Idaho State Penitentiary.[2]

Whatever the reason, it appears that Butch did consider reforming. The story of his efforts along these lines, while fraught with holes, does have substance and would have had to have come from one or both of the lawyers who were involved: Orlando Powers of Salt Lake City or Douglas Preston. As the story is told, when Butch left the WS Ranch and headed back north, possibly with some of the loot from the Folsom robbery, he seriously considered going straight.[3] But to give up outlawry and lead an ordinary life meant settling accounts. Butch's roots were in Utah, where the Parkers were solid members of the Mormon community. With the exception of his brother Dan, Butch was the only Parker who had crossed the line, and Dan had served his time and was now leading a respectable life.[4] Butch remained an embarrassment to the family, so it was natural that if he did seek the road back it should be in Utah, where family honor was so important.

Butch's first stop was the Salt Lake City office of lawyer Orlando Powers. Powers was influential and knew the right people. More important, it was apparent that he could be trusted, or Douglas Preston would not have recommended him for Matt Warner's defense at Ogden.

Butch just dropped in unannounced, telling Powers's stenographer that he wanted to see the attorney. The day must have been cold, because Butch was wearing both overalls and a blue denim jumper. He carried a battered hat, which he held in both hands. His face was weathered from months on the range, and he appeared older than his thirty-two years. Powers offered him a seat, and the following conversation took place:

Cassidy: "Is what I say to you to go as a client consulting his lawyer from now on?"

Powers: "You mean, a privileged communication?"

Cassidy: "That's it."

Powers: "All right then."

Cassidy: "I'm Butch Cassidy."

Powers: "Well, what can I do for you?"

Cassidy: "I'll tell you. There's a heap of charges out against me and considerable money offered for me in rewards. I'm getting sick of hiding out; always on the run and never able to stay long in one place. Now, when it comes to facts, I've kept close track of things and I know there ain't a man left in the country who can go on the stand and identify me for any crime. All of 'em have either died or gone away. I've been thinking. Why can't I go and just give myself up and stand trial on one of those old charges?"

Powers: "No use. You've robbed too many big corporations in your time. I do not doubt what you say, but if you were ever to go on trial, you can depend on it, some one of those companies would bring some one to the stand who'd swear against you. No, you'll have to keep on the run, I'm afraid."[5]

Discouraged, Butch thanked Powers and left. But he was not ready to give up. He would try another approach: an appeal directly to the Utah Governor, Heber Wells. Butch sought out an old friend, Parley P. Christensen, at the time Sheriff of Juab County, Utah. Christensen had known the Parker family for years and Butch had never caused trouble in his county. To show his good intentions Butch turned his guns over to Christensen: the .45 Colt revolver he had bought in Vernal in 1896 and a Winchester 44-40 Saddle-Ring Carbine.[6]

Butch's sincerity may have impressed Christensen, because he agreed to try to arrange a meeting for Butch with Wells. Christensen's request no doubt took Governor Wells by surprise. From a political, if not legal, standpoint, it was risky for a governor to give an audience to a wanted outlaw—especially one wanted in at least four states—but what may have convinced Wells to grant the request was that Christensen, as a lawman, had readily put his career on the line by interceding for Butch. For whatever reason, the governor agreed to a meeting.[7]

Butch was no doubt apprehensive, but from the beginning Wells seemed receptive. After hearing Butch's plea he told him that it might be possible that some form of amnesty could be arranged, but only if Butch was not wanted for murder. There could be no amnesty for a killer. Butch insisted that he had never committed murder so Wells promised that he would see what he could do.

If Butch had high hopes they were short-lived. At a second meeting several days later the news was not good. Wells told Butch that he had met with his attorney general who did some checking and found that Butch was in fact wanted for murder for a killing in Wyoming. Wells said that he was sorry, but under the circumstance he could not help him.[8]

It may not have made that much difference. Governor Wells may have promised more than he could deliver. As Orlando Powers would have readily told Butch, Wells could offer amnesty only as to crimes for which Butch was wanted in Utah. While Wells could have requested the same favor from the governors of other states where Butch was wanted—Wyoming, Idaho, and Colorado—he could not speak for them.

In the meantime, however, Orlando Powers had come up with another idea. For the previous decade the railroads had been ravaged by train robbers. From 1890 to 1899 there had been 261 train robberies in the nation, mostly in the western states; during that time eighty-eight persons had been killed and eighty-six injured.[9] Powers believed that the railroads, especially the Union Pacific, should have had a sincere interest in getting somebody like Butch Cassidy to agree to give up assaulting express cars. Also, the railroads had significant influence in the statehouses. If the railroads that operated in the states where Butch was wanted could be persuaded to grant their own amnesty to Butch, thus eliminating the threat he and his gang posed to financial and commercial interests that shipped by rail, perhaps the state authorities would see the overall advantage and follow suit.[10]

At the time the top Union Pacific officials may have considered Harvey Logan a greater threat than Butch to their railroad;[11] however, they agreed to discuss the offer and a plan was worked out (presumably with the help of Douglas Preston) to arrange a meeting with Butch. At Butch's suggestion the selected meeting site was near Lost Soldier Pass, about forty miles north of Rawlins and not far from the old stage road to Lander. It was desolate country, and cautious Butch probably figured that if things suddenly went sour he could easily escape into the mountains to the north. However, the meeting never came off. Douglas Preston was to bring two representatives of the railroad by buckboard, but a violent storm delayed them and they then got lost. When they finally arrived Butch had left. At the meeting site, tucked under a stone, he had left a note: "Damn you Preston, you have double-crossed me. I waited all day but you didn't show up. Tell the U.P. to go to hell. And you can go with them."[12]

To salvage the plan, Orlando Powers came up with one more idea. Butch's pal Matt Warner had been released from prison. Powers knew that Butch would trust Warner not to deceive him, and if Matt could be brought in on the deal with the railroad Butch might reconsider. Powers went to Governor Heber Wells and suggested that he summon Warner and ask him to find Butch, explain the mix-up at Lost Soldier Pass, and ask him to reconsider the deal with the Union Pacific. Warner accepted the assignment and was given $175.00 for travel expenses. The last week in August 1900, he boarded a train at Salt Lake City bound for Rock Springs, Wyoming. He was counting on Butch being either at his Powder Springs hideout or at Brown's Park. However he never reached his friend. When the train stopped at Bridger Station, just east of Evanston, Wyoming, the conductor handed Warner a telegram from Governor Wells. "All agreements off. Cassidy just held up a train at Tipton."[13]

The town of Tipton, Wyoming, lies east of the Continental Divide, midway between Rawlins and Rock Springs. While the holdup Wells referred to in his telegram is usually called the Tipton robbery, the train, the second section of Union Pacific No. 3 out of Omaha, was actually stopped by the robbers on the western slope of the divide near Table Rock. The site, also called Pulpit Rock, is a tiny settlement named after a nearby mesa where Brigham Young once delivered a much-needed sermon to a group of discouraged Mormon immigrants during their journey west for a new life in a promised land.[14]

On the night of the holdup one of the robbers probably boarded the train as it was leaving Tipton. As engineer Henry Wallenstine pulled the grade toward Table Rock, the robber, with a mask covering his face, scrambled down from the tender, shoved a pistol in Wallenstine's ribs, and ordered him to slow down when he saw a campfire alongside the track. About a mile further down the track Wallenstine saw the fire and three more masked men waiting just off the right-of-way. Once the train was stopped the robbers ordered the conductor to uncouple the mail car and express cars from the passenger coaches. As in the Wilcox robbery, the robbers used dynamite to blast their way into the express cars. When they entered the Pacific Express car, they saw a familiar face: C. E. Woodcock, the same messenger who had been on duty the night of the Wilcox robbery.[15]

If any doubt remained that the line had been hit again by the same gang that struck at Wilcox, it was removed when UP detectives took the statement of the postal clerk who had been in charge of the Railway Mail car. The clerk, identified only as Pruitt, stated that while he was lined up with the train crew and under guard, one of the robbers suddenly became very talkative. According to Pruitt (who must have had a near-photographic memory), the garrulous robber told him the following, which was later reported in the newspapers:

Don't know how we will fare here, but we did pretty well at Wilcox. We got a little short of money and come down here to get some more. This ain't the train we wanted. That one went through a week ago and carried a lot of government gold, but the man who was goin' to stop her backed out when he see two cars of bums on board, thinkin' as how they was officers. We'd have done well on that train. But bein' here and needin' money, we thought we'd better tackle this one, as we're pretty sure she' got money in the safe. We don't want to kill anybody, but we might do it just the same. We really ought to have killed that engineer in the Wilcox affair, but let him off with a rap on the head. If we ever come across him again and he acts that way we'll have to let him have it. There's no use in anybody acting smart with us.

I wish those fellows would get a move on, for we want to get away from here. We gave it to old man Hazen on Tea Pot Creek because he followed us, and if anyone follows us this time we'll give them the same dose. We ain't a skeered much as we know roads in this country that they don't and anyway if they got close we can give it to 'em.[16]

Wallenstine, the engineer, confirmed that the robber at the scene of the holdup had indeed run off at the mouth. The robber also stated that he did not want to kill anyone if he could avoid it, and neither did his companions. He said that they (the robbers) "had an agreement that if anyone killed a man unnecessarily, he himself would be killed." He added, however, that there was one member in the gang who would just as soon kill a man as not.[17]

As often happened in express car robberies, the actual amount stolen was never verified. Two days after the holdup the general manager of the Union Pacific sent a telegram to the Denver newspapers that the outlaws had taken only three money packages containing a total of $50.40 and "two packages of cheap jewelry." However, when the wrecked express car was inspected at Green River, three $20 gold pieces were found on the floor, which suggested that at least one sack of coins had broken open when the robbers blew the safe. Also, a witness at the scene stated that while the robbers were ransacking the express car they "stooped over frequently and picked up articles from the floor, which they hurriedly thrust into their pockets."[18] Later on, express messenger Woodcock let it slip to the press that the actual loss was close to $55,000.[19] It would have been even greater had he not hid several packages of money behind a trunk before the robbers broke into his car.[20]

Unlike the Wilcox robbery, where little evidence was turned up linking Butch directly to the crime, Union Pacific officials credited the Tipton holdup to Cassidy from the start. One reason was a report from a curious rancher who ran cattle near the site of the robbery. The rancher, whose name was not released, told railroad officials that he saw Butch, whom he knew on sight, and four well-armed riders on good horses in the vicinity of the holdup site two weeks before the robbery. He said that he knew it was Butch because he had watched him through his field glasses.[21] This report, combined with statements from several of the train crew that one of the robbers was "sandy complected," smooth-shaven, had gray eyes, and was about five feet ten inches tall, satisfied the authorities that Butch was the man they were after.[22]

Most writers agree that Cassidy was indeed at Tipton.[23] They also agree that he was probably accompanied by Harvey Logan and Harry Longabaugh.[24] They are less certain about the fourth man and a possible fifth.

The Pinkertons believed the robbers used a ranch on the Snake River near Dixon as their staging area. The ranch was owned by Jim Ferguson, a former butcher from Keystone, South Dakota, whom the Pinkertons believed was tied into the Wild Bunch and occasionally allowed his ranch to be used as a rendezvous site for the gang.[25]

One of the robbers at Tipton may have been Tom Welch, from near

Lonetree, Wyoming. According to a fellow who worked for Welch, Tom and Butch were pretty close. In escaping from the Tipton robbery Welch was believed to have caught a bullet in the leg forcing him to hide out at his parents' place until his wound healed. As the story goes, Welch then took his share of the Tipton loot, became partners with a doctor named Hawk, and built a hotel in Green River, Wyoming.[26]

The first reports of the robbery reached the Union Pacific Railroad offices in Omaha around 11:00 PM. Officials there wired Rock Springs, where Sheriff Pete Swanson immediately organized a posse and rushed by train to the scene, arriving near daylight. Another posse headed up by United States Marshal Frank Hadsell was dispatched by rail from Rawlins, but a mechanical breakdown near Creston delayed them, and they did not arrive until 8:30 AM the following morning.[27]

On leaving the scene of the holdup the robbers rode southeast toward Delaney Rim. The Rock Springs posse quickly picked up their trail, but just south of the rim the ground became grassy and hard and their tracks became difficult to follow. The landscape slowed Swanson and his riders considerably, and later that morning Hadsell and the Rawlins posse caught up with them. Both posses had rounded up horses quickly for the chase, which meant that some of the mounts they were riding were young and strong while others were ill-suited for the long haul. By afternoon attrition from the group had reduced the combined posses to twenty men, less than half the number that had started.[28]

Although at times the posse was strung out as much as two miles from front to back, the lead riders, guided by Deputy U.S. Marshal Joe LeFors out of Rawlins, made good time and by sundown had reached the Little Snake River just above the Colorado line, a distance of nearly 120 miles from the holdup scene. As LeFors led his horse down the bank on the north side of the river, he spotted three men and a pack horse climbing the long slope on the other side.[29]

Hadsell and LeFors quickly counted their remaining possemen: only an even dozen left, enough to handle three outlaws, but it was getting dark fast. They agreed that it would be foolhardy to ride blindly into an ambush. Moreover, the posse had been without sleep for twenty hours and the horses without rest for nearly twelve. Even though they probably were hardly out of shouting distance from the men they were after, they decided to make camp and gamble on picking up their tracks in the morning.[30]

LeFors was up early and found the outlaws' trail shortly after dawn. It led due south, which suggested to him that the outlaws probably would continue in that direction for a while then cut back west and lose themselves in the wilderness of the eastern edge of Brown's Park. LeFors rode back, awakened his men, and the posse was soon on the trail again. They had ridden about twenty miles when they came upon the robbers' pack horse. The animal had given out and was nearly dead.

Following the tracks of the remaining three horses the posse rode another fifteen miles until they saw that the trail led to a patch of low ground surrounded by a thick grove of willows. The layout did not look good: it was a perfect spot for an ambush. They unholstered their weapons and cautiously rode on, keeping their mounts at a walk. When they got closer to the grove they saw beneath the willow branches what appeared to be the legs of several horses. LeFors dismounted, picked two volunteers and the three of them crawled forward on their knees and elbows toward the trees. The remainder of the posse divided into two groups and moved off to the left and right, circling the grove. It turned out to be a waste of time. There were horses in the willows all right: three of them, but no outlaws. It was a classic Wild Bunch maneuver, one used by Butch during his very first robbery. The outlaws had used the willows to hide a relay of fresh mounts. With their fresh horses and head start, and now with the time wasted at the willows, there was no way the posse could catch the robbers before they reached the entrance to Brown's Park. The possemen rubbed their empty bellies, took a long look at their own exhausted animals, and called it quits.[31]

The authorities assumed at the time that the robbers hid out in Brown's Park until things cooled down. Some Wild Bunch historians agree. Others, however, believe that the outlaws rode through the Park and kept going west until they eventually reached Nevada, where, on September 19, 1900, they added to their treasury by robbing the First National Bank of Winnemucca.

Legend has it that on their way the Tipton robbers buried part of the loot in Uintah County, Utah, somewhere between Diamond Mountain and the Colorado line. The rumor was so persistent that treasure hunters were still searching for the cache as late as the 1950s and perhaps later— they may be still looking for it today. The "treasure" spot most often discussed is in the Dry Creek area on lower Pot Creek. This general area probably became popular because of the remains of what appeared to be a hideout that were found there. Between two large boulders someone had used tree limbs, brush, and whatever they could find to construct a makeshift roof, thereby providing a cozy, well-hidden and reasonably dry place to sleep. Further east across the Colorado line near Wild Mountain was another spot thought to have been an outlaw hideout: a cave sheltered at the entrance by a giant overhang of rock. An old-timer named White Ainge, who once owned that land, claimed that near the site he found the remnants of a corral and under the ledge near the cave he found an old tent, a can of gun powder, a ten-pound cloth bag of sugar, a box of "Federal Matches," three shirts, and a pair of hobnailed shoes of the kind worn at the turn of the century.[32]

Those who believe that the Tipton and Winnemucca robberies were not committed by the same men argue that the outlaws would not have had time after the Tipton escapade to reach Winnemucca and plan the bank job. These writers point to evidence that the Winnemucca robbers arrived there and set up camp outside of town on or before September 9.[33]

To travel by horseback from northern Colorado to Winnemucca, Nevada, in ten days would have taken some hard riding; in fact, by horseback it would have been nearly impossible. However, when the Tipton train robbers eluded Hadsell's posse they were less than a hundred miles from several stops on the Denver & Rio Grande Western Railroad. The authorities, sure that the robbers were heading for Brown's Park, may have only half-heartedly kept an eye on the railroad stations. With sufficient disguises the bandits could have boarded a train as ordinary passengers, changed trains at Salt Lake City, and arrived at Winnemucca in plenty of time to set up camp by September 9.

The fact that the outlaws were in or at least near Winnemucca as early as September 9 came from Humboldt County resident I. V. (Vic) Button, whose father, F. J. Button, managed the ranch where the outlaws made their camp. The ranch, called the CS, was fourteen miles east of town near the Humboldt River.[34] Vic Button, at the time only ten years of age, claimed that Butch Cassidy himself was at the camp and that he and the other outlaws were quite friendly. Button later said that he became quite well acquainted with the outlaws, that they were good to him and gave him candy. Also, they asked him many questions about the bank in town and about the countryside in general.[35]

Button remembered Butch as a likeable man with a broad grin.[36] He said that Butch rode a white horse that was very fast. The boy visited the camp every day and he and Butch raced their horses. He said that Butch won every time. Burton said that one day when he told Butch how much he admired the animal, Butch said "You like that horse? Someday he will be yours."[37]

During the week before the robbery the outlaws scouted the town much the same way Butch and Elzy Lay had scouted Castle Gate and Montpelier.

Lee Case, a long-time resident of Winnemucca who was then a boy of nine, remembered seeing the men at the livery stable near the bank four days before the robbery. He said they were real friendly, and they asked Case and his young friends questions about the town. He said he saw them again on several afternoons after that, and that some of the time there were three of them and sometimes four.[38]

The First National Bank of Winnemucca was on Bridge Street, Winnemucca's main thoroughfare. On Wednesday, September 19, at a few minutes after noon three men entered the front door of the bank, two armed with revolvers and the third carrying a carbine.[39] None of the men wore masks. Five persons were in the bank: the head cashier, George S. Nixon; assistant cashier, D. V. McBride; bookkeeper Malvin Hill; a stenographer named Calhoun; and just one customer, a horse buyer named W. S. Johnson.[40]

The robbers ordered everyone to raise their hands, and then told Nixon to go to the vault and bring out all of the bags of gold coins. Nixon argued that the time lock was on and he could not open the door. The robber who had escorted him to the vault, probably figuring that a bank vault would not be time-locked at twelve noon on a business day, drew a knife and informed Nixon that if he didn't open the vault he would cut his throat. Nixon wisely relented and the robbers emptied the vault's bags of coins into ore sacks they had brought with them. When done the robbers marched the four employees and Johnson out the back door and into a fenced yard behind the building. While one of the outlaws held his gun on the captives, the others leaped over the fence and ran down the alley to the rear of the F. C. Robbins store where they had left their horses. When he was sure his companions were safely mounted, the last robber vaulted the fence and ran to join them.[41]

The robbers spurred their horses toward Second Street and then turned east toward Bridge Street. George Nixon ran back inside the bank and grabbed a revolver from his desk. He dashed out the front door and fired the gun in the air to give the alarm. Johnson, the horse buyer in the bank, also ran outside, grabbed a bystander's shotgun, and drew a bead on the fleeing robbers as they crossed Bridge Street. But the weapon was not loaded. A lady standing nearby later said that, had Johnson's gun not been empty, he surely would have shot one of the bandits.[42]

In the next block a young lawyer, Edward A. Ducker, was sitting in the office of the Humbolt County District Attorney, C. D. Van Duzer, when he heard the shots: "I heard the sound of discharge of firearms and it seemed to come from the direction of the bank. I ran out and on reaching the street

I saw a man who afterwards proved to be Mr. Nixon, the president of the bank, standing in front of the institution waving a pistol, calling for the officers and shouting that the bank had been robbed. I moved down toward him and saw three men on horseback galloping across Bridge Street, two blocks farther down. They were firing their pistols as they crossed the street."[43] As the robbers passed the Reception Saloon, shooting their pistols in the air to scare people off the street, they saw Humboldt County Sheriff Charles McDeid near the saloon's front door. One of them fired a "wing shot" at him, and he quickly ducked around the corner.[44]

Young Lee Case, in the school yard at the time, added this account:
I ran to Bridge Street in time to see George Rose [then deputy sheriff] running down the street with his rifle in hand. There was shooting in the street and Mr. Lane, a resident of Bridge Street, came out to give them hell, thinking it was some celebrating cowboys.

Deputy Rose ran to a windmill and climbed it and I followed him to the top. By now the robbers, the three men I had seen every day at the stable, had crossed the bridge and were headed along the river. The sheriff leveled his rifle and fired two shots but the outlaws were moving fast and were too far away.[45]

The robbers fled east out of town, taking a road that for four or five miles ran parallel to a branch of the Southern Pacific Railroad that connected to the main line. When Deputy Rose saw the route the outlaws were taking, he ran to the train station where a switch engine was sitting with a boiler full of steam. He shouted for one of the train crew to climb up with him and get the locomotive moving. With the throttle wide open the engine quickly picked up speed and in a few minutes overtook the bandits. Rose fired at them from the cab, but the road and the tracks were several hundred yards apart and he failed to hit them.[46]

The Western Union operator at Winnemucca telegraphed the operator at Golconda, the first town east of Winnemucca, alerting the town constable whose name was Colwell. Colwell and three others rode out to head off the robbers, but they misjudged the speed the outlaws were traveling and, instead of heading them off, fell in behind them and soon met a posse of five or six men from Winnemucca led by Deputy Rose and lawyer Ed Ducker.[47]

The outlaws had left a relay of fresh horses at a ranch owned by a Francis Silve, about thirty miles east of Winnemucca.[48] According to Lee Case, after they had changed mounts one of the gang, presumably Butch, yelled to a Silve ranchhand to give the white horse to "the kid at CS Ranch."[49] The cowboy said he would; young Vic Button got his horse, and

Butch Cassidy became Vic's hero. In a letter to Pearl Baker seventy years later, Button's admiration for the outlaw had not diminished: "For a man, when he was crowded by a posse, to remember his promise to a kid—makes you think he could not have been all bad."[50]

From the Silve ranch the robbers rode northeast toward the Owyhee River, leading their pursuers to believe they were heading for "The Junipers," a nearly inaccessible wilderness on the Nevada-Idaho line where they could easily elude a posse or, even worse, lay an ambush. A second posse was quickly organized at Winnemucca and struck out toward Paradise, where they planned to pick up more volunteers and fresh horses in the hope of cutting off the outlaws before they reached the river. Officials at Winnemucca also wired Tuscarora, requesting that a posse be formed there, but they received a reply that nobody would start out after the robbers until Humboldt County guaranteed their expenses. By then Humboldt County Sheriff Charles McDeid decided the outlaws were moving too fast for the Tuscarorans to be of much help so they told them to forget it. As it turned out, if Tuscarora had launched a posse it probably could have caught up with the robbers.[51]

The robbers made a clean escape. The next day a posse found one of the robbers' abandoned horses, but that was all.[52] The authorities continued the hunt for another week but finally concluded they were following worthless trails.[53]

Because Winnemucca was so far from the Wild Bunch's usual haunts, no one gave much thought to Butch and his pals being the culprits. For suspects the authorities looked closer to home. An early suspect was an itinerant sheep shearer named Perkins, who had been working in the Disaster Peak area north of Winnemucca shortly before the robbery and who disappeared immediately thereafter. Mentioned as possible accomplices were two of Perkins's friends, Melville Fuller and Willie Wier, as well as Francis Silve, at whose ranch the robbers had stashed their first relay of fresh horses. A month or so before the robbery Fuller, Perkins, and Silve had all been seen hanging around White Rock, in Elko County, near the area where the robbers disappeared. Other names mentioned as possible confederates in crime were a Dave Jones and a Charlie Craig, thought to be acquaintances of Perkins. However, when these men were rounded up and brought before George Nixon and the other bank employees, no one could identify them as the robbers. Rumors then began to spread that if these local suspects had not held up the bank themselves, they must have brought in outsiders to do the job.[54]

This theory was confirmed when somebody searched the hayfield on

F. J. Button's cs Ranch where the robbers camped for ten days before the robbery. At the outlaws' campsite an investigator found the remains of three letters, which had been torn into tiny pieces. The pieces were carefully pasted together and handwritten copies were made and sent to the Pinkertons and to other interested parties.[55] One letter was on blue paper and bore the letterhead of Douglas A. Preston, Attorney at Law, of Rock Springs, Wyoming. Dated August 24, 1900, it was addressed to "My Dear Sir" and contained only one sentence: "Several influential parties are becoming interested and the chances of a sale are getting favorable." It was signed, "Yours truly, D. A. Preston."[56]

The second letter was on the same blue paper but without the letterhead. It contained the following: "Send me at once a map of the country and describe as near as you can the place where you found the black stuff so I can go to it. Tell me how you want it handled. You don't know its value. If I can get hold of it first, I can fix a good many things favorable. Say nothing to anyone about it." The letter was signed "P."

The third letter was addressed to C. E. Rowe, Golconda, Nevada. It was sent from Riverside, Wyoming, and dated September 1, 1900, which was nineteen days before the Winnemucca robbery:

> Dear Friend:
> Yours at hand this evening. We are glad to know you are getting along well. In regards to sale enclosed letter will explain everything. I am so glad that everything is favorable. We have left Baggs so write us at Encampment, Wyo. Hoping to hear from you soon I am as ever,
> Your friend,
> Mike

Riverside, Wyoming, is about a mile from Encampment. According to notations George Nixon later made in his journal, in the third letter, the "C" in "C. E. Rowe" was torn and may have been a different initial. Also, there could have been an initial before "Mike," possibly a "J," an "I," or an "O." The Pinkertons informed Nixon that a "C. E. Rowe" was in the agency's files and sent Rowe's description to Nixon, but nothing came of it.[57]

The Pinkertons and others involved in the Winnemucca investigation were aware that Douglas A. Preston was Butch Cassidy's lawyer, but apparently this information was not conveyed to Nixon at the time.[58]

At first some investigators interpreted the letters as suggesting that the Winnemucca robbery was a cover-up for an inside job, one that possibly involved George Nixon himself.[59] But on November 26, 1900, Homer Merrill (a Rawlins, Wyoming, attorney), reported to the authorities that an informant, Jim Rankin, told him that the parties who had robbed the Winnemucca bank were then in the Rawlins area trying to exchange "powder-burned currency" for gold.[60] This could have been the "black stuff" mentioned in the second of the three letters, the one presumably sent by Douglas Preston. No powder-burned currency could have come from the Winnemucca robbery, but dynamite was used at both the Wilcox and Tipton train robberies to blast open the express company safes.[61]

A week later the Pinkertons notified the U.S. Marshal's office in Rawlins that they may have discovered the identity of "Mike," the writer of the third letter: Mrs. Mike Dunbar of Carbon County, Wyoming. They believed that she had written the letter for her husband, who was rumored to be a contact person for Butch Cassidy's gang.[62] The Pinkertons also reported that their operatives had turned up information that an outlaw known around Rawlins as both "Alonzo" and "Swede" had arrived in that city in mid-October trying to exchange gold coins that were "blackened" or "burned," and that this individual might also have been involved in the Winnemucca robbery.[63] "Harry Alonzo" was one of the aliases used by Harry Longabaugh.[64]

Just when Butch Cassidy was finally named a suspect in the Winnemucca robbery is not known. The Pinkertons sent George Nixon a picture of Butch but he could not positively say that Butch was one of the robbers. Nixon claimed that Cassidy's face was "a great deal squarer cut" and his jaws more "massive" than those of the man in the bank who walked him to the vault and threatened him with a knife. Yet the circumstantial evidence suggesting that Butch was involved may have impressed Nixon because he eventually wrote to the Pinkertons saying that he was "satisfied that Cassidy was interested in the robbery," that he wished to name Butch as one of the robbers on the agency's wanted circular, and that "so far as Cassidy is concerned, we [the Winnemucca bank] will be willing to take chances in paying the reward for him upon the evidence now in hand."[65]

Nixon continued to waffle, however, when asked point blank whether Butch was one of the robbers. An interesting rumor then arose that Butch was not one of the armed robbers, but was in fact the customer in the bank, the horse buyer W. S. Johnson, who ran outside and fired an empty shotgun at the fleeing bandits. This gave new life to the earlier gossip that Nixon himself may have engineered the job, a rumor that continued to dog Nixon, especially after he later came into unexpected wealth and established his own bank. (The rumors did not seem to affect Nixon's long-term career, however. He prospered in the banking business and later was elected by the citizens of Nevada to the office of United States Senator.[66])

The true identity of the Winnemucca bank robbers continued to remain a mystery long after the holdup was forgotten. On April 17, 1912, a Buenos Aires, Argentina, newspaper, the *Standard*, published an article entitled "The Winnemucca Bank Hold Up," supposedly based upon an account of the robbery given to the writer by Harry Longabaugh himself, who had fled to South America ten years earlier. The *Standard* was an English language newspaper published for British expatriates living in Argentina. The article went virtually unnoticed by outlaw historians until a copy was discovered in 1994 in England by British outlaw enthusiast Mike Bell.

Although the article reads like a dime novel of its day, Bell believes it is fundamentally what it claims to be: Longabaugh's own account as told to a third party. Bell admits that the piece contains flaws and errors, which he blames on Harry's faulty memory, and that it has almost certainly been enhanced by either the writer to whom Harry gave the story or by the editors of the newspaper that published it, all of whom apparently knew little about the American West at the turn of the century. For what it's worth, the article states that the outlaws present at the Winnemucca bank that day were Butch, Harry, and Wild Bunch member Will Carver.[67]

Fort Worth and New York

1900–1901

Following the Tipton robbery, the Pinkertons again dispatched Charles Siringo to track down the robbers. Harvey Logan was highest on the Pinkertons' list of suspects, especially after they got a tip that Logan had vowed to raid the Union Pacific in revenge for the railroad's dogged pursuit of his brother Lonny.[1]

Siringo launched the chase near Grand Junction, Colorado, where Logan and a "tall" companion—possibly Ben Kilpatrick—were thought to have been spotted. After a few false starts Siringo picked up a trail that led south and then west into Utah toward Monticello and the Blue Mountains. Tracking outlaws, especially under cover, was what Siringo did best. He had a special talent for disguising himself as a hard case and persuading real hard cases to talk openly about the men he was pursuing. At the Carlisle Ranch near Monticello, a popular stop for outlaws on the run, he learned that he was only a little more than a day behind his quarry.[2]

The trail dimmed out, however, and Siringo had to guess where Logan and his tall companion were headed. He figured it was Hanksville and Robbers' Roost, so he headed for Hanksville. He questioned Charlie Gibbons, the store owner who regularly sold supplies to Butch and the Wild Bunch while they were hiding out at the Roost. Gibbons swore that he had not seen Butch, but Siringo worked on him, letting him believe that he was taking him into his confidence. Probably to protect his own hide Gibbons finally loosened up. He admitted that shortly after the Winnemucca bank robbery, Butch had left a large amount of money with him for safekeeping. Naturally Gibbons claimed that he knew nothing about the robbery and that he had no idea that he had been given stolen loot, which he said contained a generous amount of twenty dollar gold pieces. When Siringo asked him what had happened to the loot, Gibbons said that Butch eventually came and picked it up.[3]

While at Hanksville, Siringo received orders from the Pinkerton office in Denver to ride over to Circle Valley, to Butch Cassidy's boyhood home, and learn as much as he could about the outlaw's background. Then, according to his instructions, he was to head south to Alma, New Mexico Territory, to follow up on a report that the Wild Bunch might be making a ranch down there into their winter quarters. The instructions came from a man who should have known: Assistant Superintendent Frank Murray, the detective who, thanks to Butch, barely made it out of the town of Alma alive.

At Circle Valley Siringo spent a week nosing around, learning as much as he could about Butch from the Parker family's friends and neighbors. He had hoped to pick up clues but only gathered mostly trivia, such as the fact that one of Butch's childhood nicknames, which he must have detested dearly, was "Sallie." During the visit, however, Siringo got to know one of Butch's younger sisters (he didn't reveal which one) and apparently developed quite a fondness for her.[4]

Siringo did uncover a few interesting facts about the Wild Bunch while in Circle Valley. One was that the gang sometimes kept in contact through a series of "blind post offices" they had established all the way from the Hole-in-the-Wall in northeastern Wyoming to the Robbers' Roost area and possibly even further away. According to Siringo, these drops were carefully hidden in rocky crevices and hollow stumps and were used to deposit ciphered mail and items from newspapers. The ciphered mail consisted of seemingly innocuous letters with coded messages in key words. For example, by reading only every fourth word in the letter the real message would be conveyed.[5] Butch's sister later learned of one such drop in a hollow tree near Linwood, Utah. The tree had a hole in it which was hidden by a rusty metal band. Inside the hole was a bottle tied to a string. If the band was moved aside one could reach through the hole and place a message in the bottle, and could then lower it out of sight by letting out the string.[6]

On leaving Circle Valley Siringo rode south to Panguitch, loaded his pack horse with food and water, and headed for the Arizona line. After long stretches of dry desert he reached Gallup, New Mexico, where he replenished his supplies for the final leg to Alma.

Posing again as a man on the run, Siringo palavered with cowboys who drifted in and out of the saloon at Alma until he learned the details of Frank Murray's earlier visit. The story he was given was substantially the same as that reported by Murray to his superiors in Denver, except for one startling fact: the saloonkeeper, Jim Lowe, the man who had saved Murray's life, was really the outlaw Butch Cassidy.[7]

From Alma Siringo rode north into the Mogollon Mountains, where he nosed around several mining camps. At one of the camps, Frisco, he found a local cowboy who claimed to have known the former ws trail boss, Jim Lowe. Not only did he know Jim, the cowboy said, at that very moment Lowe was no more than forty miles away. Siringo immediately sent word to Frank Murray in Denver for instructions, but to Siringo's surprise Murray ordered him off the hunt and told him to return to Denver. Murray said that Siringo's source must have been mistaken about Jim Lowe being Butch Cassidy because he had met Lowe and Lowe was no outlaw.[8]

Siringo sold his two horses and caught the next stage to Silver City, the nearest town with a railroad. On the stage he got into a conversation with a fellow passenger by the name of Blake Graham who told him that he, too, knew the Jim Lowe who had worked for William French at the ws. Both Siringo and Graham had brought along a generous amount of whiskey, and before long the liquor loosened Graham's tongue: he told Siringo that Lowe was indeed Butch Cassidy, that Butch had owned the saloon in Alma. Graham also knew about Frank Murray's visit, and that not long after it Butch sold the saloon and left town with a fellow ws ranchhand named Red Weaver. Graham added that Butch himself had told him that he had saved Murray's life because he just did not have the heart to see him killed.[9]

Butch may have been hiding in the Mogollon Mountains as Charles Siringo's tipster said, but most sources suggest that following the Winnemucca bank robbery in September 1900, Butch and other members of the gang, including Harry Longabaugh, Harvey Logan, Will Carver, and Ben Kilpatrick headed for Fort Worth, Texas, for a little rest and relaxation.[10]

At the turn of the century most cowpunchers who rode into Fort Worth would at least once during their stay sample the pleasures offered by the town's tenderloin district, aptly called "Hell's Half Acre." Today the forty square blocks that once made up the "Acre"—an area that now lies just north of Interstate 30 between Jones and Houston Streets—contains a respectable Hilton Hotel and the popular Tarrant County Convention Center. But in the early 1900s the district was an embarrassment to upright city leaders. Amon Carter, founder of the *Fort Worth Star-Telegram*, was supposed to have maintained a long-standing policy that practically banned the name "Hell's Half Acre" from the pages of his newspaper.[11]

The Acre was home to Fort Worth's "Big Three" madams: Mary Porter, Jessie Reeves, and Josie Belmont, all queens of prostitution who ran the best sporting houses in the city. Their houses were all within a block of each other and they operated as friendly competitors for the better class of

customers who frequented the district. Mary Porter was often confused
with Fannie Porter, San Antonio's Queen of the Madams who was a close
friend of Butch's and who also probably had sporting interests in Fort
Worth.[12]

The Acre was also the home to a saloonkeeper named Mike Cassidy, a
dissolute character who had wandered into Fort Worth in the late 1880s
looking for work as a bartender. To his customers he was convivial "Mikey
Mike," but he was closed-mouthed about his past. Over the years he operated a number of seedy saloons in the Acre, during which time he acquired
a wife and a family and probably a long list of creditors. He also acquired a
record of minor criminal offenses, but, at least locally, they were nothing
more serious than violations of city liquor laws.[13]

Was this Mike Cassidy Butch's old pal from Circle Valley? There are
those who believe so.[14]

The trip to Fort Worth in the fall of 1900 was probably not the Wild
Bunch's first, but this one was special: gang member Will Carver was to be
married. His intended, Callie May Hunt, was also known as Lillie Davis,
one of Fannie Porter's girls from San Antonio.[15] There was a wedding ceremony but the marriage itself may have been a sham because no official record of it has been found.[16]

The party following the Carver-Davis "ceremony" may have been an
elaborate dress-up affair, which may have led to the now famous group
picture of the "Fort Worth Five": Butch, Longabaugh, Logan, Carver, and
Kilpatrick, all spiffed up in Sunday suits and jaunty derby hats. The photo
was taken by John Swartz, a prominent Fort Worth photographer who ran
his own gallery and studio, the Swartz View Company at 705 Main Street.
Swartz's enterprise was located only a few blocks from where the Wild
Bunch were making their headquarters in the Acre.[17]

Other reasons have been given for the photo: some say Butch suggested
it as a joke, others say the idea came from Longabaugh, who was fond of
dressing up and showing off.[18] Author Anne Meadows probes a little
deeper into the outlaws' psyche and speculates that maybe they were making fun of the wealthy class they professed to despise but really envied, or
perhaps they were acting out their fantasies of how life might have been
had they stayed on the straight and narrow.[19] Regardless of the explanation, the photo turned out to be a bad idea. Photographer Swartz was so
proud of his work that he put an extra print in the window of his gallery.
Somebody recognized it for what it was, had another print made and sent
it to the authorities.[20]

The man given credit for spotting the photo in Swartz's window was

Fred Dodge, a Special Agent for Wells Fargo.[21] However some doubt this theory because Dodge himself never mentioned it in his memoirs.[22] Whoever did notice the picture in Swartz's window, if that was how it was discovered, made sure that it found its way into the proper hands.[23] The authorities then had photos of five members of the inner circle of the Wild Bunch. Detectives converged on the Acre district, but by then Butch and his pals had left.[24]

Some writers credit the portrait of the "Fort Worth Five" as the cause of the Wild Bunch's eventual downfall. It's true that, for the first time, law enforcement agencies throughout the West could circulate Wanted posters displaying the faces of Harry Longabaugh, Harvey Logan, Ben Kilpatrick, and Will Carver, but Butch Cassidy's photo, taken when he entered the Wyoming State Prison in July 1894, had always been available: drawings based on the photo had appeared in newspapers nationally as early as the summer of 1899.[25]

The Swartz photo was probably the one the Pinkertons sent to George S. Nixon, head cashier of the National Bank of Winnemucca, Nevada, in an attempt to determine if Butch or any of the others in the portrait were the robbers there.[26] For years a large print of the photo has hung in the lobby of the Winnemucca bank and may have given birth to a legend that, in a display of bravado, Butch had sent a print of it directly to Nixon. In another version of this story Butch sent a print to young Vic Button, the boy at the CS ranch to whom Butch gave his white horse.[27] While many doubt this tale, it supposedly was confirmed by Button's daughter.[28]

Some writers believe that upon leaving Fort Worth, Butch and Longabaugh headed for San Antonio and Fannie Porter's house of delights.[29] If so, this was not a smart move because the Pinkertons were not far behind.

San Antonio had its own "Hell's Half Acre" district, and Fannie Porter was the Queen of the Madams there. She offered to her customers the best of services in luxurious surroundings, especially to selected members of the Wild Bunch who sometimes would stay for weeks.[30] And unlike many sporting house operators, Fannie did not discourage her girls from becoming romantically involved with their clients, at least when it came to the Wild Bunch.[31] For this reason it has been suggested that the mysterious Etta Place, who would soon became a major part of Harry Longabaugh's life, and to some extent Butch's as well, might have been one of Fannie's ladies of the evening.

There are those who say that Etta was Cassidy's companion before she was Longabaugh's, that it was she who spent the fall and winter of 1896 with Butch, first at Maeser, Utah, and later at the hideout at Robbers'

Roost.[32] It is possible this is true, but others believe that it was Longabaugh and not Butch who enjoyed the company of Etta that year, at least at the Roost.[33]

Of all the persons closely involved with the Wild Bunch, Etta Place remains the most obscure. Etta by far was the best looking of the Wild Bunch consorts; some would say even beautiful. A photograph of her and Longabaugh in 1901 shows a smallish, shapely woman with a warm, intelligent face and a quiet elegance—hardly the sort of woman who would relish the role of sidekick to a trail-hardened outlaw. But almost nothing is known about the real Etta Place.

It is unlikely that Etta Place was her real name. However, Ed Kirby, one of Longabaugh's biographers, claimed to have uncovered undocumented evidence that Etta's mother was Emily Jane Place of Oswego, New York, that she was related to the family of Harry Longabaugh's mother, Annie G. Place, and that Etta and Harry knew each other in Pennsylvania before Harry came west.[34]

Donna Ernst suggests that Etta's first name was really Ethel (a name she was using in early 1901), and that the name Etta came about later as a result of her visits to South America, where the Spanish pronunciation of Ethel would have been "Etta."[35] Dan Buck agrees about the Spanish pronunciation of Ethel—in fact, it was he who came up with the idea—but he believes that the name Etta was probably the result of a clerical error in the Pinkertons' files.[36]

There is also the theory that Etta was Ann Bassett of Brown's Park, the early girlfriend of Butch Cassidy who, with her sister Josie, competed for his affections.[37] However, in later years Ann had many opportunities to tell the world of this fact and she never did.[38]

According to another story, Etta's real name was Laura Etta Place Capel, the daughter of George Capel who also went by the name George Ingerfield. According to this story Capel was killed in 1892 while living in Arizona, and Etta, then only sixteen, ended up at Fannie Porter's sporting house in San Antonio. Butch Cassidy supposedly found her there, felt that she was worthy of a better environment, and took her to Price, Utah, where he placed her with a "good Mormon family" by the name of Thayne. At the Thaynes' place Etta took the name Ethel or Hazel and, before becoming involved with Harry Longabaugh and the Wild Bunch, taught school for a while.[39]

The above is a variant of a story that surfaced in 1970. That year a man claiming to be Harry Thayne Longabaugh, the son of Harry Alonzo Longabaugh, went around insisting to anyone who would listen that Etta Place was a woman named Hazel Tryon, a half-sister of his mother, Anna Marie Thayne. He said that after he was born in 1901, Etta (Hazel) took up with his father, eventually deserting her own children and running off with him to South America. The younger Longabaugh also said that Etta had been married two other times, to a "Johnnie" Johnson and to a man named Smith. He said that in later years she attempted to locate the two children she had abandoned but was unsuccessful. He claimed that Etta finally settled in Marion County, Oregon, where she died in 1935.[40]

On the other hand a Fort Worth newspaper editor, Delbert Willis, was convinced that Etta Place was a Fort Worth prostitute named Eunice Gray. Willis, who had interviewed Gray many times, said that she told him that she had originally come from Missouri. Gray lived to be eighty-one and died in a hotel fire in Waco, Texas, in January 1962. Although Willis apparently was convinced that Gray and Place were one and the same, he produced no concrete evidence to support his idea.[41] Willis's theory was pursued by Fort Worth historian Richard F. Selcer for his book on the "Hell's Half Acre" district of that city, but without results.[42]

In 1990 a lady from Wisconsin named Fish reported that she was pretty sure that Etta was her father's second cousin. According to Mrs. Fish, her father told her that the girl, who was from Door County, Wisconsin, "got mixed up with a bad crowd." Not only that, said Mrs. Fish, but the girl's father (Mrs. Fish's uncle) was found murdered in 1894, and it was rumored that the guilty party was none other than Harry Longabaugh.[43]

Also in the early 1990s Wild Bunch researcher Jim Dullenty thought he may have had a promising lead on Etta Place. He received a call from an outlaw enthusiast named Jesse Cole Kenworth who had what Dullenty believed was interesting information on Etta's identity. According to Kenworth, Etta could be traced to Florence, Arizona. Dullenty was ready to pack up and meet Kenworth for a trip to Florence when Kenworth broke off contact.[44]

Some writers believe that Etta eventually ended up in Denver, Colorado. Gail Drago even supplied an address: 619 Ohio Street.[45] The late F. Bruce Lamb believed that Etta might have come from the Denver area. Following these leads, author Donna Ernst, a tireless researcher, combed the census and other public records in that city but came up empty-handed.[46]

Another rumor tied Etta to the Parker clan in Utah. She was supposed to have been Butch's cousin, Amy Parker, who was born in Kanosh, Utah, in 1879 and grew up in the town of Joseph in southern Sevier County. This would have made Amy about the same age as Etta, and apparently there was some resemblance between the two women. Joseph, Utah, is less than fifty miles from Butch's parents' home in Circle Valley, and, as this story goes, Butch knew her when they were young and he later introduced her to Harry Longabaugh.[47]

What may be a variant of this story is one proposed by a Salt Lake City researcher, Steve Lacy, who claims that he has information that Etta was a schoolteacher who married a relative of Butch's and later resided in Leeds, Utah. He says that Etta's last name was Harris and that she lived until January 1959.[48]

What appears to be the most interesting lead in the search for Etta's roots came from additional digging by Donna Ernst. At least one Pinkerton detective who had been assigned to find the Wild Bunch believed that Etta's parents lived in Texas.[49] Picking up on this, Ernst had the 1900 census records for Texas searched for every Ethel born between 1875 and 1880 who lived in or near Fort Worth or San Antonio.[50] (She chose these two cities because they were two of Harry Longabaugh's favorite hangouts.) Ernst also searched old city directories and marriage, death, and tax records. Women named Ethel who had large families were tossed out. Eventually all of the Ethels were eliminated except one, and that one was an almost-perfect match. Her name was Ethel Bishop, and she lived in San Antonio with four other women—all young and single—at 212 South Concho Street, just around the corner from Fannie Porter's den of pleasure. In one of the directories Ethel had listed herself as an unemployed music teacher; however, like Fannie's place, the building at 212 South Concho Street was a bordello.[51]

Ernst then conducted a nationwide census search but it turned up little further information. She did find two Ethel Bishops in the 1880 census for West Virginia, both of whom roughly matched the San Antonio Ethel. In writing to persons named Bishop that were living in West Virginia, Ernst was encouraged by a letter from a man who wrote "the past is best left in the past anyway" and included a confusing family tree on the back of his letter. But before Ernst could probe the matter further the man died.[52]

Utah outlaw writer Kerry Ross Boren has suggested that Butch may have had stronger feelings for Etta than is generally believed. Boren claims that his source for this information was his (Boren's) grandfather, Willard Schofield, who supposedly knew Butch. Boren says that sometime shortly before Butch, Longabaugh, and Etta fled to South America, Butch spent an evening in the saloon in Linwood, Utah, where his grandfather tended bar. Boren says that his grandfather recalled that Butch talked quite a lot about Etta that night. "He talked about her like he thought an awful lot of her. He didn't come right out and say anything, but I could tell that he was anxious to tell someone about it and he spent nearly an hour just telling about things she did."[53]

Whatever Etta's early relationship with Butch, by late fall 1900 she had clearly paired up with Harry Longabaugh and was his companion at both Fort Worth and San Antonio.

By 1900 it appears that Longabaugh had also replaced Elzy Lay as Butch's closest pal among the Wild Bunch. Whether Butch and Harry ever shared the same lover is debatable, but they probably shared other traits. Unlike Harvey Logan they were not killers, at least so far they had not been put to the test. They also probably shared the belief that things were getting out of hand, that in their escape from Fort Worth they had cut it too close, and that it was probably time for the gang to call it quits.

Butch later described his uneasiness that year as a restlessness: a feeling that, as vast as the West was, it was getting too small for him.[54] He may have been right. For example, in one of his favorite hideout areas, desolate Grand County, Utah, which in 1900 probably had less than 750 inhabitants, telephone (not telegraph) lines began linking the major towns.[55] To another friend Butch later remarked that the law had also become so familiar with the Wild Bunch's practices that it was only a matter of time before all the members of the gang would be killed or captured.[56]

Charles Kelly suggests that Butch's uneasiness that year was a sign of an uncanny judgment about such things—that Butch usually knew when the game was played out and when it was time to toss in his cards.[57] But predicting a possibly bleak future for the Wild Bunch would not have been that difficult. The West was beginning to get its crime problem in hand. For one thing, robbing a train was becoming more difficult. In the early years it was fairly easy to crack open an express car, but the railroads had entered the steel era in car construction and it appeared that express cars would soon become nearly impregnable.[58] Also, train crews were beginning to stiffen their spine when robbers came calling. A train robbery was a blight on a crew's record: even though fault might not be laid on any one member of the crew, every mishap, every delay, every error in judgment could be a black mark against a crew and affect its individual members' chances for future advancement.[59]

Not only were train crews getting more tough-minded, the federal commissioner of railroads had recommended that extra guards be put on runs carrying valuable express shipments, and that these guards should be armed with repeating shotguns and extra rounds of buckshot. Rumors were afloat that incredible devices were being explored by express companies and railroad lines to thwart bandits: Gatling guns and searchlights; globular steel cars with revolving turrets; battery-powered, electrically charged steel floor plates near express car doors that could cook an intruder alive; messengers armed with hand grenades that could be thrown out of the express car windows; hoses connected to the locomotive boiler from which live steam could be sprayed on attackers; and devices designed to pour burning oil on would-be robbers.[60]

As to giving up the outlaw's life, it was probably as good a time as any. No one knows how the Wild Bunch loot had been split up during the previous several years, but if Butch and Longabaugh had managed to hang on to much of their shares they probably had sizable stakes. But if they did decide to start a new life, where would they go? The West was no longer safe: Fort Worth proved that. The East was out: their money would be used up too fast there, and then what would they do? They were used to working the range: they weren't dirt farmers or city laborers.

Canada was probably no option: Longabaugh had been there and knew what it was like—too much law and order. The word was that it was nearly impossible to be a successful outlaw north of the U.S.–Canadian border, thanks to the damnably efficient Canadian Mounties.[61]

On the other hand there was South America. South America had a lot of jungle, but there were also supposed to be mountains and prairies not unlike those of the North American West. South America was definitely a possibility, especially for Butch. He had seen all of the U.S. that he "thought was good" and felt that he wanted to see more of the world.[62]

The choice was eventually made: South America it was and, more specifically, Argentina.

Why Argentina? Butch or Longabaugh may have read about the country in a magazine. *National Geographic* had recently run several articles on Patagonia, a vast area in southern Argentina that stretches between the Andes Mountains and the Atlantic Ocean.[63] Or maybe the boys had met someone who had been to Argentina, or someone who knew someone who had.[64]

Turn-of-the-century Argentina was on the verge of an economic boom, a boom that a North American cowboy could share in. Because of an outbreak of hoof and mouth disease in England, the importation of live cattle and sheep from that country was prohibited. Argentina was not only growing its own beef and mutton, it was beginning to export both. Foreigners were finding that cattle and sheep ranches in the Argentine interior were a sound investment.[65]

Once the decision was made to leave the United States, Butch severed one of his last ties to Wyoming: the disposition of his remaining interest in the ranch he and Al Hainer acquired on Horse Creek in Fremont County in 1889.

Just what legal rights Butch and Hainer retained in the Horse Creek property by that time are not known. Butch's banker friend, Eugene Amoretti Jr., may have used the Horse Creek property to graze his own cattle when Butch was sent to prison in 1894. Local records are unclear, but it appears that in the early 1890s Butch and Hainer added to their original acquisition of 160 acres. Then in 1898, according to one source, these acres, which included the portion containing Butch and Hainer's cabin, were acquired as relinquished homestead land by an Iowa couple, Francis B. Nicol and his wife. The Nicols had come to Wyoming in 1891. At the time he acquired the land, Nicol held the U.S. Mail contract between Fort Washakie and Dubois. According to this source, Nicol improved the land with an irrigation ditch that diverted water from Horse Creek. He and his wife held the land until 1919, when they sold it to the Dubois Mercantile Company.[66]

Another source says that Amoretti purchased the property directly from Butch and Hainer in 1900. This source, however, may have been referring to Butch and Hainer's later-acquired land. According to local history, Amoretti operated a hunting lodge for tourists on the land called "The Ramshorn Lodge in the Rockies." In promoting the lodge Amoretti advertised that there were more deer, elk, bear, bobcats, and mountain sheep in the area than anywhere else in the world.[67]

Plans for South America were laid and the details were gradually worked out. Longabaugh informed Butch that Etta Place was going along too. How Butch felt about this isn't known for certain. According to Butch's sister, he did not like the idea at first, pointing out that the country down there was no place for a woman. But he eventually relented, possibly after Harry reminded him that they would need a good cook and housekeeper.[68] According Charles Kelly, Butch also tried to persuade Harvey Logan to join them, but he declined.[69]

Before leaving the country, Etta and Harry decided to do a little sightseeing. Their eventual destination was New York City, where they later embarked by ship, but it was then winter and some believe that rather than head directly for the frigid northeast, Etta and Harry spent New Year's Eve and early January 1901 in much warmer New Orleans.[70] When they did board a train for the north their first stop was Pennsylvania, where Harry, enjoying a rare return to his hometown, introduced Etta to his relatives.[71]

High on the list of family members to visit were Harry's sister and brother-in-law, Samanna and Oliver Hallman, who lived in Mont Clare, Pennsylvania. But according to family records, all was not joyous: the pair's visit with Samanna and Oliver had to be clandestine because by then the Pinkertons had discovered Harry's Pennsylvania roots and at times had the Hallman home under surveillance. While visiting with his sister and brother-in-law, Harry mentioned his and Butch's plans to go to South America and probably buy a ranch.[72]

Harry and Etta left Pennsylvania in mid-January, bound by train for New York City. During this period Harry may have been experiencing some health problems. Shortly after their arrival in New York, Harry scheduled an appointment with a Manhattan physician, Isaac Weinstein, M.D., whose office was located at 174 Second Avenue.[73] While in Pennsylvania Harry had mentioned to his family that he was having trouble with an old gunshot wound in his left leg.[74] Whether Dr. Weinstein actually treated Longabaugh is not known; however it is possible that he referred him to another physician in Buffalo, New York.

The Buffalo physician, Ray V. Pierce, M.D., operated what would be called a clinic today, but in 1901 was known under the names of its joint facilities, "Dr. Pierce's Invalids Hotel," and "Dr. Pierce's Medical Institute." The Institute, a grand five-story brick building with a stained glass entry and lush paneled walls located at 653 Main Street in Buffalo, offered its guests/patients, among other things, Turkish baths and holistic remedies for "chronic diseases—specifically those of a delicate, obscure, complicated or obstinate character."[75]

Although the Pinkerton files reveal that both Harry and Etta checked into Dr. Pierce's hotel, no records have ever been found that disclose the medical reason for their visit.[76] While Harry may have sought treatment for the old leg wound, some have speculated that since Etta checked in with him, their problem may have been venereal.[77] On the other hand, in the days of the popular health spas it was common for spouses to share accommodations with patients.

It also is possible that Longabaugh may have been suffering from a lung disorder. According to Elton Cunningham, a saloonkeeper in Mogollon, New Mexico, and a pal of the Wild Bunch when Butch worked at the ws Ranch, Harry Longabaugh was a "lunger" who occasionally spit blood when he coughed.[78] That Harry might have had something as serious as tuberculosis was never mentioned by family members; however, he did suffer from severe "catarrh," which today would be considered chronic sinusitis.[79]

Whatever the reason for their stay at Dr. Pierce's, when they left, Harry and Etta were feeling well enough for a side trip to Niagara Falls before returning to New York City.[80]

Once back in New York, on February 1, 1901, Harry and Etta checked into Mrs. Catherine Taylor's boarding house at 234 West 12th Street, taking the best suite on the second floor.[81] They signed the guest register as Mr. and Mrs. Harry Place. Throughout their trip Harry called himself Harry A. Place and Etta, Ethel Place. Harry told Mrs. Taylor that he was a cattle buyer from Wyoming.[82]

A third guest from Wyoming signed in too. Butch, using the name James Ryan, informed Mrs. Taylor that he was Ethel Place's brother.[83]

For the next three weeks Butch, Harry, and Etta did the town. According to witnesses later interviewed by the Pinkertons, the trio took in the popular vaudeville shows of the day and enjoyed the city's many taverns and night spots, among them Connelly's Bar at 3rd Avenue and 23rd Street, Pete's Tavern at Irving Place and 18th Street, and Joe's Bar on Union Square. After their excursions through the city they would return to their boarding house a little unsteady and probably a little too noisy for Mrs. Catherine Taylor's liking.[84] Among the shows they may have caught were Weber and Fields, who were playing that month at the Music Hall. Also, while Etta may have spent an afternoon shopping, the boys might have slipped over for a matinee at the Dewey Theatre on East 14th to see the "Merry Maiden" Burlesque Girls.[85]

The trio dropped in at Tiffany's, then at the corner of 15th Street and Union Square and already famous for its fine jewelry, where, possibly for Valentine's Day, either Butch or Harry bought Etta a fancy gold lapel watch costing $150. While there Harry also purchased a diamond stickpin for himself.[86] Later, Harry, all spruced up in fancy Eastern duds, and Etta, in a sweeping full skirt, high collar, and lace (and proudly displaying her new watch) had their pictures taken at DeYoung's on Broadway, at the time one of New York's top photography studios.[87] Harry is believed to have sent a print of the picture to a friend from his cowpunching days in Wyoming's Little Snake River Valley, a clerk at Robert McIntosh's General Store in Slater, Colorado.[88]

When Butch, Harry, and Etta arrived in the city, the weather had been mild, at least for the first of February. The temperature was in the mid-twenties with only a hint of snow. By February 10 the temperature had dropped to the teens and the East Coast was in the grip of a snowstorm. New York City fared better than most areas, but still the city was forced to send out over 1,800 street sweepers and nearly 1,000 carts and trucks to haul off the snow and keep traffic moving.[89]

On February 13, if the trio had ventured outside their rooms they could have caught a hack down to the Battery for a spectacle that New Yorkers would talk about for years. A sudden warm front upstate had caused massive chunks of ice, in some places stretching from shore to shore, to break up and move down the Hudson River to the harbor. As these chunks rounded the Battery and met a similar ice flow from the East River, the two merged and held every boat and ship in their path: from the smallest tugs to giant ocean liners, the harbor traffic was paralyzed. As cold as it was—and made worse by gale-force winds of over sixty miles per hour—spectators gathered by the thousands to view the sight. One witness later said he counted sixty-two vessels caught in the sea of ice, while another man claimed he counted twice as many.[90]

Despite the weather, Butch, Longabaugh, and Etta frolicked in Manhattan for nearly three weeks. According to one version of the story, their holiday ended when Butch boarded a train bound for the West and one more robbery. Harry and Etta then checked out of Mrs. Taylor's boarding house and headed for Pier 32 on the East River, now well free of ice, and booked passage on the ss *Herminius*, a British freighter illegally converted to carry a few passengers. The ship was bound for Buenos Aires, Argentina, by way of Montevideo, Uruguay.[91]

In the other version of the story, which seems to make more sense, Butch did not leave his friends but instead sailed with them to Argentina, either on the *Herminius* or on some other ship.[92]

Wagner

1901

The Wild Bunch's last express car robbery in the United States took place on the Great Northern Railroad near Wagner, Montana. The date was July 3, 1901, and the victim was the Great Northern's westbound Express No. 3, the Coast Flyer.[1]

Why did the gang ride hundreds of miles in the blazing sun almost to the Canadian border to strike the Great Northern, when Union Pacific flyers were conveniently making daily runs across Wyoming? It probably had little to do with the promise that Butch had allegedly made to Wyoming Governor William A. Richards on his release from prison that he would stay clear of his state. If he had made such a promise he probably broke it with the Tipton train robbery. A raid on the Great Northern may have been Harvey Logan's idea, since Logan was familiar with that area of Montana. Maybe the gang had fled Wyoming and were hiding out in Montana. Or it is possible they had received a tip that an especially large shipment was aboard the Coast Flyer.

The gang may have bypassed the Union Pacific Railroad because the risk was too great. The Wilcox holdup had convinced Union Pacific officials that express car robberies were likely to become a major problem, especially in the Wyoming division. The UP's Wyoming division was a train robber's dream. In many stretches along the route, mountains, or at least rugged foothills, were within a hundred miles or less of the tracks. With a reasonable head start, bandits could easily escape. And while whistle stops and tank towns dotted the line in Wyoming, towns large enough to produce a fast-moving posse on quick notice were scarce.[2]

But railroad baron E. H. Harriman, who had taken control of the Union Pacific in 1898, believed that he had the answer. Like Butch Cassidy, Harriman knew almost everything there was to know about horses, and, also like Butch Cassidy, he knew that a successful express car robbery usually depended upon good animals capable of making fast getaways.[3] It was Harriman who pushed for adoption of the Union Pacific's "posse cars": special railroad cars that could be loaded with men and horses in a moment's notice. When fully implemented a posse car operation consisted of gutted baggage cars equipped with ramps ready to be coupled to fast locomotives stationed at strategic points along the line. Once steam was up these lightning-fast trains were capable of transporting animals and men to the scene of a holdup in record time. To occupy these cars Harriman insisted on experienced manhunters and sturdy horses that could easily go a hundred miles a day without faltering.[4]

The Wild Bunch was well aware of the Union Pacific's innovation, having been introduced to an early version at the Tipton robbery. Had the posse out of Rawlins been equipped with hand-picked horses that night, and had the locomotive selected to rush to the scene not broken down, the gang might have been put out of business then and there.[5]

Perhaps the gang was also concerned that the Union Pacific, unlike most other railroads, was offering rewards for train robbers, dead or alive.[6] Before then the railroads had taken the position that it was bad for public relations to offer rewards that invited the killing of suspected train robbers, but the word was out that the Union Pacific was taking the opposite view, and, moreover, the UP might even begin offering rewards that paid more for dead robbers than for live ones.[7]

The Great Northern Railroad was not yet offering dead-or-alive rewards and had no lightning-fast horse cars. The Wagner robbery, staged many miles from the nearest town in which a posse could be organized, was a complete success. Some reports said the gang rode away with $40,000.[8] Butch, however, may have felt differently. If he was as adverse to gunplay as most people believed, he could not have been proud of how the holdup was carried off.

While the combined baggage-express car was being assaulted, somebody in the gang with a Winchester must have begun fretting about the passengers interfering and nervously peppered the sides of the coaches to keep them in line. Eighteen-year-old Gertrude Smith from Tomah, Wisconsin, foolishly leaned out the window to see what was happening and took a bullet in the shoulder. Fortunately the bullet missed the bone, but, according to a witness, blood spurted everywhere.[9]

There were at least four robbers at Wagner, although some say five and maybe even six.[10] Butch was mentioned as being there, as well as Harvey

Logan, Ben Kilpatrick, and O.C. (Camilla) Hanks.[11] Kilpatrick had been with the gang since before Fort Worth, but Hanks was a newcomer to the Wild Bunch, having recently been released from the Montana State Penitentiary at Deer Lodge after serving an eight-year sentence for train robbery.[12] Some sources later reported that Harry Longabaugh was also along, but for a while Kilpatrick was mistaken for Harry.[13] If Butch was present, he may have let Logan lead the assault because of Harvey's familiarity with the area.[14] Also, by then, Logan probably had more personal experience in robbing express cars than Butch did.[15]

Unlike most train robberies, which for tactical reasons were usually pulled off at night or just before dawn, the robbers at Wagner struck in the early afternoon. From statements given by witnesses the authorities believed that Harvey Logan may have slipped aboard behind the tender at an earlier stop.[16] Possibly this was at the water tank at Malta, ten miles east of Wagner.[17] Ben Kilpatrick may also have boarded there as a paying passenger.[18] The others, all armed with Winchesters, waited at a designated spot along the track near a site called Exeter Switch.[19]

Shortly after leaving Malta, someone, probably Logan, climbed forward over the tender, took command of the locomotive and ordered the engineer, Tom Jones, to stop at the switch. Jones had no choice but to comply. Closely adhering to the procedure followed in their earlier holdups, the gang ordered a trainman to cut loose the baggage-express car from the passenger coaches and then commanded engineer Jones to pull ahead again.[20] According to a witness, two trainmen, fearing a collision if the train was stalled too long on the tracks, ran back to put out warning flares. The robbers, apparently taken by surprise, began firing at them. Both trainmen were hit and one of them later died from the effects of his wound.[21]

Once the robbers were in the baggage-express car they went to work on the safe with dynamite. Witnesses said they heard up to four explosions. Harvey Logan was said to have remarked later that it was the hardest safe he had ever tried to open.[22]

Back in the coaches the sound of the dynamite blasts sent the already unnerved passengers into near-panic. Ira Merritt of Republic, Washington, then only a boy, remembered the scene well. "When the second blast went off women began crying and men wringing their hands and a lot them wondering out loud if they were going to blow the whole train up one car at a time." The conductor came down the aisle and tried to calm the passengers down by joking that it was just a little Fourth of July celebration.

"Of course that didn't go over very big," Merritt said. Someone asked the conductor to take a look at Gertrude Smith's wound and explain how a July Fourth celebration caused that. "I'll never forget the look on that man's face when he saw the blood spattered all over the girl's clothes," Merritt said. "He turned white as the driven snow and had to clutch one of the seats to keep from crumpling to the floor."[23]

Ira Merritt recalled that a sheriff was on the train, a man traveling from somewhere in Montana. This sheriff also made a trip down the aisle, with "his coat thrown back showing off his star, letting it be known he had a six-gun and what he would do if the bandits tried to enter the coaches." Some of the passengers pleaded with him not to start a fight, said Merritt. Then Merritt added, "but as I think about it now, I don't think he needed any convincing on that score."[24] According to another account, the sheriff, whose name was Griffith, then went to back to the last coach, jumped off the train and began firing at the robbers, but the gang's Winchesters quickly persuaded him to climb back on and cause no further trouble.[25]

If the passengers were concerned about the gang coming through the cars, they need not have worried. Robbing passengers was never the Wild Bunch's style. The take in the coaches was seldom worth the risk, thanks mainly to travelers' checks, which became popular in the mid-1890s. Once travelers' checks caught on, well-heeled passengers began carrying less and less cash, especially on long trips.[26]

When they had finished emptying the express company safe, the bandits jumped down from the car and ran to their horses, which had been staked near the tracks, and rode off to the south toward the Milk River, which ran almost parallel to the tracks.[27] Apparently not satisfied that they had already nearly paralyzed the passengers with fear, they turned and fired a few more rounds toward the train as they rode away.[28]

When news of the holdup reached Glascow, a posse was formed and struck out after the robbers. It was a large force and they apparently expected to be on the trail for quite a while because they brought along a cook and a chuck wagon. It was wasted effort, however, because they never caught up with the bandits. Someone suggested that it was because the posse refused to get too far ahead of their food supply.[29] Also they may have been discouraged by sarcastic messages the outlaws sent back by way of travelers that the gang had passed along the trail.[30]

The bandits were supposedly sighted several times during the first twenty-four hours, which sent a couple of additional posses off on unsuccessful searches. A few days after the robbery a rancher named Morton was picked up after cashing some bank notes from the express car. On being questioned he said that the outlaws had come by his ranch and had convinced him to trade four of his good saddle horses for four of their tired mounts plus $100 in bank notes. Lawmen departed quickly for the ranch, but the trail had grown cold.[31] Staying well away from civilization the outlaws probably rode in a southwesterly direction toward the headwaters of the Missouri. According to one account they split up at about 150 miles, after arranging to rendezvous later somewhere in the Little Rockies.[32]

Cholila

1901–1904

According to Buenos Aires journalist Francisco Juárez, Butch Cassidy arrived in Argentina at the same time as Harry Longabaugh and Etta Place did.[1] If true, it means that Butch, too, may have left New York on the British freighter ss *Herminius* in February of 1901.[2] However, nearly all other writers and apparently the Pinkertons as well place Butch at the Wagner robbery.[3] Some say he then caught a cattle boat for Liverpool, England, and from there hopped a freighter for Argentina.[4]

If Harry Longabaugh and Etta Place were on the *Herminius* they probably arrived in Buenos Aires during the last week of March, 1901.[5] That week they registered at the city's fashionable Hotel Europa as Mr. and Mrs. Harry A. Place, and shortly thereafter they deposited approximately $12,000 in the Buenos Aires branch of the London and River Platte Bank.[6] According to Ed Kirby, at the bank Harry jokingly questioned the banker who took his money about the bank's security system, suggesting that he was concerned about bandits.[7]

At this point it is difficult to track Harry and Etta for a while. They may have traveled the Argentinian back country looking for a ranch or land to buy.[8] At some time during the following year Butch joined them. According to the Pinkerton files, in early March 1902 the trio were again registered guests at the Hotel Europa, and Butch was once again posing as Etta's brother.[9]

On April 2, 1902, Butch petitioned the Registry of the Colonial Land Department in Buenos Aires to purchase some public land. In the petition, signed by Butch and Longabaugh as James Ryan and Harry A. Place, the two men stated that they had settled on four square leagues of government land within the Territory of Chubut, Argentina, and as proof of their intentions to improve it they had acquired 1,300 sheep, 500 head of cattle, and 35 horses.[10] Chubut is in southern Argentina, by steamer more than 750 miles from Buenos Aires. The land described in the petition was in western Chubut, in the valley of Cholila at the foot of the Andes Mountains not far from the Chilean border.

Four square leagues was a lot of land—over 25,000 acres. At the time the value of land in Argentina varied considerably. Property located near Buenos Aires or other Argentine cities the size of Rosario or Santa Fé commanded a high price. Away from civilization the land value largely depended upon how close it was to a railroad.

Why the American outlaws chose to settle in this particular region is also not known, but they may have felt very much at home. In Patagonia, as in the western United States, ranchers ranged their livestock far and wide in common herds, and, also like the American West, cattle stealing was a major industry.[11] Some observers believed the practice flourished because it was encouraged by dishonest law enforcement officials who themselves were on the take.[12]

According to one story the trio came by their land as a result of a trip to the interior by way of the Chubut River. While on the trip, Butch, Harry, and Etta happened to meet a Scotsman, John "Jock" Gardiner, who had come to Argentina in 1890 for his health. After teaching school for a while, Gardiner began trading with the local Indians, did very well at it, and eventually established a ranch in western Chubut province. As the story goes, Gardiner and Butch hit it off from the start and he was instrumental in the trio's success at finding available land near Cholila and assisted them in acquiring their first livestock.[13]

Only Butch was present to file the petition for the land the following April. Longabaugh, possibly having a recurrence of his health problems, had decided to return to the United States. According to the Pinkerton files, on March 3, 1902, Harry and Etta boarded the *Soldier Prince* bound for New York. If Harry was in poor health he must have appreciated the accommodations. This time the couple did not travel undocumented on a rusty freighter. They clearly went first class. The *Soldier Prince* was a brand new steamer of the Prince Line making only its second voyage. Launched the previous October, the vessel carried some cargo but was also equipped with a spacious deck of large and airy cabins and an elegant oak-paneled dining salon, all of which were illuminated in the evenings with the latest in electric lighting.[14]

The *Soldier Prince* arrived at Bush Terminal in Brooklyn, New York, on April 3, and shortly thereafter Harry and Etta took a room at 325 East 14th Street in Manhattan's lower east side. The following month Harry checked into a New York hospital.[15] The Pinkerton report did not say which one, but it may have been Bellevue, which, at 27th Street and First Avenue, was the nearest general hospital.[16]

Harry may have been expecting the stay to be expensive. In late March or early April a check for $3,546 was drawn on Longabaugh's account at the London and River Platte Bank in Buenos Aires. The Pinkerton records are not clear but it probably was drawn by Butch. According to one story the check was sent to Harry in New York.[17] According to another, Butch cashed it in Trelew (a town in eastern Chubut province) where it was endorsed by one Angel M. Botaro who owned the Del Globo Hotel where Butch, Harry, and Etta usually stayed when they were traveling in and out of the interior.[18] The second version of the story is probably correct. Harry probably would have taken enough money with him to New York to meet emergencies. It is unlikely that the check would have been for unanticipated expenses after the couple reached New York, because it was drawn before Harry and Etta even arrived there.

Following Harry's hospital stay the couple returned to Pennsylvania for another visit with Harry's sister, Samanna, and her family in Mont Clare. According to family history, Harry told Samanna and her husband about the ranch in Cholila and suggested that someday Samanna's two sons should come to Argentina for a visit. On leaving Mont Clare, Harry and Etta went to Atlantic City, New Jersey, where they visited Harry's brother, Harvey. William Longabaugh, Harvey's seven-year-old son, later told of going to the beach with his uncle Harry and playing in the surf.[19]

While Longabaugh and Etta were in the United States, Harry and Butch were named as suspects in a train robbery in the Midwest. On the evening of July 3, 1902, two men stopped a Rock Island, Omaha and Denver express near Dupont, Illinois. It was a typical express car robbery except that the robbers had the help of an innocent citizen. That citizen, Charles Nessler, had sneaked aboard at Englewood with the intention of hitching a free ride on the front of the baggage car to his home in Rock Island. When he found two other men had the same idea he thought they were just tramps, but then he saw that they were armed and were wearing masks. They informed him that they were planning to rob the train and that he was going to help. Then they forced him to climb over the tender and tell the engineer to put on his breaks.[20]

After the train had come to a stop the two men marched the engineer and fireman back to the express car, where they commanded the express messengers to open up under the threat of blowing up the car with dynamite. The messengers opened up, but in doing so one of them slipped on the door sill. The robbers thought that he was trying to escape and they shot him in the leg.

The car carried the usual two safes, and the robbers scooped out between $100 and $500 from the smaller one. They had intended to blast open the larger safe, but when some of the passengers became curious and started to come forward to the front of the train, they stuffed their loot into a bag and ran to a wagon standing near the tracks.

Although during the peak of the train robbery era the state of Illinois had experienced its share of robberies by amateurs, the authorities suspected that this holdup might have been committed by professionals. They showed Charles Nessler pictures of Butch and Longabaugh, but since it was dark and the two men had their faces covered he could only suggest that there might be a "general resemblance." However, one local farmer, L. P. Moss, came forward and said that earlier in the day he had met two strangers on the road who had asked directions to Chicago. When he was shown the photographs of Butch and Harry he identified them as the men he had talked to. Then the engineer, Charles Goodall, in giving his statement said that he believed that one of the robbers was bowlegged.[21]

Other witnesses appeared: one of them, J. W. Holstein, who ran a local hotel, said that he had seen the men, that there were actually three of them, and that one of them did resemble the photograph of Harry Longabaugh. Finally, when a witness said that he believed that the two men in the photographs could be the same men who had rented a room in Englewood for two weeks before the robbery, the authorities told the press of their suspicions. On July 6 the *Chicago Tribune* published a follow-up article on the robbery with pictures of Butch and Harry.

If Harry Longabaugh was involved in the robbery he would have had to have made a quick trip back to New York City because on July 10, Harry and Etta sailed from New York on the *Honorius*.[22] According to the Pinkerton files, the couple again chose a freighter that was not officially supposed to carry paying passengers. Because of this Harry was designated on the ship's crew list as the purser, and Etta was listed as a steward or stewardess. The ship arrived in Buenos Aires on August 9, and Harry and Etta again checked into their favorite hotel, the Europa. Five days later Harry went to the London and River Plate Bank and closed his account.[23]

In the meantime, back in Chubut, Butch, perhaps feeling lonely, decided to write a letter to Mathilda Davis, mother of Maude Davis and mother-in-law of Elzy Lay. Although he had been gone from the United States for little more than a year, Butch may have become homesick; he mentioned to Mrs. Davis that "when I think of my old friends you are always the first to come to my mind." In the next paragraph he referred to a photograph, apparently of Maude and Elzy, which someone had sent to him. Noting that in the photo "Maude looks very sad," he wrote that he wished that he had the persons in the picture with him there in Argentina since he believed that he could "liven them up."[24]

Next, in a tongue-in-cheek manner Butch brought Mrs. Davis up to date on his exploits. "Another of my Uncles died and left $30,000 Thirty Thousand to our little family of 3 so I took my $10,000 and started to see a little more of the world. I visited the best Cities and best parts of the countries of South A. till I got here. And this part of the country looked so good that I located, and I think for good, for I like the place better every day."

Butch described the ranch, which he said included a good four-room house, a stable, a warehouse, and a chicken house, and he also listed his and Longabaugh's livestock holdings. If the numbers he gave Mrs. Davis were accurate, he had done a little dealing in the previous six months. Since petitioning the Registry of the Colonial Land Department in Buenos Aires for the right to purchase the land he and Longabaugh were improving, he had increased their herd of cattle by two hundred head, sold off two hundred sheep, and reduced their horses by seven.

Harry and Etta had been gone those six months and Butch, running the ranch alone, was blue. He apparently felt he was suffering from the lack of a cook to keep him fed and from companionship in general. He complained that he was "living in Single Cussidness" and that he was alone all day. While he was, as he said, liking his Cholila retreat "better every day," he wasn't that enthused about his fellow Argentine ranchers. "[M]y neighbors don't amount to anything," he said. Besides, "the only language spoken in this country is Spanish, and I don't speak it well enough to converse on the latest scandals," without which, he said, the conversations "are very stale."

Life at the ranch was no doubt lonely. North American travelers generally avoided Patagonia, finding it desolate and monotonous. At the turn of the century its vast pampas, hemmed in between an inhospitable, harborless coast and the nearly inaccessible Andes Mountains, was still occupied mainly by Native Indians. The meager number of European and North American settlers there were found in the few small villages that dotted the territories or here and there on ranches, which in some areas were separated from one another by a three- to five-day ride.[25]

Cholila Valley probably offered Butch little in the way of entertainment, but there were books he could borrow from a few English-speaking neighbors. He could ride over to the village of Esquel, which occasionally held fiestas, or to Leleque, where, as much as his limited Spanish would permit, he could talk cattle and sheep with the boys at the Lands of the South Company where local ranchers bought their livestock.[26] Of course, at the end of the day after the traditional Argentine heavy late supper he could always seek comfort from one of the local ladies of the evening.[27]

When totally bored, if he felt comfortable leaving the ranch for several weeks he may have ridden over to more civilized Trelew at the opposite end of the Chubut River. It was a tiring ride across practically the entire width of the province, but he may have found the trip enjoyable, perhaps bringing back memories of his youth when he and Mike Cassidy gathered up strays in the canyons below Circle Valley. While southern Patagonia, with its rounded hills, tiny lakes, and broad stretches of prairie has been said to resemble western Nebraska, further north the land has been described as "a treeless jungle of badlands, peaks, ridges, and minor valleys," and could easily have been mistaken for southern Utah.[28]

Butch probably found eastern Chubut province much like Utah in other ways, too. The area around Trelew, more arid than the western end of the province, had been settled in 1865 by a colony of emigrants from Wales who, like the Mormons, had left their home country to escape persecution. In Argentina these determined Welsh formed a world unto themselves. Like Butch's ancestors they conquered droughts and floods with picks and shovels, constructing an elaborate system of irrigation canals that allowed them to grow grain and raise sheep and cattle.[29]

Western Chubut province, however, was far from arid and was first-class land for raising livestock. "It can't be beat for that purpose," Butch wrote Mrs. Davis. "I have never seen a finer grass country, and lots of it, hundreds and hundreds of miles . . . unsettled and comparatively unknown . . . good agricultural country."

Livestock was only one way to make a living, Butch wrote: "[A]ll kinds of small grain and vegetables grow without irrigation . . . there is plenty of good land along the mountains for all the people that will be here for the next hundred years."

The climate was much milder than in Utah, Butch said. The summers were beautiful and not hot. The winters, on the other hand, were very wet and disagreeable, but "it never gets cold enough to freeze much."

Butch also may have been unhappy with the remoteness of the ranch. "I am a long way from civilization," he wrote. "It is 16 hundred miles to Buenos Aires, the Capitol of the Argentine, and over 400 miles to the nearest RailRoad or Sea Port in the Argentine Republic." But things were looking up, he said. The Pacific coast towns of Chile were only about 150 miles to the west, and while at present it was necessary to cross the mountains to get there—a very difficult undertaking in itself—the Chilean government was in the process of cutting a road through the Andes that would allow them to get their beef to the coast in one tenth the time it was currently taking. What's more, he said, they could buy supplies in Chile for one-third of what they cost in Cholila.[30]

Butch may have felt very secure in his Argentine hideaway because for as cautious as he had always been, he did a rather careless thing: at the top of the first page of the letter he clearly indicated his whereabouts: "Cholila, Ter. Chubut." Because they were so many miles from the United States, both Butch and Harry may have become complacent. According to Pointer, information supposedly obtained from the Argentine provincial police reports and published in a Buenos Aires newspaper suggested that at times Harry and Etta may have carelessly traveled as Mr. and Mrs. Harry Longabaugh, and Butch as George Parker.[31]

The trio may have acquired a low opinion of the law enforcement authorities there and of Argentine government officials in general. A story often repeated by North Americans and Europeans in Argentina at the time concerned the Curumalan estancia (one of the largest ranches in the country) and how it got its beginning. In the 1880s the Argentine government offered to sell a former cavalry officer a huge tract of land under an arrangement whereby he would stock it with 50,000 mares from which he would supply the army with remounts. Under the arrangement he would be paid for the horses and use the money to pay off the land. The officer-turned-rancher, however, had another plan in mind. As the story was told, he would periodically sell a large number of horses to the army, see that they were loaded on a train, but also see that somewhere during the long trip over the desolate pampas the train was stopped and the horses taken off. As a result, the army bought the same lot of horses over and over. Before the paperwork was untangled and the plot uncovered, the enterprising schemer had paid off the land, sold it for cash to an Irish speculator, and gone merrily on his way.[32]

Butch and Longabaugh had more to deal with than the Argentine authorities. By early 1903 the Pinkertons had discovered their whereabouts: "ranching in a new country 350 miles inland," according to a February 14 letter from Robert Pinkerton to the president of the Union Pacific Railroad.[33] The Pinkertons may have obtained this information from postal employees who were persuaded to open mail addressed to the outlaw pair's friends and relatives in the United States.[34]

Braced with what appeared to be solid information, the Pinkertons sent an experienced operative, Frank Dimaio, to Buenos Aires. Dimaio knew that Butch was still using the last name Ryan, and that Harry and Etta were still posing as Harry and Ethel Place. Since the fugitives had continued to use these aliases and had apparently made little effort to keep them off documents and records, it did not take Dimaio long to learn about the ranch in Cholila. In fact, George Newbery, the U.S. vice-consul in Buenos Aires, owned an *estancia* on the north shore of Lake Nahuel Huapi in Neuquén Territory, just 130 miles north of Cholila, and was aware of the three North Americans and their sheep ranch.[35] Dimaio, however, reported to his superiors in New York that Newbery advised him not to try to go to Cholila until the end of the rainy season, that the roads were so flooded that it would be impossible to reach the ranch.[36] Newbery promised Dimaio that if the outlaws were not apprehended by the next time he visited his own ranch, he would go over to Cholila and try to lure Butch and Longabaugh to Buenos Aires on some pretext such as having them appear personally to sign more papers regarding their petition for government land. Taking Newbery's advice, Dimaio returned to New York, but before he left he had Wanted circulars for the trio printed in Spanish for distribution to local law enforcement departments and the steamship companies.[37]

Also, before he left Buenos Aires, Dimaio secured Newbery's promise to keep in touch by telegraph. Newbery was to wire the Pinkertons at once if he learned anything new about the outlaws. Concerned that Cassidy and Longabaugh might have contacts in Buenos Aires, a code was worked out for sending messages. The code name for Cassidy was to be "citron," for Longabaugh, "lemons," for Etta, "peaches," and for both Longabaugh and Etta, "apricots."[38]

At this point, however, the bandit pair got a break. When the Pinkertons tried to solicit funds from former Wild Bunch victims in the United States—western railroad and express companies and the American Bankers Association—for an expedition to Argentina to bring back Butch and Harry, the detective agency received no cooperation. It wasn't the money: the cost of the expedition was estimated at only around $5,000. It was more a matter of common sense. Why not leave things as they were? Why bring these bandits back to the United States where they might escape and begin robbing all over again?

The Pinkertons, unwilling to spend their own funds, reluctantly put the idea of an expedition on hold.[39] Later, to explain why the agency had not apprehended the outlaw pair as they had many other criminals, William A. Pinkerton, in addressing an annual convention of police chiefs, told his audience that "being expert ranch men they [Cassidy and Longabaugh] engaged in cattle raising on a ranch they had acquired, located on a piece of high table land from which they commanded a view of 25 miles in various directions, making their capture practically impossible."[40]

Frank Dimaio's efforts in Buenos Aires did not go unnoticed, however, and as a reward he was promoted to general superintendent of the agency's newly formed Pittsburgh division.[41]

While the Pinkertons were fairly sure they knew where Butch and Longabaugh were hiding, others believed the Wild Bunch were still engaged in mischief. In November 1903, Tom Horn was awaiting his hanging in Cheyenne, Wyoming, for the killing of fourteen-year-old Willie Nickell, a rancher's son whom Horn apparently mistook for the boy's father, Kels Nickell, thought to be on Tom's hit list. Someone slipped Horn word that arrangements were being made to break him out of jail, and that Butch Cassidy and his gang had been hired to do it. The Cheyenne authorities heard the same rumor and troops were called out to patrol the courthouse square. Horn's execution was scheduled for November 20. On the eighteenth, Tom received another message that he would be freed the following day. Throughout the night gamblers in most of Cheyenne's saloons were giving odds that Butch would set Tom free. When Horn awoke the next morning, outside his cell someone had written in the snow in large letters, "Keep Your Nerve." Tom waited all day for Butch to come. The next day at 11:08 AM, Horn, now knowing that help was not on its way, still managed to smile at the crowd before the rope was slipped around his neck.[42]

Thousands of miles away the Cholila ranch was doing well. Butch and Harry had increased their herds by purchases from the Lands of The South Company in Leleque and from Jarred Jones, a transplanted Texan who owned a large spread in neighboring Neuquén Territory.[43] While the cabin the "family of three" called home was far from fancy, it was comfortable by local standards. Built with rough-split cypress logs, it stood out from neighboring ranch houses that were usually built of stone. Not surprisingly, the bandit trio's house resembled a frontier cabin of the American West, with a few added features such as four-pane, double-hung glass windows that had been specially ordered from the United States. Another feature was a small cellar that could have been used as a hiding place in an emergency.[44]

Apparently Etta was a tidy housekeeper. Primo Capraro, an Italian immigrant who had spent an evening at the cabin, recalled that the house was "simply furnished and exhibited a certain painstaking tidiness, a geometric arrangement of things, pictures with cane frames, wallpaper made of clippings from North American magazines, and many beautiful weapons and lassos braided from horsehair."[45] Etta also was known to be a genial hostess and an excellent cook, especially of Mexican dishes.[46]

According to Raúl Cea, a local historian interviewed by Anne Meadows and Dan Buck during one of their trips to Argentina, Cea's grandparents were neighbors of Butch, Harry, and Etta when they built their cabin. Cea's father, Pedro, then a teenager, passed on many stories to Raúl and other family members about the three "North Americanos." The Ceas considered the trio very cultured by local standards and persons obviously accustomed to living well. At first the locals thought their new neighbors were probably too refined to make a success out of ranching Chubut style, but to their surprise they discovered that Butch, whom they knew as "Santiago Ryan," and Harry Place were in fact competent cowboys.[47] Etta, too, impressed the neighbors with her horsemanship.[48]

Etta's other attributes did not go unnoticed either. Local gossip was that both Butch's friend Jock Gardiner and the local *comisario*, Edward Humphrys, were clearly smitten with the beautiful Mrs. Ethel Place.[49]

Butch and Harry, with Etta's help, may have operated the ranch by themselves the first year. It wasn't that ranchhands could not be found. In fact there were probably many from which to choose. Most Argentine gauchos found work on ranches only a few weeks or months a year, usually hiring themselves out by the day during roundup and branding time. In most cases that was all the help most ranchers needed, since the average Patagonia ranch could be operated with a small staff of peons (unskilled laborers). Probably in a little more demand were the broncbusters, or *domadores*, but even they usually traveled from ranch to ranch and were paid by the day. Only a few gauchos held positions on ranches on a year-round basis.[50]

Butch's and Harry's hesitancy to take on more ranchhands that first year might have been due to the pair's unfamiliarity with the Spanish language. According to Raúl Cea they eventually hired a foreman, Alejandro Villagrán, who turned out to be a loyal and conscientious employee. Probably with Villagrán's help they also picked up at least two additional hands, Juan Vidal, a local peon, and Wenceslao Solís, a Chilean.[51]

Butch and Harry likely found that the life of the average cowpuncher in Patagonia differed little from that of his counterpart in the American West. William Buffin, a North American freelance writer visiting the pampas the same year the outlaw pair began ranching, described the Argentine gaucho's life as "seasons of marking calves and foals, of shearing, of maize picking, and of sheer idleness . . . they have their horse racing, and card playing, and cock fighting, and dancing, and love making—all in their own gutsy, untamed manner."[52]

Gaucho horse racing in Argentina was far from the docile sport Butch was familiar with in Utah and Colorado. There were the usual races, but there were also popular variations. A favorite of the gauchos was "crowding horses," in which two riders attempted to push each other off the track while they raced. Argentine gauchos were famous for mistreating their horses. Another popular game, *cinchada*, was a form of tug-of-war in which two horses were fastened together tail-to-tail with rawhide lassos tied to the saddles. The rider who could pull the other backward past a mark was the winner. An even more brutal contest was *pechando*, or "breasting," where two mounted riders facing each other at about a furlong's distance would gallop at top speed and crash head-on. These charges would be repeated until one rider or his horse could no longer continue.[53]

As in the North American West, card playing was popular on the Argentine pampa. Butch, fond of gambling but not necessarily adept at it, was probably introduced to *truco*, a favorite of the gauchos.[54] Played with a forty-card deck, the game included a good bit of clever signaling and table talk, probably not to Butch's liking because of his difficulty in speaking and understanding Spanish.[55] Butch may have preferred taba, a gaucho form of dice in which the players threw the anklebone of a cow or horse and bet on whether it came up heads or tails.[56]

Cockfighting was abundant in most of Latin America, and raising birds and staging contests was nearly an industry in itself. Many towns maintained special cockfighting arenas, collected license fees from the bird owners, and taxed the proceeds of the bouts.[57]

As to lovemaking, women were in short supply on the Argentine pampa. Ranch owners had families of course, but married gauchos found it difficult to get jobs. Ranchers believed that the presence of women on a working ranch only roused jealousy and fighting among the workers, so usually only bachelors were hired. Some of the larger Patagonian towns had prostitutes, but the gauchos were most often served by mobile madams who transported their "girls" from village to village in high-wheeled carts. The arrival of a cart meant an impromptu fiesta. Tents were set up and customers formed lines. As they paid the madam she would give each gaucho a candle, the length of which was based upon how much time they purchased with the lady of choice. When the candle went out the time was up.[58]

While Cassidy may have found little difference between Argentina and the American West when it came to cowpunching, according to one of his pals back in the States Butch had trouble finding a saddle in Argentina that suited him. Elton Cunningham, the saloonkeeper in Mogollon, New Mexico, said that Butch had given him a saddle when he left the ws Ranch. Later, after Butch had settled in Argentina, Cunningham said he received a letter from Butch in which he mentioned that most of the saddles there were the Mexican type with wide pommels and not to his liking. According to Cunningham, Butch wanted the saddle back. He suggested that Cunningham come down and join them in Cholila, and be sure to bring the saddle.[59]

Apparently Butch considered the native Argentine saddle ill-suited to his needs and out of the question. Compared to a North American saddle it was flat and lumpy and probably felt strange to Butch's tail end. Also it had tiny, rounded wooden "toe" stirrups that offered little room for a western boot. Toe stirrups were essential on the Argentine pampa because it was honeycombed with animal burrows that could easily trip a horse and pin a rider if the rider couldn't slip his feet from the stirrups.[60] This risk was so great that the gauchos practiced the survival procedure called *pialar* in which a single rider would gallop down a gauntlet of fellow gauchos with lassos and, as the rider rode past the men would lasso his horse's legs and throw it to the ground. The rider's goal was to slip out of the stirrups and land on his feet with the reins still in his hands. Holding on to the reins was important because on the vast pampa a solitary gaucho who lost his horse might have difficulty making it back to the ranch alive.[61]

In late 1903 Harry and Etta may have left Cholila for another trip to the States. According to the Pinkertons the couple was spotted that winter near Fort Worth, Texas.[62] Also, private records kept by Longabaugh's family, presumably passed on by his sister, Samanna, suggest that Harry and Etta visited the 1904 World's Fair at St. Louis.[63] However, Longabaugh was back in Argentina by late February of that year. It is possible that he and Etta had to cut their trip short because Harry was needed at the ranch. Bulls had to be procured and Butch was unable to straddle a horse, being laid up with his "dose of Town Disease," presumably the result of a risky evening with one of the local ladies.[64]

The following month provincial authorities might have put a momentary scare into Butch. He was detained briefly by the Chubut police on suspicion of having helped a bandit—believed to be a North American named Robert Evans—escape following the robbery of a land company manager.[65]

Moving On

1904–1907

Life at the Cholila ranch for the remainder of 1904 was apparently uneventful; however, by the following spring the situation had changed. On May 5, 1905, in a letter to neighbor John C. Perry, a former Texas lawman who had settled in Cholila about the same time as Butch and Longabaugh, Butch announced that he, Harry, and Etta were leaving Cholila. He did not say where they were going or whether they would be returning, but he gave the impression that he was winding up affairs at the ranch.[1]

According to the records of the Chubut province law enforcement authorities, the outlaws' ranchhand Wenceslao Solis reported that on May 9, 1905, he accompanied Butch, Harry, and Etta to Lake Nahuel Huapi, a two-day ride north into Río Negro Province. From there, Solis said, the trio embarked for Chile and he returned to the ranch with their saddles. Police records also contained a statement by Daniel Gibbon, a Welsh neighbor who had become a close friend of the outlaws, that sometime later in 1905 the trio's ranch buildings and livestock were sold to an Englishman, Thomas T. Austin, manager of a local branch of a Chilean land company.[2] According to Raúl Cea, son of the outlaws' neighbor Pedro Cea, Etta gave their furniture to their ranch foreman, Alejandro Villagrán, who in turn gave some of it to Pedro.[3]

The Chubut authorities, however, believed that before the trio departed for Chile in May, they paid a visit to the town of Río Gallegos (on the southern tip of Argentina) and robbed a local bank: del Banco de Tarapacá. The robbery took place in February 1905, and several versions of the incident have been reported. According to one version the provincial police found witnesses who claimed that three North Americans rented a small house on the edge of town a week or so before the robbery. According to these witnesses, the trio rode into town to buy provisions several times a week. When they did, they rode at a fast gallop both coming and going. The neighbors thought it amusing, and called the trio "those crazy Yankees." It was later decided, however, that there was a method to their madness, because when they robbed the bank and raced out of town on horseback no one thought a thing about it.[4]

It was speculated that the third robber was not Etta but Wild Bunch member Harvey Logan, who supposedly fled the United States in 1904 by way of Mexico, took a ship to Uruguay, and joined his companions at the Cholila ranch sometime shortly after the first of the year.[5] Logan had become a celebrity in the States after breaking out of a Knoxville, Tennessee, jail in 1903, and it was presumed at the time that he had teamed up with his old Wild Bunch pals in South America.[6]

Probably the most accurate version of the Río Gallegos robbery comes from Argentine historian Osvaldo Topcic, whose works were uncovered by Anne Meadows and Dan Buck. In Topcic's account, taken from the contemporary newspaper *El Antárico* and local police files, two North Americans who called themselves Brady and Linden arrived in Río Gallegos and checked into the Hotel Argentino. They claimed to be representatives of a livestock company in Río Negro province looking for land. They opened an account at the Banco de Tarapacá and then circulated around town, dining at the best restaurants and putting on quite a show. They even made a point of buying a telescope and compass, presumably to use in scouting the hinterlands.[7]

But on February 13, 1905, the two men returned to the Banco de Tarapacá and closed their account, giving the impression that their business in Río Gallegos was done and they were returning to Río Negro. The next day, however, they were back at the bank, this time brandishing long-barrelled revolvers.

It was just before closing time and the assistant manager, Arturo Bishop, and the cashier, Alexander Mackerrow, were totaling up the day's business. The gunmen forced the two men to put all of the bank's loose cash into a large, white canvas sack. The shorter of the two robbers, the man who called himself Brady, also picked up a small cash box containing some silver. Later estimates put the value of the cash and silver at about $100,000 in today's money. Once finished with their work, one of the robbers covered Bishop and Mackerrow while the other went outside and tied the canvas sack to his horse. A few minutes later they both rode off toward the Gallegos River. Police and soldiers scoured the back trails for days, but could only come up with a pair of abandoned horses and the empty cash box.[8]

Despite the similarity in methods between this holdup and the Wild

Bunch bank robberies in the United States, there is no conclusive proof that Cassidy, Longabaugh, or Etta were the culprits. The descriptions given to the authorities—the shorter bandit had green eyes, a sunburned complexion, and a closely cropped beard that was somewhere between chestnut and black, and the taller one was about five feet ten inches, had a narrower face with a light complexion, green eyes, blond hair, a regular nose, and an upper lip that moved a lot when he spoke—could have matched Butch and Harry (if Butch had dyed his beard dark), but the robbers were also described as being between twenty-five and thirty years of age. In 1905 both Butch and Harry were pushing forty.[9]

Furthermore, at a recent historical conference Butch and Harry (and presumably Etta) were all but cleared of the Río Gallegos affair. On February 26, 1997, a three-day conference of interested historians was held at Esquel, Chubut. Called the First International Symposium on the Adventures of North American Outlaws in Argentina, Chile, and Bolivia, the gathering brought together scholars and outlaw enthusiasts from both North and South America. Among the participants were Anne Meadows and Dan Buck. After reviewing the results of an exhaustive research effort, the participants concluded that Cassidy and Longabaugh could not have been involved in the Río Gallegos holdup because: (1) the physical descriptions of the perpetrators did not match those of Butch and Harry; (2) several neighbors swore that Butch and Harry were in Cholila at the time of the robbery; (3) Butch's name (the alias he was using) appears on a purchase order at a store in Súnica, a town near Cholila, about the time of the holdup; and (4) a government agricultural survey taken in Cholila during the month of February 1905 indicated that both Butch and Harry were present at their ranch 750 miles from Río Gallegos.[10]

It now appears that the trio departed from Cholila once they learned they were suspects in the Río Gallegos holdup. On June 28, 1905, Harry wrote to their neighbor, Dan Gibbon, from Valparaíso, Chile, that they had just arrived and that "our business went well and we received our money." Harry then informed Gibbon that in two days he and Etta were leaving for San Francisco, adding that "I don't want to see Cholila ever again, but I will think of you and all of our friends often, and we want to assure you of our good wishes."[11]

Butch and Harry may have received word that the law was closing in from the local *comisario*, Edward Humphrys. It was rumored that Humphrys had been ordered by the authorities in Buenos Aires to investigate the duo's criminal activities, but instead he warned his friends that it might be wise to start packing. Humphrys was later relieved of his position, according to a fellow policeman, for "failing to carry out his orders and conducting himself in a manner unbecoming a police officer."[12]

Longabaugh and Etta may or may not have gone to San Francisco.[13] According to Raúl Cea, the three North Americans spent the next several months hiding in the mountains west of their ranch. But still other reports suggest they spent those months somewhere in Chile, possibly Antofagasta, a seacoast town near the northwestern corner of Argentina. In the Pinkerton files there is a memorandum that Longabaugh, using the alias Frank Boyd, became involved in some unidentified legal trouble and had to call upon the U.S. vice-consul in Antofagasta to get it straightened out. This information was supposed to have come from the postal worker in Pennsylvania whom the Pinkertons apparently recruited to read Harry's letters to his family.[14]

Nothing further was heard from Butch, Harry, and Etta until December 1905, when, on the day before Christmas, they made the headlines of Buenos Aires's two leading newspapers, *La Prensa* and *La Nacion*. The robbery at Río Gallegos, over a thousand miles from Buenos Aires, had nearly been forgotten. The suspects' trail had gone cold and local authorities had just about given up any hope of making an arrest. But on December 19, at Villa Mercedes, Argentina, about four hundred miles west of Buenos Aires, another bank was hit. Five days later, thanks to background information provided by Pinkertons' National Detective Agency, the newspapers announced that the suspects were James Ryan, Harry Longbaugh [*sic*], Miss H. A. Place, and Harvey Logan, whom the articles described as bold members of a gang of North American bandits who had been hiding out in Chubut province. In the *La Prensa* article, Miss Place, identified as "Longbaugh's" wife, was described as "an interesting woman, very masculine, who wears male clothing with total correctness, and who is dedicated more to the occupations of men than to those of women." She also was a "fine rider, handles with precision all classes of firearms, and has an admirable male temperament."[15]

Villa Mercedes was well chosen for a bank robbery. The town was a busy commercial center for rich cattle country. Beef was shipped daily by rail to both Buenos Aires and Rosario, and the banks did a thriving business.

The robbery itself was vintage Cassidy: well-planned down to the last detail. It was timed to coincide with the town's major monthly cattle sale, which meant that the bank's cash drawers would be full, and a clean getaway was assured through relays of fresh horses and supplies stashed along the way.[16]

The Banco de la Nación was at the corner of Belgrano and Riobamba streets. According to newspaper accounts, on December 19 four "well-mounted horsemen" rode up to the bank. One stayed with the horses while the other three barged through the lobby door, loudly demanding that the safes be opened. Witnesses said the robbers brandished both guns and knives. The manager of the bank, a Señor Harleb, and a customer, Carlos Ricca, apparently failed to respond quickly enough and the intruders struck them with the butt ends of their revolvers. The treasurer of the bank, whose name was Garcia, grabbed a gun and hastily fired off three shots but failed to hit any of the robbers. Across the street a man named Ventura Domínguez ran over from his office when he heard the gunfire. He was taken inside and lined up with the others, but in the confusion he slipped away. He returned to his office, got his gun, and fired five times as the bandits were fleeing, but he, too, missed. According to bank officials the robbers took between 12,000 and 14,000 pesos, which in today's money would be about $130,000 to $137,500.[17]

The bandits had planned their escape well. After several zig-zags through Mercedes's streets they rode at a hard gallop south out of town. The police, however, were not far behind. According to one account, at one point (probably just north of Buena Esperanza) the outlaws reined up, giving the appearance that they were going to make a fight out of it, but after a few minutes of heavy firing they remounted and were off again.

The bandits rode first south and then west toward the Chilean border. Soon other posses joined the chase, but the robbers were well-mounted and with fresh relays of horses along the way they gradually outdistanced their pursuers. The leader of one of the posses claimed that when the outlaws had worn out their horses they shot them, rather than let the posse-men use them to keep up the chase. Although there were reports that one of the outlaws had been wounded and that the outlaws had to stop now and then to care for him, the posses never did catch up. When a series of torrential rains swelled the rivers and streams the lawmen gave up and returned home.[18]

As the weeks passed the police continued to gather additional information about the bandits. Witnesses said that just before the robbery they saw the suspects drinking whiskey at a bar two blocks from the bank. When shown photos of Butch, Longabaugh, Etta, and Harvey Logan, the owner of the bar identified the first three as being the customers in question. Logan he couldn't identify. Also, the foreman of a ranch outside of town recognized photos of Butch, Harry, and Etta as three Americans who had stayed several days at the ranch and had left only a few hours before the holdup.[19] And on interviewing residents along the bandits' getaway route, the authorities were told that it appeared that the suspects were very familiar with the route they had selected and that they had stashed away supplies at strategic spots along the way. At one spot the police found a raincoat believed to have belonged to one of the robbers. The label had been torn out but it was identified as having been made in North America. Little else was found.[20]

After the Villa Mercedes robbery, Butch, Harry, and Etta may have returned to Antofagasta, Chile.[21] Since Antofagasta is well north of Villa Mercedes, their initial escape route that led south may have been intended to throw off their pursuers, or possibly to take them to a little-known pass where they crossed the Andes into Chile. From there they may have followed one of the many winding sheep and cattle trails down the western slope of the mountains and caught a coastal steamer heading north to Antofagasta.

At this point our outlaw trio slipped into the shadows for a while. On January 10, 1906, the *Buenos Aires Herald* reported that three of the suspected robbers of the Villa Mercedes bank had been arrested in Neuquén Territory, midway between Villa Mercedes and Cholila. However, three days later the police admitted they had made a mistake and that the persons who had been arrested, apparently also North Americans, had been released. Later the three filed claims against the Argentine government for illegal detention.[22]

Sometime in 1906 Longabaugh hired on with a railroad construction contractor named Roy Letson to drive mules to La Paz, Bolivia. Letson remembered Harry as a rather shy man who kept to himself most of the time. He was also the restless type, Letson said, and before long, he moved on.[23]

By then Etta Place may have been long gone. According to Butch, Etta had been stricken with what appeared to be appendicitis, and Longabaugh had taken her back to the States to a hospital in Denver for surgery. He apparently left her there and returned to South America alone.[24]

After leaving the employ of Roy Letson, Longabaugh is believed to have gone to work for the Concordia Tin Mines at Tres Cruces, Bolivia, about seventy-five miles southeast of La Paz. This information was later obtained from a North American mining engineer, Percy Seibert, who at the time was also working at the Concordia site.[25] Shortly thereafter Butch also showed up at Concordia looking for a job. At the time, the manager of the mine, Rolla Glass, needed a man to travel into La Paz with purchase orders for livestock and other goods and equipment, as well as bring the payroll back out to the workers at Tres Cruces. Apparently Glass saw in Butch a man he could trust, and he offered him the position. Seibert said that Glass found Butch an "excellent and trustworthy employee." He was also "a good bargainer and always rendered a strict account of funds turned over to him." Seibert said Butch often carried cash that reached six figures, yet as far as he knew he never betrayed the trust Glass placed in him.[26] At Concordia Butch used the name Santiago Maxwell, and Harry Longabaugh called himself Enrique Brown.[27]

Seibert, like Rolla Glass, was impressed with Butch. Years later he wrote: "Butch Cassidy was an agreeable and pleasant person. . . . He took well with the ladies and as soon as he arrived in a village he made friends with the little urchins and usually had some candy to give them."[28] Seibert could never get close to Longabaugh, however. While he had no trouble getting along with him, to Seibert Harry seemed to remain somewhat distant.[29]

In September 1906, Cassidy's and Longabaugh's criminal escapades in South America were the subject of an article in the magazine section of the *New York Herald*. The title of the piece blared "Yankee Desperadoes Hold Up the Argentine Republic." The piece was mostly fiction; in his description of the Villa Mercedes robbery the author wrote that one of the bandits shot the bank manager in the head, which never happened. Also, perhaps to make the article more interesting, Wild Buncher Harvey Logan was resurrected from the grave and added as a third outlaw. In one account Logan and Butch were supposed to have been traveling through the mountains on a stagecoach when they discovered that a fellow passenger had with him a trunk containing a large amount of gold. The two outlaws, in what the author described as a "playful mood," waited until the coach reached a place where the road ran adjacent to a deep ravine and pitched both the passenger and the driver "headlong into the abyss below." They then gathered up the gold, unhitched two horses from the coach, and rode off bareback, "escaping unmolested to their distant plateau" (wherever that was).[30]

Sometime in April 1906, Longabaugh returned to Cholila; according to Wenceslao Solís, Longabaugh came back to arrange for the sale of two hundred sheep and thirty mares that he and Butch had left under the care of Dan Gibbon.[31]

In November 1907, both Butch and Harry took leaves of absence from the Concordia mine and, with a third man (probably a co-worker) made a trip three hundred miles east to Santa Cruz, Bolivia, possibly with the intention of finding land in which to invest. Butch was clearly impressed with the area. In a letter to his fellow workers back at the mine, some of whom may have been interested in doing the same thing, Butch wrote that land was cheap and a good investment, mainly because a railroad was being built from Puerto Suárez that would connect Santa Cruz with towns in southwestern Brazil. Except for periodic water shortages, said Butch, the area was ideal for both crops and cattle yet neither was being raised. (Butch believed that this was because the locals were too lazy to dig wells.) Game was also plentiful, he said, and could be taken right along the mountain roads.[32]

Butch was also impressed with the town of Santa Cruz, joking that it had a population of 18,000, of which "14,000 are females," one of whom he evidently wasted little time in romancing. About her, he wrote: "The lady feeds me on fine wines and she is the prettiest little thing I ever seen." However, he did not expect the relationship to last, complaining that the lady had a "nasty" papa who was likely to bring an end to his little arrangement.

When Butch wrote the letter, he and Longabaugh had been in Santa Cruz for about three weeks. He told his friends that the two of them were planning to head south in a few days and would be returning to Concordia in about a month.[33]

One thing that Butch did not mention was that while they were looking for a place to stay in Santa Cruz, they dropped into the local sheriff's office. There on the wall were Wanted posters for Butch Cassidy and Harry Longabaugh. According to the story, Butch jokingly told the sheriff that he would keep his eyes open for these men, and if he saw them he would notify the sheriff and they would split the reward. Butch and Longabaugh were apparently in little danger of being arrested, however; according to the friend who went with them, by then Butch was wearing a heavy bushy beard that made him nearly unrecognizable, and Longabaugh had put on quite a bit of weight since the photograph on the Wanted poster was taken.[34]

The boys at Concordia eventually learned that Butch and Longabaugh were outlaws. As Seibert told it, Longabaugh, while on a trip in the southern Bolivian province of Potosi, had stopped in the town of Uyuni. While having a few drinks in a local taberna he met a fellow North American. They got talking about life back in the States, and one thing led to another. Harry, well into his cups, began boasting about the holdups he and Butch had pulled off before coming to South America. Word got back to Concordia and their secret was out.[35]

According to another story, Rolla Glass learned from one of his engineers that Butch and Longabaugh were fugitives; his employee had identified them from a Pinkerton Wanted circular he had seen in Buenos Aires.

Glass decided to say nothing, hoping that the two men would continue to behave themselves at Concordia. However, one night a fellow employee thought he overheard Butch and Harry discussing a holdup. The employee assumed that they were talking about robbing the Concordia mine office and he ran to tell Glass. When Glass confronted them, Butch admitted that they were on the law's Wanted list, but he assured Glass that they did not rob people they worked for. That seemed to satisfy Glass.[36]

The revelation about the pair's past did not seem to bother Percy Seibert either, who still welcomed Cassidy and Longabaugh at the supply camp he operated near mine headquarters. Butch especially enjoyed these visits; Seibert had a large Gramophone record collection and Butch loved to listen to the music on the wind-up player. Eventually Butch's outlaw reputation turned out to be an advantage for Seibert, who later wrote: "He allowed no other bandits to interfere with my camp and told them when they needed an animal shod or they needed a meal I would take care of them, but that they should move on and keep their backs toward my camp and not give it the reputation of being a bandit's hangout."[37]

Apparently Seibert was not the only one to benefit from Cassidy's contacts with the local outlaw element. Seibert said that sometime during late 1907 Butch learned of a plot to kidnap and hold for ransom one of the owners of a competing mining operation. According to Seibert, Butch warned the intended victim and even secured a bodyguard for him.[38]

Once the word was out, Butch talked freely with Seibert about his outlaw career in the States, which he claimed he and Longabaugh finally had to abandon because the Pinkertons, the American Bankers' Association, the railroad detectives, and even the U.S. Cavalry were constantly on their trail.[39] One of their closest calls, he said, was right there in Argentina, following the Villa Mercedes robbery. The posse that was quickly formed after the holdup got a lot closer to them than was mentioned in the newspapers.[40]

When Seibert asked Butch why he and Longabaugh had given up the straight life in South America and returned to banditry, Butch told him that settling down was impossible. There was no use trying to hide out and go straight, Butch told him. "There's always an informer around to bring the law on you. After you've started, you have to keep going, that's all. The safest way is to keep moving all the time and spring a holdup in some new place. In that way you keep the other fellows guessing."[41]

Seibert said that Butch apparently could never relax and forget that he was a wanted man. After Rolla Glass left as manager of Concordia, Seibert took over and he and his wife moved into a house near the mine. He said that Butch often came over for Sunday dinners. Seibert remembered that Butch always sat in a chair near the window that overlooked the valley, and when not at the table he always took a seat on a small sofa that gave him full view of all three outside doors to the house.[42]

One day Butch talked to Seibert about Harvey Logan. Butch considered him the most fearless member of the gang. He said that he had used every effort to induce Logan to join them in South America, but Logan had turned him down. Next to Logan, he said the bravest man he had ever known was an express messenger on a train the gang had held up in Wyoming. When Butch ordered the messenger to come out of the express car he had refused. Butch finally had to throw in sticks of dynamite to flush him out, nearly wrecking the car. When the messenger finally came to the door, Butch warned him to come out unarmed. The messenger replied that he was unarmed but Butch didn't believe him, thinking that any man who could stand as much dynamite as he did had nerve enough to shoot it out. Butch was right: when he searched him Butch found a gun. Butch added that when he took the gun from him, the messenger clearly expected Butch to kill him, yet even then he never flinched a bit.[43]

San Vicente

1908

According to Percy Seibert, not long after the boys at the Concordia mine learned of Butch's and Longabaugh's outlaw past, Butch settled up his and Harry's accounts at the company stores and informed Seibert they were leaving. Seibert believed that it was because Butch did not want to bring disgrace to the company by letting it be known that it employed wanted outlaws.[1] However, this probably is giving Butch too much credit. More than likely Butch decided that it was safer to move on.

After Concordia, Butch and Longabaugh may have gone to work for a transportation company in southern Bolivia operated by a Scot, James "Santiago" Hutcheon. The company hauled passengers and freight in mule-drawn coaches and wagons. Hutcheon may have known them as Maxwell and Brown, but it is possible they introduced themselves to others as the Lowe brothers.[2]

Percy Seibert later heard that the two outlaws went across the border to Peru, where they held up a stagecoach they thought was carrying remittance money belonging to the Santo Domingo Mine. However, the Santo Domingo officials, wary of robbers on the lonely mountain trails, had sent a dummy coach ahead of the money coach and the boys rode off empty-handed. Their next holdup, said Seibert, was a train robbery back in Bolivia, near the town of Eucalyptus in Oruro Department, about fifty miles southwest of Concordia.[3] Seibert did not give the date of this holdup, but the newspapers of the day reported two robberies near Eucalyptus in 1908. In May a railroad paymaster was robbed of what in today's currency would be about $90,000. The suspects were believed to be two North Americans who had worked for the railroad that ran between Eucalyptus and La Paz.[4]

After the Eucalyptus robbery, Seibert said Butch and Longabaugh returned to Peru and hid out on the eastern slope of the Andes Mountains at

Sacambaya, an abandoned Jesuit mission near the headwaters of the Amazon. According to Seibert the local authorities knew they were there but would not risk going in after them.[5] The following August the paymaster of a construction company was robbed of an undetermined payroll while traveling on the same railroad. Whether Butch and Longabaugh were responsible isn't known, but the authorities believed that this robbery was committed by the same men who struck at Eucalyptus.[6]

On November 4, 1908, Butch and Harry may have held up an official of the Aramayo, Francke y Compañia mining company and took the firm's payroll. The official, Carlos Peró, was traveling by mule on an isolated trail south of Quechisla, Bolivia, with his son, Mariano, and a servant, Gil González. At a place called Huaca Huañusca they were surprised by two well-armed "Yankees" whose faces were covered with bandannas.[7] According to Peró, one of the bandits was "thin and of normal stature," and the other was "heavyset and taller." They both wore "new, dark-red, thin wale corduroy suits with narrow, soft-brimmed hats." Peró said that when the bandits ordered them to dismount it was in English and "in a very pleasant manner." However, he added that the bandits' rifles "were cocked and ready to fire." He added that they also each carried a Colt revolver and possibly a small Browning revolver on their cartridge belts, which were filled with rifle ammunition.[8]

The bandits knew that Peró was carrying the company payroll. They also knew which package among several contained the money. According to Peró there were two "very similar" packages in his saddlebag, and they immediately picked the correct one without bothering to check the other. They did, however, apparently overestimate the size of the payroll: asking if Peró was not carrying 80,000 *bolivianos* when the actual amount was 15,000.[9]

Before they left they ordered Peró's servant to turn over his mule to them, but left the other two mules where they were. According to Peró, "they undoubtedly planned their retreat carefully; otherwise, they would not have left us with our animals or they would have killed us in order to avoid accusations or to gain time."[10]

Three days later, on November 7, Malcom Roberts, the manager of Aramayo, Francke y Compañia, received a message from a Captain Justo P. Concha of the Bolivian army that the bandits who had stolen the Aramayo payroll had been confronted by an armed patrol in San Vicente, a small village some thirty miles southwest of the site of the robbery. According to the report both robbers had been killed, and the payroll had been recovered.[11]

There are several versions of this shootout. Percy Seibert, who was convinced that Butch and Longabaugh were the two payroll robbers, said that after the holdup they rode to the village of Tupiza, which is southeast of the holdup site. There they learned that word of the robbery had preceded them and the authorities were looking for two North Americans. Worried, they made a hasty departure, intending to go north to Uyuni and possibly from there leave Bolivia for their sanctuary in the Peruvian Andes at Sacambaya.[12]

At San Vicente, which was on the way to Uyuni, they made a fatal mistake. Rather than camp somewhere along the trail the two bandits, in an act uncharacteristic of Butch, rode boldly into the village and rented a room for the night in a small house. Apparently somebody became suspicious of the pair of well-armed "foreigners" and sent word to a Bolivian army patrol that was stopping in Uyuni. The captain of the detail, Justo P. Concha, accompanied by two soldiers and the local sheriff, Timoteo Rios, embarked for San Vicente to check matters out. According to an article that later appeared in *La Manana*, a newspaper published in the nearby town of Sucre, the four-man posse confronted the two foreigners in their casa. Shots were fired and one of the soldiers was killed. Concha ordered the two men to surrender but they answered with more shots, and a gun battle erupted that lasted for more than a half-hour and ended when both foreigners were killed. On searching the bodies, Captain Concha found the stolen Aramayo payroll plus a map of Bolivia on which the outlaws had marked the route they were taking. Marked were the towns of La Paz, Santa Cruz, Cochabamba, and Potosí. After San Vicente they had intended to go to Santa Catalina and then to La Quiaca.[13]

According to Anne Meadows and Dan Buck, who searched local records for reports of eye-witness accounts and any and all other evidence of the incident, the article in *La Manana* seemed to be fairly accurate, except that Captain Justo P. Concha was probably not with the first group that approached the casa and engaged the two bandits.[14]

Meadows's and Buck's search eventually uncovered a file containing a Bolivian magistrate's investigation of the shootout. Included was a statement by the local corregidor, or mayor, who testified that he had encountered the two bandits earlier in the evening when they were looking for a place to spend the night. The corregidor, Cleto Bellot, said that he saw the strangers at the door of a local resident, Bonifacio Casasola, inquiring about a place to spend the night. Since there were no hotels or inns in San Vicente, Casasola, at the urging of Bellot, gave them a room. Bellot said that the two men unsaddled their mules and gave them fodder, then went into their room to chat with Bellot. In doing so, Bellot said, they left their weapons and saddles outside. Bellot said they told him that they had come from La Quiaca and wanted to know the road to Santa Catalina. Later they asked about the road to Uyuni and Oruro. Finally they said they wanted some beer and sardines, and Bellot sent Casasola off to buy them with money provided by "the taller one."

Bellot said that when he left he went directly to the "lodging of the commission" (presumably the equivalent of the town council) and told them about the arrival of the two foreigners. The "commissioners," with loaded rifles, plus two Bolivian soldiers, returned with Bellot to the house. One of the soldiers, a Victor Torres, went ahead and, according to Bellot, "from the door he was shot once with a revolver, wounding him, to which he responded with a rifle shot." Bellot apparently decided that this sort of an affair was not for him and he headed home. On the way he encountered Captain Justo P. Concha, who asked him to try to round up help from the villagers.[15]

While gathering up volunteers, Bellot said that he heard "three screams of desperation" but did not say whether they came from the house or from the men that were now surrounding it. Bellot says that at about midnight one shot was fired by the "inspector," apparently a local policeman, but nothing was heard from the foreigners the rest of the night. Around six in the morning the men approached the room and found the two men dead: "one was in the doorway and the other behind the door on a bench."[16]

Bellot's statement regarding the shootout is probably accurate, and repudiates the account offered by Arthur Chapman as conveyed by Percy Seibert, whose sources were never determined. Seibert's version, more than likely embellished by New York journalist Chapman, is more dramatic. According to Chapman the two bandits did choose to stay all night at San Vicente. Apparently the only accommodations were a one-story collection of casas in the same adobe complex as the office of the town constable, with the two facilities possibly sharing a common courtyard.[17]

Chapman says that the two bandits stopped at the constable's office and let it be known that they needed a place to spend the night. After being given a room they returned to their mules, took off their saddles and blankets and piled them and their rifles in the courtyard across from the door of their hut.

The constable, perhaps simply following a routine practice, checked out the strangers' mules. He recognized one of them as belonging to his friend Gil González, the servant of Carlos Peró, the official of the Aramayo company who was robbed of the company payroll three days earlier. As luck would have it, at the time there was a detail of Bolivian cavalry camped just outside of town, and the constable sent a messenger to the captain telling him of what he had discovered.[18]

The soldiers hurried to San Vicente and surrounded the courtyard. The captain in charge walked to the door of the hut where the two outlaws were preparing to eat and demanded that they surrender. One of the strangers—Harry Longabaugh, according to Seibert/Chapman—was pretty drunk, but Butch was still fairly clear-headed. Although the captain had his gun drawn, Butch turned and drew his pistol and, shooting from the hip, killed him instantly.[19] The outlaws then opened fire on the rest of the soldiers. As Chapman later wrote it, their "revolvers blazed from door and window, and men began to stagger and fall in the courtyard. . . . Cassidy and Longabaugh were firing rapidly, and with deadly effect. Those of the detachment who remained on their feet were firing in return. Bullets sank into the thick adobe walls or whistled through the window and door. Other soldiers began firing from behind the shelter of the courtyard wall."[20]

Chapman says that without their Winchesters the two outlaws stood little chance. Longabaugh decided to try to reach them, shouting for Butch to cover him. Shooting as he ran he got halfway across the courtyard before he fell. When Butch saw that Harry was hit he ran to him and dragged him back inside. Butch tried several times to reach the rifles himself, but each time the gunfire drove him back.

It began to grow dark and shots from the outlaws came less often, suggesting that their ammunition was low. Sometime between nine and ten o'clock the soldiers heard two shots from the hut and then silence. Thinking it was a ruse they continued to fire but did not move in. They waited throughout the night and into the dawn. Around noon of the next day, after having heard no more shots from the outlaws for nearly ten hours, they advanced. On entering the hut they found both men dead. From the appearance of the bodies Butch had put a bullet into Longabaugh's brain, and then used his last cartridge for himself. When the soldiers searched the outlaws' saddlebags they found the money from the Aramayo payroll, as well as gold and silver coins from the holdup at Eucalyptus. They also found a generous supply of antiseptic drugs, a pair of field glasses, and a man's Tiffany watch.[21]

According to Victor Hampton, a mining engineer who worked in San Vicente during the 1920s, the two bandits were buried in an Indian graveyard near where they were killed. Hampton claimed he got this information from Malcom Roberts, the Aramayo company manager.[22]

When Butch's pals back in the States heard rumors that he and Longabaugh had been killed they did not give it much thought. It wasn't the first time that Butch had been reported dead and later turned up very much alive. Some of Butch's acquaintances suspected that he and Longabaugh had started the rumor themselves so that they could return to the United States and live in peace. Supposedly Butch had written some of his friends that things were "getting a little hot" down in South America and that he might be returning some day. But the letters from Butch eventually stopped coming, and letters to him, addressed to various aliases and addresses per his instructions, were eventually returned unclaimed.[23]

While Butch's letters ceased, newspaper accounts of the outlaw pair's antics in South America did not. On February 1910, western papers carried an eastern dispatch about the State Department in Washington having received word from Argentina that Butch and Longabaugh, believed to have been joined by Harvey Logan, had formed a bandit gang so powerful that the government was paying them tribute to keep them from wreaking havoc throughout the country.[24]

That same month Pinkerton hearts may have skipped a beat when a report was received at the Denver office that a train robber arrested in St. Louis had given the authorities the name of Jim Lowe. But the excitement over the arrest soon subsided when further checking revealed that the suspect was a small-time outlaw from Kansas City.[25]

There would be other reports. In 1914 the Pinkertons were notified that Butch had been arrested for murder and was confined to a prison in Antofagasta, Chile. According to the informant, Butch had been working out of Antofagasta as a mule driver for the Nitrate Mining Company. His duties involved leading pack trains loaded with mineral down to the city and returning to the mines with remittances and supplies. As part of his responsibilities Butch was required to make routine visits to a local bank. According to the report, one day he appeared at the bank with an American woman. While the woman distracted the bank officers, Butch attempted to gather up some of the cash lying around but things went sour, and during the fracas Butch shot and killed an Antofagasta city official. In attempting to escape, Butch's horse stumbled and fell and he was captured. The Pinkertons wrote the Antofagasta chief of police in an effort to verify the story, but the agency files did not contain his answer. Also, the report did not mention what happened to the woman. Ann Meadows and Dan Buck attempted to confirm the story but were unsuccessful.[26]

Butch's old outlaw pal Matt Warner apparently accepted the story that Butch was dead. In 1937 or 1938 Matt wrote that Butch and Longabaugh were killed in a fight with soldiers that had been chasing them. Whether Matt based this on Arthur Chapman's account isn't known for sure. Matt's version varied from Chapman's to some extent. Matt wrote that Butch and Longabaugh had stolen an army mule and a reward was offered for their capture. Soldiers then "got on their trail and one night found a mule near their hide-out in some deserted army barracks. Butch and Harry held the whole company off for hours and killed a lot of 'em. But their ammunition give out, and they was killed. Some say Longabaugh was killed first and that Butch kept his last shot for himself." In Warner's opinion it would not have been like Butch to shoot himself. He believed that Butch would have kept all of his shots for the men that were trying to kill him, but otherwise Warner appears to have believed the story.[27]

Warner claimed that some of Butch's friends sent a man named Walker down to South America to find out for sure whether Butch was dead. Warner said that he reported back that the story about the shooting was true and that he had found Butch's grave.[28] According to Charles Kelly, Walker's trip was financed by Matt Warner, Elzy Lay, and others, including Hanksville, Utah, storekeeper Charley Gibbons and a retired rancher, Dr. J. K. W. Bracken. Walker supposedly spoke with soldiers who had been involved in the battle and had even found a photograph of the two dead outlaws. (If there was such a photograph it has been lost.) According to Charles Kelly, although Warner seemed convinced of Butch's demise Dr. Bracken, who supposedly examined the photo, was not so sure.[29]

Dan Buck, for one, does not buy the idea that Butch's pals sent men to Bolivia to check out the shooting story, dig up the grave, and take photographs. "There is no evidence, aside from these old-timer tales, that such a team was ever dispatched, although versions of the story have circulated for years. Even under the best of circumstances, it would have taken several months to a year for Butch's friends to learn of his demise, organize a team, and get it to San Vicente. Not a hint of such an event has ever surfaced in Bolivia in the expatriate mining community, the American diplomatic corps, or Bolivian government circles."[30]

The expedition story does seem far-fetched; however, as to the time factor mentioned by Buck, exactly when Butch's friends learned of his death isn't clear. Also, as to the fact that no hint ever surfaced locally regarding such an expedition, the team may not have been dispatched to San Vicente or even Bolivia. At the time Matt Warner believed that Butch was killed in Argentina.[31] The team may have been looking in that country.

Will Simpson, the prosecuting attorney who sent Butch to prison in 1894 also believed that Butch met his end at San Vicente. In 1939 Simpson, then in the private practice of law in Jackson, Wyoming, said that he knew two men who went to South America to verify the story and that he had talked to one of them "no more than three months ago."[32] This would have been around February 1939.[33]

Over the years those who believed that Butch and Sundance did not die in Bolivia point out that the Bolivian officials never identified the two men who were killed at San Vicente. While the Bolivian authorities apparently believed that the dead men were the same ones who stole the Aramayo payroll, the men's names, if they were known at the time, were not released to the public. However, aliases believed to have been used by Butch and Longabaugh have been indirectly linked to the shootout. Anne Meadows and Dan Buck discovered copies of correspondence written in July and September 1909 between the American legation in La Paz, Bolivia, and the American consulate in Antofagasta, Chile, regarding an inquiry into the identities of the dead outlaws. Frank Aller, vice-consul in Antofagasta, wanted a copy of the death certificate of one of the victims, a man he said was named either Boyd or Brown who had been living in Antofagasta. Aller said a Chilean judge needed proof of his death to settle his estate. In one of the letters it was mentioned that the other victim at San Vicente was named Maxwell.[34] According to the 1906 Pinkerton report on Butch and Longabaugh, Harry was using the alias Frank Boyd in Chile, possibly in Antofagasta, and according to Percy Seibert, Brown and Maxwell were the names Longabaugh and Butch had used when they signed on with the Concordia Tin Mine.[35]

The Bolivians replied to inquiries that the identities were not known. However, two years later, on January 21, 1911, a Bolivian official sent a letter to Aller stating that he was enclosing "a complete record of the case of Maxwell and Brown, drawn up by the authorities of the district where they were killed, and which I hope will be of some use to you."[36] Meadows and Buck found a copy of the letter but not the record it was supposed to have contained; apparently the sender had sent the original to Aller without making a copy.[37]

While nothing has been found to conclusively identify the two men killed at San Vicente, Buck's and Meadows's dogged efforts did turn up further details on the shootout, including the missing judicial records (the Bolivian equivalent of an inquest file). The documents had been taken by another Cassidy-Longabaugh researcher, Roger McCord of New York City. McCord learned of Dan's and Anne's search, got in touch with them, and the three shared their information.

In the judicial records was a summary of the statements of Carlos Peró, victim of the Aramayo holdup, his son Mariano, and his servant Gil González. Although their attackers had been masked, all three stated that they recognized the bodies laid out in San Vicente as the same men who robbed them. Carlos Peró stated: "[D]espite having seen no more than the robbers' eyes and the corresponding parts of their faces at the time of the robbery, I recognized both of them, without any sort of doubt, as well as the hats they wore, with the exception of their clothing, which is different from what they wore at Huaca Huañusca." Peró added that one of the mules captured with the robbers was the Aramayo mule taken during the holdup.[38]

The judicial records also contained a statement from one Remigio Sànchez, who claimed to have been an eyewitness to the gun battle at San Vicente. According to Sànchez, when the shooting was over the soldiers entered the hut and found "the smaller gringo stretched out on the floor, dead, with one bullet wound in the temple and another in the arm. The taller one was hugging a large ceramic jug that was in the room. He was dead, also, with a wound in the forehead and several in the arm." Both of the dead men, said Sànchez, were "unshaven blonds, with somewhat turned-up noses, the small one a bit ugly and the large one good-looking."[39]

A Bolivian official, Aristides Daza, who apparently was formally involved in the investigation, testified that he had also entered the hut where the battle had taken place and found a body in the threshold of the door "with a revolver that appeared to have been fired. Presently, I focused in on the other individual, who was on a bench, having used an earthen jug as a shield, finding him dead. . . . I proceeded to remove the bodies, beginning with the first one, who was in the doorway. In his pockets were money, personal effects, and some pounds, as described in the inventory."

The list of personal effects of the dead men contained several interesting items. On the body of the smaller victim (presumed to have been Butch) were the usual personal items (money, comb, pocket mirror, etc.,) and also seven personal cards inscribed with the name Enrique B. Hutcheon. In addition there was an ammo belt with 121 unspent Winchester cartridges. On the body of the other man were similar personal items plus 149 Mauser and Winchester cartridges and an English dictionary (apparently not a Spanish-English dictionary, but an English dictionary). Also, in the pair's saddlebags were 14,400 *bolivianos*.[40]

The cards with the name Enrique B. Hutcheon were a mystery. If it was Butch, why would he have seven cards of a person named Hutcheon? Was Butch intending to establish a new alias? Or was the body really that of a man named Enrique B. Hutcheon? Dan Buck doubts that it was Hutcheon.

For one thing, Hutcheon's name turned up in a Tupiza, Bolivia, newspaper on November II, 1908, as being registered at a local hotel.[41] Also, thinking that Enrique B. Hutcheon might have been related to James "Santiago" Hutcheon of Tupiza, Bolivia, for whom Butch and Longabaugh supposedly worked following their stint at the Concordia mines, Buck and Anne Meadows wrote to James Hutcheon's descendants, who said they thought Enrique might have been James's half-brother. Buck believes that if the authorities had reason to suspect that James's half-brother was one of the Aramayo bandits, that fact would have been known.[42]

As unlikely as it may seem, the possibility that the dead man could have been Enrique Hutcheon does raise an interesting question: local legend had it that one of the two bodies buried in the San Vicente cemetery after the shootout was that of a Chilean.[43] Also, several reports of the South American robberies attributed to Cassidy and Longabaugh (including the holdup of the Aramayo payroll) mentioned that one of the robbers appeared to be Chilean rather than a North American.[44] However, Dan Buck cautions not to make too much of this. He writes: "There were half a dozen Bolivian newspaper accounts of the holdup and shootout and, like newspaper accounts of crimes in the U.S., they vary widely in accuracy. The Bolivian newspapers described the bandits as two Yankees, a Yankee and a Chilean, and a Yankee and a Dane." Also, says Dan, "Carlos Peró, the man they held up, says the bandits were Yankees and spoke English."[45]

The officials at the American Legation at La Paz were apparently satisfied that Butch was one of the dead bandits. In May 1913, while traveling in South America, a carpenter from Missouri named James Lowe was arrested by the Bolivian authorities on suspicion of being "George Parker," the North American bandit. According to State Department records, Lowe sought help from the American Legation. He was eventually released, presumably after legation officials produced evidence that included "assertions by certain Englishmen and others that a man known as George Parker had been killed in one of the provinces two or three years ago while resisting arrest."[46]

To Dan Buck and Anne Meadows, who became consumed by the riddle of Cassidy's and Longabaugh's fate, the only logical solution was to try to have the bodies in the San Vicente cemetery exhumed. Again, the researchers met with good fortune. While looking up names of forensic experts in hopes of persuading one to join them in digging up the bodies, an expert found them. He was Clyde Snow, a forensic anthropologist from Oklahoma. Snow was just the man they needed. Identifying bodies was his specialty, and he had an impressive record of working on high-profile cases, including the identification of Nazi war criminal Josef Mengele in Brazil. It was pure serendipity: while on a project in Argentina, Snow had become curious as to what really happened to Butch Cassidy and Harry Longabaugh.[47]

With Snow's reputation and Meadows's and Buck's enthusiasm, it was not difficult to find a sponsor for the expedition. Since the project seemed ideal for a PBS documentary, Boston public television channel WGBH and the producers of the TV program *Nova* signed on.[48]

From Froilán Risso, the son of the former caretaker of the cemetery at San Vicente, based upon information obtained from the inquest documents, Dan and Anne had located what was believed to be the graves of the outlaws. Next, they obtained the necessary permissions from the appropriate Bolivian officials to exhume the bodies. Once this was done, an exhumation team led by Snow, accompanied by Dan and Anne, headed for San Vicente.[49]

After several stops and starts, the team was eventually able to remove one skeleton from the grave, plus a piece of a skull from a second corpse.[50] According to Snow's estimate, the skeleton was of a man between five-feet eight-inches to six-feet two-inches in height. From the shape of the bones, Snow figured he probably was caucasian. Because of decomposition, it was difficult to tell if there were any bullet holes, but there did appear to be one in the frontal sinus area. Furthermore, there were copper stains near the eye socket and also near the elbows, both of which may have come from metal fragments. Among several items found with the body was a button of the type mentioned on the inventory list of the bandits' personal effects in the inquest file. More importantly, however, were the boots. Loosely attached to the corpse's feet, Snow and his companions found the decaying soles of a pair of small men's boots. This was encouraging, because for a man of his height (probably somewhere between five-feet nine-inches to six feet), Harry Longabaugh was said to have had small feet.[51]

Clyde Snow obtained permission to take some of the bones back to his laboratory in Oklahoma for a detailed forensic analysis, where x-ray studies of the skeleton confirmed the presence of metal fragments embedded in the skull and also revealed an old wound, possibly from a gunshot, in the lower left leg. This sparked interest because of rumor that Longabaugh had once been treated for a gunshot wound. The next obvious step was DNA analysis. Here, however, the investigators ran into a temporary problem. For a DNA comparison with a living Longabaugh relative, a maternal descendent of Harry's was needed, and none could be found.[52]

However, this obstacle would eventually be overcome, apparently by a refinement of the DNA testing process that allowed comparison with a paternal descendent. But when an analysis was finally performed and a DNA comparison made with Longabaugh's relatives, no match could be found, thus excluding the possibility that the skeleton was Harry's.[53]

The DNA from the remains was also compared with Parker family samples, with the same results—no matches.[54] The partial skull from the second corpse was found to be that of a Native American and not Caucasoid.[55]

Then came disheartening news (or was it disheartening?). The exhumation team had probably been digging in the wrong grave. Photographs taken of the exhumed grave in 1972 revealed a headstone with a plaque bearing the name of a German miner, Gustav Zimmer. Sometime between 1972 and Dan's and Anne's first visit to the cemetery, the plaque had been removed.[56]

While the search for the true identity of the victims at San Vicente is not over, Buck and Meadows believe that the evidence, though not conclusive, strongly points to Butch and Harry being the bandits who died that night.[57] One cannot ignore, they say, the statements of Aramayo official Carlos Peró and Frank Aller of the U.S. consulate in Antofagasta, Chile; the aliases the bandits used; their physical descriptions, which so closely match Butch's and Harry's; the similar modus operandi used in the Aramayo and earlier robberies; and the pair's apparent disappearance after the shooting.[58] Dan and Anne are fairly certain that Butch's and Harry's remains lay resting in San Vicente, either in the cemetery in an unmarked grave or just outside the cemetery confines in unconsecrated ground that rural Bolivians sometimes reserve for uninvited guests.[59] Clyde Snow believes that he and his crew probably had the right grave but just need to dig deeper. He expects to give it another try. "I have a feeling," he says, "that I'll be going back to San Vicente someday and get into the other graves under that headstone."[60]

The exhumation of the graves had a decided effect on the village of San Vicente. With the publicity generated by Buck's and Meadows's visits and the later Snow expedition, Froilán Risso became San Vicente's self-appointed oral historian on the 1908 shootout. After the exhumation team's departure, Risso, in his late fifties and one of the oldest residents of the town (apparently living in San Vicente is not conducive to old age), seemed to acquire many additional facts surrounding the battle, which he originally claimed came from his father who had entrusted him with the solemn duty to pass the story on for the ages. When asked why he never told these stories before Buck's and Meadows's visit, Froilán's answered "No one ever asked me."[61]

Today the town proudly displays its own small collection of bones—presumably those unearthed by Snow and his crew and left in San Vicente—as the remains of the famous North American bandits. It is hoped, say the townspeople, that these remains will eventually attract many tourists and make the town rich.[62] Fame may not come easily. To reach San Vicente travelers must endure a fourteen-hour train ride from La Paz, the Bolivian capital, and then a treacherous three-hour trek by four-wheel-drive vehicle over the mountains.[63] Unfortunately the town has little else to attract tourists. Although it has over 1,600 inhabitants, San Vicente still has but one school and one church and overall conditions there have improved little since 1908. It is not uncommon, even today, to see pigs and dogs fighting in the streets for the scraps of food that float along in the open sewers.[64] Except for devout Wild Bunch fans, San Vicente does not have much to recommend it as a remarkable place to visit.

Horizons

Death may be inevitable, but it's not always determinable. It has been compared to an horizon which, unlike life, is limited by our sight.

Rossiter Worthington Raymond, *A Commendatory Prayer*

Word of the San Vicente shootout was slow to reach the United States. As late as 1921 the Pinkertons still assumed that Butch and Longabaugh were alive and still living somewhere in South America. In fact, nothing has ever been found in the Pinkerton files to suggest that the Pinkerton agency ever officially declared the two outlaws dead.[1]

When Lula Parker Betenson and the family heard the news that her brother and Harry Longabaugh were killed, she said at first they doubted the stories but later they began to fear that it might be true. They were especially sickened, Lula said, with the thought that in the fatal shootout Butch may have added murder to his crimes.[2]

Then one day—Lula did not give the year—a childhood friend of Butch's, Circleville neighbor Jim Gass, came home from a trip to California with startling news that he had seen Butch getting on a train in Los Angeles. He said that he was sure that it was Butch—they had even waved at each other—but then the train pulled out and he was gone. According to Lula this was the first of several rumors the family would hear, rumors that would keep up their hopes that her brother might still be alive.[3]

According to Lula the Parker family's prayers were answered in 1925. By then the family had moved to town but still owned the homestead in Circle Valley. It was a fall day, she said, and her brother Mark was working out at the ranch fixing fence. As Mark told it later, a new black Ford touring car pulled up to the house and a man got out and started across the field to where Mark was working. From a distance Mark thought it was his cousin, Fred Levi, but as the man got closer he recognized that "characteristic Parker grin." It was Robert LeRoy Parker.[4]

After much back-slapping the two brothers drove into town to the old brick house where their eighty-one-year-old father, Max Parker, was living with several of his bachelor sons. Lula, now married and with her own family, lived only a short distance away and was summoned to fix supper for the men. At first she did not recognize her brother. When their father finally told her who he was, she said: "My knees felt like rubber, and my insides turned upside down."[5]

Why had Butch waited so long to get in touch with his family? He said he had wanted to but he was too ashamed; he said he felt too much sorrow for bringing them such embarrassment.

According to Lula, Butch said that he and Harry Longabaugh had planned to return from South America together, but he had developed a leg problem (he thought from a scorpion bite) and was laid up for several weeks. When the time came to go he was still too weak and Harry returned without him.[6]

When asked about the shootout in San Vicente, Butch said that he read more about it after he returned to the States than he knew about it in South America.[7] He had heard that Percy Seibert had identified him and Longabaugh as the victims, apparently thinking he would do them a favor by allowing them to bury their past.[8]

Lula said Butch told her that after leaving South America he spent a good bit of time in Mexico. While in Mexico City he ran into Etta Place, who told him that she and Longabaugh were living right there in the city. He said he visited with them for several days, but then apparently got restless and decided to move on. He said that he had not seen them since. After Mexico he did some traveling in Europe, especially Italy, which he liked very much. He also spent a year or so in Alaska but didn't like the cold. He did, however, like the Northwest—apparently meaning the northwestern United States—which he said was now home to him.[9]

According to Lula, Butch and the family visited long into the night, recalling childhood events and special good times. Butch stayed with his father for several days and then he and Mark rode up into the hills southwest of Circle Valley to visit with his other brothers who had a cabin there. All in all Butch's visit lasted a little more than a week. Before he left he asked that nobody mention that he had been there. Lula said that everyone agreed to do as he asked, and that for years they kept it their little secret.[10]

When news leaked out in the early 1970s that Lula was writing a book about her brother, it created quite a stir among the handful of Wild Bunch historians in existence at the time. At first Lula was receptive to their letters, but then she began complaining about being misquoted and she clammed up, telling those who wanted to know more about Butch that they would have to wait for her book.[11] Before she quit answering questions, some of what she had to say about her brother may have been reported inaccurately. One tabloid account had Butch revealing to her that the victims of the shootout at San Vicente were just a couple of "greenhorns," that on the night of the shootout Longabaugh was off somewhere tending to business matters and Butch was several miles away in an Indian hut recovering from a scorpion bite.[12] This version never appeared in her book.

While Lula's book was eagerly awaited by outlaw enthusiasts, the publishing industry did not get overly excited about it. Lula had begun putting her story together in the late 1960s, shortly after the filming of the movie *Butch Cassidy and the Sundance Kid*. By 1970 she assumed that it would soon see the light of day.[13] However, she was turned down, and a rumor spread that it was because she would not reveal the date and place of Butch's death.[14] Another publisher was found—Brigham Young University Press—which brought the book out in 1975 to immediate success.

But Lula had her detractors. Foremost was Wild Bunch researcher Jim Dullenty, who at the time was working on his own book on Butch. Dullenty doubted the accuracy of Lula's story about Butch's return, and he found similar doubts among members of Lula's own family. Dullenty had interviewed Max and Ellnor Parker, son and daughter-in-law of Dan Parker, Butch's brother and, according to Dullenty, Max and Ellnor said that Butch came back all right, though not in 1925 as Lula had said, but five years later.[15]

Larry Pointer also interviewed Max and Ellnor. Pointer says that they told him that Butch visited them in Milford, Utah, in 1930, while they were taking care of Dan, who was then in his early sixties and in ill health. The Parkers said that Butch came to the house with two other men and talked to Dan Parker for several hours. Ellnor Parker said that she remembered the day clearly because Butch sat and rocked her young son, Max Jr. The Parkers said that following the visit, Dan regularly received letters from Butch, some of which contained money. Dan always destroyed the letters but the Parkers said that he did reveal to Ellnor that Butch was living in Spokane under the name William Phillips. According to Pointer, in 1970 when Lula began releasing information about Butch's return, Ellnor Parker wrote her about the 1930 visit and told her what Dan Parker had said about Butch using the alias William Phillips. Ellnor said that Lula wrote back, asking her not to share that information with anyone else.[16]

According to Bill Betenson, Lula's grandson, some members of the Parker family did not want Lula to write the book because of the agreement made by Butch's father and the family that they would never reveal the true details of Butch's return.[17] Bill Betenson clearly challenges Jim Dullenty's view that Lula's statements deserve scrutiny. "Lula did not lie," Betenson says.[18] He insists that Butch's visit to Circleville in 1925 was confirmed by Lula's son Mark.[19]

Lula Parker Betenson and her brothers were not the only persons who claimed to have seen Butch after he was presumed killed in South America. Josie Bassett, who sometimes considered Butch her "Brown's Park Beau," claimed that she visited with him several times in the late 1920s and early 1930s. The first time was in Nevada in 1928 and the second, in 1930, was in Baggs, Wyoming. According to Josie, Elzy Lay was with Butch in Baggs, and he and Elzy came to where she was staying. "We had a good visit, talking over old times." Josie said she saw Butch two more times, once in Rawlins and again in Rock Springs, Wyoming.[20] Harv Murdock, Elzy Lay's grandson, said that Josie's recollection of the date of the meeting in Baggs with Butch and Elzy was probably accurate because Elzy visited Harv's mother at the Murdock ranch near Baggs about the same time.[21] Still curious about Josie's recollections, Harv Murdock decided to test her during a visit to her home in her later years. He said he challenged her with "You know very well Butch was killed in South America." Josie answered, "I know Butch Cassidy a hell of a lot better than I know you. He was here in Baggs in about 1930." Murdock said that three more times he challenged her but she repeated the story in almost the same words every time.[22]

A Rock Springs resident also reported seeing Butch but at a much earlier time. John Taylor, a local auto dealer and garage man, told Brown's Park historian John Rolfe Burroughs that one day in 1922 Cassidy drove into Taylor's shop in a Model T to get some work done on the car. "He was pulling a two-wheel trailer loaded with camping gear," Taylor said, and he "asked me a lot of questions about old-timers around Rock Springs. He didn't tell me who he was, but I recognized him."[23]

According to Larry Pointer, two years later, Tom Welch, a Wyoming pioneer who claimed to have also known Butch in the old days, said that Butch stopped to visit him in Green River, Wyoming. Welch also said that Butch was driving a Model T and was towing a two-wheel trailer with camping gear.[24]

Another old-timer from Butch's Wild Bunch days, Tom Vernon, the unofficial "mayor" of Baggs, told of a reunion with his friend "sometime in the twenties." Vernon said that Butch stayed with him in Baggs for two days. There was no mistake that it was Butch, Vernon said, recalling the days when Butch and his gang had the run of the town. "I played at the dances he and the other members of the Wild Bunch threw in Baggs."[25]

In the summer of 1925 Butch was spotted near Jackson, Wyoming. Boyd Charter, then a boy of seventeen, said that a man whom his father knew from the old days spent part of the summer camped in a grove of trees near the Charter ranch. Boyd said that Butch didn't talk much, but he did invite Boyd to hunt sage chickens with him. Later, after the man had left, Boyd overheard his father tell Will Simpson, the prosecuting attorney who sent Cassidy to prison in 1894, that it was Butch who had camped on his ranch.[26]

Another eyewitness who claimed to have seen Butch and recognized him from bygone days was Edith MacKnight Jensen, daughter-in-law of Josie Bassett. Edith was seventeen when her family moved to Brown's Park. Her father, Stephen Embrey, homesteaded in Moffat County, Colorado, on the lower end of Pot Creek. According to Edith, in 1928, following her marriage to Chick MacKnight (Josie's son), she and Chick went on a trip to Nevada with her aunt, Ann Bassett Willis, and Ann's husband, Frank Willis. The trip was presumably to check on a mining claim Ann had an interest in, but the real reason, said Edith, was to see Butch, who had a cabin in Pahrump Valley about fifty miles west of Las Vegas. Edith said she knew for sure it was Butch. "If you ever got a close look at his eyes, you'd never forget those eyes."[27]

Crawford MacKnight, Ann Bassett's nephew, tells of an earlier trip by Ann to the Nevada mining camp and her first reunion with Butch. MacKnight said that a man known around the area as Doc Masson came into camp one day and kept "looking Ann over." Later, when the man got Ann alone he asked about certain events that occurred at Brown's Park when Ann was young. He would not come right out and tell her who he was, but he did say that she knew him. Finally, he said, "When we were young I knew you well. I had many a meal at the Bassett cabin." Then she recognized him. It was Butch, wearing a black goatee. Afterward, when he wasn't looking, Ann took pictures of him and later compared them to earlier pictures of Butch that Maude Davis had kept. According to MacKnight, if you held your hand over the lower part of the man's face in the picture you could clearly see it was Butch.[28]

Gold was first discovered at the gold camp in Pahrump Valley in 1890 when the mine was called "Chispas," a Spanish word used locally for "gold nugget." This mine pinched out in 1899 but a new vein was found nearby. The new mine was named "Johnnie" after the Indian guide who first brought prospectors to the area. This vein showed real promise, and a camp grew up around the diggings. To work the site properly the owners saw they needed outside help, and around 1900 they leased the claim to a group of Mormons from Salt Lake City. The claim produced so well that when the lease was up the owners declined to renew, having decided to take it over themselves. But the Salt Lake City group refused to leave and continued to work the claim with armed guards. A series of gun battles erupted, and several men were killed.[29]

In 1908 a prospector from Goldfield, Nevada, found a nearby vein that promised even more gold than the Johnnie mine; however, it was eventually abandoned when it was found connected to the Johnnie vein. The Johnnie mine was worked until 1940 when the owner died. In 1941 a couple of promoters out of Hollywood talked the widow of a movie industry big shot into investing in a revival of the mine, but within months they were accused of embezzlement and the project folded.[30]

There are rumors that Butch worked at one of the Johnnie mines. One version claims that he posed as a mining engineer named "Topping," while another says he was simply a night watchman.[31] Some say that Butch died there, a story believed to have originated with Josie Bassett.[32] Lula Parker Betenson herself must have taken these tales seriously, because a close friend, Barbara Ekker of Hanksville, Utah, said that Lula went to the Johnnie and inquired about the stories of Butch's death.[33]

In the early 1980s, Butch Cassidy biographer Ed Kirby visited Johnnie looking for traces of Butch. The place was nearly deserted by then, but Kirby did find an old-timer, Fred S. Cook, who claimed to have once been a reporter for the *New York Daily Mirror*. Cook showed Kirby a grave that some people thought was Butch's. It sat just off the road into town and was surrounded by a small picket fence. The wooden cross said "Bill Kloth." Cook said legend had it that Kloth was a prospector who got careless one day and blew himself up with dynamite.[34] Kirby believes that Butch lived in the Johnnie from the late 1930s until the 1940s, and that he died there in 1944.[35]

A Colorado old-timer, Ray Merrick, believed that he may have met Butch Cassidy once. He says it was in 1923 or 1924, at a spot about fifty miles east of Grand Junction, Colorado. Merrick, probably six years of age at the time, was standing at the side of the road watching his father and another man fix a culvert. A Model T carrying two men and camping gear stopped nearby, and the men got out, took shovels out of the car, and started digging in the ground. The fact that there were two strangers and a boy standing nearby didn't seem to bother them. Eventually the men found what they were digging for: a cache of ten-dollar gold pieces. When they finished they gave Merrick ten dollars and his father and the other man twenty dollars each and said, "Remember, you never saw a thing." Merrick said that several weeks later his father brought home some old cardboard Wanted posters that bore the photograph of Butch Cassidy. He showed them to Merrick and said, "that's the man in the Model T."[36]

According to Lula Parker Betenson, Butch lived until 1937. She said her father received a letter that year from one of Butch's friends, a man calling himself "Jeff," who said her brother died of pneumonia. The writer assured Mr. Parker that his son was "laid away very nicely." Lula said Butch was living in the "Northwest" when he died. She added that where he is buried and under what name is still the Parker family's secret. She said that upon learning of his son's death, Maximillian Parker remarked, "All his life he was chased. Now he has a chance to rest in peace, and that's the way it must be."[37] Lula's grandson Bill says that his grandmother swore that she would never tell where Butch was buried in order to protect Butch's gravesite, figuring that if the public found out where it was it would be desecrated.[38]

But did Butch die when Lula said he did? One of the strangest stories involving his appearances occurred in Price, Utah, in 1939. Two years earlier Butch's old outlaw pal Matt Warner had written in his autobiography that he was convinced that Butch had died in South America. When he heard that persons were claiming that Cassidy was seen back in the United States, Matt called it "poppycock."[39] However, according to Matt's daughter Joyce, her father eventually changed his mind. In later years Matt insisted that Butch had survived the shootout in Bolivia and was, indeed, still alive somewhere. "I believe up until the last few months of his life," Joyce Warner said of her father, "he expected to hear from him."[40]

According to Joyce, Matt almost did. In November 1939, eleven months after Warner's death, a man came to Joyce's home in Price asking for Matt. When she told him that her father had died, the man asked her if Matt had ever talked about a fellow he knew named Butch Cassidy. Joyce said of course he had and that Matt did not believe the story that Butch had died in South America. The stranger then suddenly became talkative, telling Joyce that he had known Matt well and that he, too, had been to South America, and that one time he and Matt had robbed a bank together: the Moffat Bank in Denver, Colorado. Joyce said that she remembered her father telling about that robbery, and that the stranger's version was virtually the same as her father's. Finally, Joyce asked point blank, "You are Butch Cassidy, aren't you?" The stranger admitted that he was and told her how he had left Harry Longabaugh in South America and had returned to the States, and how Longabaugh had found another partner whom he began calling "Butch" apparently as a joke.[41]

The man said that he had moved to the eastern part of the United States, had married and had two daughters. He said that he had worked for the railroad for about twenty years and was now retired. In 1925 he had returned to Circleville to visit his family, but there was a "family argument" and he never went back. He implied that the argument was over his family's contention that his mother had died of a broken heart because of him.[42]

Joyce said the man told her that he had wanted to visit her father earlier but did not know where he was living. He said that he happened to see an old copy of *Cosmopolitan* magazine that contained an article about Matt's book and decided to look him up. Joyce and her mother invited the stranger to stay over but he declined. As he was leaving he asked that they not tell anyone of his visit. Joyce said that he later wrote to them, at least three times, but the letters stopped coming in the spring of 1941.[43]

Steve Lacy, a Salt Lake City Wild Bunch buff who interviewed Joyce Warner about Cassidy's visit, followed up on this story and claims to have discovered that Butch did in fact work for a railroad as Joyce said, and that, over the years, he had resided in several towns using the name Frank Ervin, including El Paso, Texas, Fresno, California, and Goldfield, Nevada. Other than Joyce Warner, Lacy won't reveal his sources, claiming to have all of this interesting information in book form, which he will soon publish.[44]

Goldfield, located in south central Nevada on U.S. Highway 95 about thirty miles south of Tonopah, has been mentioned more than once in connection with Butch Cassidy's post–South America years. Wild Bunch researcher Dan Callan of Etna, California, reported in 1991 that he had discovered that Butch, while working for the railroad (Callan did not give the date) had spent his vacations in the Goldfield area prospecting in the hills around the town. Callan also heard that at one time Butch may have maintained a post office box in Goldfield under the alias "Irwin," "Erwin," "Irving," or "Erving."[45] Goldfield, as the name suggests, was once a boomtown, boasting a population of 30,000 in 1906 and producing gold at an annual rate of $10 million during its peak years. The strike lasted about a decade, but production eventually declined and by the 1920s Goldfield was mostly an afterthought. A few die-hard prospectors stayed on, however, hoping for another mother lode.[46]

The rumor that Butch was in Goldfield may have stemmed from a former would-be member of the Wild Bunch who was hired in 1907 by the Goldfield mine owners to help keep a lid on local labor troubles. The man's name was Thomas Bliss, but he also went by the name Maxwell, an alias used by Butch in South America. Sally Zanjani, whose father was a young attorney in Goldfield at the time, says that the man was actually "Gunplay Maxwell," whom Wild Bunch researchers have described as a "wannabe" member of the gang who never made the grade.[47] Some sources say this may have been the same Maxwell who served time with Butch in the Wyoming Territorial Prison.[48]

The evidence connecting Butch to Goldfield is pretty weak, but an interesting coincidence does exist. One of the early investors in Goldfield was George S. Nixon, the bank official at Winnemucca, Nevada, who was rumored to have conspired with Butch to rob his bank in September 1900.[49] Another interesting coincidence is that the boxing impresario Tex Rickard, who once was mentioned in connection with a rumor that Etta Place took up with an American fight promoter in South America after she left Harry Longabaugh, also was an early Goldfield entrepreneur.[50]

In February 1973, while Ed Kirby was gathering material for his book on Butch Cassidy, he received a letter from Mary Agnes Haymes of Silver City, New Mexico. Haymes said that in 1936 or 1937, when she was around nine or ten years old, her mother introduced her to a Mormon cowboy whom she said was Butch Cassidy. The man had come to Haymes's parents' home to visit Haymes's grandmother. Haymes said the man appeared to be a kind gentleman who seemed to get along well with children. He had a quiet sense of humor, but "laughed easily at others' stories." Haymes said that the man spent most of the time discussing mutual friends and incidents with her grandmother. Before he left the man let the family take his picture.[51] The photo, which appears in Kirby's book, does somewhat resemble Butch, who would by then have been seventy years of age, but the resemblance was not enough to be considered proof that the man was indeed Cassidy.

Was Butch still alive in the 1940s? Kirby thinks he was still living in Johnnie, Nevada, and Joyce Warner claimed that she had received letters from him as late as 1941. Also, in July of that year a young Utah state trooper, Merrill Johnson, was patrolling U.S. Highway 89 between Panguitch and Kanab in southern Utah when he stopped a car with California license plates at Mount Carmel Junction because the driver had ignored a stop sign. He wrote the driver a warning ticket and went about his way.

Trooper Johnson and his wife, who had recently been married, were living with her parents in Kanab. When Johnson pulled into his in-laws' driveway that night he was surprised to see the car with the California plates parked nearby. When he entered the house, still wearing his uniform, the driver of the car looked startled, but Johnson's father-in-law, John Kitchen, said, "It's all right, it's my son-in-law, he lives here. He's O.K." John Kitchen then said, "Merrill, this here's an old friend of the family, Bob Parker—Butch Cassidy—he was passing through and dropped in to say hello."

Trooper Johnson sat down with his father-in-law and the stranger and listened to them trade reminiscences about their youthful days in Utah. Johnson did not remember much of what was said, but did remember that the man said that he had once been in Bolivia and had later been in an automobile accident in California and spent some time in a hospital. He was then on his way to visit his brother, Bill Parker, in Fredonia, Arizona, just south of the Utah line. Johnson said that his father-in-law and the man talked for hours, but he didn't pay too much attention to them and finally went to bed.

The man spent the night with the Kitchens and the next day Johnson drove him down to Fredonia. That afternoon the man's brother drove him back and he left, saying that he was going to Wyoming. Later Johnson tried to remember the name the man had given when he got the ticket, but could not recall it. Apparently Johnson lost his copy. He said that he was later shown pictures of Cassidy and there was no question that the man was Butch.[52] Merrill's wife Ramona backed up his story. She said that Cassidy did indeed visit her parents' home and that her father knew him well.[53]

And then there is the bizarre tale of "The Two Butch Cassidys." According to a Utah miner named Art Davidson, in addition to the Butch Cassidy that most people are familiar with—Robert LeRoy Parker of Circleville, Utah—there was also another Bob Parker. The other Bob Parker was from near Joseph, Utah, and was Robert LeRoy's uncle. The uncle Bob Parker was born in 1875, which made him nine years younger than Robert LeRoy. When uncle Bob Parker was eight years old he was sent to live with Robert LeRoy's parents on their ranch near Circleville. Although this was about the same time Robert LeRoy left home for Telluride, Colorado, during the next twenty-five years Bob and Robert LeRoy crossed paths many times. According to Davidson, it was uncle Bob Parker and not Robert LeRoy Parker who was the leader of the Wild Bunch.[54]

Davidson claimed that he met uncle Bob Parker in Leeds, Utah, in the late 1940s and learned some of the details of the Wild Bunch's adventures from him, but he says that Parker never came right out and admitted that he was one of the two Butch Cassidys.

It appears that Davidson may have been the victim of a colossal practical joke. A family by the name of McMullen who operated the Log Cabin Inn in Leeds made a habit of spreading outrageous tales about the Parker family and the activities of Butch Cassidy. Two of the McMullens, Willard and Bob, were Butch's distant cousins and probably did have access to enough family details to make their fanciful stories halfway believable.[55]

Phillips

In December 1937, while working on the first edition of his book *The Outlaw Trail*, Charles Kelly received a letter from Mart T. Christensen, former Treasurer of the State of Wyoming and at the time the state director of the Wyoming Writers Project, a federally funded WPA program created to provide income to unemployed writers.[1] Christensen wrote that he had heard that Kelly was contemplating a book on Butch Cassidy and the Wild Bunch and he wanted him to know facts that he and his Wyoming field workers had recently discovered, facts that could be highly important to his book.[2]

Butch Cassidy, Christensen wrote, apparently did not die in South America but was seen in Lander, Wyoming, two years previous "by some old friends whom I know personally and whose veracity and memory I do not question for a moment. He [Cassidy] lives in Seattle, Washington, and goes by the name William Phillips."[3]

Christensen felt compelled to write Kelly because of the rumors the field workers were picking up around Lander and because of a letter he had received the previous August from Tacetta B. Walker, author of *Stories of Early Days in Wyoming: Big Horn Basin*. Walker had written Christensen that Butch Cassidy had returned to the Lander vicinity in 1934 and was recognized by two Lander residents who had known him in the early days: Ed Farlow and Hank Boedeker. According to Walker, Farlow said that he knew it was Cassidy because "of an incident he related that only he, Cassidy, and one other knew," and the other man was dead. Walker added that Farlow told her that he believed Cassidy "was going by the name of Bill Phillips in Spokane, Washington."[4]

Kelly was aware of the stories. He and Walker had already been corresponding, and she had given him the same information that she had shared with Christensen. After an exchange of letters she assumed that Kelly would follow up on the stories and get in touch with the mysterious Mr. Phillips.[5]

Kelly's response to Mart Christensen, however, was not what he expected, leading Christensen to believe that Kelly considered the Lander stories of little value. Undaunted, in June 1937 Christensen again wrote to Kelly, suggesting sarcastically that anyone who was interested in the life of Butch Cassidy enough to write a book would certainly want to check these stories out. He said that he had personally talked to Boedeker and Farlow in Lander and believed that they were telling the truth. He added that Hank Boedeker was the deputy sheriff who had assisted in taking Cassidy to the penitentiary in 1894, that during Butch's recent visit to Lander Boedeker had spent the best part of a day reminiscing with him, and that Cassidy gave Boedeker some of the details of the shootout in San Vicente at which Butch was supposed to have been killed. Also, Christensen said there was a third man who could testify to Butch's recent visit: Harry Baldwin, a local merchant who had sold Cassidy some supplies.[6]

If this letter piqued Kelly's interest he was slow to move on it—much too slow—because later that year Kelly learned that William Phillips of Seattle, Washington, had died.[7]

During his research on *The Outlaw Trail*, Kelly had come across several rumors that Butch did not die in South America but had instead escaped, returned to the United States, and been seen in various parts of the West in recent years. Kelly placed very little value in these tales, believing that if they were true, Butch would have returned to his home in Circleville, Utah, to visit his father, who was then in his nineties.[8]

The William Phillips story may have troubled Kelly a little, however, because sometime in late 1937 he wrote to the city of Seattle to see if a death record under that name actually existed. The city's department of health had no information on the man, but the registrar of health records suggested that Kelly write to the State of Washington Bureau of Vital Statistics. He did just that and found a record of the death of a William T. Phillips of Spokane, Washington, on July 20, 1937.[9]

William T. Phillips left a widow, Gertrude, and Kelly wrote to her, asking for information about her deceased husband. At first Mrs. Phillips avoided Kelly's inquiries, but in October 1938 she finally agreed to give him a brief summary of her husband's life.

Her husband was not Butch Cassidy, she wrote; however, both she and her husband had known Cassidy and his family. In fact, she said, her husband "thought he knew Cassidy very, very well." She went on to say that Phillips had been born in the east and came west when he was fourteen. He first settled in the Black Hills of Dakota and later worked on a farm or a ranch somewhere in the corn belt. He "fell in" with Cassidy around the time of Wyoming's Johnson County War. Afterward, Phillips traveled throughout the country some more, spending time back east as a mural decorator in New York City and later operating a machine shop in Des Moines, Iowa. It was about this time that she and Phillips were married. They spent a year in Arizona and then moved to Spokane, where they lived until Phillips's death.[10]

Mrs. Phillips's letter seemed genuine. She concluded with: "So, I'm afraid there is little of interest that I can acquaint you with, concerning the western experiences, tho' I wish I could, for I would very much like to figure out some way whereby I could better myself financially; the depression of '29 is responsible for my present circumstances."[11]

Kelly considered Mrs. Phillips's letter proof that the story of her husband being Butch Cassidy was a hoax.[12]

With the excitement over the coming of World War II, the William Phillips–Butch Cassidy connection was largely forgotten. Then, on May 7, 1942, an article, entitled "Phillips Was Not Butch Cassidy, Say Regan Who Knew Both Men," appeared in the Lander newspaper, the *Wyoming State Journal*. James Regan had operated a sheep camp between Red Bank and Kaycee, Wyoming, at the turn of the century. He claimed that Butch had stopped there several times and that he got to know him. Later, in the 1930s Regan claimed that he also met the man called William T. Phillips during one of his visits to Wyoming. According to Regan, Phillips was not Cassidy. Phillips was a much larger man, Regan said, at least five-feet eleven-inches tall, and weighed 210 to 215 pounds. Cassidy, as Regan recalled, only weighed about 150 to 160 pounds.[13]

The story lay relatively dormant for another thirty years, until December 1972, when an item on the Associated Press wire brought life back into it. On December 18, 1972, a fire broke out at the Priess Hotel in Missoula, Montana. Killed in the blaze was a man identified as Robert Harvey Longabaugh. Further investigation revealed that for several years this man had been going around claiming to be Harry Longabaugh Jr., the son of the Sundance Kid.[14]

Buried in the story was an item stating that Robert Harvey Longabaugh had once claimed that he had been a pallbearer at the funeral of Butch Cassidy in Spokane, Washington. When the wire containing the story came across the desk of the city editor of the *Spokane Daily Chronicle*, he saw the gist of a good local piece. He handed the wire to a young reporter, Jim Dullenty, and suggested that he follow it up.[15]

Jim Dullenty was a good choice to do the story. He had grown up on a Montana ranch and had a strong interest in outlaw history. He immediately went on the hunt.

Gertrude Phillips, William's widow, had died in 1959. However, Dullenty found that the couple had adopted a child in 1919. His name was William R. Phillips and he was still living in Spokane. When Dullenty interviewed him, William calmly told the reporter that the story that his father was Butch Cassidy was an accepted fact, but that his mother had preferred to keep it a secret. Dullenty also discovered that a close friend of the Phillips', a Mrs. Blanche Glasgow, was still living. From Phillips's son and from Mrs. Glasgow, Dullenty was able to piece together much of William T. Phillips's life.[16]

As Dullenty was preparing his article for the *Chronicle*, another writer, Larry Pointer, showed up in Spokane looking for information on William Phillips. Pointer and his wife had been married in Lander the previous year, and their best man was Allan Robertson, a Lander businessman whose grandmother was Dora Lamorreaux, one of Butch Cassidy's girlfriends during the early 1890s. Robertson mentioned this to Pointer and also that Dora had claimed that Butch, whom she then knew as George Cassidy, came back to visit his Lander friends in the 1930s, long after he and Harry Longabaugh were supposed to have been killed in South America. Pointer and his bride were fascinated by the story and spent the summer of 1972 at the University of Wyoming Western History Research Center gathering information on Cassidy. The following year their search led them to Spokane where they crossed paths with reporter Dullenty.[17]

When photographs of William T. Phillips (supplied by his son and by Blanche Glasgow) showed a strong resemblance to Butch, Dullenty and Pointer were sure they were onto something. The two writers joined forces, pooled their resources, and continued the hunt as a team.

As Dullenty and Pointer dug deeper into Phillips's life, evidence suggesting that he and Cassidy were one and the same began to accumulate at a remarkable rate. Interviews with friends and relatives of persons living in Lander, Wyoming, in the 1930s confirmed that Butch had visited there, and that these visits corresponded in time to visits to Wyoming by William Phillips. During one such visit Phillips was accompanied by a friend, Ellen Harris, and her young son, Ben. The son, when interviewed by Dullenty in 1973, recalled that as Phillips walked around the town of Lander, old acquaintances came up to him immediately and called him "George."[18]

From 1935 through 1937 Phillips had exchanged letters with another Wyoming girlfriend of Cassidy's, Mary Boyd, and on one occasion Phillips sent Mary an opal ring inscribed "Geo C. to Mary B." When Phillips died in July 1937, Mary Boyd wrote to a friend of Phillips's in Spokane, stating that she had been Phillips's common-law wife while he was in Wyoming and asked if he would help her secure the return of a tie pin she had given him.[19]

For additional proof that Phillips and Cassidy were the same man, Dullenty and Pointer arranged for a comparison of their handwriting. A letter from William Phillips to Mary Boyd written on December 17, 1935, was given to a handwriting analyst, Jeannine Zimmerman of Aurora, Colorado. She was asked to compare it to a copy of the letter from Butch Cassidy to Mathilda Davis written while Butch was in Cholila, Chubut Province, Argentina. Zimmerman was of the opinion that the letters were written by the same person.[20]

In his book Pointer identified Zimmerman as a "Master Certified Graphoanalyst and Questioned Document Examiner."[21] However, Dan Buck, who reviewed Zimmerman's communications with Pointer, says that she was not a forensic document examiner but a graphologist. Buck points out that graphologists, who "are not held in high regard among forensic document examiners," usually study handwriting and "personality profiling" (as revealed by a person's handwriting) from a correspondence school, and their conclusions are open to question. In addition, says Buck, Zimmerman "didn't conduct a blind test, since Pointer hinted at the outcome he was seeking." Buck says Pointer asked Zimmerman if the two letters, one written in 1902 and the other in 1935, could possibly have been written by the same person given the age difference and health complications at the later age. Taking this into consideration, Zimmerman said yes, they were written by the same person.[22]

Zimmerman also conducted a personality profile on Cassidy-Phillips but, according to Buck, she later cautioned Pointer not to mention this in his book because such an analysis "is not fully accepted in the United States" and "my efforts will appear much more authentic" if the personality business were left out.[23]

The *Spokane Daily Chronicle* also engaged a handwriting analyst to examine the two handwriting samples. This expert, also a graphologist and not a certified forensic document examiner, was of the opinion that the letters "could have been" written by the same person. A third graphologist who saw the articles on Phillips in the *Daily Chronicle* and had volunteered to examine the letters was of the opinion that the letters were not written by the same person.[24]

In the meantime, more interesting evidence turned up. When Dullenty's series of articles on William Phillips began to appear in the *Spokane Daily Chronicle* in the fall of 1973, Blanche Glasgow remembered that William T. Phillips had written a story about Butch Cassidy and the Wild Bunch. According to Glasgow, Phillips had penned the manuscript in 1934 following one of his trips to Wyoming. In the words of Larry Pointer, Phillips had written the story to "set the record straight on the life of Butch Cassidy."[25]

On completing the manuscript, which he titled "The Bandit Invincible," Phillips sent it to his friend Ellen Harris to have it typed. Neither Phillips's original hand-written manuscript nor the typed version has ever been found. However, sometime in the mid-1930s, when Phillips showed Blanche Glasgow his original manuscript, Blanche and her then-husband Bill Lundstrom became fascinated by it. Blanche wrote to Ellen Harris, asking her to send her a typed copy so that she could copy it. When it arrived, Blanche and her daughters, Cleo and Veryl, and her sister, Madge Fields, having no typewriter sat down and copied the entire story in longhand in spiral-bound notebooks.[26]

The original manuscript was replete with spelling, grammatical, and punctuation errors, which Ellen Harris had reproduced in type with little attempt to edit. When copied in longhand by the four women some of these errors were corrected by Madge Fields in the portion she copied; otherwise, Pointer believes the copy that has survived is pretty much as Phillips wrote it.[27]

In amateurish, third-person prose, Phillips awkwardly attempted to portray Butch as a turn-of-the-century Robin Hood. It was hardly an objective effort. Phillips, a former entrepreneur who had once owned his own successful machine shop, had lost his business in the Depression. As a result he had begun to strongly espouse socialist notions, which came across clearly in the manuscript.[28]

Although parts of the manuscript seem to ring true, which suggests that Phillips may have been acquainted with at least some segments of Butch's life, other parts range anywhere from vague and inaccurate to obvious fabrications. Whether the inaccuracies are the result of Phillips's lack of knowledge of the true facts, are the result of a fading memory, or are simply an attempt to write what he believed to be an interesting story isn't clear. In his foreword to the manuscript Phillips states that it was "essential to substitute some of the real names of both persons and places," including holdup sites.[29] If Phillips was actually on the scene during the Wild Bunch's forays, this of course could have been his attempt to protect participants who were still alive at the time of the writing.

To date no one has placed William Phillips in Butch's gang. However,

Will Simpson, the prosecuting attorney who sent Butch to prison in 1894, believed that the man who came to Lander in the 1930s representing himself as Butch was a man who had earlier spent some time in Fremont County under the name of Ed McClellend. According to Simpson, McClellend, also known locally as "Big Ed," left the Wind River area in 1888 but returned five years later to the Lander valley and settled on Willow Creek.[30]

According to Ellen Harris's son Ben, who with his mother had accompanied Phillips on one of his Wyoming trips, it was they who had persuaded Phillips to write the story. By 1934 Ben had changed his name from Harris to Fitzharris and was working in Hollywood as a little-known actor and property man. He thought that the story might be picked up by one of the studios, which in 1934 were cranking out westerns by the hundreds. However, when given the manuscript to send around, Ben backed out, giving as the reason Phillips's inclusion of Butch's adventures in South America, which Ben apparently thought were unrealistic (western outlaws did not run off to places like Argentina and Bolivia).[31] Of course the manuscript was also poorly written and Ben, having his own career goals, may have been embarrassed to endorse it.

When he got nowhere in Hollywood, Phillips shopped the story around among magazine publishers but was repeatedly turned down.[32] He finally gave up and, dejected, probably threw away the original manuscript.

Despite bits and pieces of what could be considered possible inside information on the activities of the Wild Bunch, Phillips's fabrications rendered the manuscript practically useless as source material on Butch Cassidy. It also fails to answer the question as to whether Phillips was Cassidy.

Jim Dullenty's articles on Phillips in the Spokane *Daily Chronicle* created an interesting debate among Wild Bunch fans as to whether Butch and Phillips were one and the same. One writer not convinced was Utah historian Faun McCorkie Tanner. While presenting a paper on Butch before the Westerner's Corral in Phoenix, Arizona, Tanner met a former Rawlins, Wyoming, resident named Sam Adams. Adams told Tanner that his brother, George Adams, had known Cassidy personally. Tanner's paper apparently rekindled Sam Adams's interest in Butch, and a short time later he returned to Lander and sought out as many persons as he could find who had claimed to have seen Butch when he visited the area in the thirties. Adams later reported to Tanner that he had talked to two men, George and Al Smith, whose father, John Smith, had rustled steers in Johnson County and had later operated a ranch near the Hole-in-the-Wall. In describing his conversation with the Smiths, Sam Adams convinced Tanner that they and their father, all of whom met with Cassidy in Lander in 1933, knew Butch far too well to have been taken in by William Phillips.[33]

Tanner claimed that Robbers' Roost historian Pearl Baker was another writer who was not taken in by the Phillips story. Baker, says Tanner, was convinced that Butch himself returned to Lander in the 1930s. She did not deny that Phillips also visited Wyoming, but she said that her research suggested that Butch's visit was in 1933 and that Phillips was probably there in 1934. Baker believed that Phillips might have been closely associated with the Wild Bunch, possibly may even have ridden with them, and that this would explain how he knew so much about them and Butch.[34]

After Dullenty's articles, the Phillips-Cassidy story slipped to the back burners until 1977, when the University of Oklahoma Press published Larry Pointer's *In Search of Butch Cassidy*. Based largely upon Dullenty's earlier research, Pointer's book contains much additional information on Butch and includes a detailed annotation of Phillips's manuscript. While the manuscript itself is too flawed to offer much evidence that Phillips was Cassidy, Pointer's collateral research makes an impressive argument that they were the same man. His book swayed many outlaw writers, including yours truly. However, in the two decades since the book was published, generally accepted thinking on the subject has tended to drift in the other direction.

There is now strong documentation that Phillips was born in Michigan and not in Utah. Also, there are letters believed to have been written by Butch in South America that would place him there when Phillips was in the United States.[35] Moreover, a computer analysis of the photos of the two men conducted in 1991 all but rules out the likelihood that Phillips was Cassidy.[36]

Jim Dullenty, who launched the investigation in 1972 and who has since spent more time researching the question than any other person, also has his doubts. In 1991 he wrote "I have reached the conclusion that William T. Phillips probably was not Butch Cassidy, but that has not been proven. It certainly has not been proven that Phillips was Cassidy."[37] As of early spring 1997, Dullenty had not changed this view.[38]

Dullenty believes that Gertrude Phillips was probably telling the truth, as she knew it, when she wrote to Charles Kelly that her husband was not Butch. Near the end of their marriage the couple drew apart. Phillips was known to be a womanizer, and Gertrude grew to hate him, refusing even to care for him during his last illness. Life was not easy for Gertrude at the time. Dullenty believes that, if Phillips had been Cassidy, Gertrude would have taken advantage of the fact and profited by it.[39]

Dan Buck and Anne Meadows, in researching Anne's book on the years Butch and Longabaugh lived in South America, spent considerable time looking into the William Phillips case. They concluded that his claim to be Butch was dubious to say the least. While Phillips did seem to provide some details about Bolivia that would not be readily known to the average person, he could have obtained this information from the library.[40] In general, Buck and Meadows consider the portion of Phillips's manuscript devoted to Butch's adventures in South America to be "hogwash."[41]

As captivating as the William Phillips story is, an even more intriguing sidelight was uncovered by Buck and Meadows in the early 1990s involving mining engineer Percy Seibert, the source of writer Arthur Chapman's article that first revealed that Butch and Longabaugh had been killed in the shootout at San Vicente. Seibert's son-in-law, Wayne Graham, once lived in Spokane *and was acquainted with William T. Phillips*. Graham knew Phillips in the 1920s and early 1930s. They were, in fact, close friends, occasionally spending long evenings together. Phillips sponsored Graham's membership in the Masons and the Elks. Wayne Graham, however, told Dan Buck that Phillips never discussed Butch Cassidy with him. When Dan asked Graham if he thought Phillips could have been Cassidy, Graham's reply was: "I don't know. He could take care of himself. He was all man, but I never saw him with a gun or anything like that."[42]

To add a little more flavor to this tidbit, Graham's wife, Stella Seibert Graham, told Dan and Anne that Butch and Longabaugh did not die in Bolivia, but that they both had returned to the United States. However, when Dan asked Wayne Graham about this, Graham answered, "I'm not sure her memory is reliable. If it conflicts with what her father said in the history books, I'd stick with her father's version."[43]

Since we can assume that William Phillips was not Butch Cassidy, one wonders what effect Phillips's activities had on the theory that Butch survived the San Vicente shootout and returned to the United States.[44] Jim Dullenty believes that the effect was significant, suggesting that most of the sightings of Butch were probably sightings of Phillips. Possible exceptions, says Dullenty, are reports by Josie Bassett, Tom Vernon of Baggs, Wyoming, and Lula Parker Betenson.[45] But there is room for argument here. In addition to these sources, there were other sightings of Butch in the 1920s, yet little evidence exists that Phillips began his trips to Wyoming posing as Cassidy until at least the summer of 1929.[46]

One exception comes from Bert Charter. According to Charter, in 1925 during a visit to Jackson Hole by a man whom Charter believed to be

Butch Cassidy, he (Charter) thought he heard the man say that his name was Phillips.[47] On the other hand, Pearl Baker offered an interesting explanation for this. She suggested that since it is possible that Phillips and Cassidy were acquainted, Butch may have used the name of William Phillips on occasion, and this might even have been a private joke between the two men.[48]

Afterthoughts

Not only is death sometimes indeterminable, it does not treat everybody the same. Ordinary people usually rest in peace, but the public occasionally makes this peace difficult for outlaws, especially its oppressed heroes. Why do they have a problem staying dead? Michael Zuckerman, history professor at the University of Pennsylvania, thinks he knows. "America has always been a place where you have a lot of people who feel suckered, who are prepared to believe that things are not what they seem. For these people, wish joins with reality and it's easy to believe that an underdog hero is still around."[1]

In a way this describes some members of the Wild Bunch. It took years to convince some people that it was Harvey Logan who lay dead with a bullet in his head following the June 1904 robbery of a Denver & Rio Grande express car near Parachute, Colorado. Lawmen at the scene identified the body as Logan's but others felt differently. Pinkerton officials in Denver had a photograph taken of the body and affirmed that it was indeed Logan, yet there were still some who were not convinced. So the Pinkertons brought in an agent from Nashville who had become acquainted with Logan when he was in jail there. The body was exhumed and the agent reconfirmed that it was Harvey. This appeared to settle the dispute until a special officer of the Union Pacific Railroad, William T. Canada, stated that the Pinkertons were wrong and that he was positive that it was not Logan. The Pinkertons brought in more witnesses, including several federal officers who had known the outlaw. They all agreed that it was Harvey.[2]

One would have thought that this would have ended the controversy but three years later William Pinkerton himself, while addressing a convention of police chiefs at Jamestown, Virginia, announced that Harvey Logan was still on the loose and was robbing banks with Butch and Longabaugh in South America.[3] Pinkerton's doubts aside, years of additional research seem to have finally laid the matter to rest. Harvey Logan did die at Parachute.[4]

Then there was Wild Bunch member George Currie, killed near Price, Utah, in April 1900. Although Currie's father identified the body and took it home to Chadron, Nebraska, for burial, a rumor persisted that it was not really George in the coffin, that his father had only wanted the authorities to think so.[5]

The controversy dragged on for nearly two years; finally a hearing was held in Denver in January 1902 to resolve the matter once and for all. Pinkerton detective Frank Murray was called to verify that the corpse buried in Nebraska was Currie. Murray testified under oath that it was, which should have settled the issue; however, although Murray was supposed to have known Currie quite well, his testimony at the hearing actually suggested that in arriving at his opinion he had placed much importance on the reactions of Currie's family members on the return of the body to Nebraska.[6] (Such proof, of course, didn't mean much if Currie's father had indeed plotted to fool the authorities.) Currie, however, was never seen again, so he's probably resting at peace in Chadron.

Then there was Harry Longabaugh. According to Lula Parker Betenson, Butch told her that the Sundance Kid had survived their South American escapades and the last he knew Harry was living peacefully with Etta Place in Mexico City. Writer Ed Kirby followed this up and found evidence that led him to believe that after Mexico Longabaugh headed for San Francisco where his brother Elwood lived. Kirby said that Harry traveled under several aliases, including George Hanlon, Hiram Bennion, and Hiram BeBee. Kirby wrote that Harry, as George Hanlon, was arrested in California in 1919 for grand larceny and sentenced to San Quentin for one to ten years. After serving one year and seven months he was released. He traveled some more and finally settled in southern Utah in the late 1930s or early 1940s under the name Hiram BeBee.[7]

According to Kirby, while living in Utah BeBee was considered a "grouch" by his neighbors, some of whom thought he was a whiskey bootlegger. In 1945 he got into an argument with an off-duty town marshal in a saloon in Provo. The marshal ushered him outside and threw him into the cab of his pickup truck. Bebee reached into the glove compartment, pulled out a revolver, and shot the marshal dead. He was convicted of murder and sentenced to death, but the Utah Board of Pardons commuted the sentence to life imprisonment. He died in prison on June 1, 1955.[8]

Kirby's evidence is hardly convincing. It consists of Hiram BeBee's revelations to close friends that he was Harry Longabaugh, the Sundance Kid; an unidentified source who said that Butch Cassidy told some friends that Longabaugh was going by the name Hiram BeBee; the suggestion that Longabaugh and Hiram BeBee were similar in appearance; and the suggestion that both men possessed a "tremendous ability to shoot fast and straight," both "displayed great intelligence," and "around both was wrapped an aura of mystery."[9]

Kirby's tireless tracking was in vain. Hardly anybody accepts his theory, not even Wild Bunch researcher Jim Dullenty, who was the editor of Kirby's book.[10] At a 1996 gathering of Wild Bunch researchers at Craig, Colorado, a panel of eight participants was asked to vote on whether photographs of BeBee and Longabaugh suggested they were the same person. The vote was seven against to one in favor.[11]

Besides the Wild Bunch, the outlaw who probably has experienced the greatest problem staying dead is Jesse James, although serious historians agree that Jesse's killing in St. Joseph, Missouri, in 1892 is probably one of the best-documented events in outlaw history.[12] Over a dozen books have attempted to explain how Jesse could not possibly have been the man who was shot that day. According to Jesse's son, Jesse Edwards James, who died in 1951, Jesse junior was personally aware of fifteen persons who came forward pretending to be his outlaw father, most of whom have been characterized by authentic historians as "maudlin, illiterate, vague, confused [and] pathetic."[13]

But what about Butch Cassidy? Admittedly there have been similar crackpot claims and outlandish stories about Butch's later years. But unlike the Jesse James saga, on the surface there seems to be some evidence from reliable witnesses that Butch lived long after he was supposedly killed in Bolivia. Persons who knew Butch during the peak of his outlaw years swore that they saw him and talked to him during the 1920s and early 1930s—and some of the conversations or sightings took place before the imposter William Phillips appeared on the scene. Yet, as Dan Buck and Anne Meadows insist (and their argument is certainly persuasive), there is strong circumstantial evidence that both Butch and Harry Longabaugh died in the 1908 shootout at San Vicente.

Until Buck's and Meadows's search, there was much doubt that a shootout even occurred. Evidence now supports the theory that there was indeed a shootout, and that two bandits, probably North Americans, perished at the scene. There is little question these two had stolen the Aramayo payroll, and their descriptions closely matched those of Butch and

Longabaugh. Moreover, the dead outlaws were using aliases that Butch and Harry were known to use.[14]

Is there an answer? On the one side is the testimony of individuals who claimed they saw Butch as late as the 1940s, and on the other side is strong circumstantial evidence that he died in 1908. How can such inconsistency be resolved? If a jury were asked to decide, the evidence would be weighed and the jurors would determine the greater weight of the proof, commonly known as the "preponderance" of the evidence, a term used in civil law (as opposed to criminal law) to mean evidence that is more convincing to the mind—evidence that best accords with reason and probability.[15] Some refer to it simply as fifty-one percent of the evidence.

The circumstantial evidence obtained by Buck and Meadows that Butch and Longabaugh were the victims at San Vicente is convincing indeed. Buck and Meadows are solid investigators and their conclusions cannot be ignored; however, their evidence is slightly stronger for Longabaugh than it is for Butch.

Frank Aller, vice-consul at the American Legation in Antofagasta, Chile, was interested in determining whether one of the bandits killed at San Vicente was a man known in Chile as Boyd or Brown (presumably Longabaugh) because a Chilean probate judge needed proof of death to settle the man's (or someone's) estate.[16] Aller and the judge were primarily interested in Boyd/Brown; their interest in the other man, Maxwell (presumably Butch), was only to assist in identifying Boyd/Brown. The fact that the judge may have eventually obtained enough information to close the Boyd/Brown matter (it isn't clear that he did) does not mean that the judge had come to any conclusion about Maxwell.[17]

In several reports about the South American robberies attributed to Cassidy and Longabaugh, including the Aramayo payroll robbery, the media, presumably from information gained from the authorities, reported that one of the robbers appeared to be Chilean rather than a North American.[18] Also, according to local legend, one of the two bodies buried in the San Vicente cemetery after the shootout was that of a Chilean.[19]

In the possession of the shootout victim believed to be Butch were seven cards bearing the name Enrique B. Hutcheon, which led the Bolivian officials to initially identify the body as Hutcheon.[20] Why the cards? This has never been explained.

Joyce Warner, Matt Warner's daughter, who claimed that Butch visited her in 1939, said that Butch told her that after he returned to the States, Longabaugh found another partner whom he also called "Butch," apparently as a joke.[21] Could the dead man have been Butch Number Two?

This leads us to the "Dilly theory": the possibility that the dead man with Longabaugh was a rustler named Tom Dilly who had once operated in Carbon, Emery, and Grand Counties in Utah.

Little is known about Tom Dilly's background. He may have come from Texas, where it was rumored that he was wanted in a murder case. He is believed to have drifted into western Colorado sometime in the late 1890s and taken a job with the Webster City Cattle Company. While with Webster he got into a fight with the manager of the spread and another cowboy named Sam Jenkins and pretty much whipped them both.[22] He also may have worked for the Pleasant Valley Coal Company at Castle Gate and might have been there in April 1897 when Butch and Elzy Lay robbed the company paymaster.[23]

Dilly was short-tempered, but when he was not out of sorts he could be congenial. He was fairly close to a family named Warner (no relation to Matt) who had a ranch on the Price River above Woodside, Utah. He would often bring candy and toys to the Warner children and was always a welcome guest. He also stayed a few winters with Jim McPherson, a rancher east of the Green River on Florence Creek. One winter, apparently as a joke, Dilly rebranded a bunch of Webster City cattle with McPherson's brand, and McPherson had to hurry over to Webster headquarters and square matters.[24]

Dilly also gathered up a few Webster cows for himself and began putting together his own herd. He teamed up with George Currie for a while in late 1899.[25] When an inspection of Dilly's ranch near Woodside revealed that he probably had acquired a couple hundred head a little faster than he should have, the law began to keep an eye on him.[26] And when Grand County Sheriff Jess Tyler and another man named Sam Jenkins, a member of Tyler's posse (and Dilly's nemesis at Webster) were shot in the back while searching for rustlers along the Uintah-Grand County line east of Green River, Dilly became a prime suspect.[27] (It was reported that just as Jenkins was shot he shouted "Dilly!") An all-out manhunt was launched—some say the largest of its kind up to that time—but it was slow getting organized. The killers' trail was easily followed to a ranch about twelve miles from the scene of the killing, where they had picked up supplies and fresh horses. Their tracks then led northeast, as if they were heading for Brown's Park, but after that no further trace of them was found.[28] Although during the chase Dilly was at the top of the suspect list, the authorities eventually decided that he was not one of the killers or, if he was, they did not have enough evidence to convict him.[29]

Could this Tom Dilly have been mistaken for Butch in Bolivia? Several sources place Dilly in South America.[30] Also, J. K. W. Bracken, the Utah doctor-turned-cattleman who supposedly helped finance an expedition to see if Butch really did die in San Vicente, said a photograph he saw of one of the two the victims of the 1908 shootout at San Vicente looked more like Tom Dilly than it did Butch.[31] According to one report, an American outlaw named "Dey" had helped Butch and Harry rob the Banco de la Nación in Villa Mercedes.[32] Could this have been a misspelling from a mispronunciation of "Dilly?" (In some Spanish dialects the pronunciation of Dilly could conceivably sound something like "Dey-yeh.")

One of the persons who placed Tom Dilly in South America was Brown's Park pioneer Avvon Chew Hughel. Sometime in 1901, Dilly was involved in another shooting, this time in a saloon in Sunnyside, Utah, located in southern Carbon County just above the Emery County line. The victim was Steve Chapman, a sheepman. Dilly fled north to Nine Mile Canyon where the Chew family had a cattle camp. When Dilly arrived at the camp he was only minutes ahead of a posse. At the camp were two Chew children, Avvon and Harry. Dilly dismounted, jerked off his saddle, and slapped it on one of the Chew horses. He then persuaded Avvon and Harry, both of whom were fond of "Uncle Tom" because of the candy he brought them, to hide in the rocks and fire their rifles at the trail in front of the posse. This delayed the posse enough to give Dilly time to escape. Avvon, who later wrote about her family's adventures in Carbon County and Brown's Park, said that Dilly eventually escaped to Rock Springs, Wyoming, where he caught a westbound train. He later wrote the Chews from San Francisco, telling that he was bound for South America.[33]

The Dilly theory is interesting but admittedly far-fetched. While Butch and Tom Dilly did have common traits—they both played the harmonica, enjoyed pulling practical jokes on their friends, and were popular with children—Dilly and Butch were not similar in appearance. Dilly was tall and thin with curly black hair and black eyes.[34]

Furthermore, even if Dilly was in South America in 1908, he too may have survived unscathed. Pearl Baker tells of an incident during World War I involving a Utah boy named Lee Bryner who was stationed in England. Young Bryner, who was from Price, met a young Englishwoman at a dance in Selfridge. During their conversation the young lady mentioned that her father was named Tom Dilly and was originally from Utah. Bryner later dined with the Dillys and recalled that the father was tall and rawboned, and appeared to be well-to-do financially. Bryner said that during the evening the man seemed eager to learn something about several old-timers who lived in and around Price.[35]

If Butch did die at San Vicente, what accounts for the story told by his sister, Lula Parker Betenson, that he had returned and visited the family in 1925? On the surface Lula's revelation should have been enough proof that Butch had survived his South American adventure. Why should we doubt the word of this charming old lady? Serious Wild Bunch researchers offer several reasons for doubt. One is lack of verification from the Parker family. Dan Buck points out that with only one exception, all members of the Parker clan who should have known whether Butch returned—including his siblings (most of whom, according to Lula, were present during his visit in 1925)—have not gone on record in support of Lula's story. Butch's brother Dan Parker was the possible exception: he may have believed that Butch returned, but, as Buck reminds us, he apparently also believed that William Phillips was Butch (which Lula denied and which has all but been disproved).[36]

Another weakness in Lula's story is her record of inconsistencies, especially surrounding Butch's death, many of which were revealed by Jim Dullenty, who corresponded with Lula and kept track of her interviews while she was preparing her book. Says Dullenty, "Lula Parker Betenson changed her story about her brother many times, and when this was pointed out to her, she claimed she had been misquoted. I have a file full of her statements and she gives various dates and places of her brother's death."[37]

Dan Buck points out another inconsistency that he believes sheds light on the lack of credibility of Lula's story. Buck discovered that Lula's husband, Jose Betenson, in filling out genealogy forms provided by the Church of the Latter-Day Saints for deceased members of the faith, had originally entered the date of Butch's death as 1909. Later, sometime during or after 1950, the information on this form was changed. The new form says Butch died in 1937, the date Lula settled on for her book.[38]

Another apparent Lula detractor is Cassidy biographer Ed Kirby, who was an early Lula supporter. While he was writing *The Saga of Butch Cassidy and the Wild Bunch*, published in 1977, Kirby, who had interviewed Lula, said that he was convinced that Butch did not die in San Vicente.[39] However, he later revealed to Dan Buck and Anne Meadows that Lula once implied to him that "she was just having fun," and that, in fact, she "had no idea what happened to her brother."[40]

Returning to the shootout at San Vicente, those who believe that Butch may not have been one of the outlaws who came to an end that night point to the way the two men died as supporting evidence. It would appear that they died primarily because they were either careless or stupid, and Butch

Cassidy was neither. The two outlaws who were killed were eventually proven to be the ones who robbed the Aramayo payroll. Would Butch Cassidy have ridden into San Vicente on a mule stolen from the Aramayo victims? Outlaws traditionally wore bandannas over their faces during robberies and changed clothes afterward to reduce the chance of being identified should they later be picked up by the authorities. But such precautions could be a waste of time if an outlaw were picked up riding the same horse he used in his getaway. How long did Butch Cassidy ever stay astraddle a horse he used in a robbery? It can be argued that the reason outlaws like Butch had a relay of fresh horses stashed away along an escape route was not only to outdistance a posse, but also to eliminate one means by which witnesses could identify them.

Furthermore, those who really knew the ever-cautious Butch would wonder why he would have even considered spending the night in San Vicente. It was three days after the Aramayo robbery. News of the loss of the payroll had spread throughout the area, and the suspects were believed to be North Americans. It would have been more like Butch to have avoided the town and camp somewhere off the trail.

Was it Butch with Harry Longabaugh that night in San Vicente? As absurd as some of the claims of Butch's reappearance seem to be, and many are indeed absurd, should the entire list of sightings be so quickly swept aside? Should we be influenced by the notion that volume dilutes? Why should multiple sightings be taken as a negative? Some of these persons—maybe even just one—could have really met him.

Notes

Circle Valley

1. Betenson and Flack, *Butch Cassidy*, 43–46; Heidt, "Cassidy Came to Coonville," 58.

2. Betenson and Flack, *Butch Cassidy*, 43–47.

3. *Eastern Utah Advocate*, May 19, 1897. (Interview of Ryan by correspondent from *Salt Lake City Tribune*.)

4. Betenson and Flack, *Butch Cassidy*, 33, 40; Pointer, *In Search of Cassidy*, 43.

5. Betenson and Flack, *Butch Cassidy*, 32–33; Pointer, *In Search of Cassidy*, 44. Circleville is in Piute County, but the Parker property lay just across the line in what is now Garfield County.

6. Baker, *Wild Bunch at Robbers Roost*, 9–10; Betenson and Flack, *Butch Cassidy*, 9–13, 20. An erroneous story has been handed down that Robert Parker, Maximillian's father, froze to death on the trip west near Green River, Wyoming, and that Maximillian and his mother buried him in a shallow grave scratched in the snow. This account, wholly untrue, was repeated in Kelly's *Outlaw Trail*, 11.

7. Betenson and Flack, *Butch Cassidy*, 31–32.

8. Betenson and Flack, *Butch Cassidy*, 31.

9. Pointer, *In Search of Cassidy*, 43.

10. Poll, *Utah's History*, 223.

11. Baker, *Wild Bunch at Robbers Roost*, 184.

12. Taylor, "Silver Reef," 18–19.

13. The Silver Reef mining district had a short but active career as a source of both silver and lead. Silver was discovered in the mid-1860s, but no serious mining was done until 1875. A rush soon followed, and within a few months the camp grew to some 1,500 inhabitants. Production tapered off somewhat in 1879, but continued intermittently until 1909. Poll, *Utah's History*, 222; Taylor, "Silver Reef," 17–20. For Max at Frisco, see Betenson and Flack, *Butch Cassidy*, 34; Pointer, *In Search of Cassidy*, 44.

14. The mine at Squaw Springs eventually became known as the Horn Silver Mine and proved to be the richest silver producer in Utah. The mine got its name from a local tale that one ledge of ore was so rich it could be whittled, with slivers curling off the ore shaped like the horns of a mountain sheep. Poll, *Utah's History*, 222.

15. Betenson, "Lula Parker Betenson," 4.

16. Baker, *Wild Bunch at Robbers Roost*, 184; Betenson and Flack, *Butch Cassidy*, 34; Pointer, *In Search of Cassidy*, 43–44.

17. Eventually Bob had twelve brothers and sisters: Dan, Arthur, Jen, Bill, Knell, Eb, Blanch, Lula, Mark, Nina, Leona, and Rawlins. Betenson, "Lula Parker Betenson," 2.

18. Stegner, *Mormon Country*, 171.

19. Betenson and Flack, *Butch Cassidy*, 34; Pointer, *In Search of Cassidy*, 44.

20. Stegner, *Mormon Country*, 38.

21. Pointer, *In Search of Cassidy*, 44.

22. Pointer, *In Search of Cassidy*, 43.

23. Kelly, *Outlaw Trail*, 11. The theft of the saddle was later confirmed during an interview of rancher Pat Ryan by the *Salt Lake City Tribune* (*Eastern Utah Advocate*, May 19, 1897).

24. Pointer, *In Search of Cassidy*, 43. As to the overalls incident, Pointer suggests that since young Bob was raised as a Mormon and had what Pointer terms "a frontier ethic" that a man's word is his bond, Bob must have considered the note he left the store owner in which he promised to pay for the merchandise an "inviolate pledge" that should not have been questioned.

25. Betenson and Flack, *Butch Cassidy*, 33–34.

26. Stegner, *Mormon Country*, 174–75.

27. Betenson and Flack, *Butch Cassidy*, 33–34.

28. Betenson and Flack, *Butch Cassidy*, 40. Prior to Lula Parker Betenson's clarification of this arrangement it was thought that Max Parker had somehow scraped together enough money to purchase the Marshall ranch (see Kelly, *Outlaw Trail*, 40).

29. Poll, *Utah's History*, 289–90.

30. Poll, *Utah's History*, 263–64. The federal marshals used the town of Silver Reef as one headquarters site for their "polyg hunts" because it was predominantly a non-Mormon community. The marshals were unable to understand why the polygamists always seemed to know just when to go into hiding. Years later it was discovered that the local telegraph operators, all of whom were Mormons, found a way of learning of the marshals' intended raids and were sending coded warnings by wire to other towns throughout the area (Taylor, "Silver Reef," 19).

31. Boren and Boren, "Anna Marie Thayne: Mrs. Sundance," 22–23. According

to the Borens, whose sources include descendants of persons whom the Parkers helped to escape, Bob Parker continued to assist polygamists after he became Butch Cassidy the outlaw by helping them hide in the desolate canyons of the Robbers' Roost area and by contributing money to underground leaders to defray the expenses of transporting families to Mexico.

32. Betenson and Flack, *Butch Cassidy*, 40; Pointer, *In Search of Cassidy*, 45.

33. Baker, *Wild Bunch at Robbers Roost*, 184.

34. Kelly, *Outlaw Trail*, 11.

35. Ryan interview as reported in *Eastern Utah Advocate*, May 19, 1897.

36. Betenson and Flack, *Butch Cassidy*, 41–42.

37. Betenson and Flack, *Butch Cassidy*, 42; Baker, *Wild Bunch at Robbers Roost*, 184–85.

38. Betenson and Flack, *Butch Cassidy*, 45.

39. Betenson and Flack, *Butch Cassidy*, 44–45; Baker, *Wild Bunch at Robbers Roost*, 18–19.

40. Kelly, *Outlaw Trail*, 12; Baker, *Wild Bunch at Robbers Roost*, 19.

41. Kelly, *Outlaw Trail*, 10; Betenson and Flack, *Butch Cassidy*, 19, 31–32.

42. Betenson, "Lula Parker Betenson," 6.

43. Betenson and Flack, *Butch Cassidy*, 46–47.

44. Baker, *Wild Bunch at Robbers Roost*, 1, 13.

45. Baker, *Wild Bunch at Robbers Roost*, 14, 18–19; Betenson and Flack, *Butch Cassidy*, 45.

46. Baker, *Wild Bunch at Robbers Roost*, 24–25.

47. Kelly, *Outlaw Trail*, 303.

48. Baker, *Wild Bunch at Robbers Roost*, 17–27.

49. Warner, *Last of the Bandit Riders*, 107.

50. Kelly, *Outlaw Trail*, 12–13. Utah writer Kerry Ross Boren claims that the story was true, that his grandfather, Willard Schofield, whose family were close friends with the Parkers, had asked Bob about the incident in later years and Bob had confirmed it. According to Boren, Bob told his grandfather: "I've done a few things in my time, Willard, but I wouldn't leave nobody to die like that. Besides, a man don't know when he might need a favor himself someday" (Boren, "My Grandpa Knew Butch Cassidy," 44).

51. Betenson and Flack, *Butch Cassidy*, 39, 50.

52. Betenson and Flack, *Butch Cassidy*, 48–49.

Telluride

1. Poll, *Utah's History*, 283–84.

2. Stegner, *Mormon Country*, 68.

3. Betenson and Flack, *Butch Cassidy*, 55–56.

4. Warner, *Last of Bandit Riders*, 106.

5. Lavender, *Telluride Story*, 16, 21, 22.

6. Lavender, *Telluride Story*, 22.

7. Lavender, *Telluride Story*, 22.

8. Lavender, *Telluride Story*, 23, 25–26.

9. Bob's experiences during his first stay in Telluride were chronicled by his sister, who says that their father described them to her. Betenson and Flack, *Butch Cassidy*, 53–57.

10. Pointer, *In Search of Cassidy*, 48, quoting a Wyoming sheepherder, James Regan, in an article that appeared in the *Wyoming State Tribune*, May 7, 1942.

11. Pointer, *In Search of Cassidy*, 48.

12. Betenson and Flack, *Butch Cassidy*, 55.

13. Betenson and Flack, *Butch Cassidy*, 56.

14. Brown, *American West*, 331.

15. Horan, *Desperate Men*, 377, quoting an old cowpuncher, John F. Kelly.

16. Lavender, *Telluride Story*, 27.

17. Warner, *Last of Bandit Riders*, 27; Baker, *Wild Bunch at Robbers Roost*, 56.

18. Warner, *Last of Bandit Riders*, 21–39.

19. Warner, *Last of Bandit Riders*, 105.

20. Silvey, *Northern San Juan County*, 32.

21. Cress, *Match That Broke Saguache*, 62–64.

22. Warner, *Last of Bandit Riders*, 105–7.

23. Warner, *Last of Bandit Riders*, 106–7.

24. Warner, *Last of Bandit Riders*, 105–9.

25. Warner, *Last of Bandit Riders*, 111.

26. Warner, *Last of Bandit Riders*, 80, 112; Kelly, *Outlaw Trail*, 17.

27. McCarty, *McCarty's Own Story*, vi, 1; Jessen, *Colorado Gunsmoke*, 217.

28. Kelly, *Outlaw Trail*, 17–19.

29. Hughel, *Chew Bunch*, 23.

30. McCarty, *McCarty's Own Story*, 28.

31. Jessen, *Colorado Gunsmoke*, 163–64.

32. Kelly, *Outlaw Trail*, 26–27.

33. Jessen, *Colorado Gunsmoke*, 165–74. Jessen's primary source is the unpublished account of the robbery by Cyrus Wells "Doc" Shores, the lawman who tracked down the robbers. Shores's manuscript is entitled "The First Train Robbery on the Denver & Rio Grande in 1887," and is on file in the Western History Department of the Denver Public Library. A contemporary account of the robbery appears in the *Rocky Mountain News*, November 4, 1887. The four men eventually arrested and convicted of the robbery were Jack Smith, Bob Smith, Ed Rhodes, and Bob Boyle (*Rocky Mountain News*, November 4, 1887; Jessen, *Colorado Gun-*

smoke, 163–74). See also Patterson, *Train Robbery Era*, 242–44. In his memoirs Tom McCarty does describe a train robbery in which he and his pals placed "a few obstructions" on the track, but as best one can tell (McCarty was terrible with dates), this robbery occurred several years later. Also, in this robbery McCarty claimed to have cleaned out the express car of about $3,000 in cash (McCarty, *Mc-Carty's Own Story*, 30–31).

34. Transcript of interview with Frank Silvey, Sept. 14, 1936, on file at the Utah Historical Society (Document A1006–1). McCarty rode Silvey's horse, Whitey, to three wins on July 4, 1888, at Cortez.

35. Warner, *Last of Bandit Riders*, 117.

36. *Dolores Star*, Feb. 11, 1938.

37. *Dolores Star*, Feb. 11, 1938.

38. Warner, *Last of Bandit Riders*, 117.

39. McCarty, *McCarty's Own Story*, 28.

40. Kelly, *Outlaw Trail*, 27; Burroughs, *Where West Stayed Young*, 121; Jessen, *Colorado Gunsmoke*, 217–19.

41. Jessen, *Colorado Gunsmoke*, 219.

42. Kelly, *Outlaw Trail*, 34. In his book, Matt Warner mentions settling down for a while in Star Valley but does not mention the $10,000 bill.

43. McCarty, *McCarty's Own Story*, 50.

44. Warner and Lacy, "Warner's Daughter," 17.

Return to Telluride

1. Warner, *Last of Bandit Riders*, 118.

2. Fetter and Fetter, *Telluride*, 55–56; Lavender, *Telluride Story*, 32.

3. Warner, *Last of Bandit Riders*, 118–19.

4. Baker, *Wild Bunch at Robbers Roost*, 58.

5. Kelly, *Outlaw Trail*, 30.

6. Webb, "Outlaw Trail: Never Was," 30–31; Kelly, *Outlaw Trail*, 30. Dan, who was nineteen months younger than Bob, left home not long after Bob, reasoning that he could earn more money elsewhere and thus help out the family. According to his great-grand nephew, however, Dan soon fell in with a "rough crowd," presumably the Carlisle Ranch bunch (Betenson, "Alias 'Tom Ricketts,'" 4). According to local history, the Telluride robbery was planned in San Juan County, most likely at the Carlisle ranch. See McPherson, *San Juan County*, 326. Also, according to local history, Bob himself worked for the Carlisles at one time (Tanner, *Far Country*, 177).

7. Webb, "Outlaw Trail: Never Was," 30–31. For the cattle and sheep conflict, see Walker, "The Carlisles," 280.

8. Webb, "Outlaw Trail: Never Was," 30.

9. Walker, "The Carlisles," 280.

10. Walker, "The Carlisles," 282.

11. Walker, "The Carlisles," 275, citing the diary of Henry L. A. Culmer (Utah State Historical Society, Salt Lake City).

12. Kelly, *Outlaw Trail*, 30.

13. *Rocky Mountain News*, June 27, 1889.

14. Warner, *Last of Bandit Riders*, 120–21.

15. *Pueblo Daily Chieftain*, June 26, 1889 (four men involved); *Colorado Springs Gazette*, June 29, 1889 (four men involved); *Rocky Mountain News*, July 1, 1889 (six men involved).

16. Baker, *Wild Bunch at Robbers Roost*, 158.

17. *Rocky Mountain News*, June 27, 1889.

18. *Pueblo Daily Chieftain*, June 30, 1889.

19. Kelly, *Outlaw Trail*, 30. In his book Kelly refers to a Bert and Bill "Maddern." Kelly may have meant that Bert held the robbers' horses on the street while they were in the bank. Pearl Baker, on the other hand, believes that Bert was responsible for holding the first relay of fresh horses on Keystone Hill (Baker, *Wild Bunch at Robbers Roost*, 160).

20. Ernst, *Sundance*, 53–55.

21. Ernst, *Sundance*, 23–29.

22. Kelly, *Outlaw Trail*, 30.

23. Betenson, "Alias 'Tom Ricketts,' " 5. Bill Betenson is the great-grand nephew of Bob and Dan Parker. His source for Dan's involvement at Telluride is a statement by Joe Bush, a deputy U.S. Marshal, that appeared in the *Salt Lake City Herald* on September 13, 1896.

24. Warner, *Last of Bandit Riders*, 120.

25. Baker, *Wild Bunch at Robbers Roost*, 159.

26. *Rocky Mountain News*, June 27, 1889.

27. *Pueblo Daily Chieftain*, June 26, 1889; *Colorado Springs Gazette*, June 28, 1889.

28. Warner, *Last of Bandit Riders*, 121–22.

29. Warner, *Last of Bandit Riders*, 122.

30. McCarty, *McCarty's Own Story*, 28.

31. Warner, *Last of Bandit Riders*, 122. The site of the holdup can still be visited today. The bank itself is gone, but the building, a small, two-story, white storefront structure now known as the Mahr building, remains. It is located on the north side of Colorado Street (Telluride's main street) in the middle of the block between Fir and Pine Streets. Although the building was rebuilt, or at least substantially remodeled three years after the robbery, old photos suggest that it still closely resembles the original structure. A brass plaque adorns the door of the building, com-

memorating it as the site of "Butch Cassidy's first bank robbery." Unfortunately, many outlaw buffs who travel to Telluride to see the site visit the wrong building. Both Lula Parker Betenson, in her *Butch Cassidy, My Brother*, and Larry Pointer, in his *In Search of Butch Cassidy*, mistakenly identify Telluride's First National Bank building as the robbery site. The First National Bank building, an impressive stone structure that really looks like an 1880s bank, was in existence at the time of the robbery, but it was down the street, at the corner of Fir and Colorado, a half a block west of the bank that Butch and his friends struck that day.

32. *Dolores Star*, Feb. 11, 1938.

33. *Rocky Mountain News*, June 27, 1889.

34. Baker, *Wild Bunch at Robbers Roost*, 159.

35. McCarty, *McCarty's Own Story*, 28.

36. Baker, *Wild Bunch at Robbers Roost*, 160; Kelly, *Outlaw Trail*, 30. In his book, Matt Warner makes a point of saying that "instead of having a relay or two of horses hid up to make that run, we picked out our fastest and toughest nags and decided to make that run without relays." Warner, 120. This may have been true, but it must be remembered that throughout his account of the Telluride robbery, Warner clearly avoids implicating anyone except himself, Bob Parker, and Tom McCarty. To admit that fresh horses were waiting along their escape route would suggest that others were involved.

37. Rambler decided to tell his story in an article sent to the editor of a local newspaper, the *Shenandoah Tribune*. The article, titled "The Telluride Bank Holdup," was later reprinted in the *Telluride Republican* and probably the *Norwood Leader* as well. A clipping of the article was found by a San Miguel County resident, William Greager, who lives near Norwood. A copy was obtained from Greager by Butch Cassidy researcher Daniel Buck, who kindly shared it with me. The clipping is undated, but had to have been written sometime after September 7, 1893, because Rambler mentions the Delta, Colorado, bank robbery of that date that resulted in the death of both Tom McCarty's brother and his nephew.

38. Rambler's story seems to contradict another version of the bandits' escape, the source of which is unknown, which claims that the three outlaws tricked the local authorities by heading west out of Telluride toward Keystone Hill then backtracking to south of town, where they picked up Bear Creek Trail (a steep and treacherous mountain path that followed the creek south past its east fork), then looped to the west north of Palmyra Peak. See Casebier, "Horseback Bandits," 1. It is unlikely that the outlaws would have taken this route but it would have been possible. After leaving Bear Creek Trail, the outlaws could have picked up a second seldom-used trail at Alta lakes, which led southwest to Gold Creek and eventually to the San Miguel River's south fork just north of Ames.

39. Rambler, "Telluride Bank Holdup," *Shenandoah Tribune*.

40. Jessen, *Colorado Gunsmoke*, 219, 225.

41. *Dolores Star*, Feb. 11, 1938.

42. Warner, *Last of Bandit Riders*, 123. Such a comment from Tom McCarty would not be unusual, according to Utah rancher Pat Ryan, to whom Bob Parker may have described this scene several months later when he visited Ryan's ranch. In a later interview with a correspondent from the *Salt Lake City Tribune*, Ryan called McCarty "one of the most cold-blooded and heartless members of the gang" (*Eastern Utah Advocate*, May 19, 1897). Warner and McCarty were apparently identified immediately; within a week most newspapers in the area were listing them as two of the robbers (*Pueblo Daily Chieftain*, June 30, 1889; *Rocky Mountain News*, July 1, 1889; *Colorado Springs Gazette*, July 6, 1889).

43. McCarty, *McCarty's Own Story*, 28.

44. *Pueblo Daily Chieftain*, June 26, 1889.

45. *Dolores Star*, Feb. 11, 1938.

46. Rambler, " Telluride Bank Holdup."

47. Johnny Nicholson was Matt Warner's jockey when he raced his mare, Betty. In Rambler's letter to the *Shenandoah Tribune*, in which he had admitted having a hand in the Telluride robbery, he said that Tom McCarty had three partners who helped him pull off the job: Matt Warner, Bert Madden, and John Nicholson. Rambler did not mention Bob Parker. Does this mean Parker was not one of the robbers? Maybe, but there are other possibilities. Rambler's article was probably submitted to the *Tribune* in the mid-1890s, before Parker became the well-known Butch Cassidy. Even at this late date Rambler may not have known that he had participated in a robbery with the famous Butch Cassidy. Rambler said that he was brought into the Telluride scheme by Tom McCarty. According to Warner, McCarty did not meet Bob Parker until the fall of 1888. Rambler suggests that he, Rambler, was recruited by McCarty in the spring of 1889, only after the plans were laid to raid the Telluride bank. Therefore, it is possible that Rambler never met Parker until just before the robbery. Maybe in the last-minute rush to put the job together there were no formal introductions and at the time Rambler mistakenly thought Parker was Nicholson.

48. Warner, *Last of Bandit Riders*, 125.

49. Old-timers around Mancos say that the law was led to the trio's camp by Tom McCarty's horse, a white gelding that followed the outlaws after being replaced at one of the early relay points. Casebier, "Horseback Bandits," 1.

50. Ernst, *Sundance*, 53.

51. McCarty, *McCarty's Own Story*, 29.

52. Warner, *Last of Bandit Riders*, 127–28.

53. McCarty, *McCarty's Own Story*, 28.

54. Kelly, *Outlaw Trail*, 31.

55. Rambler, "Telluride Bank Holdup."

56. On July 1 the *Rocky Mountain News* reported that one of the robbers was a "Bob Porter."

57. Kelly, *Outlaw Trail*, 31.

58. Kelly, *Outlaw Trail*, 31; *Colorado Springs Gazette*, July 6, 1889.

59. *Rocky Mountain News*, July 1, 1889.

60. Kelly, *Outlaw Trail*, 32.

61. Warner, *Last of Bandit Riders*, 125.

62. Pointer, *In Search of Cassidy*, 52; Jessen, *Colorado Gunsmoke*, 246–47. Marshal Clark was apparently bad clean through. It has been said that he would find out when gold shipments were being made and tip off his outlaw friends. He was also a highway robber himself. He would put on black whiskers to disguise himself and hold up miners coming into Telluride for a Saturday night's fun. Then, the following morning he would impishly take their report of the robbery in his marshal's office. He served as Telluride town marshal until August 6, 1895, when, around midnight as he was walking down Colorado Street on his way back to his cabin he was killed by a shot from the shadows (Jessen, *Colorado Gunsmoke*, 247).

63. Baker, *Wild Bunch at Robbers Roost*, 160.

64. *Dolores Star*, Feb. 11, 1938.

65. Warner, *Last of Bandit Riders*, 129.

Flight

1. Baker, *Wild Bunch at Robbers Roost*, 160–61.

2. Baker, *Wild Bunch at Robbers Roost*, 160–61.

3. Warner, *Last of Bandit Riders*, 125–26.

4. Rambler, "Telluride Bank Holdup."

5. Warner, *Last of Bandit Riders*, 128–29.

6. McPherson, *San Juan County*, 326.

7. Warner, *Last of Bandit Riders*, 127.

8. Casebier, "Horseback Bandits," 1. Stopping at Tom McCarty's brother's ranch may have been a risky decision. According to Casebier, McCarty's horse had been identified as one of those used by the bank robbers, and a Wanted poster for Tom was already being printed in Telluride. Bill McCarty, Tom's brother, was one of the early ranchers in the general area that is now La Sal, Utah, and was fairly well known (McPherson, *San Juan County*, 96, 172; Silvey, *Northern San Juan County*, 30).

9. Tanner, *Far Country*, 160.

10. The Taylor family operated the ferry at Moab for years. According to local legend, the founder, Norman Taylor, got the idea during his first visit to the town when he saw the bodies of two men who had tried to swim the river the day before.

The ferry was a God-send to travelers, and the Taylors got rich off the operation, charging up to $4.00 for a wagon and a team of horses to cross when the river was high. The county finally took over the enterprise in 1897 and reduced the rate to fifty cents per wagon. Firmage, *Grand County*, 115–17.

11. Baker, *Wild Bunch at Robbers Roost*, 162–63; Warner, *Last of Bandit Riders*, 127–28. Baker's source for this conversation was Don Taylor, another son of Lester Taylor. Don Taylor was not there that night, but probably heard the story many times from his father and brother. Don Taylor did tell of an incident that happened years later during the prohibition era, when the Taylors were visiting Price, Utah, where Matt Warner, who eventually served his time and had gone straight, was then operating a pool hall. The Taylors went over to the hall, walked up to Warner, and asked if he could get them anything to drink. Not recognizing them, Warner began naming soft drinks that he had to offer. One of the Taylors then leaned forward and said, "Matt, just like you were one morning before daylight on the Grand River, our business lies rolling." Warner's eyes lit up and he called for somebody to take his place, saying that he was on the wrong side of the bar. Then he and the Taylors spent the remainder of the evening enjoying hard liquor and recalling the good old days (Baker, *Wild Bunch at Robbers Roost*, 163).

12. Tanner, *Far Country*, 160, 306. While the outlaw trio's visit to Moab that night was brief, it remains a colorful part of local history. Years later, during the town's annual "Butch Cassidy Days" celebration, local residents no doubt enjoyed telling tourists of how a reformed Matt Warner once returned to Moab to attend one of the town's horse racing events. During the races, when Matt was seen betting heavily, somebody in the crowd called to him, "Where did you get so much money, Matt?" He supposedly waved the money over his head and shouted back, "At the Telluride bank, years ago."

13. Warner, *Last of Bandit Riders*, 131.

14. Warner, *Last of Bandit Riders*, 133–35.

15. Warner, *Last of Bandit Riders*, 135.

16. Firmage, *Grand County*, 135.

17. Firmage, *Grand County*, 172.

18. McCarty, *McCarty's Own Story*, 29.

19. Warner, *Last of Bandit Riders*, 131–33; McCarty, *McCarty's Own Story*, 29.

20. Warner, *Last of Bandit Riders*, 132.

21. Warner, *Last of Bandit Riders*, 136.

22. Kelly, *Outlaw Trail*, 63–67.

23. Kelly, *Outlaw Trail*, 67–68.

24. Warner, *Last of Bandit Riders*, 136.

25. Burton, "Crouse's Robbers' Roost," 2.

26. Burton, "Crouse's Robbers' Roost," 7–8.

27. Burton, "Crouse's Robbers' Roost," 8–9.

28. DeJournette and DeJournette, *One Hundred Years*, 21.

29. According to local historians Dick and Daun DeJournette, the cabin was located about five miles southwest of Charlie Crouse's ranch, just east of an area called Rye Grass. DeJournette and DeJournette, *One Hundred Years*, 328.

30. Warner, *Last of Bandit Riders*, 136; Burton, "Crouse's Robbers' Roost," 8–9.

31. Burton, "Crouse's Robbers' Roost," 9.

32. Warner, *Last of Bandit Riders*, 136.

33. Warner, *Last of Bandit Riders*, 136.

34. Warner, *Last of Bandit Riders*, 76.

35. Warner, *Last of Bandit Riders*, 136–37.

36. This theory is pure conjecture, based mainly upon Matt Warner's statement that the nearest town from their hideout was Green River and that they had ridden in from the north; it also presumes that once they had reached Roost country they would have wanted to leave the main trails as soon as possible for the safety of a hideaway.

37. Warner, *Last of Bandit Riders*, 138.

38. Betenson and Flack, *Butch Cassidy*, 64–65; Lula Betenson, during an interview reported in the *Waterbury Republican*, May 25, 1975, as quoted in Kirby, *Saga of Butch*, 97.

39. Betenson and Flack, *Butch Cassidy*, 181.

40. Betenson, *Waterbury Republican*, May 25, 1975, as quoted in Kirby, *Saga of Butch*, 97.

41. Lula said that Bob was surprised to see his brother, but it is possible that the two had somehow arranged the meeting, considering the implication that Dan may have been aware of or even involved in the preparations for the Telluride robbery.

42. Betenson and Flack, *Butch Cassidy*, 64–65.

43. Warner, *Last of Bandit Riders*, 138. Matt Warner, the only source for this incident, says the man's name was Gillis, but Bob also had an uncle named Dan Gillies, who was the postmaster at Circleville (Baker, *Wild Bunch at Robbers Roost*, 187; Betenson and Flack, *Butch Cassidy*, 56). It is doubtful, however, that Bob would have expected his uncle to report him to the authorities.

44. Warner, *Last of Bandit Riders*, 142. Although mentioned by several Wild Bunch historians, this story is almost too cute to take seriously. It or something like it may have happened, but Matt Warner or his co-author, Murray King, may have embellished it greatly. Writer Charles Kelly once said that Warner, in his later years, "was one of the best storytellers I have ever met; but he never told a story the same way twice, and over the years his memory got a little tangled up" (Kelly, *Outlaw Trail*, 35).

45. Warner, *Last of Bandit Riders*, 137–41.

On Upper Wind River

1. We know definitely that Bob Parker was calling himself George Cassidy by March 1890 and probably earlier. In a letter he wrote that month to his brother, he apologized that it "has been so long since I have written" and closed by saying: "Direct your letters to George Cassidy as before and burn this up as you read it," which suggests that he had written before using his new name. George Cassidy to Dan Parker, March 13, 1890. Reprinted in Dullenty, *Cassidy Collection*, 8.

2. Betenson and Flack, *Butch Cassidy*, 70–72.

3. With the reader's permission he'll be called Butch from here on.

4. Warner, *Last of Bandit Riders*, 144–45.

5. Warner, *Last of Bandit Riders*, 146–48. The description of the flight from Robbers' Roost to Wyoming is taken from Matt Warner's account. Tom McCarty, in his memoirs, does not mention the incident at the saloon in Lander. According to McCarty, who was often vague and never named names, two of his companions left and went off to buy horses (giving the impression that there were more than three in the group). As McCarty told it, "two of my partners concluded to purchase a band of horses for their money. Finding a gentlemen who had a very desirable lot of horses a bargain was made, the horses received, and bidding me goodbye they took their horses to a shipping point on the Union Pacific Railroad in Wyoming, loaded their horses on the cars and started for some eastern state, where they sold out a fair figure, and I suppose remained in the states a few days." McCarty says he then bought a new horse for himself and headed "into the western part of Wyoming," which, "being a place that had no outlet in the winter season on account of the snow being too deep on a large range of mountains that it was necessary to cross to get to where civilization could be found, I felt quite secure" (McCarty, *McCarty's Own Story*, 29).

6. See Moulton, *Roadside History*, 50–51.

7. Baker, *Wild Bunch at Robbers Roost*, 17, 24–25.

8. DeJournette and DeJournette, *One Hundred Years*, 164.

9. Both Brown and Dan Parker were eventually captured, and after being held briefly in the Wyoming Territorial Penitentiary at Laramie they were convicted of the robbery and sentenced to the Detroit House of Correction. Parker was pardoned in 1897, but Brown, who developed mental problems and tuberculosis while in prison, was transferred to the Saint Elizabeth's Insane Asylum in Washington DC, where he died in July 1900 (Frye, *Atlas of Outlaws*, 116, 259). For the story of the robbery, see Reust and Davidson, "Daniel Sinclair Parker," 4–5; Betenson, "Alias 'Tom Rickets,'" 2–28. Another Brown was Charley Brown, who apparently resided for a while in the Lander area and probably knew Butch (Pointer, *In Search of Cassidy*, 77). This Brown, a cowboy with roots in Texas, was indeed a rustler. In 1894 he was convicted of horse stealing and sentenced to the penitentiary for three years. But what appears to elimi-

nate him from consideration was his age. If the penitentiary records are correct, he would have been only eleven years old when Butch and his pals rode into Wyoming in the fall of 1889. Brown was a common name in Wyoming at the time, at least among miscreants. Between 1872 and 1900, eighteen men named Brown either served time in the penitentiary at Laramie or were temporarily housed there (Pointer, *In Search of Cassidy*, 77; Frye, *Atlas of Outlaws*, 4, 155).

10. McClure, *Bassett Women*, 7.

11. McClure, *Bassett Women*, 7.

12. Spafford, "Ann Bassett: 'Queen of the Cattle Rustlers,'" 24–25.

13. McClure, *Bassett Women*, 57.

14. DeJournette and DeJournette, *One Hundred Years*, 223.

15. Betenson and Flack, *Butch Cassidy*, 68.

16. *Fremont Clipper*, April 15, 1892; Greene, "Cassidy in Fremont," 1.

17. *Fremont Clipper*, April 15, 1892; Kelly, *Outlaw Trail*, 53. Will Simpson, a neighbor, did not remember that Cassidy and Hainer "dealt in horses," but he recalled that they did have plenty of money (Simpson to Charles Kelly, May 5, 1939, reprinted in Dullenty, *Cassidy Collection*, 31–34).

18. Lacy and Dullenty, "Revealing Letters," 11. Al Hainer remains a shadowy character. Although he admitted to the name "Hainer" on legal documents, it is possible that his name was spelled "Haymer," and he may have spent some time in Thermopolis, Wyoming, both before and after he joined up with Butch (Dullenty, personal communication, August 12, 1997). There is at least one Wild Bunch writer doing research on Hainer: Tim G. Palmieri, 602 Golf Course Road, Aliquippa PA 15001. Anyone having information on the man is invited to write to Palmieri.

19. Greene, "Cassidy in Fremont," 1. Cassidy biographer Larry Pointer, citing information obtained from the descendants of local residents, says that Butch and Hainer moved into an existing cabin that had been recently constructed by two bachelors, Charlie Peterson and Hughie Yoeman. As his sources, Pointer lists current or former Upper Wind River residents Harriet Woolery, Essie McCullough, Frankie Moriarty, Frank Welty, "Dutch" Nipper, Bill Burlingham, Mae Shippen, and George Peck (Pointer, *In Search of Cassidy*, 56).

20. In a letter written in 1937, Simpson said "As you know, Cassidy and Harmer [*sic*] took up a ranch on Horse Creek a little above Dubois and constructed some cabins. One of my ranches was right across the creek from where they lived. I was pretty well acquainted with both of them." Simpson to Harry Logue, February 4, 1937, reprinted in Dullenty, *Cassidy Collection*, 17. Simpson did not believe that Cassidy and Hainer purchased the property from Peterson and Yoeman but had instead taken up a homestead. Simpson to Charles Kelly, May 5, 1939. (Of course, Peterson and Yoeman may have homesteaded the land earlier and abandoned it.)

21. Greene, "Cassidy in Fremont," 1.

22. McPhee, "Former World," 41.

23. Greene, "Cassidy in Fremont," 1; William L. Simpson to Charles Kelly, May 5, 1939, reprinted in Dullenty, *Cassidy Collection*, 31.

24. Moulton, *Roadside History*, 206–7.

25. Pointer, *In Search of Cassidy*, 56.

26. Simpson to Kelly, May 5, 1939.

27. Betenson and Flack, *Butch Cassidy*, 83–84.

28. Allison, *Dubois History*, F7, T53.

29. Pointer, *In Search of Cassidy*, 56–57, citing as his source the younger Amoretti's son-in-law, George Peck. Lula Parker Bentenson also mentions Amoretti (but spells the name "Amaretti") and gives as her source a letter from Will Simpson's sister, Ida Simpson Redmond (Betenson and Flack, *Butch Cassidy*, 83).

30. Betenson and Flack, *Butch Cassidy*, 83. The authors' source was Ida Simpson Redmond.

31. Allison, *Dubois History*, T53. Eugene Amoretti Jr. became one of the most successful businessmen in the area, with interests in the Stock Grower's Bank in Bridger, Montana, and the Lander Electric Light Company. He also acquired extensive real estate holdings in and around Fremont County, and later served two terms in the Wyoming State Legislature (Allison, *Dubois History*, F7).

32. Allison, *Dubois History*, F147; Warner, *Last of Bandit Riders*, 306; Kelly, *Outlaw Trail*, 95.

33. Will Simpson and his wife settled in the area first. He moved his mother and father there in 1888. Simpson to Kelly, May 5, 1939.

34. Greene, "Cassidy in Fremont," 1–2. Alick F. C. Greene's account gives the impression that he was at the party; however, he probably heard the story some years later from the Simpsons. According to biographical data obtained from the Wyoming State Archives by Wild Bunch historian Dan Buck, Greene was living in Montana at the time of the party. He came to Wyoming in 1904 and may have become acquainted with the Simpsons while residing in Fort Washakie, Wyoming, where from 1904 to 1913 he was employed by the U.S. Indian Service as a disbursing agent. He returned to Montana in 1913 and worked at the Tongue River Agency for a year, and then transferred to the Cheyenne River Agency in South Dakota. He returned to Ft. Washakie in 1932 and apparently retired there. His monograph on Butch in Fremont Country was probably written in the early 1940s.

35. Greene, "Cassidy in Fremont," 2.

36. Betenson and Flack, *Butch Cassidy*, 21, citing a letter from Dorothy Hubbard, daughter of Ida, dated September 12, 1972.

37. Moss, "Bertha Picard, 1895–97," 48.

38. Betenson and Flack, *Butch Cassidy*, 84, citing an article about Ada Calvert Piper in the *Rawlins Daily Times*, December 9, 1967. Mrs. Piper was apparently

broad-minded when it came to defining devilment. She recalled that Butch would steal horses now and then when he needed money, and that one night he and some friends even broke into her father's corral and stole thirty head. She said he later paid for them, however.

39. Betenson and Flack, *Butch Cassidy*, 87, citing a letter from Bill Marion of Lander, an acquaintance of Mrs. Robertson. Over the years Lander newspapers frequently reported that Mrs. Robertson had been Butch's girlfriend. However, during a speaking engagement before a local women's group, Mrs. Robertson admitted that she had gone on exactly one horseback ride with Butch (Dullenty, "Outlaw or Imposter?" 22).

40. Pointer, *In Search of Cassidy*, 58–59, citing interviews with residents of Lander, Riverton, and BarGee, Wyoming, in 1972. In 1937 Mary Boyd would claim (so it seems) that she had once been Butch's common-law wife. This assertion is open to question, however, because of Mary's involvement with William T. Phillips, a Spokane, Washington, businessman who posed as Cassidy during several trips to Wyoming in the early 1930s. Mary Boyd may or may not have been duped by Phillips. According to a Lander, Wyoming, historian, Blanche Schrorer, Mary once confided to a close friend that she and Phillips "had planned the phony identity." Mary Boyd Rhodes to W. Fields, August 9, 1937, reprinted in Pointer, *In Search of Cassidy*, 23–24; Dullenty, "Outlaw or Imposter?" 22; Meadows, *Digging Up Butch*, 123. Dan Buck creates even greater doubt about the Mary Boyd–Butch Cassidy relationship. He believes that Pointer misinterpreted Mary Boyd's letter; that she probably meant that she had been the common-law wife of William T. Phillips not of Butch, during William Phillips's earlier visits to Wyoming. Buck, personal communication, August 30, 1997.

41. Betenson and Flack, *Butch Cassidy*, 87, citing an article by Maude Baker Eldredge, Baker's daughter, that appeared in the Craig, Colorado, *Daily Press*, February 12, 1971. Mrs. Eldredge, who was about seven years of age when Butch helped her father learn the ranching business, said that Butch gave her a mule and taught her how to ride it (Betenson and Flack, 89).

42. Greene, "Cassidy in Fremont," 2.

43. Why Butch chose to give New York City as his place of birth is not known, but it may have been because he knew that, should anyone have reason to check on his past, it would be difficult to do so in a city so distant and so large as New York City.

44. Greene, "Cassidy in Fremont," 2.

45. Simpson to Charles Kelly, May 5, 1939. Kelly noted this fact in the next edition of his book. Both Kelly and Lula Parker Betenson mention the epidemic as occurring in the winter of 1892–93 rather than during the winter of 1889–90, the date given by Greene (Kelly, *Outlaw Trail*, 55; Betenson and Flack, *Butch Cassidy*, 83). Larry

Pointer, citing Dubois resident Mae Shippen as his source, says that one of the Simpson children was down with the flu, and Cassidy rode through a blizzard to obtain medicine from a doctor at Fort Washakie, a 120-mile round trip (Pointer, *In Search of Cassidy*, 57).

46. Betenson and Flack, Butch Cassidy, 83.

47. Cassidy to Dan Parker, March 13, 1890, reprinted in Dullenty, *Cassidy Collection*, 8–9.

48. This statement, that Butch was staying in a house "18 miles from Lander" has caused some confusion, because in those days Horse Creek was about 75 miles from Lander. But Butch was shrewd: it could have been an intentional misstatement in case the authorities intercepted the letter.

49. George Cassidy to Dan Parker, March 13, 1890.

50. Greene, "Cassidy in Fremont," 2.

51. Greene, "Cassidy in Fremont," 2.

52. *Eastern Utah Advocate*, May 19, 1897 (Ryan interview in *Salt Lake City Tribune*); Kelly, *Outlaw Trail*, 51–52.

Blue Creek and Afterward

1. Larson, *History of Wyoming*, 271.

2. The site was originally called the Riverside Post Office. Apparently the source for this information was Guy's son, John. According to local historian Gatchell Condit, Butch's ownership of the property could be verified by the abstract of title, which was in the possession of the latest owner (Condit, "The Hole-in-the-Wall," 19–22). Larry Pointer however, claims that Butch purchased the property from a "squatter." Pointer's source appears to be Ethyl Taylor, whom he does not further identify, but whom he interviewed at the property in July 1974. It is doubtful that Butch would have purchased the property from a squatter, since a true squatter would have had no rights to sell. Pointer may have meant an "adverse possessor." (Pointer, *In Search of Cassidy*, 68). Under the law in Wyoming at the time, one could acquire title to land by settling on it and openly maintaining possession for ten years if, during such time, the true owner was aware of the adverse possessor's presence but made no effort to put him off the land (Ackerman and Johnson, "Outlaws of the Past," 82, 84). According to Wild Bunch researcher Jim Dullenty, Butch Cassidy built the pair of attached cabins on the property (Dullenty, "Historic Outlaw Sites," 18). However, Condit's source claimed that the cabins were on the land when Butch purchased it. A photo in Condit's article of the original cabins shows that they are indeed similar to the cabins Dullenty photographed in the early 1980s, but they are not identical. It is possible, of course, that the original cabins deteriorated and had to be restored, and were modified during restoration.

3. Kelly, *Outlaw Trail*, 129, citing an interview with Wheelwright, then in his nineties, probably sometime in the 1930s.

4. Hawthorne, "Johnson County," 4.

5. Spring, *Near the Greats*, 35, citing a personal interview with Manseau.

6. Hawthorne, "Johnson County," 4.

7. There are several ways to reach the Hole-in-the-Wall, none of which is recommended without first obtaining detailed instructions from the Bureau of Land Management (BLM) office in Buffalo, Wyoming. While the Hole itself is on public land, it is nearly surrounded by private property. Heck, *Pass Patrol*, 78. According to Heck, who explores outlaw trails throughout the West from his Denver headquarters (Pass Patrol 4x4 Travel Club, PO Box 470309, Aurora CO 80011), the local authorities do not go easy on trespassers in the Hole-in-the-Wall country.

8. Dullenty, "Outlaw Hangouts," 30.

9. Pointer, *In Search of Cassidy*, 68; Dullenty, "Houses Butch Built," 9.

10. Baker, *Wild Bunch at Robbers Roost*, 186.

11. Edgar and Turnell, *Brand of a Legend*, 69–70.

12. Greene, "Cassidy in Fremont," 2; Marion, "He Bit the Hand," 45; Pointer, *In Search of Cassidy*, 66, 71, citing a November 21, 1972 interview with Raymond Picard at Lost Cabin.

13. Simpson to Kelly, May 5, 1939, reprinted in Dullenty, *Cassidy Collection*, 30.

14. Warner, *Last of Bandit Riders*, 212.

15. Warner, *Last of Bandit Riders*, 213–14.

16. Spahr, "Industrial America," 628.

17. Smith, *War on the Powder*, 155–56.

18. Warner, *Last of Bandit Riders*, 215.

19. Smith, *War on the Powder*, 156; Woods, *British Gentlemen*, 1.

20. Warner, *Last of Bandit Riders*, 215.

21. Warner, *Last of Bandit Riders*, 216–18.

22. Kelly, *Outlaw Trail*, 52.

23. Betenson and Flack, *Butch Cassidy*, 87, citing Maude Baker Eldredge, daughter of Butch's friend, rancher C. E. Baker; Ernst, "Friends of the Pinkertons," 35. According to Ernst, Ayers later became a Pinkerton informant who spied on Butch and his companions. For information on Butch's work for Beason and the Two-Bar see Kelly, *Outlaw Trail*, 52–53, which cites an interview with George Streeter of Ogden, Utah, who said he worked with Butch at the Two-Bar.

24. Betenson and Flack, *Butch Cassidy*, 69. Betenson does not give the source of her information. Larry Pointer, citing as his source a Wyoming pioneer named Joe Gras, says the Rock Springs butcher shop Cassidy worked for was owned by one "Otto Schnauber." Gras claimed he also worked at the shop in 1893, after Cassidy had moved on (Pointer, *In Search of Cassidy*, 262). Cassidy also may have worked

at yet another Rock Springs butcher shop, one owned by a John Maulson who had a cattle ranch twenty miles south of town. The source of this information is Pete Parker, the grandson of Harry S. Parker, Rock Springs town marshal in the early 1890s (Betenson and Flack, *Butch Cassidy*, 72).

25. Betenson and Flack, *Butch Cassidy*, 69.

26. Dullenty, personal communication, August 12, 1997.

27. Burroughs, *Where West Stayed Young*, 119; Betenson and Flack, *Butch Cassidy*, 70.

28. Warner, *Last of Bandit Riders*, 110.

29. Pointer, *In Search of Cassidy*, 53, 262.

30. Boren, "Grandpa Knew Butch," 47.

31. Burroughs, *Where West Stayed Young*, 112.

32. *Helena Weekly Herald*, Dec. 8, 1892.

33. Burroughs, *Where West Stayed Young*, 119 (source not cited).

34. Greene, "Cassidy in Fremont," 2.

35. Harry Logue to William Marion, reprinted in *Wyoming State Journal*, April 6, 1950.

36. Will Simpson to Harry Logue, Feb. 4, 1937, reprinted in Dullenty, *Cassidy Collection*, 29.

37. Greene, "Cassidy in Fremont," 2. According to some card game historians, success at faro in Butch's day did not depend so much on skill at the game but rather on spotting a crooked dealer (Beman-Puechner, "Bucking the Tiger," 255).

38. Kelly, *Outlaw Trail*, 52.

39. Betenson and Flack, *Butch Cassidy*, 72–74, citing a 1973 interview with Harry George Parker's son Pete Parker, of Jackson, Wyoming. The original source of this story could be either the marshal or his son, since both were present in Rock Springs at the time. These Parkers were no relation to Butch.

40. Betenson and Flack, *Butch Cassidy*, 70. According to a friend of Preston's, Finley P. Gridley, manager of one of the Union Pacific Railroad's coal mining companies near Rock Springs, Preston told him that Butch once saved his (Preston's) life, and that, to show his appreciation, Preston promised that he would defend Butch or his friends whenever they got into trouble (Kelly, *Outlaw Trail*, 237). Marshal Harry S. Parker's grandson, Pete Parker, said that Butch also helped save his grandfather's life one day when a crowd of drunken Rock Springs miners threatened the lawman with knives and broken whiskey bottles. According to Pete Parker, Butch, clutching a meat cleaver from the butcher shop, and a Union Pacific Railroad detective named George Pickering, who was fortunately armed with a rifle, managed to back down the troublemakers (Betenson and Flack, *Butch Cassidy*, 72).

A Five-Dollar Horse

1. Apparently there was some doubt about Nutcher's correct name. In the crimi-

nal proceedings that were brought against Butch and Al Hainer, Nutcher was referred to in the beginning as "Joseph A. Nutcher" and later as "William H. Nutcher." The records of the Wyoming State Penitentiary list him as "Joseph Nutcher."
Frye, *Atlas of Outlaws*, 145.

2. Pointer, *In Search of Cassidy*, 70.

3. Will Simpson to Charles Kelly, May 5, 1939, reprinted in Dullenty, *Cassidy Collection*, 31–34.

4. Baker, *Wild Bunch at Robbers Roost*, 186–87. Baker's source for this incident
was a file she found in the Utah Historical Society archives entitled "Morals, Colorado Project." This material also said that before Butch and Hainer disappeared
they sold their Horse Creek Ranch, which is an error. According to local land records, they did not sell the ranch until 1900. The buyer was Butch's friend and
neighbor, banker/rancher Eugene Amoretti Jr. (Allison, *Dubois History*, F7).

5. Pointer, *In Search of Cassidy*, 72. The material in the files of the Utah Historical Society cited above by Baker also contains an error regarding Bob Calverly: that
he was a Fremont County deputy, a mistake that has been picked up by several
writers.

6. Edgar and Turnell, *Brand of a Legend*, 72, and Kelly, *Outlaw Trail*, 56.

7. Hawthorne, "Johnson County," 7.

8. Kelly, *Outlaw Trail*, 56.

9. Hawthorne, "Johnson County," 7, 22.

10. Walker, *Early Days in Wyoming*, 97.

11. Pointer, *In Search of Cassidy*, 72.

12. Kelly, *Outlaw Trail*, 56–57.

13. Simpson to Kelly, May 5, 1939.

14. Kelly, *Outlaw Trail*, 57; Pointer, *In Search of Cassidy*, 72.

15. Kelly, *Outlaw Trail*, 57.

16. Besides John Chapman, Kelly says Calverly was also accompanied by Charlie
Davis, who later became sheriff of Park County, Wyoming. He says Davis was the
brother of Kate Davis, the girl who led Calverly and Chapman to the ranch where
Butch and Hainer were hiding. Kelly, *Outlaw Trail*, 57.

17. Letter from Bob Calverly, date unknown, published in the *Wyoming State
Tribune*, June 16, 1939, and reprinted in Pointer, *In Search of Cassidy*, 72–73. The letter was obtained from Bob Calverly's son, James.

18. The account of the prosecution of Butch and Al Hainer is based upon the
court records of State v. George Cassidy & Albert Hainer, Case No. 144 (District
Court, Fremont County, Wyoming) and State v. George Cassidy & Albert Hainer,
Case No. 166 (District Court, Fremont County, Wyoming). These cases are also discussed in Pointer, *In Search of Cassidy*, 71–77, and Betenson and Flack, *Butch Cassidy*, 91–93, 101–7.

19. Butch and Hainer were charged in an "Information," or "Criminal Information," a document used in setting forth criminal charges by a public officer (usually
the prosecuting attorney). The Information is still used in most states today. It differs from an "Indictment," which is a document containing charges returned by a
grand jury stating that the jurors believe there is sufficient evidence to bring an accused to trial.

20. Otto Franc was Otto Franc von Lichenstein, a former German nobleman
who came to America probably sometime in the 1870s. In 1879 he founded the Pitchfork Ranch in western Big Horn County near the Greybull River with 1,200 Here-
fords brought down from Montana. By 1884 he was running nearly 15,000 head. An
innovator, Franc installed on the Pitchfork an underground drainage system using
pipes made out of redwood trees. Also, he was one of the first ranchers in the Big
Horn Basin to grow winter feed, primarily alfalfa. Sandoval, *Historic Ranches of
Wyoming*, 30. Just what Franc's role was in bringing the complaint against Cassidy
and Hainer is not clear. For many years, Franc served as a Justice of the Peace for
Fremont County. He may merely have signed the complaint in this capacity (Edgar
and Turnell, *Brand of a Legend*, 61).

21. Little is known about the men who agreed to testify for the prosecutor
against Butch. John Chapman, the man who helped track Butch down, was a Big
Horn Basin rancher, who with his brother owned a ranch in the Sage Creek Basin.
James Thomas was the acquaintance who had learned that Butch had departed for
southwestern Wyoming. Speed Stagner, a Missourian who had married a Shoshone woman and had been adopted into the tribe, may have been at the Shoshone
Agency at Fort Washakie when Butch and Hainer stopped there. Walker, *Stories of
Early Days in Wyoming*, 124, 227. David Stewart either worked for Otto Franc or
was a neighboring rancher (Edgar and Turnell, *Brand of a Legend*, 72).

22. Leonard Short had been in the hotel business in both Lander and Fort Wash-
akie; later he became a rancher and also operated the mail route between Fort
Washakie and Meeteetse, Wyoming. He was either owner or part-owner of the
Mail Camp where Butch was staying when he bought the three horses from Joe
Nutcher. Walker, *Early Days in Wyoming*, 120.

23. The trial was probably postponed only until the next term of court, which
would have been in the fall. However, since the case was not tried until the following July, apparently it was postponed again.

24. Simpson to Kelly, May 5, 1939.

25. Unlike most of the big ranchers, Colonel J. A. Torrey, owner of the M-Bar
ranch, encouraged homesteaders to settle around his spread. Walker, *Early Days in
Wyoming*, 86.

26. Christian Heiden interview by Jack Plane on "Labor Broadcast," December
15, 1937. A portion of this interview is reprinted in Kelly, *Outlaw Trail*, 54, 55. Accord-

ing to Edward M. Kirby, Butch was actually a moderate drinker who indulged sparingly in blended whiskeys. Without giving the source of his information, Kirby adds that Butch's favorite brands were "Mount Vernon" and "Old Crow" (Kirby, *Saga of Butch*, 7–8).

27. Frye, *Atlas of Outlaws*, 170.

28. Walker, *Early Days in Wyoming*, 86.

29. Boren and Boren, "Anna Marie Thayne," 24. The Borens believe that the young girl was Etta Place, who later became Harry Longabaugh's consort and accompanied Longabaugh and Butch to South America shortly after the turn of the century. However, few if any other writers support this theory.

30. Simpson to Kelly, May 5, 1939.

31. *Fremont Clipper*, June 23, 1893.

32. State v. George Cassidy and Al Hainer, No. 166, District Court, Fremont County, Wyoming.

33. Pointer, *In Search of Cassidy*, 75.

34. Harry Logue, a Fremont County deputy sheriff in the early 1890s, says that the Fremont County sheriff, Charley Stough, went to the Horse Creek Ranch, presumably to bring Hainer to Lander to stand trial with Cassidy. According to Logue, Hainer persuaded Stough to allow him to keep his guns on the ride from the ranch to the courthouse, explaining later that "there were some men laying for me and I wanted a chance which I would not have had if you had all the guns." *Wyoming State Journal*, April 6, 1950. In his *In Search of Butch Cassidy*, Larry Pointer says that Hainer was instrumental in causing Butch to be arrested. Pointer cites William T. Phillips's unpublished manuscript, "The Bandit Invincible: The Story of Butch Cassidy," in which Phillips claimed Hainer helped lay a trap for Butch (Pointer, *In Search of Cassidy*, 75–76). When Pointer wrote his book he was convinced that Phillips was Butch Cassidy, and that the "Bandit Invincible" manuscript was Cassidy's authentic autobiography. This idea has since lost favor with Wild Bunch historians, and Phillips is now considered to have been an imposter; however, it is possible that Phillips knew Butch—at least he knew a lot about his early life. See Meadows, *Digging Up Butch*, 115–16.

35. Richard Ashworth was a colorful and, to some extent, mysterious character. If not the owner, he had a major interest in the Grey Bull Cattle Company, the corporate entity associated with the operation of Ashworth's Big Horn Basin ranch, the z-t. Ashworth apparently kept a low profile. Although a successful rancher and originally from Birmingham, England, he is not mentioned in Lawrence Woods's *British Gentlemen*, a history of Englishmen who were involved in ranching in Wyoming. Ashworth suffered from alcoholism and died of delirium tremens while yachting in the Mediterranean in 1901. Edgar and Turnell, *Brand of a Legend*, 81, 109.

36. Frye, *Atlas of Outlaws*, 145.

37. Greene, "Cassidy in Fremont," in Dullenty, *Cassidy Collection*, 3.

38. Simpson to Kelly, May 5, 1939. There is some confusion here on dates. Simpson says the jury reached a verdict on a Saturday, yet the cover of the written verdict, as contained in the court records, is dated July 4, 1894, a Wednesday. Simpson may have been mistaken as to the day of the week; July 4 was a holiday, which probably meant the courthouse was closed and caused Simpson to misremember it as a weekend. Also, the date on the cover of the verdict may be the date the verdict was filed rather than the date it was rendered by the jury.

39. Simpson to Kelly, May 5, 1939.

40. Simpson to Kelly, May 5, 1939. Simpson thought Butch had horse-whipped Blanchard, but Hainer was later convicted for the crime, fined $25.00, and sentenced to thirty days in the county jail (Pointer, *In Search of Cassidy*, 77). Apparently, Simpson did not bring charges against Hainer, Armento, or Lamareaux for attempting to assault him.

41. Simpson to Kelly, May 5, 1939.

42. Simpson to Kelly, May 5, 1939.

43. State v. Cassidy and Hainer.

44. Diary of Otto Franc, reprinted in part in Edgar and Turnell, *Brand of a Legend*, 78.

45. Wyo. Stat. § 4984 (1892).

46. The "common law" is the law originally derived from England and is based upon court decisions rather than upon the statutes created by Congress or the state legislatures. As to the crime of receiving stolen property, see Perkins, *Criminal Law*, 322.

47. Perkins, *Criminal Law*, 322.

48. Wyo. Stat. § 4988 (1892). This is not a typographical error. Under the common law, "neat" cattle means "straight-backed, domesticated animals of the bovine genus regardless of sex, and is not generally, but may be, taken to mean calves or animals younger than yearlings." Neat cattle includes cows, bulls, and steers, but not horses, mules, goats, hogs, or sheep. *Black's Law Dictionary*, 4th ed.

49. This fact was confirmed only two years later by the Supreme Court of the United States in a case involving a Texas defendant who was wrongfully convicted of murder. Stevenson v. United States, 162 U.S. 313, 16 S. Ct. 839, 40 L. Ed. 980 (1896). This rule of law is still in effect today, being reaffirmed most recently in 1980 by the Supreme Court in Beck v. Alabama, 447 U.S. 625, 100 S. Ct. 2383, 65 L. Ed. 980, which cited the Stevenson case as precedent.

50. Allison, *Dubois History*, F7, T53. According to Allison, Amoretti would eventually take title to the Horse Creek property. Allison's book includes a copy of a receipt dated January 6, 1894, signed by Douglas Preston acknowledging receipt from Amoretti of $76.40 "on account of George Cassidy and Al Hainer, the same re-

ceived on standing order of George Cassidy and E. Amoretti, Jr." The account may have been a special legal defense fund, or it may have been set up to receive money from Amoretti.

51. Greene, "Cassidy in Fremont," 3 [104].

52. Betenson and Flack, *Butch Cassidy*, 95, citing a letter from Dorothy Hubbard, Will Simpson's niece.

53. Betenson and Flack, *Butch Cassidy*, 95 (Hubbard letter). According to Lula Betenson, Butch did bear a grudge against Bob Calverly, the Uinta County deputy sheriff who captured him in 1892. However, he apparently got over it. Betenson and her co-author tell a story about an old-timer, Tom Welch, a resident of Evanston, the Uinta County seat. Welch was supposedly acquainted with both Cassidy and Calverly, and he claimed to have once had in his possession an exchange of letters between the two men that indicated that Butch had passed up a chance to get revenge against the deputy when he, Butch, slipped into Evanston one night unnoticed (Betenson and Flack, 98). The authors' source for the story was Utah outlaw writer Kerry Ross Boren who said he saw the letters and made copies of them while they were in Welch's possession. No other writer has reported seeing the letters.

The Big Stone House

1. Frye, *Atlas of Outlaws*, 153–56.

2. Huett, "Locked Up," 22.

3. Moulton, *Roadside History*, 229.

4. Moulton, *Roadside History*, 229.

5. Frye, *Atlas of Outlaws*, vii–viii.

6. Frye, *Atlas of Outlaws*, 148.

7. Frye, *Atlas of Outlaws*, 138, 153–54.

8. Pointer, *In Search of Cassidy*, 77–78, citing an interview with Hank Boedeker Jr. at Dubois, Wyoming, March 14, 1973.

9. Huett, *Locked Up*, 22.

10. Frye, *Atlas of Outlaws*, 121, 132–33, 152, 155.

11. Frye, *Atlas of Outlaws*, 153.

12. Betenson and Flack, *Butch Cassidy*, 95–96.

13. However, Butch's great-great nephew, Bill Betenson, suggests that the family did know about Butch's confinement. Betenson writes that when Butch entered prison in July 1894, it was "an exceptional burden on Dan's mother, Annie, to have her two sons in prison." Betenson, "Alias 'Tom Rickets,'" 14.

14. Betenson, "Alias 'Tom Rickets,'" 12–16.

15. Betenson, "Alias 'Tom Rickets,'" 17.

16. Betenson and Flack, *Butch Cassidy*, 96. In commenting upon Lula's state-

ment, Dan Buck points out that regardless of whether Butch was embittered by his confinement to the Wyoming penitentiary, before he was sent there he was well on his way to a career as a rustler and horse thief (Buck, personal communication, August 30, 1997). This, of course, is true; however, it is likely that in his sister's mind and in the minds of many of his friends, Butch did not become a true outlaw until he began robbing banks and express cars.

17. Yochelson and Samenow, *The Criminal Personality*, 238.

18. Frye, *Atlas of Outlaws*, 153.

19. Frye, *Atlas of Outlaws*, 155.

20. Frye, *Atlas of Outlaws*, 155–56.

21. Frye, *Atlas of Outlaws*, 152.

22. Pointer, *In Search of Cassidy*, 79; Frye, *Atlas of Outlaws*, 146.

23. Stoner, "My Father was a Train Robber," 20–21; Hadley and Dullenty, "Cokeville," 7.

24. Frye, *Atlas of Outlaws*, 145.

25. Adams, "Rawhide Robbery," 13.

26. Frye, *Atlas of Outlaws*, 147; Marion, "He Bit the Hand," 45, 49. The deed conveying the property to Thorn was declared void, and it was rumored that before Tom Osborne left for prison he deeded the property to Butch, who redeeded it back to him when Tom was pardoned in August 1896. This Tom Osborne, whose real name was Thomas O. Shepherd, is sometimes confused with a Tom Osborne (or Osborn) who worked for Otto Franc on his Pitchfork Ranch (Edgar and Turnell, *Brand of a Legend*, 43).

27. Frye, *Atlas of Outlaws*, 145.

28. Frye, *Atlas of Outlaws*, vii.

29. Frye, *Atlas of Outlaws*, vii, 148.

30. Frye, *Atlas of Outlaws*, 140, 159.

31. Frye, *Atlas of Outlaws*, 149, 155–56, 159.

32. Frye, *Atlas of Outlaws*, 142, 143.

33. Larson, *History of Wyoming*, 295–96.

34. Larson, *History of Wyoming*, 295–96.

35. Poll, *Utah's History*, 237.

36. McPherson, *San Juan County*, 173–74. Ranchers in southeastern Utah attempted to upgrade their herds by bringing in Hereford and other shorthorn bulls. In 1892 the Utah Legislature passed a law requiring at least one halfbreed shorthorn bull for every twenty cows but it was too late (Walker, "The Carlisles," 273–74, 284).

37. Edgar and Turnell, *Brand of a Legend*, 81.

38. Kelly, *Outlaw Trail*, 60.

39. Baker, *Wild Bunch at Robbers Roost*, 188.

40. Kelly, *Outlaw Trail*, 60.

41. Collins, "Butch and the Wild Bunch," 292.

42. Frye, *Atlas of Outlaws*, 153.

43. Elnora L. Frye to Jim Dullenty, "Letters," *The Journal of the Western Outlaw-Lawman History Association*, spring-summer 1991, 1.

Free Again

1. Warner, *Last of Bandit Riders*, 155–56.

2. Warner, *Last of Bandit Riders*, 156–60, 258–69, 283–93.

3. Warner, *Last of Bandit Riders*, 293–95.

4. Burton, *Uintah County*, 414.

5. Warner, *Last of Bandit Riders*, 293–95.

6. Warner, *Last of Bandit Riders*, 293; McClure, *Bassett Women*, 57.

7. Betenson and Flack, *Butch Cassidy*, 159–60; Burton, *Uintah County*, 374. According to Burton, the sales slip was found among the store records (Burton, *Uintah County*, 390). Someone then traced the history of the weapon, which bore the Serial No. 158402, and found that it was manufactured in 1895 and shipped from the Colt factory to J. F. Schmeizer, a firearms wholesaler in Leavenworth, Kansas, who in turn sold it to the Ashley Valley Co-op in Vernal (Betenson and Flack, 160).

8. McClure, *Bassett Women*, 57.

9. Kirby, *Saga of Butch*, 14. Kirby interviewed Lay's daughter, Marvel Lay Murdock, of Heber City, Utah, in August 1973.

10. DeJournette and DeJournette, *One Hundred Years*, 279.

11. Kelly, *Outlaw Trail*, 85.

12. Baker, *Wild Bunch at Robbers Roost*, 170.

13. Burroughs, *Where West Stayed Young*, 122.

14. Betenson and Flack, *Butch Cassidy*, 79, citing information from the family records of Marvel Lay Murdock, daughter of Elzy Lay, and Harvey Murdock, Elzy's grandson. Flack interviewed the Murdocks in 1972. Lay's birthplace has also been given as Mount Pleasant, Ohio, twelve miles north of McArthur (Dullenty, "Gentleman Outlaw," 24). According to Marvel, the family name was originally "Leigh," but people had so much difficulty with the spelling that they changed it (Kirby, *Saga of Butch*, 90, citing an interview with Marvel Murdock in the summer of 1970). However, Jim Dullenty, who has conducted extensive research on Elzy's family, says in all the early records the name is spelled "Lay" (Dullenty, personal communication, August 12, 1997).

15. Betenson and Flack, *Butch Cassidy*, 79; Dullenty, "Gentleman Outlaw," 24; I. B. Allen to Charles Kelly, November 18, 1949.

16. Dullenty, "Gentleman Outlaw," 24.

17. Dullenty, "Gentleman Outlaw," 24. About the time Elzy committed his first

bank robbery, his friend William McGinnis was on his way to becoming a bank vice-president.

18. McClure, *Bassett Women*, 57; Kelly, *Outlaw Trail*, 85. Many a future cowboy came west with the haying crews in 1887. Having been spoiled by what appeared to be unlimited grass on the high plains, cattlemen in Nebraska, Colorado, Wyoming, and Montana were taken by surprise by the hot dry summer of 1886 which was followed immediately by a bitter winter of heavy snow. Livestock losses the following spring reached 90 percent for some ranchers. It was a hard lesson, but it convinced ranchers that it was prudent to cut and stack hay during good years in case of a bad one. Hundreds of haying operations were launched in the summer of 1887. Robinson, "Hay Gatherers on the High Plains," 62–63.

19. Harvey Lay Murdock's conversation with Josie Bassett Morris, as told to Dora Flack, April 1972. Betenson and Flack, *Butch Cassidy*, 249, 251.

20. Burton, *Queen Ann Bassett*, 6, citing an interview with Meacham's son. The Bassett sisters' quarrels were known to sometimes culminate in fist fights. McClure, *Bassett Women*, 52.

21. Baker, *Wild Bunch at Robbers Roost*, 171.

22. McClure, *Bassett Women*, 57.

23. Kirby, *Saga of Butch*, 12. Kirby says that Lay could be found reading or studying around the campfire or in the bunkhouse while others played cards. Kirby gives no source for this information but it probably came from Lay's daughter, Marvel Lay Murdock. Mrs. Murdock said that her father was once compared to the 1960s television character "Paladin," the frontier intellectual who was equally adept at quoting Shakespeare and handling a six-gun (Kirby, *Saga of Butch*, 14).

24. Betenson and Flack, *Butch Cassidy*, 251.

25. Burton, *Queen Ann Bassett*, 21–22.

26. Kelly, *Outlaw Trail*, 21; Dullenty, "Gentleman Outlaw," 29.

27. Walker, "Recollections of the Duchesne Strip," 2.

28. Burton, *Uintah County*, 377.

29. Dullenty, "Gentleman Outlaw," 51; Frye, *Atlas of Outlaws*, 142.

30. Boren and Boren, "Tom Vernon," 53; Dullenty, "Gentleman Outlaw," 51.

31. Baker, *Wild Bunch at Robbers Roost*, 171.

32. Warner, *Last of Bandit Riders*, 296.

33. McClure, *Bassett Women*, 57.

34. Dejournette and DeJournette, *One Hundred Years*, 266, 279–80.

35. Baker, *Wild Bunch at Robbers Roost*, 166, citing a 1957 interview with Ben Laycock, an eyewitness to the robbery; Jessen, *Colorado Gunsmoke*, 221–22. For contemporary newspaper articles on the robbery, see *Rocky Mountain News*, Sept. 8, 9, and 11, 1893.

36. Baker, *Wild Bunch at Robbers Roost*, 166; Jessen, *Colorado Gunsmoke*, 223.

37. Jessen, *Colorado Gunsmoke*, 223.

38. McCarty, *McCarty's Own Story*, 50.

39. McCarty, *McCarty's Own Story*, 50. One wonders why the McCartys stashed their second relay of horses so near town, since their first horses would not have tired that quickly. One possibility is that witnesses to the robbery would have described the horses the robbers were riding when they dashed away from the bank. By changing horses (and also perhaps changing clothes) they would have been more difficult to identify if they were later picked up.

40. McCarty, *McCarty's Own Story*, 50–53.

41. DeJournette and DeJournette, *One Hundred Years*, 280, 287.

42. DeJournette and DeJournette, *One Hundred Years*, 48, citing an interview with Ralph Chew.

43. Hughel, *Chew Bunch*, 86; Skovlin, "McCarty Names NOLA," 2. Brown's Park old-timers say that Charlie Stevens died in March 1899 (DeJournette and De-Journette, *One Hundred Years*, 47, 288). According to Jim Dullenty, however, Tom McCarty may have spent his final days in eastern Oregon and is buried there—so says writer Jon Skovlin, of Cove, Oregon, who is presently conducting extensive research on McCarty (Dullenty, personal communcation, August 12, 1997).

44. Kouris, *Brown's Park*, 79.

45. Kouris, *Brown's Park*, 79; Warner, *Last of Bandit Riders*, 296. Crouse apparently continued to play host to his outlaw friends. According to local gossip, he and Overholt kept a room over their saloon for overnight guests, the type of travelers that were not generally welcome at Vernal's respectable boarding houses (Burton, *Uintah County*, 374). Crouse may have extended more than a night's sleep to Butch Cassidy and his friends. According to Pinkerton files, four years later he was suspected of getting rid of "bad money" for the Wild Bunch, which may have meant loot damaged from the gang's overuse of dynamite in robbing express cars (Ernst, "Blackened Gold," 4).

46. Bill Wall had worked for one of the Telluride mines as a packer and, therefore, he and Butch may have known each other as early as 1884, when Butch held a similar job, possibly with the same mine. Kelly, *Outlaw Trail*, 99.

47. Warner, *Last of Bandit Riders*, 296–97.

48. *Vernal Express*, May 14, 28, and Sept. 24, 1896; *Ogden Standard*, September 9, 10, and 11, 1896. Warner, of course, denied that he had been hired to be a gunfighter and claimed that he was as surprised as anyone when Milton and the Stauntons began shooting at him (Warner, *Last of Bandit Riders*, 229; *Vernal Express*, Sept. 24, 1896).

49. *Vernal Express*, May 14, 1896; Kelly, *Outlaw Trail*, 93. According to Warner, on hearing of his and Wall's arrest, Butch and Elzy Lay rode to Vernal and, assisted by Charley Crouse and Bob Swift, helped Sheriff Pope and his deputies guard the jail (Warner, *Last of Bandit Riders*, 303).

50. *Vernal Express*, Sept. 24, 1896. Matt Warner described the trip to Ogden as agonizing. To get to Ogden from Vernal they had to ride eighty miles north to the Union Pacific Railroad at Carter, Wyoming. Worried that Butch or other pals of Warner's might attempt a rescue, or that the vigilance committee from Vernal would try to lynch the prisoners, Sheriff Pope brought along four deputies. To prevent Warner and Wall from escaping they tied them to mules. According to Matt, they handcuffed him and tied his hands to the saddle horn, then tied his ankles together with a rope that was stretched under the mule's belly. They slipped the prisoners out of Vernal at night and rode as fast as they could. By the time they reached Carter, Matt's hands and ankles were raw and bleeding. Although Matt and the sheriff had been friends for years, Matt claimed that he warned Pope that if he did ever get free he would kill him (Warner, *Last of Bandit Riders*, 304–5).

51. *Vernal Express*, May 28, 1896.

52. Kelly, *Outlaw Trail*, 94.

53. Warner, *Last of Bandit Riders*, 306.

54. Allison, *Dubois History*, F147.

55. Pointer, *In Search of Cassidy*, 100, citing interviews with descendants of the Meeks family.

56. Walker, *Early Days*, 129–30.

Montpelier

1. Sweet, "Gramps, Butch Cassidy," 38.

2. Dullenty, *From the Editor*, 3; Behymer, "You Don't Chase!" 27. The Montpelier bank was located at 833 Washington Street. The building still stands today; it's now a print shop. Kathy Corgatelli, "Cassidy Robs Again," *Idaho Falls Post Register*, http://www.idahonews.com/horse/August/butch.htm (16 Aug. 1996).

3. Hayden, "Cassidy and Montpelier Robbery," 2.

4. Wilde, *Treasured Tidbits of Time*, 221.

5. Wilde, *Treasured Tidbits of Time*, 221; Kelly, *Outlaw Trail*, 95; Hayden, "Cassidy and Montpelier Robbery," 4.

6. *Idaho Daily Statesman*, Aug. 14, 1896.

7. *Idaho Daily Statesman*, Aug. 14, 1896; Hayden, "Cassidy and Montpelier Robbery," 3; Wilde, *Treasured Tidbits*, 221. According to one of the witnesses, it appeared that the gunman was not angered much by McIntosh's answer, but rather he had seen McIntosh's rifle and thought that he was about to reach for it (Hayden, "Cassidy and Montpelier Robbery," 3).

8. A story is still told around Montpelier that a local freight hauler, Fritz Teuscher, had met the three robbers as they were riding into town. Teuscher had several empty sacks on his wagon and one of the robbers, which Teuscher believed to be Cassidy, asked if he could borrow it. When Teuscher asked for what, he said that

Cassidy grinned and answered, "Oh for all you know we might be going to rob the bank in Montpelier." Teuscher said that he gave the men the sack and then joked, "When you get through, I live in Geneva. My name is Fritz Teuscher, and if you come by, drop it off." Wilde, *Treasured Tidbits,* 221–22.

9. Wilde, *Treasured Tidbits,* 221.

10. *Idaho Daily Statesman,* Aug. 14, 1896; Hayden, "Cassidy and Montpelier Robbery," 3.

11. *Idaho Daily Statesman,* Aug. 14, 1896; Hayden, "Cassidy and Montpelier Robbery," 3–4.

12. Behymer, "You Don't Chase!" 27; Sweet, "Gramps, Butch Cassidy," 9, 38.

13. Behymer, "You Don't Chase!" 27; Sweet, "Gramps, Butch Cassidy," 9, 38.

14. Behymer, "You Don't Chase!" 54. Since witnesses claimed that the robbers had brought a sack with them to carry the money from the bank, it is possible that the oat sack was used in dividing up the loot.

15. *Idaho Daily Statesman,* Aug. 14, 1896; Hayden, "Cassidy and Montpelier Robbery," 4.

16. *Montpelier Examiner,* Aug. 15, 1896; *Idaho Daily Statesman,* Aug. 17, 1896; Hayden, "Cassidy and Montpelier Robbery," 4.

17. *Idaho Daily Statesman,* Aug. 15, 1896.

18. Hayden, "Cassidy and Montpelier Robbery," 4.

19. *Idaho Daily Statesman,* Aug. 17, 1896.

20. Hayden, "Cassidy and Montpelier Robbery," 4. A report came in that Malone's posse spotted the outlaws' little sorrel mare, which, because it was carrying the heavy stolen coins, could not keep up with Butch and his companions. The possemen tried to catch it but were unsuccessful. Out of this incident has grown a fanciful tale that the little horse was able to elude Malone's posse and eventually find its way to the outlaws' hideout on her own.

21. *Idaho Daily Statesman,* Aug. 14, 1896; Kelly, *Outlaw Trail,* 96; Hayden, "Cassidy and Montpelier Robbery," 5.

22. *Montpelier Examiner,* Aug. 27, 1896; Wilde, *Treasured Tidbits,* 223.

23. Wilde, *Treasured Tidbits,* 223.

24. *Montpelier Examiner,* Aug. 27, 1896.

25. Hayden, "Cassidy and Montpelier Robbery," 5; Warner, *Last of Bandit Riders,* 306.

26. Warner, *Last of Bandit Riders,* 306; Kelly, *Outlaw Trail,* 96.

27. These principles have not changed: it is how things are done today.

28. Warner, *Last of Bandit Riders,* 306.

29. Kelly, *Outlaw Trail,* 98.

30. *Salt Lake City Herald,* Sept. 9, 1896, partially quoted in the *Ogden Standard* of Sept. 10, 1896. See also Kelly, *Outlaw Trail,* 99; and Betenson and Flack, *Butch Cassidy,* 112.

31. *Salt Lake City Herald*, Sept. 9, 1896.

32. *Ogden Standard*, Sept. 10, 1896; Kelly, *Outlaw Trail*, 100; Betenson and Flack, *Butch Cassidy*, 112.

33. *Ogden Standard*, Sept. 10, 1896.

34. *Ogden Standard*, Sept. 10, 1896.

35. *Ogden Standard*, Sept. 10, 1896.

36. *Ogden Standard*, Sept. 10, 1896.

37. This story appears in Kelly's *The Outlaw Trail*, beginning on page 100. Although Kelly says that Decker and Smoot's account of meeting Butch and Meeks was published in the *Salt Lake Tribune* "during the trial," a search of the *Tribune* archives on file at the Salt Lake City Public Library failed to turn up the article in any of the archived editions published during the month of September 1896. It is of course possible that the article appeared in an early edition of the paper but was pulled from a later edition, and only the later edition was preserved for the archives.

38. Kelly, *Outlaw Trail*, 100.

39. Kelly, *Outlaw Trail*, 100. Charles Kelly claimed that, in 1935, he interviewed the police chief, who was supposed to have intercepted the notes, as well as a jailor who was on duty while Warner, Wall, and Coleman were awaiting trial. Kelly said that both men affirmed that they had seen the notes and that they had allowed them to be passed between Warner and Cassidy.

40. Kelly, *Outlaw Trail*, 100.

41. A copy of the letter appears in Dullenty, *Cassidy Collection*, 36–37.

42. *Vernal Express*, Sept. 24, 1896. Warner later claimed that Staunton changed his testimony because Matt had attended to his wounds while waiting for the sheriff to arrive (Kelly, *Outlaw Trail*, 98).

Castle Gate

1. Boren and Boren, "Tom Vernon," 53–64. Tom Vernon was the uncle of the late Clinton Vernon, former Attorney General of Utah. According to the Borens, Vernon, then eighteen years of age, witnessed the events described in this account of Butch and Elzy Lay at the Jones ranch. In addition, Kerry Ross Boren says that his own grandfather and grandmother were also staying at the Jones ranch during the time Cassidy and Lay were there—in fact, Boren says, in the cabin next door.

2. Maude claimed that she and Elzy were married that fall. In later years, Elzy's second wife, Mary Calvert Lay, said that Elzy told her that the marriage was performed in Grand Junction, Colorado. However, Marvel Lay Murdock (Maude and Elzy's daughter), doubts that her parents ever made it official. Dullenty, "Gentleman Outlaw," 27–28.

3. Tom Vernon says that it was Etta (Boren and Boren, "Tom Vernon," 54). Mar-

vel Lay Murdock, daughter of Maude and Elzy, says that Etta was with the Wild Bunch that fall, possibly with Butch (Baker, *Wild Bunch at Robbers Roost*, 173). Etta Place biographer Gail Drago is not sure (Drago, *Etta Place*, 46–47). Ann Bassett and the woman who became known as Etta Place were similar in appearance. Although Maude Davis should have known who shared Butch's bed at Maeser, she and Ann Bassett were close friends and Maude may have gone along with the story that Butch's companion was Etta Place to protect Ann's reputation. Doris Burton, throughout her book, points out how Ann could have frolicked with the Wild Bunch many times as Etta Place; however, her thesis that Bassett and Etta were one and the same has not been accepted by most writers (Burton, *Queen Ann Bassett*, 14–15).

4. *Salt Lake City Herald*, Sept. 9, 1896, quoted in the *Ogden Standard*, Sept. 10, 1896. See also Kelly, *Outlaw Trail*, 99; and Betenson and Flack, *Butch Cassidy*, 112.

5. Burton, "Sheriff Pope," 8.

6. Pete Dillman was also part owner of Vernal's only funeral parlor, an interesting and possibly at times advantageous business for a deputy sheriff. For a while Dillman also operated a drug store and, in the absence of a doctor, served in that capacity (an interesting line of work for a funeral parlor owner). Burton, *Uintah County*, 162, 404.

7. Boren and Boren, "Tom Vernon," 55; Burton, "Sheriff Pope, 8.

8. Boren and Boren, "Tom Vernon," 55; Burton, *Uintah County*, 375.

9. *The Vernal Express*, May 14, 1896; Burton, *Uintah County*, 274.

10. Burton, "Sheriff Pope," 9, citing Ann Bassett's diary. Butch, however, may not have shared Ann's opinion regarding John Pope's loyalties. According to Pope's granddaughters, several weeks after he left Vernal, Pope received a postcard from Butch, saying: "Pope, Gawd damn you, lay off me. I don't want to kill you." Burton says that the granddaughters told her that the postcard was placed in the Daughters of Utah Pioneers Museum in Salt Lake City (Burton, *Uintah County*, 390).

11. Burroughs, *Where West Stayed Young*, 43.

12. Burroughs, *Where West Stayed Young*, 130, citing correspondence by Sizer on file in the records of the Routt National Forest.

13. Kelly, *Outlaw Trail*, 236–37.

14. Kelly, *Outlaw Trail*, 136. Kelly's source was probably Gridley, who supplied him with other stories about his days in Rock Springs working for the Union Pacific mine, but neither he nor Kelly mentions how he knew the would-be robbers were Butch and his gang.

15. McClure, *Bassett Women*, 58–60. In recalling the event, Ann Bassett remembered it as occurring in 1895. While Ann may have been good at remembering menus and how people dressed, she apparently was a little weak in remembering dates, since Butch was in prison that fall. McClure believes that the party actually took place on Thanksgiving Day, 1896 (McClure, *Bassett Women*, 224).

16. McClure, *Bassett Women*, 59–60.

17. McClure, *Bassett Women*, 60.

18. Baker, *Wild Bunch at Robbers Roost*, 173.

19. Utah Archives, "Robbers Roost and Butch Cassidy, Criminals," file 1899–1900, papers of Governor Heber M. Wells. Reprinted in part in Betenson and Flack, *Butch Cassidy*, 116.

20. Baker, *Wild Bunch at Robbers Roost*, 29. Buhr would later move his ranch headquarters to Granite Wash, about seventeen miles south of Hanksville at the north edge of the Henry Mountains. The authorities believed that Butch and the Wild Bunch later established a hideout near there, just north of the wash. This site was also near a spring and was more elaborate than the Horseshoe Canyon site. It consisted of three log cabins with a cellar and a nearby corral sheltered by an overhanging bluff (Utah Archives, "Robbers Roost and Butch Cassidy, file 1899–1900; Betenson and Flack, Butch Cassidy, 119). There were rumors that Buhr was actually the "King Bee" of rustlers in the Robbers' Roost area because they were always welcome at his ranch (Kelly, *Outlaw Trail*, 148). Buhr's foreman, Jack Moore, and Moore's brother-in-law, Monte Butler, were said to be heavily involved in the rustling business (Kelly, *Outlaw Trail*, 147; Frank Silvey, *Northern San Juan County*, 58).

21. Baker, *Wild Bunch at Robbers Roost*, 171–72.

22. Geary, *Emery County*, 108–9.

23. Kelly, *Outlaw Trail*, 157–58.

24. Baker, *Wild Bunch at Robbers Roost*, 172–73.

25. Utah Archives, "Robbers Roost and Butch Cassidy," file 1899–1900; Betenson and Flack, Butch Cassidy, 116.

26. Baker, *Wild Bunch at Robbers Roost*, 173. Marvel Lay Murdock, the daughter of Elzy and Maude, believes that she was conceived while her parents were at the Robbers' Roost hideout. Dullenty, "Gentleman Outlaw," 27.

27. Baker, *Wild Bunch at Robbers Roost*, 173. Marvel said that her mother "loved and admired" Etta and thought that she was the most beautiful woman she had ever seen. Brown's Park historians Dick and Daun DeJournette also believe that it was Etta, and that she was there to be with Butch (DeJournette and DeJournette, *One Hundred Years*, 216). Marvel's son, Harv Murdock, grandson of Elzy, said that Pearl Baker once told him that Butch, Elzy, Maude, and Etta had carved their initials on the mantle above a fireplace in a cabin at Robbers' Roost, but the cabin later burned down (DeJournette and DeJournette, *One Hundred Years*, 340).

28. Baker, *Wild Bunch at Robbers Roost*, 173. Baker claimed that she personally interviewed several men who had seen Butch's companion that winter, but none of them were sure of her true identity. However, in 1974 in an interview with Ed Kirby, Pearl said that she herself believed that it was Etta (Kirby, *Saga of Butch*, 89).

29. Burton, *Queen Ann Bassett*, 19, 28, 32, 37–38.

30. Baker, *Wild Bunch at Robbers Roost*, 173.

31. Kelly, *Outlaw Trail*, 170–71; Baker, *Wild Bunch at Robbers Roost*, 174.

32. This raises the possibility that three women were present. If the mysterious Etta Place was there (as some say), and if Ann Bassett and Etta were not one and the same, and Ann Bassett was with Butch, then Etta may have been Longabaugh's companion, which may have been the beginning of their long-standing relationship.

33. Baker, *Wild Bunch at Robbers Roost*, 174.

34. Van Cott, *Utah Names*, 69.

35. Geary, *Emery County*, 112.

36. Except where otherwise noted, this account of the Pleasant Valley Coal Company robbery and Butch and Elzy Lay's escape has been taken from the April 22, 1897, issue of the *Eastern Utah Advocate* (Price, Utah) and from Baker, *Wild Bunch at Robbers Roost*, 201–11, and Kelly, *Outlaw Trail*, 133–40.

37. According to Arden Stewart, former Uintah County sheriff whose father worked on a ranch near Castle Gate at the time of the robbery, the locomotive engineer gave the signal with his whistle when the payroll was on board. Stewart, "Dad Nearly Rode with Butch," 45.

38. That cowboys on horses were a novelty in Castle Gate and how Butch and his pals overcame the problem comes from Baker, *Wild Bunch at Robbers Roost*, 202.

39. DeJournette and DeJournette, *One Hundred Years*, 336–39. The source of this story was Arden Stewart, former sheriff of Uintah County, whose father, John Henry "Hank" Stewart, was working at the Murning-Meeks ranch at the time.

40. Geary, *Emery County*, 128.

41. Baker, *Wild Bunch at Robbers Roost*, 48–49, quoting from the notes of the April 1897, meeting of the Carbon County Commissioners, contained in the *County Court Minute Book*, 163–64. Smith's petition was successful and Sheriff Donant submitted his resignation. At the same meeting the Commissioners appointed a new sheriff, C. W. Allred.

42. Several writers tell of Butch using this time to train his horse not to fear a noisy, steaming locomotive. As the story goes, Butch was concerned that when the day came to relieve the coal company of its payroll, his horse would be skittish because the company offices were so near to the railroad. So while hanging around Castle Gate, when a train would come in Butch would ride to the front and make his horse stand as close to the locomotive as possible, until the animal eventually realized that a belching engine was nothing to fear. Stewart, "Dad Nearly Rode," 45; Kelly, *Outlaw Trail*, 134; Stegner, *Mormon Country*, 290.

43. Charles Kelly is believed to have obtained this information during a personal interview with Caffey in 1938. Kelly, *Outlaw Trail*, 136.

44. Stewart, "Dad Nearly Rode," 46.

45. Baker, *Wild Bunch at Robbers Roost*, 205. Charles Kelly believes that Carpenter commandeered a switch engine instead of the passenger train locomotive that brought the payroll from Salt Lake City. He says that townsmen from Castle Gate piled on, apparently intending to join the posse that would surely be formed in Price, and that on the way one of the men, David Kramer, fell off and was injured (Kelly, *Outlaw Trail*, 137). The report in the *Eastern Utah Advocate* does not mention Carpenter appropriating a locomotive of any kind.

46. Donant was still on the job; apparently Allred, the new sheriff, did not take office until the following month.

47. Kelly, *Outlaw Trail*, 134, 137.

48. Geary, "Emery County," 127.

49. The outlaws may have had a camp of some sort near the cliffs just above the San Rafael River, at a spot called San Rafael Swell. The report on Butch Cassidy's hideouts found by author Dora Flack in the archives of Utah Governor Heber M. Wells listed the spot as "Robbers Roost No. 6" and notes that the outlaws passed through there after the Castle Gate robbery. Betenson and Flack, *Butch Cassidy*, 116–19. While Charles Kelly's account of the escape assumes that Butch and Lay were still together at this point, later on Kelly raises the possibility that they may have split up somewhere along the route. Kelly says that there was "undisputed evidence" that Lay and one of the gang members rode to Robbers' Roost by way of Torrey, a small town in western Wayne County, and then to Hanksville, which is directly to the east and midway between Torrey and Robbers' Roost. Kelly's evidence came from an eyewitness, Albert Morrill, then a boy of twelve, who said that Lay and the other man spent an afternoon and evening at Torrey. As to Hanksville, Kelly's source was a local resident, Court Stewart, who said that the two men spent two or three days camped at the edge of town (Kelly, *Outlaw Trail*, 139).

50. Kelly, *Outlaw Trail*, 138. At the point where the outlaws turned south, the number of riders may have grown to as many as eight. It was reported that during the night at a ranch near Ninemile Wash, eight horses were taken from the corral and eight weary animals were left in their place (Kelly, *Outlaw Trail*, 139).

51. Baker, *Wild Bunch at Robbers Roost*, 206–7. For a retracing of the route taken by Joe Walker, see Heck, *Pass Patrol*, 43.

52. It was probably Tom Lloyd, a former sheriff. See Betenson and Flack, *Butch Cassidy*, 126.

53. Baker, *Wild Bunch at Robbers Roost*, 209–10.

54. Betenson and Flack, *Butch Cassidy*, 126.

55. *Eastern Utah Advocate*, Apr. 22, 187. Elzy Lay was not mentioned. According

to the article, Cassidy's accomplice was believed to be a "Tom Gissell," a name still unfamiliar to Wild Bunch researchers.

56. This supposedly occurred at a meeting of coal company executives in Denver. Finley P. Gridley had brought a picture of Butch to the meeting. Carpenter was sitting at the opposite end of a long table. Gridley took out the picture and slid it down the table toward Carpenter. He looked at it and jokingly threw up his hands, exclaiming, "For God sakes, Grid, don't ever give another scare like that!" Kelly, *Outlaw Trail*, 238.

57. Kelly, *Outlaw Trail*, 152–53.

58. Burroughs, *Where West Stayed Young*, 123. Burroughs says Butch's favorite song was "The Texas Ranger."

59. Betenson and Flack, *Butch Cassidy*, 126.

60. Geary, *Emery County*, 124, 128.

61. Kelly, *Outlaw Trail*, 155–56.

62. Geary, *Emery County*, 325.

63. Kelly, *Outlaw Trail*, 155–57.

64. Baker, *Wild Bunch at Robbers Roost*, 174.

Longabaugh

1. Ernst, *Sundance*, 17–18; Kirby, *Rise and Fall*, 22.

2. Kirby, *Rise and Fall*, 28.

3. Perkins, "Historic Triangle," 20–21; Silvey, *Northern San Juan County*, 25.

4. Ernst, *Sundance*, 19, 23; Kirby, *Rise and Fall*, 28.

5. Kirby, *Rise and Fall*, 29, citing a 1901 article in the *Great Falls Tribune*.

6. Ernst, *Sundance*, 23.

7. McPherson, *San Juan County*, 149, 173.

8. Walker, "The Carlisles," 283.

9. Walker, "The Carlisles," 270–71.

10. Baker, *Wild Bunch at Robbers Roost*, 110–13.

11. According to southeastern Utah historian Faun McCorkie Tanner, Butch himself may have worked for the Carlisles. However, Tanner does not give us the source of her information. Tanner, *Far Country*, 177.

12. Kirby, *Rise and Fall*, 28. For more on the Pittsburgh Land and Cattle Company see McPherson, *San Juan County*, 172.

13. Ernst, *Sundance*, 33–34.

14. Horan, *Desperate Men*, 377, quoting "an old cowpuncher," John F. Kelly.

15. Warner, *Last of Bandit Riders*, 111.

16. Kirby, *Rise and Fall*, 30.

17. Buck, "Surprising Developments," 34.

18. Brown, *American West*, 331.

19. Brown, *American West*, 331.

20. Woods, *British Gentlemen*, 106.

21. Brown, *American West*, 331.

22. Sandoval, *Historic Ranches*, 11; Clay, *My Life*, 93.

23. Kirby, *Rise and Fall*, 30. The incident was reported in *The Sundance Gazette*, March 18, 1887.

24. Kirby, *Rise and Fall*, 30–31. Longabaugh was fortunate that Clay simply sent the sheriff after him because Clay gave no quarter when it came to punishing thieves. One day Clay heard that a man whom he suspected of stealing his cattle had been found dead in an arroyo with a bullet hole in him. His comment was "The moral stickler of the East would call this murder. Knowing the circumstances, I call it retribution—well merited at that" (Clay, *My Life*, 82–83).

25. It seems observers had a difficult time agreeing on a description of Longabaugh once he reached maturity. In August 1887, he was described as being five feet ten and a half inches tall and having a light complexion, light hair, and blue eyes. Kirby, *Rise and Fall*, 35. Eighteen months later, upon leaving jail, Harry's official prison record listed him as five feet nine inches and having black hair, a dark complexion, Creole-type features, and weighing 165 pounds (Frye, *Atlas of Outlaws*, 273). Over the years, between age twenty-one and forty-one he was also described as being anywhere from five feet seven to six feet in height and weighing as much as 190 pounds. His hair ranged from light brown to black (which, of course, could have been the result of a dye). However, his eyes were at various times reported to be blue, gray, black, and brown (Kirby, *Rise and Fall*, 35; Meadows, *Digging Up Butch*, 279).

26. Ernst, *Sundance*, 40–41; Kirby, *Rise and Fall*, 30–31. Ernst raises the possibility that the confederate may have been Butch Cassidy. It was believed that Longabaugh may have had assistance in this escape because of the obvious difficulty in personally removing the shackles and handcuffs; however, his later escape attempts suggest that he was adept at doing so.

27. Ernst, *Sundance*, 41–42; Kirby, *Rise and Fall*, 32.

28. Ernst, *Sundance*, 41–43; Kirby, *Rise and Fall*, 32–33. The article on Longabaugh appeared in *The Daily Yellowstone Journal*, June 7, 1887, and his letter to the editor appeared on June 9. The newspaper was published in Billings.

29. Ernst, *Sundance*, 43–45; Kirby, *Rise and Fall*, 33–35.

30. United States v. Harry Longabaugh, U.S. District Court for the Territory of Wyoming. Indictments Nos. 33, 34, and 44, Grand Jury of the County of Crook, Territory of Wyoming, August 2, 1887.

31. Frye, *Atlas of Outlaws*, 273; Ernst, *Sundance*, 45; Kirby, *Rise and Fall*, 34–35.

32. Frye, *Atlas of Outlaws*, 96. Illinois readily entered into these arrangements with various territorial prisons because that state was allowed to turn a profit from the use of prison labor.

33. Frye, *Atlas of Outlaws*, 108.

34. Frye, *Atlas of Outlaws*, 273.

35. It is not certain just who first tagged Longabaugh with the nickname Sundance Kid. Utah writer Kerry Ross Boren believes that it was Cleophas J. Dowd, a Brown's Park character and former Pinkerton agent who over the years was pals with several members of the Wild Bunch. Boren, "Pinkerton," 28. Boren does not give the source of this information.

36. Ernst, *Sundance*, 45. This incident was reported in *The Sundance Gazette*, May 4, 1888.

37. Frye, *Atlas of Outlaws*, 273.

38. Kirby, *Rise and Fall*, 35; Ernst, *Sundance*, 45; Frye, *Atlas of Outlaws*, 273. The pardon is listed as Document No. 124 in Volume I of the *Record of Pardons* of the Secretary of the Territory of Wyoming.

39. Kirby, *Rise and Fall*, 37; Ernst, *Sundance*, 45–47. The shooting of Bob Minor, alias Buck Hanby, was reported in *The Sundance Gazette*, May 17, 1889.

40. Ernst, "Sundance: Missing Years," 21; Ernst, *Sundance*, 53, 55. For her source Ernst cites correspondence and interviews with descendants of George Longenbaugh, especially Walter Longenbaugh, George's son. Ernst also states that the Longenbaugh family history includes information that George's wife Mary provided provisions for the Telluride robbers when they were hiding out at Tom McCarty's ranch. The McCarty place was only a mile and a half from the Longenbaugh ranch. Other members of the family may know the truth, but apparently they are hesitant to talk much about their outlaw ancestor (William D. Longabaugh, "Sundance Kid," 35, 39). For more on this possibility, see Richard Patterson, "Sundance Kid in Telluride Robbery?" 10–12.

41. Kirby, *Rise and Fall*, 37.

42. Kirby, *Rise and Fall*, 37, 39.

43. Buck, "Surprising Development," 34.

44. Buck, "Surprising Development," 10.

45. It has been suggested that the complaint may have been filed by Herb Millar after he spotted the hacksaw blade under Harry's saddle, thinking that the blade would injure the horse. Ernst, "Sundance: Missing Years," 23.

46. Buck, "Surprising Development," 10, quoting from Ings's memoirs, published locally in 1980 under the title *Before the Fences*.

47. Buck, "Surprising Development," 10.

48. Ernst, "Sundance: Missing Years," 21.

49. Ernst, "Sundance: Missing Years," 23.

50. Harry and Bill Madden may have first met in Montana in 1892, but it is more likely that they knew each other in Colorado since the town of Mancos was less than twenty miles from Harry's cousin's ranch near Cortez. That Madden also

knew Butch Cassidy in Colorado lends more support to the suggestion that Harry and Butch may have first met there.

51. Patterson, *Train Robbery Era*, 245–48. For an account of the Verdi robbery, see Beebe and Clegg's *U.S. West: The Saga of Wells Fargo*, which contains many details not reported in the newspaper accounts.

52. Patterson, *Train Robbery Era*, 14, 113–16. The history of the James gang is best covered in William A. Settle Jr.'s *Jesse James Was His Name*. The Big Springs robbery was reported in most major newspapers of the day, including *The New York Times*, September 20, 1877. On the career of Sam Bass, see Gard, *Sam Bass*. Bass's record haul was topped four years later. In October 1881 three robbers attacked an express car on the Colorado & Southern Railroad a few miles north of Colorado Springs. Unverified reports estimated the loss at $145,000—$105,000 in cash and $40,000 in jewelry and other valuables. The robbers were captured, but the money and valuables were never found. For an interesting account of the robbery, see Kildare, "Bear River Loot," *Real West*, September 1968.

53. Patterson, "Train Robbery," 48.

54. The brief slump in train robberies may have been due partially to the rumor that the express companies were no longer shipping vast sums by rail because of the advent of money orders. But there were still plenty of currency and coin being shipped to and from banks, and payrolls in the West were usually met with cash. The treasures were still there for those who chose the right express cars to rob. Hatch, *American Express*, 84–86.

55. Patterson, "Train Robbery," 48–49.

56. Patterson, "Train Robbery," 49–50.

57. Kirby, *Rise and Fall*, 46–47.

58. The blind baggage was the windowless platform area at the front end of an express or baggage car, just behind the tender. It was so named because a person hidden there could not be seen by the locomotive crew. For years the spot was the favorite boarding place for both tramps and train robbers. The blind baggage became so popular among train robbers in the 1890s that the editors of the railroad industry periodical *Railway Age* urged car builders to abolish the front platform on express and baggage cars. The idea was resisted; railroad cars had both front and rear platforms to allow trainmen to move freely from one end of a train to the other. However, in 1895 the U.S. Post Office Department adopted the idea of eliminating the front platform for some of its railway mail cars. An alternative to eliminating the blind baggage was to install a window in the front door of the cars. In the 1870s a few cars had such windows, but they were discontinued probably because the glass could be easily broken, allowing bandits, even if the window was barred, to shoot into the car. Patterson, *Train Robbery Era*, 16. The details of the Malta robbery appeared in most Montana newspapers, including the November 30

editions of *The River Press* (Malta) and *The Great Falls Daily Tribune*. This account was taken mainly from the *Helena Weekly Herald*, December 8, 1892. See also Ernst, *Sundance*, 79–83, and Kirby, *Rise and Fall*, 46–48.

59. Most railway express cars carried two safes: a "through safe" that was locked at the point of origin and was not to be opened until the terminus or a division point, and a "local safe" that the messenger used during the run for shipments picked up and delivered along the line and for cash and valuables being held for passengers.

60. In 1891 word spread that on some long runs express companies were installing through safes with variable combination locks (locks that could be given new combinations each time a train departed on a run). These combinations, sent by telegraph (presumably in code) to the terminus or division point were not given to the express car messengers and, therefore, the messengers could not be forced to open the safes. It was rumored, however, that this was more fiction than fact, that the story was concocted to discourage potential train robbers. Some express companies did experiment with spring-operated time locks on long shipments. If held up by robbers the messengers were expected to show the bandits the elaborate time mechanism and explain that absolutely no one could open the safe until the expected time of arrival at the destination point. Patterson, *Birth, Flowering*, 120.

61. Harlow, *Old Waybills*, 463.

62. *Helena Weekly Herald*, Dec. 8, 1887.

63. Ernst, *Sundance*, 82–83; Kirby, *Rise and Fall*, 47.

64. Ernst, *Sundance*, 83, citing a memo contained in the files of Pinkerton's National Detective Agency pertaining to the Malta robbery. The memo, dated November 29, 1892, was from a J. D. B. Greig, apparently a Pinkerton operative.

65. Kirby, *Rise and Fall*, 48.

The Wild Bunch

1. Kouris, "Lynching Calamity," 61–62.

2. DeJournette and DeJournette, *One Hundred Years*, 240–43.

3. Kelly, *Outlaw Trail*, 162. Just when Butch put together his "gang" is difficult to determine. Probably it was sometime in late summer of 1896. Only Butch, Elzy Lay, and Bub Meeks have been directly connected with the robbery of the Montpelier bank, but Butch and Elzy may have had considerable help in making their escape following the robbery at Castle Gate. Kerry Ross Boren, without citing a source, thinks that the gang was officially organized at Charley Crouse's ranch in Brown's Park on August 18, 1896, five days after the Montpelier holdup (Boren, "Badges and Badmen," 42). Pearl Baker seems to generally agree as to the time frame (Baker, *Wild Bunch at Robbers Roost*, 188). In the beginning the gang may have been called the "Diamond Mountain Boys" (Armstrong, *Story of Maxwell*, 14).

4. Baker, *Wild Bunch at Robbers Roost,* 188.

5. Buck, personal communication, August 30, 1997. According to Buck it is possible that the Pinkertons dreamed up the "fearsome moniker," "The Wild Bunch," to impress upon the American Bankers Association the need for the kind of protection that the detective agency could provide.

6. Parsons, "Burial Plot," 56.

7. Baker, *Wild Bunch at Robbers Roost,* 188. Baker gives no source for this information.

8. Kirby, *Rise and Fall,* 54. Some believe that the gang may not actually have been Butch's to lead in the beginning, that the group may have been without a true leader for a while, and that several of the early members may have looked to Logan for leadership while others favored Currie. At least one outlaw historian, Ed Bartholomew, carries this further. He believes that Butch has been highly overrated as the leader of the Wild Bunch and that whatever fame and success the gang enjoyed should be credited to other members. Bartholomew feels the same way about Harry Longabaugh. He thinks the popularity of both Butch and Harry is the product of "romantic mythmaking" (Selcer, *Hell's Half Acre,* 318, citing correspondence with Bartholomew).

9. That there were both a Kid "Curry" and George "Currie" in the gang has troubled Wild Bunch researchers for years. The two names were frequently confused, mainly because "Currie" was often spelled "Curry," even by George's acquaintances. See, for example, Brock, "A Timely Arrival," *Annals of Wyoming,* Jan. 1943.

10. Kelly, *Outlaw Trail,* 117–18. An account of the fight by a man who was there that night appears in the *Great Falls Tribune,* January 20, 1935.

11. Kelly, *Outlaw Trail,* 117–18; Lamb, *Wild Bunch,* 4–5.

12. Condit, "The Hole-in-the-Wall," 22.

13. Pointer, *In Search of Cassidy,* 253.

14. Kelly, *Outlaw Trail,* 162.

15. Kelly, *Outlaw Trail,* 163; Wilde, *Treasured Tidbits,* 223.

16. Kelly, *Outlaw Trail,* 163.

17. Kirby, *Rise and Fall,* 55–57; Ernst, *Sundance,* 85–87.

18. For years Wild Bunch researchers have accepted as fact that Harry Longabaugh was one of the participants in the robbery at Belle Fourche. Included among these researchers was Donna B. Ernst, author of *Sundance, My Uncle.* However, in August 1997 Ernst reported finding an unpublished manuscript in the archives of the University of Wyoming that suggested otherwise. The manuscript was written by John F. Gooldy, a rancher in the Snake River Valley who claimed to have known Longabaugh well and said that, at the time of the Belle Fourche robbery, Longabaugh was in the valley working for a neighboring rancher, A. R.

Reader. According to Ernst, Gooldy's account was verified by two clerks at a general store in nearby Slater, Colorado. An interview of one of these clerks, Oliver St. Louis, is on file at the Museum of Northwest Colorado, Craig, Colorado. Ernst, "Sundance Kid," 6.

19. The bank had purchased a new pistol that was kept under the counter where Marble was working, but a few days earlier, a local stock detective, Billy Cathey, had borrowed it, leaving his gun, which was unreliable. Martin, "A Lively Day," 47.

20. Kirby, *Rise and Fall*, 57–58; Ernst, *Sundance*, 87.

21. Martin, "A Lively Day," 47; Ernst, *Sundance*, 87–88; Kirby, *Rise and Fall*, 58–59.

22. Martin, "A Lively Day," 47; Kirby, *Rise and Fall*, 59–60. Accounts of the robbery appeared in most of the Black Hills newspapers of the day, including *The Pioneer Times*, June 29, 1897, and *The Sundance Gazette*, July 2, 1897.

23. Kirby, *Rise and Fall*, 60.

24. Kirby, *Rise and Fall*, 60. According to Kirby, who does not give his source, Sheriff Fuller shot Longabaugh's horse, and one of the possemen, W. R. Glassie, confiscated Harry's saddle, which remained in the possession of the Glassie family for years.

25. Griffith, "Sundance Kid," 30. Elizabeth Griffith, the author of this article, is the granddaughter of Ben F. Hilton.

26. In her account of her grandfather's encounter with Harry Longabaugh, Elizabeth Griffith does not explain how Longabaugh knew about the attic. Possibly it was sheer luck; he may have discovered it after he had barged into the office, or he may have guessed that there was an attic from the shape of the building. A third possibility is that he had asked somebody on the street if they knew of a sleeping room for rent.

27. Griffith, "Sundance Kid," 31.

28. Pointer, *In Search of Cassidy*, 121–23. Pointer interviewed Fred Hilman, then 88 years of age, in July 1972.

29. Pointer, *In Search of Cassidy*, 121–23.

30. Pointer, *In Search of Cassidy*, 123. It is difficult to believe that Cassidy would leave a note containing both his true name and his alias, and imply that he was an outlaw, which clearly casts some doubt on the accuracy of at least this part of Hilman's story.

31. DeJournette and DeJournette, *One Hundred Years*, 282–83. The authors' source was Rex Taylor, Daun DeJournette's father, who obtained the story from Henry Lee.

32. Kelly, *Outlaw Trail*, 163.

33. DeJournette and DeJournette, *One Hundred Years*, 282. According to the

DeJournettes, Lee gave a different version of the robbery. In Lee's version Meeks was in the bar talking to Guild while Lee and two others robbed the store, which was adjacent to the bar.

34. Kelly, *Outlaw Trail*, 234–35.

35. Kelly, *Outlaw Trail*, 160; Pointer, *In Search of Cassidy*, 130. Pointer cites interviews with two eyewitnesses to the celebration at Baggs: Carley Jebens and Janette Magor. At the time, Janette Magor's mother ran a boarding house in Baggs (Pointer, 217).

36. Siringo, *Riata and Spurs*, 246–47. The place Ryan opened in Rawlins was called the Home Ranch Saloon. Ernst, "Wanted: Friends," 45.

37. Kirby, *Rise and Fall*, 61; Ernst, *Sundance*, 89–90; Pointer, *In Search of Cassidy*, 130. This incident was reported in the *Billings Gazette*, September 24, 28, and 30, 1897.

38. Pointer, *In Search of Cassidy*, 131; Ernst, *Sundance*, 92.

39. Pointer, *In Search of Cassidy*, 132; Ernst, *Sundance*, 94.

40. Kirby, *Rise and Fall*, 63.

Busy Times

1. *Denver News*, Mar. 6, 1898.

2. Burroughs, *Where West Stayed Young*, 112–13.

3. Burroughs, *Where West Stayed Young*, 112–13.

4. Hughel, *Chew Bunch*, 99.

5. *Denver News*, Mar. 6, 1898.

6. Dullenty, *Harry Tracy*, 29–30; Kouris, *Brown's Park*, 84–86.

7. Ernst, "Powder Springs," 49–50. A visiter to either springs today will find the faint remains of what might have been the foundations of the outlaws' cabins. At the lower springs, in a small hillside, there are also the remains of a dugout, lodgepole, and part of a wall.

8. Burton, *Uintah County*, 376–77.

9. Dullenty, *Harry Tracy*, 29; Kouris, *Brown's Park*, 84–86.

10. Kouris, "Lynching Calamity," 23; Dullenty, *Harry Tracy*, 31.

11. Dullenty, *Harry Tracy*, 32.

12. Dullenty, *Harry Tracy*, 32.

13. Dullenty, *Harry Tracy*, 33–37.

14. Boren, "Grandpa Knew Butch," 46. Boren claims Butch told his grandfather: "Tracy was a bad breed and troublemaker of the worst sort. He was with me awhile but after his friend shot down a fifteen-year-old boy in my own territory, I went to him and ordered him out of the Park. I thought there would be trouble but Tracy was already pressed by the ranchers who were out for revenge and several posses from Vernal and Rock Springs, and I guess he was anxious to leave anyway."

15. Dullenty, *Harry Tracy*, 19.

16. A story was passed around Brown's Park that Butch and Jack Bennett were acquainted enough for Butch and his friends to have given Bennett a nickname. As the tale goes, following the robbery of the Pleasant Valley Coal Company at Castle Gate in April 1897, while Butch and the gang were engaging in one of their celebrations at Baggs, Wyoming, it was learned that a friend, "Old Man" Bender, had died from pneumonia. Apparently the local doctor who had treated him was also in the saloon, and the gang, well-liquored up and playful, organized a "kangaroo court" to try the doctor for negligence in allowing his patient to die while under his care. Patrick Johnson and Jack Bennett were present, and the gang appointed Jack Bennett as judge. From then on Jack was known as "Judge" Bennett. Kouris, *Brown's Park*, 84–85; Dullenty, *Harry Tracy*, 29.

17. *Fremont Clipper*, Mar. 25, 1898.

18. *Denver News*, Mar. 6, 1898. Hoy paid for his outburst. After his diatribe appeared in the Denver newspaper, his ranch was raided and much of his livestock, wagons, equipment, and supplies were stolen or destroyed (*Fremont Clipper*, Mar. 25, 1898).

19. Mathisen, "Rocky Mountain Riders," 30–31.

20. Mathisen, "Rocky Mountain Riders," 30 (citing an article in the *Cheyenne Sun Leader*. No date was given).

21. Greene, "Cassidy in Fremont," 8. According to Edna Robison (daughter of Hanksville merchant Charley Gibbons, who, in addition to his general store, also ran a small hotel in Hanksville), some kind of "document" was sent to Butch and his pals suggesting amnesty in return for joining the war effort. Betenson and Flack, *Butch Cassidy*, 129, 134.

22. Kelly, *Outlaw Trail*, 213–15. (Interviews with J. P. O'Neill, Gen., U.S. Army [ret.] and Frederick H. Sparrenberger, Maj., U.S. Army [ret.].) It is believed that outlaw Dave Lant also may have served in the Philippines and may have won several medals for courage and bravery (Dullenty, *Harry Tracy*, 37).

23. Mathisen, "Rocky Mountain Riders," 31–32.

24. Candee, "Oklahoma," 328.

25. Greene, "Cassidy in Fremont," 7.

26. *Wyoming State Tribune*, June 16, 1939; Pointer, *In Search of Cassidy*, 147.

27. *Wyoming State Tribune*, June 16, 1939; Pointer, *In Search of Cassidy* 147.

28. Flack, "Living Dead," 21.

29. *Eastern Utah Advocate*, May 19, 1898. Cattle rustling was certainly frowned upon in Carbon County, but seldom called for a posse and all-out manhunt; in this case, Billy McGuire and one of the Whitmores had been jumped and beaten badly before the thieves ran off with their horses and 25 head of cattle (Kelly, *Outlaw Trail*, 174).

30. *Eastern Utah Advocate*, May 19, 1898.

31. Kelly, *Outlaw Trail*, 175.

32. *Eastern Utah Advocate*, May 19, 1898.

33. *Eastern Utah Advocate*, May 19, 1898. According to J. W. Warf, one of the members of the posse, Sheriff Allred had a high-pitched voice that occasionally cracked when he was excited. When Allred first called out for the outlaws to surrender, the result was an "unintelligible squawk" (Kelly, *Outlaw Trail*, 176).

34. *Eastern Utah Advocate*, May 19, 1898; Flack, "Living Dead," 22–23. According to one version of the story, at first the posse was all for cutting off the heads of the two dead men and burying their bodies where they lay rather than carry the corpses fifty miles into Thompson Springs. But Jim McPherson talked them out of it, complaining that he did not want any bodies buried on his land (Bristow, "Rude Awakening," 41).

35. *Eastern Utah Advocate*, May 19, 1898.

36. *Eastern Utah Advocate*. May 19, 1898. Walker and Herring were killed on Friday, May 13 (although some newspapers, including the *Denver Daily News*, reported that Butch died on a Sunday). Had it been Butch who was killed that day, it would have meant that he was born and died on a Friday the 13th.

37. Flack, "Living Dead," 21, citing a letter dated April 18, 1898, to Utah Governor Heber Wells from M. F. Tillery, Sheriff of Montrose County, Colorado.

38. Kelly, *Outlaw Trail*, 178. At first, some thought the man who called himself Schultz was Elzy Lay (*Salt Lake City Herald*, May 14, 1898).

39. Flack, "Living Dead," 23.

40. Kelly, *Outlaw Trail*, 178.

41. Betenson and Flack, *Butch Cassidy*, 126. Notwithstanding Lula Betenson's verification of this tale, one has to wonder if it was not borrowed from Mark Twain's *Adventures of Tom Sawyer*.

42. Kelly, *Outlaw Trail*, 179.

43. Spring, *Near the Greats*, 35.

44. Siringo, *Riata and Spurs*, 232.

45. DeJournette and DeJournette, *One Hundred Years*, 2, 3, 11, 82.

Alias Jim Lowe

1. Yochelson and Samenow, *Criminal Personality*, 158.

2. Webb, "The Outlaw Trail," 24, 27.

3. French, *Further Recollections*, ix-xii.

4. Siringo, *Riata and Spurs*, 240.

5. French, *Further Recollections*, xiv.

6. Siringo, *Riata and Spurs*, 240.

7. French, *Some Recollections*, 258.

8. French, *Some Recollections*, 259.

9. French, *Some Recollections*, 259–60. Miguel A. Otero, at the time governor of the Territory of New Mexico and a good friend of William French, years later said that he believed that French knew full well that he had members of the Wild Bunch in his employ and was probably in collusion with them all along (Miguel Otero to Charles Kelly, Sept. 14, 1935).

Wild Bunch historians have speculated as to whether Harry Longabaugh was among the gang members who joined Butch and Elzy at the ws Ranch. Ed Kirby places Longabaugh in southeastern Arizona in late 1897, but does not give a source for this information. This was probably at least eight or nine months before Butch and Elzy signed on at the ws. According to both Donna Ernst and Dick and Daun DeJournette, Longabaugh spent the winter of 1898–99 working for a rancher named Beeler in Carbon County, Wyoming (Ernst, "Sundance Kid," 17; DeJournette and DeJournette, *One Hundred Years*, 335).

10. *The Denver Times*, June 2, 1899.

11. *The Denver Times*, June 2, 1899; *Carbon County Journal*, June , 1899; *New York Times*, June , 1899.

12. *Buffalo Bulletin*, June 8, 1899 (statement of railway mail clerk Robert Lawson).

13. *Buffalo Bulletin*, June 8, 1899.

14. *Buffalo Bulletin*, June 8, 1899.

15. Kelly, *Outlaw Trial*, 235, 241.

16. Kelly, *Outlaw Trial*, 237.

17. Kelly, *Outlaw Trial*, 237–38.

18. Spring, *Near the Greats*, 34.

19. Kelly, *Outlaw Trial*, 242–43.

20. Kelly, *Outlaw Trial*, 242–43.

21. An account of the shooting appears in the *Natrona County Tribune*, June 8, 1899.

22. Sheriff Josiah Hazen was one of the most highly respected law officers in Wyoming. The town of Douglas shut its doors on the day of his funeral and hundreds attended the services, including the governor of the state. Lawmen for miles around volunteered to search for his killers. *The Denver Republican*, June 8, 1899.

23. Kelly, *Outlaw Trial*, 245; Pointer, *In Search of Cassidy*, 153.

24. Brock, "A Timely Arrival," 66. The robbers may have picked up their supplies and horses at the Brock ranch. According to Elmer Brock (Albert's son), who was seventeen at the time, the Brock family knew George Currie quite well.

25. *New York Times*, July 10, 1899.

26. At the time, the Logans were known locally as "the Roberts boys."

27. Kelly, *Outlaw Trial*, 244.

28. *New York Herald,* June 25, 1899.

29. Robert E. (Bob) Lee was captured on February 28, 1900 at Cripple Creek, Colorado, and the following May was convicted in federal court of robbing the United States mail during the Wilcox holdup. He was sentenced to the Wyoming State Penitentiary (which was still housing federal convicts) on May 31, 1900, and served six years and nine months (Frye, *Atlas of Outlaws,* 215). Bruce Lamb claimed that, besides George Currie and Harvey Logan, the Wilcox robbers were Harry Longabaugh, Butch, and Wild Bunch member Bill Cruzan (Lamb, *Wild Bunch,* 13). However, Lamb gives no source for this information. Donna Ernst says that Texans Will Carver and Ben Kilpatrick, who had recently joined the Wild Bunch, were in on the Wilcox affair (Ernst, *Cowboy to Outlaw,* 7). Like Lamb, Ernst also offers no source.

30. Siringo, *Cowboy Detective,* 306; Kelly, *Outlaw Trail,* 245.

31. Burroughs, *Where West Stayed Young,* 129. Burroughs implies that his source was the family of the friendly rancher, "who must remain anonymous because his descendants are among the leading citizens of southern Wyoming."

32. Boren, "Grandpa Knew Butch," 44. Boren says the witness was his grandfather, Willard Schofield, whose family were close friends of the Parkers. According to Boren, his grandfather was tending bar in the saloon where the outlaws were drinking. After they left, the owner of the saloon told Schofield that the gang "just came back from Wyoming—they held up the train at Wilcox."

33. Burton, *Queen Ann Bassett,* 22–23. In telling the story years later, Ann may have exaggerated the amount of the cache ($20,000). It is unlikely that Elzy's share of the Wilcox job was that much.

34. Ernst, *Sundance,* 113, citing John Cornelison, "The Wilcox Train Robbery," Wyoming State Archives.

35. DeJournette and DeJournette, *One Hundred Years,* 335.

36. Kennan, *Harriman,* 174, quoting W. H. Park "Recollections of E. H. Harriman in Connection with the Union Pacific" (unpublished manuscript).

37. Pointer, *In Search of Cassidy,* 153.

38. Simpson to Kelly, May 5, 1939, reprinted in Dullenty, *Cassidy Collection,* 31.

39. Kelly, *Outlaw Trail,* 245–46.

40. Simpson to Kelly, May 5. 1939. In the letter Simpson says that he saw Butch immediately after the Wilcox robbery, having "met him on the Muddy, between Fort Washakie and Thermopolis, Wyoming, and spent an hour with him." During the summer of 1996, Will Simpson's grandson, former Wyoming Senator Alan Simpson, was being interviewed by reporters on network TV. In an off-hand remark, while discussing his Wyoming roots, Senator Simpson mentioned that his grandfather "had been Butch Cassidy's attorney." (Note that Senator Simpson did not say that his grandfather had prosecuted Butch or that he had been his friend,

but that he had been his attorney.) Was it possible that both Douglas Preston and Will Simpson counseled Butch between robberies? Dan Buck thinks not. He suggests that Senator Simpson may have merely confused Douglas Preston with his grandfather or possibly telescoped their two roles into one, which Buck believes would have been easy to do, since Will Simpson both prosecuted and befriended Butch. Buck, personal communication, August 30, 1997.

41. Pearl Baker to Faun McCorkie Tanner, June 14, 1973, cited in Tanner, *Far Country*, 168.

42. *New York Herald*, June 25, 1899. While the drawing of Butch was accurate, Butch was identified in the caption and in the article as "Buck Cassiday." This mistake was apparently made in New York. In newspapers in the West, by 1899 Butch was usually properly identified.

43. Years later, Hanksville storekeeper Charley Gibbons revealed that Butch had visited him that week. Gibbons knew Butch well, having sold supplies to the Wild Bunch when they were hiding out in nearby Robbers' Roost. Kelly, *Outlaw Trail*, 154, 247. Butch Cassidy biographer Ed Kirby interviewed Charley Gibbons's daughter, Edna Gibbons Robison, in 1970. In recalling Cassidy's visits to Hanksville, Edna told Kirby: "Yes, I remember the Wild Bunch. They used to ride into Hanksville for supplies from my father's store. Usually there were nine to twelve of them at any one time. They were good customers and behaved like gentlemen. They had many friends in town" (Kirby, *Saga of Butch*, 84–85).

44. Siringo, *Cowboy Detective*, 306. In Siringo's memoirs he identifies his fellow detective as O. W. Sayles. Most writers have assumed that this was his name. However, on publication of Siringo's book, the Pinkerton agency filed suit and forced him to delete certain sensitive material and also change some names. For example, in editions of the book published after the lawsuit was resolved, Pinkerton became "Dickenson" and Tom Horn (who for a while was also a Pinkerton operative and a close friend of Siringo's) became "Tom Corn." It is possible that there was no O. W. Sayles, that Siringo's partner was actually Pinkerton detective Frank P. Dimaio, who would later lead the hunt for Butch and Harry Longabaugh in Argentina. See Morn, *Eye That Never Sleeps*, 161. Morn states "Siringo spent four years with Dimaio in search of Butch Cassidy and the Wild Bunch gang." Dan Buck thinks not. He believes that if Dimaio had joined Siringo in the hunt for the Wild Bunch in the American West, he (Dimaio) would have mentioned it in his reminiscences. Buck wonders if Morn's statement, which was not footnoted, was not a vague reference to Dimaio's hunt for the Wild Bunch in Argentina (Buck, personal communication, August 30, 1997).

45. Morn, *Eye That Never Sleeps*, 159–61.

46. Morn, *Eye That Never Sleeps*, 159–61.

47. Siringo, *Cowboy Detective*, 306–10.

48. Siringo, *Cowboy Detective*, 311.

49. Siringo, *Cowboy Detective*, 311–12.

50. Siringo, *Cowboy Detective*, 313.

51. Siringo, *Cowboy Detective*, 312–24.

52. The robbery occurred on July 11, 1899.

53. French, who by the time he wrote his *Recollections* had apparently forgotten the man's name, identifies him only as the "special officer." Reno worked out of the Colorado Southern Railroad's Denver office. Dullenty, "Farm Boy," 5; Kelly, *Outlaw Trail*, 252.

54. By then the posse included Sheriff Farr; William Reno; Jonathan N. Thacker, a special officer for Wells Fargo; and F. H. Smith of New York City, who was probably either a railroad or express company official. Local volunteers included H. N. Love, James H. Morgan, Perfecto Cordova, and Miguel Lopez. Kelly, *Outlaw Trail*, 252.

55. French, *Some Recollections*, 263–64.

56. French, *Some Recollections*, 265.

57. Burton, *Dynamite and Six-Shooter*, 81–85.

58. Burton, *Dynamite and Six-Shooter*, 84–85.

59. Burton, *Dynamite and Six-Shooter*, 86.

60. Many Wild Bunch writers believe that Tom Capehart was Harvey Logan. See Kelly, *Outlaw Trail*, 250; Baker, *Wild Bunch at Robbers Roost*, 107; Lamb, *Wild Bunch*, 52. However, according to Jeff Burton, who did extensive research on New Mexico outlaws of this period, this claim is without foundation. Burton believes that Capehart was a cowboy turned bandit whose origins have never been determined (Burton, *Dynamite and Six-Shooter*, 5). Philip J. Rasch is in agreement with Burton, saying that from his study of the physical descriptions of the two men, Capehart could not have been Logan (Rasch, "Death Comes to Saint Johns," 4).

61. French, *Some Recollections*, 266.

62. French, *Some Recollections*, 266–69. For details of the capture, derived mainly from testimony of the members of the posse and newspaper accounts, see Burton, *Dynamite and Six-Shooter*, 94–97.

63. Burton, *Dynamite and Six-Shooter*, 110–11.

64. Burton, *Dynamite and Six-Shooter*, 111–21.

65. Betenson and Flack, *Butch Cassidy*, 187.

66. French, *Some Recollections*, 270–71.

67. French, *Some Recollections*, 272.

68. French, *Some Recollections*, 273–74.

69. Siringo, *Riata and Spurs*, 240–41.

70. Siringo, *Riata and Spurs*, 240.

71. French, *Some Recollections*, 274–75.

72. Kyacks were containers that were draped over pack saddles to carry extra loads. Most were just large leather pockets that hung on each side of the horse. On the ws Ranch, however, somebody had designed special kyacks made of rawhide stretched over wooden frames to form box-like contraptions that were light and strong and could carry pots and pans and other heavy objects—even fifty-pound sacks of flour—without galling the horse's sides. Also, since these special kyacks were flat, blankets and other gear could be piled on top of them, considerably increasing the total amount that could be carried. French, *Some Recollections*, 275–76.

73. French, *Some Recollections*, 276.

74. French, *Some Recollections*, 276–77.

75. Rasch, "Death Comes to Saint Johns," 2, citing the *Socorro Chieftan*, Apr. 28 and May 12, 1900.

76. French, *Some Recollections*, 277. French assumed that Butch was looking for the loot taken from the robbery. After the Turkey Canyon shootout, the posse found scattered about the scene thirty to forty sticks of dynamite, a saddle and bridle, a bloodied hat and slicker, a coffee pot, cooking utensils, and tin cans used for cups. Also buried nearby were a rifle and ammunition. (Why these were buried is anybody's guess.) No money from the holdup was found, or at least not reported (Burton, *Dynamite and Six-Shooter*, 86).

Tipton and Winnemucca

1. Webb, "Elton Cunningham," 16.

2. Burton, *Dynamite and Six-Shooter*, 121. As to Bub Meeks, see Hayden, "Cassidy and Montpelier Robbery," 7. Within six months two more members of the gang would be gone. In February 1900, Harvey Logan's brother, Lonny, would be killed by lawmen at his aunt's house in Dodson, Missouri, where he was tracked down by Pinkertons following his flight from Harlem, Montana, after trying to cash a $1,000 bill from the Wilcox robbery (*Kansas City Star*, Feb. 28, 1900; Mike Bell, "The Killing of Lonny Logan," 27–8). Two months later Flat-Nose George Currie would meet his end at the hands of a posse near the Green River in Uintah County, Utah, when he was mistaken for a rustler they were chasing (Kelly, *Outlaw Trail*, 261).

3. Kelly, *Outlaw Trail*, 266.

4. Betenson, "Alias 'Tom Ricketts,'" 18. There are stories told within the Parker family that some of Butch's other brothers wanted to follow in his footsteps but that he did his best to discourage them, in one instance telling one brother that he was "too slow and too stupid" to be a member of this gang (Betenson, 5).

5. Greene, "Cassidy in Fremont, 8–9. Charles Kelly provides a description of the conversation between Butch and attorney Powers that differs slightly from

Greene's version (See Kelly, *Outlaw Trail*, 267–69). Neither author gives his source, but a good attorney would have kept a memorandum of the meeting, to which both Greene and Kelly may have eventually had access.

6. Betenson and Flack, *Butch Cassidy*, 159–60.

7. Kelly, *Outlaw Trail*, 269.

8. Kelly, *Outlaw Trail*, 269–70. According to Butch's sister, while Butch whiled away time in Salt Lake City waiting to hear about his offer to reform, he embarked on a new romance. Lula would not reveal the young lady's real name, but she did include a picture. See Betenson and Flack, *Butch Cassidy*, 151–53.

9. Harlow, *Old Waybills*, 437, citing figures compiled by the editors of the express industry trade paper, *Express Gazette*. See also *Rail Age*, March 15, 1895.

10. Kelly, *Outlaw Trail*, 270–71. Although Kelly may have obtained this story from Orlando Powers or Douglas Preston, whom he says worked together to arrange the deal between Butch and the railroad, the tale gets a little fanciful. Kelly says that Powers's offer to the Union Pacific included an agreement by Butch to hire on as an express guard, which Powers suggested would discourage outlaws from attempting robberies.

11. Kennan, *Harriman*, 174, quoting Park, "Recollections of E. H. Harriman."

12. Kelly, *Outlaw Trail*, 271. According to Lula Betenson, the aborted meeting between Butch and the railroad officials took place in October 1899. Her source for the date was outlaw writer Kerry Ross Boren, who claimed it came from author Agnes Wright Spring, "who was secretary to Douglas Preston for many years" (Betenson and Flack, 153). It is doubtful that Agnes Wright Spring was ever Preston's secretary. Spring probably became acquainted with Preston when he later served as Attorney General of Wyoming and she was Wyoming State Librarian. See Rosa, "Agnes Wright Spring," 54.

13. Kelly, *Outlaw Trail*, 271–72. For the most part Matt Warner's version of the story is the same. However, Warner claimed that it was a later robbery, the holdup of the National Bank of Winnemucca, Nevada, that lost Butch his chance to reform (Warner, *Last of Bandit Riders*, 320–21). Lula Betenson offers yet another version. She claims that Butch lost his chance for amnesty and a job with the Union Pacific when he was suspected of being involved in the killing of lawmen Jesse Tyler and Sam Jenkins near Thompson Springs, Utah, in May 1900 (Betenson and Flack, *Butch Cassidy*, 155).

14. Moulton, *Roadside History*, 275.

15. Carlson, "The Tipton Train Robbery," 16. According to one report the train carried a mail car, a Pacific Express car, and an Oregon Short Line Express car. The robbers blasted their way into the Pacific car, only slightly damaged the Oregon Short Line car, and left the mail car untouched. *New York Herald*, Sept. 1, 1900.

16. *The Denver Republican*, Sept. 2, 1900. The robber's ramblings, as related by

the postal clerk, are printed here just as they appeared in the newspaper, dialect and all, which suggests that the piece was generously doctored by an editor for flavor.

17. Carlson, "Tipton Robbery," 16.

18. *The Denver Republican*, Sept. 2, 1900.

19. Baker, *Wild Bunch at Robbers Roost*, 191; Kirby, *Rise and Fall*, 79.

20. *The Denver Republican*, Sept. 2, 1990. For another account of the robbery, see *Wyoming State Tribune*, Aug. 31, 1900.

21. *The Denver Republican* Sept. 2, 1900.

22. Kelly, *Outlaw Trail*, 275. Butch's eyes were actually blue, but the rest of the description seemed to fit.

23. Kelly, *Outlaw Trail*, 275; Baker, *Wild Bunch at Robbers Roost*, 191; Pointer, *In Search of Cassidy*, 165; Kirby, *Saga of Butch*, 35, 78. One writer who did not agree was the late F. Bruce Lamb, who believed that the job was pulled off by Wild Bunch members Harvey Logan, Ben Kilpatrick, Bill Cruzan, and Billy Rose (Lamb, *Wild Bunch*, 13, 50). Lamb, however, failed to give his source. Also, according to Donna Ernst, the Pinkertons did not believe that Butch was at Tipton (Ernst, *Sundance*, 127, citing an undated Pinkerton file on the robbery).

24. Kelly, *Outlaw Trail*, 275; Kirby, *Rise and Fall*, 78. Ernst, citing the undated Pinkerton file, says that Longabaugh was to join the others at Tipton, but changed his mind at the last minute and went with Butch to Nevada, apparently to plan the gang's next robbery, the holdup of the First National Bank of Winnemucca. Ernst, *Sundance, My Uncle*, 127.

25. Ernst, "Wanted: Friends," 47.

26. DeJournette and DeJournette, *One Hundred Years*, 200.

27. Carlson, *Tipton Robbery*, 12. Both posses were early versions of the Union Pacific's innovative "horse cars," in which mounted riders were dispatched to robbery sites in baggage cars converted to carry men and animals (Kennan, *Harriman*, 174, quoting from "Recollections").

28. Carlson, *Tipton Robbery*, 13–14.

29. LeFors discovered later that the robbers had stopped about a mile down river to eat supper and repack their load. At the site, the posse found money wrappers and paper that had been torn off of express packages. Carlson, *Tipton Robbery*, 14.

30. Carlson, *Tipton Robbery*, 14.

31. Carlson, *Tipton Robbery*, 14–15. On September 5, the *Rawlins Republican* reported that the posse gave up the chase because they lost the trail when the robbers resorted to an "old trick" of riding along with a bunch of range horses to make their own tracks difficult to follow.

32. DeJournette and DeJournette, *One Hundred Years*, 353.

33. Ernst, *Sundance*, 130. As if the controversy over whether the Tipton bandits

had time to reach Winnemucca and rob the bank there was not enough, outlaw writer James D. Horan threw another log on the fire. Horan came up with a story that, following the Tipton holdup, Cassidy, Longabaugh, and Will Carver headed to South Dakota, not Nevada, intending to rob a bank in Deadwood. On the way, claimed Horan, the trio ran into an acquaintance from the Hole-in-the-Wall who warned them that the people in Deadwood were "riled up" over earlier robbery attempts and were armed and waiting for another gang of bandits to show up. This friend suggested that, instead of Deadwood, Butch and his pals should rob the Winnemucca bank in Nevada. Horan and Sann, *Pictorial History*, 199–200. Horan was a prolific writer and responsible for uncovering many valuable sources on western outlaw history, but much of his writing was not footnoted and must be read with caution.

34. Ernst, *Sundance*, 130.

35. I. V. Button to Pearl Baker, November 21, 1970. Reprinted in Baker, *Wild Bunch at Robbers Roost*, 192.

36. Pointer, *In Search of Cassidy*, 170.

37. Button to Baker, November 21, 1970.

38. Kirby, *Rise and Fall*, 82–8. Kirby's source was Case himself, whom Kirby interviewed at Winnemucca. He did not give the date of the interview.

39. Most writers agree that it was Cassidy, Harry Longabaugh, and Will Carver who entered the bank. Kelly, *Outlaw Trail*, 277; Baker, *Wild Bunch at Robbers Roost*, 191; Kirby, *Rise and Fall*, 83. Ernst believes it was Longabaugh, Carver, and Harvey Logan (Ernst, *Sundance*, 130).

40. *The Silver State*, Sept. 19, 1900; *The Denver Republican*, Sept. 20, 1900; Ernst, *Sundance*, 130–32.

41. *The Silver State*, Sept. 19, 1900; *The Denver Republican*, Sept. 20, 1900; Berk, "Butch Cassidy Didn't Do It," 24. Berk's source was George S. Nixon's private journals.

42. *The Silver State*, Sept. 20, 1900.

43. Reynolds, "Winnemucca Bank Robbery," 26. In some accounts George Nixon is mentioned as president of the bank but in others, head cashier. It is generally believed that he was a part owner and head cashier at the time of the robbery (Berk, "Cassidy Didn't Do It," 23).

44. *The Silver State*, Sept. 20, 1900.

45. Kirby, *Rise and Fall*, 85. The town of Winnemucca would later commemorate the robbery with an annual "Butch Cassidy Days" celebration and parade. Lee Case was the grand marshal of the first parade. Landsberg, "He Remembers Butch," *The Sunday Camera*, Oct. 31, 1982.

46. *The Silver State*, Sept. 19, 1900; Reynolds, "Winnemucca Robbery," 26.

47. *The Silver State*, Sept. 20, 1900.

48. *The Silver State*, Sept. 20, 1900.

49. Kirby, *Rise and Fall*, 86.

50. Button to Baker, November 21, 1970.

51. *The Silver State*, Sept. 20, 1900.

52. *The Silver State*, Sept. 22, 1900.

53. *The Silver State*, Sept. 27, 1900.

54. Berk, "Cassidy Didn't Do It," 25, citing George S. Nixon's journals.

55. Berk, "Cassidy Didn't Do It," 26.

56. Berk, "Cassidy Didn't Do It," 26. See also Ernst, "Blackened Gold," 1, 4.

57. Berk, "Cassidy Didn't Do It," 26.

58. Berk, "Cassidy Didn't Do It," 27.

59. Ernst, "Blackened Gold," 4, citing the private papers of U.S. Marshal Frank P. Hadsell, who led one of the posses that pursued the robbers following the Tipton train robbery. These papers are held at the Wyoming State Archives in Cheyenne. Ernst does not explain why the letters were so interpreted.

60. Ernst, "Blackened Gold," 4, citing Hadsell papers.

61. Ernst, "Blackened Gold," 4.

62. Ernst, "Blackened Gold," 4. This lead failed to develop into anything. Little information has been uncovered about Mike Dunbar, except that he might have been the brother of a Jeff Dunbar, known to be an outlaw, who was killed in a saloon fight in Dixon, Wyoming, in July 1898. Ernst, "Friends," 35; DeJournette and DeJournette, *One Hundred Years*, 282.

63. Ernst, "Blackened Gold," 4.

64. Frye, *Atlas of Outlaws*, 276.

65. Berk, "Cassidy Didn't Do It," 27, citing letters from Nixon to the Pinkertons dated January 8, 1901 and February 21, 1901.

66. Berk, "Cassidy Didn't Do It," 23, 64.

67. The entire article is reprinted in the Summer 1995 issue of *The Journal of the Western Outlaw-Lawmen History Association*. See Bell, "Interview with the Sundance Kid," 13–16.

Fort Worth and New York

1. Siringo, *Riata and Spurs*, 229.

2. Siringo, *Riata and Spurs*, 229. Some writers have said that Charles Siringo actually infiltrated the Wild Bunch. Possibly so; at least he said he did. In 1928, after reading an article on the Wild Bunch in *Frontier Times*, Siringo wrote to the editor of the magazine, J. Marvin Hunter, stating that he was a "member of the Wild Bunch for four years under many assumed names" (Siringo to editor, *Frontier Times*, November 1928).

3. Siringo, *Riata and Spurs*, 235.

4. "I had hard work to keep from falling in love with Miss Parker, the pretty young sister of Butch Casiday [*sic*]. She was the deputy post-mistress in Circleville." Siringo, *Riata and Spurs*, 238. Regarding this visit to Circleville, Siringo later wrote: "There I made the acquaintance of the whole Parker family. I became attached to George Parker's pretty black-eyed sister, who was deputy post-mistress in Circleville. From her I gained many important secrets of the 'Wild Bunch'" (Siringo to editor, *Frontier Times*, November 1928).

5. Siringo, *Riata and Spurs*, 247–49.

6. Betenson and Flack, *Butch Cassidy*, 157.

7. Siringo, *Riata and Spurs*, 240–41.

8. Siringo, *Riata and Spurs*, 241.

9. Siringo, *Riata and Spurs*, 242.

10. Kelly, *Outlaw Trail*, 281; Baker, *Wild Bunch at Robbers Roost*, 193; Selcer, *Hell's Half Acre*, 254; Ernst, *Sundance*, 147.

11. Selcer, *Hell's Half Acre*, xii.

12. Selcer, *Hell's Half Acre*, 153, 250.

13. Selcer, *Hell's Half Acre*, 246–47, 319. Selcer's sources are the Fort Worth City Directories and Tarrant County Criminal Court records. According to Donna Ernst, in the fall of 1900 Mike Cassidy's saloon was at 1600 Calhoun Street (Ernst, *Sundance*, 147).

14. Boren and Boren, "Anna Marie Thayne," 27. The Borens cite as their source James McClamy of Missoula, Montana, a nephew of Mike Cassidy.

15. Ernst, *Cowboy to Outlaw*, 10; Selcer, *Hell's Half Acre*, 249. The Borens say that Lillie also worked out of Mike Cassidy's saloon. Boren and Boren ("Anna Marie Thayne," 27).

16. Selcer, *Hell's Half Acre*, 249. Lillie Davis claimed that she did have a marriage certificate and that she sent it home to her father in Palestine, Texas, to show that she intended to give up prostitution and settle down. Selcer, *Hell's Half Acre*, 249, citing a statement by Lillie contained in the Pinkerton Archives. Donna Ernst gives the date of the certificate as December 1, 1900, and says that it was signed by a Tarrant County Justice of the Peace. Carver used the alias William Casey (Ernst, *Cowboy to Outlaw*, 11). Ernst does not give the source of her information.

The fact that Lillie had a certificate to send to her father, even though no record of the marriage exists, can be explained. Outlaws shied away from leaving paper trails. Carver may have paid the justice of the peace a little extra money not to enter the marriage in his records.

17. According to Pinkerton files, the photo was taken on November 21, 1900, ten days before the date of Will and Lillie's alleged marriage certificate (Ernst, *Sundance*, 149; Ernst, *Cowboy to Outlaw*, 11). The wedding party could have been on November 21st following the sham ceremony, and Lillie could have talked Carver into obtaining a marriage certificate later so that she could send it to her father.

18. Selcer, *Hell's Half Acre*, 257.

19. Meadows, *Digging Up Butch*, 78.

20. Selcer, *Hell's Half Acre*, 257–58.

21. Ernst, *Sundance*, 149, citing Pinkerton files; Kelly, *Outlaw Trail*, 281.

22. Over the years, Dodge kept copious journals, diaries, and letters covering his career, which were later used by writer Carolyn Lake for her book, *Fred Dodge: Under Cover for Wells Fargo*. Nowhere is the photo mentioned, nor does Dodge mention a visit to Fort Worth during the fall or winter of 1900. However, during that period Dodge and his family were living in San Antonio and, although he was no longer working under cover for Wells Fargo, he was still in their employ. Lake, *Fred Dodge*, 223, 231. Also, in 1900 Wells Fargo maintained an office in Fort Worth at 817 Main Street, little more than a block away from the Swartz gallery and studio (Selcer, *Hell's Half Acre*, 262).

23. According to another version of the story, nobody spotted the photo in the window of the Swartz gallery. One of the prints was discovered when the authorities raided the rooming house where the gang had been hiding out. Selcer, *Hell's Half Acre*, 263.

24. Selcer, *Hell's Half Acre*, 262.

25. *New York Herald*, June 25, 1899.

26. Berk, "Cassidy Didn't Do It," 27.

27. Ernst, *Sundance*, 140.

28. According to the story, Butch sent several photos to Button but young Vic was interested in only one: a picture of Butch posing with an Indian chief. Button put the rest of the photos away in a trunk and forgot about them until 1914, when he dug them out and gave them to the sheriff of Humboldt County as a memento of the Winnemucca robbery. Selcer, *Hell's Half Acre*, 261–62, citing a telephone interview in February 1986 with Button's daughter, Lenore Conway, of Sacramento, California.

29. Ernst, *Sundance*, 149.

30. Drago, *Etta Place*, 149.

31. Selcer, *Hell's Half Acre*, 248.

32. Boren and Boren, "Tom Vernon," 54; Baker, *Wild Bunch at Robbers Roost*, 173.

33. Ernst, *Sundance*, 70.

34. Kirby, *Rise and Fall*, 71–72. Kirby does not describe this undocumented evidence.

35. Ernst, "Identifying Etta Place," 10–11.

36. Dan Buck, panel member of symposium "What Ever Happened to Butch and Sundance," held at Craig, Colorado, by the Western Outlaw-Lawman History Association, July 20, 1996. On this question, Buck writes: "I once suggested to

Donna Ernst that perhaps Etta came to us by way of a Spanish mispronunciation of Ethel—the "h" being silent in Spanish. But now we know that she used and was known as Ethel, not Etta, in North and South America, and that Etta comes to us compliments of the Pinkertons." The Pinkerton clerks, says Buck, copying down anything and everything they could find on the woman, used both "Etta" and "Ethel," and even "Eva" in their files. "For reasons unknown," he says, "they settled on Etta for their Wanted posters." Buck, personal communication, August 30, 1997.

37. Burton, *Queen Ann Bassett*, 65–66. Neither Jim Dullenty nor Dan Buck buy this theory. Dullenty points to evidence that Bassett was seen in Colorado on the same day Etta Place was supposed to have been in New York (Dullenty, personal communication, August 12, 1997), while Buck flatly rejects Burton's proof as "idle speculation" (personal communication, August 30, 1997). Although challenged, Burton sticks to her basic premise, but she does suggest that there may have been several women who, at times, assumed the role of Etta Place (telephone interview with Doris Burton, December 5, 1996). Buck dismisses this as an "even shakier" theory, but does not explain why (personal communication, August 30, 1997).

If Etta's real name was not Place, it is possible that she did not use that name until she met up with Harry Longabaugh, who at times used Harry A. Place as an alias. When in Argentina with Longabaugh and Butch, Etta was said to have used the name "Anna Marie Place" (Meadows, *Digging Up Butch*, 6).

38. Buck and Meadows, "Etta Place," 13.

39. Boren and Boren, "Anna Marie Thayne," 24.

40. Kirby, *Saga of Butch*, 93–94. According to Kirby, this information was obtained during an interview with Harry Thayne Longabaugh in Hanksville, Utah, in July 1970. Longabaugh, who called himself "Harry Jr.," entertained Wild Bunch enthusiasts for several years with yarns about his "father," the Sundance Kid, but few of his tales checked out. On December 18, 1972, "Harry Jr." died in a hotel fire in Missoula, Montana. In appearance he did resemble the Longabaugh family, but extensive research by Donna Ernst has failed to turn up a connection (Ernst, *Sundance*, 192–94).

41. Drago, *Etta Place*, 63–65.

42. Selcer, *Hell's Half Acre*, 249–50.

43. Buck and Meadows, "Etta Place," 13.

44. Jim Dullenty, symposium panel member, "What Ever Happened to Butch and Sundance," Craig, Colorado, July 20, 1996.

45. Drago, *Etta Place*, 237.

46. Ernst, "Identifying Etta Place," 11. In his book, *Kid Curry: The Life and Times of Harvey Logan*, Lamb quotes Butch Cassidy as saying that he thinks "a Denver gal has her hooks" into Harry Longabaugh. He obviously meant Etta. This book, however, is a narrative taken from the memory of Lamb's various family

members who either knew Harvey Logan or heard stories that were passed along by other members. While the book is footnoted in parts, Lamb gives no source for this reference to Etta.

47. Drago, *Etta Place*, 65. This story has a glaring weakness, however. As the tale was passed along by Drago, Butch also grew up in the town of Joseph, a fact Lula Betenson, Butch's sister, failed to mention.

48. Steve Lacy, panel member of symposium, "Butch and Sundance," Craig, Colorado, July 20, 1996. Lacy claims that he has other startling information on Etta and Butch, which he will soon reveal in a book.

49. Buck and Meadows, "Etta Place," 14.

50. San Antonio was a good bet because of the town's Mexican influence. According to persons who knew her later in Argentina, Etta spoke some Spanish and was adept at cooking Mexican dishes. Meadows, *Digging Up Butch*, 64; Burns, "A Secret Hoard in Argentina," 29.

51. Ernst, "Identifying Etta Place," 11.

52. Ernst, "Identifying Etta Place," 11–12.

53. Boren, "Grandpa Knew Butch," 46.

54. Butch Cassidy to Mathilda Davis, August 10, 1902, reprinted in Dullenty, *Cassidy Collection*, 39. The original letter is on deposit at the Utah State Historical Society, Salt Lake City.

55. Firmage, *Grand County*, 166.

56. Chapman, "'Butch' Cassidy," 61.

57. Kelly, *Outlaw Trail*, 287.

58. *Railroad Car Journal*, Apr. 1897:82; Harlow, *Old Waybills*, 438.

59. Warman, "Soldiers of the Rail," 461.

60. Patterson, *Birth, Flowering*, 122–25.

61. The fact that Canada rarely suffered a train robbery did not go unnoticed in the United States. A few American railway officials had been pushing for something similar to the Canadian mounties since the early 1890s. In 1894, the editors of *Railway Age* wrote: "Mounted police are what is wanted for the robber-cursed regions of Kansas, New Mexico, Indian Territory, Texas and wherever railway trains are being plundered without protection or redress from the government. This remedy is worth more than all the devices for protection that have been suggested." *Railway Age*, Dec. 14, 1894.

62. Cassidy to Mathilda Davis, August 10, 1902.

63. Meadows, *Digging Up Butch*, 52.

64. On one of their visits to Argentina, Wild Bunch researchers Anne Meadows and her husband, Dan Buck, talked to a Patagonian photo historian named Ricardo Vallmitjana, who speculated that Butch and Harry came to Argentina through the efforts of a local bandit, Mansel Gibbon, whom the two outlaws may

have met during one of Gibbon's trips back to the United States. Meadows, *Digging Up Butch*, 52. However, Dan Buck and Anne Meadows, in checking the 1895 Argentina census, found Gibbon to be only seven years old at that time, which meant that he could not have been more than thirteen years old when Butch, Longabaugh, and Etta arrived in Argentina (Buck, personal communication, August 30, 1997).

65. Shaw-Lefevre, "A Visit to the Argentine Republic," 835.

66. Allison, *Dubois History*, F170.

67. Allison, *Dubois History*, F7.

68. Betenson and Flack, *Butch Cassidy*, 161.

69. Kelly, *Outlaw Trail*, 285.

70. Kirby, *Rise and Fall*, 88. Reference to the pair's visit to New Orleans can be found only in Kirby's work, and he does not give the source.

71. Ernst, *Sundance*, 157, citing Pinkerton files and Longabaugh family records.

72. Ernst, *Sundance*, 157, citing Pinkerton files and Longabaugh family records.

73. Kirby, *Saga of Butch*, 54. Kirby does not give his source for this information.

74. Ernst, *Sundance*, 159.

75. Drago, *Etta Place*, 156–57. Instead of being referred by Dr. Weinstein, Harry and Etta may have learned of Dr. Pierce's miraculous cures from the doctor's best-selling book *The People's Common Sense Medical Advisor in Plain English*, which was believed to have sold in the millions of copies and stayed in print for almost fifty years. Author Drago's information on Dr. Pierce and his Institute comes from articles in the *Buffalo Courier Express*, June 2, 1907; June 23, 1941; June 25, 1941; and Feb. 2, 1966, and the *Buffalo Evening News*, July 2, 1907, and June 23, 1941.

76. Ernst, *Sundance*, citing a memo from William A. Pinkerton to Robert A. Pinkerton dated July 20, 1902.

77. Drago, *Etta Place*, 157.

78. Webb, "Elton Cunningham," 13. Cunningham, who was from Ontario, Canada, may have known something about lung disorders. He himself suffered from tuberculosis and had come to the Southwest in hopes that the dry air would improve his health. The idea that Longabaugh was troubled with lung problems may not be far-fetched. A former girlfriend of Harry's, Emma Florence Stanford, was said to have died from tuberculosis sometime between 1893 and 1895 (Boren and Boren, "Anna Marie Thayne," 26).

79. Ernst, *Sundance*, 161. Elton Cunningham's exact words were: "He [Longabaugh] was a lunger. He was coughing and was bad, that fella there." But later, when asked if Longabaugh was "pretty sick," Cunningham replied: "No, not bad, but you could see he was short-breathed [sic], you know, a little bit and he coughed a good deal" (transcript of interview of Elton Cunningham by Blachly, on file at the Center for Southwest Research Collections, University of New Mexico). After re-

viewing this tape, Ernst wrote: "Sounds to me more like catarrh, a sinus problem inherent in the family" (Ernst, personal communication, January 20, 1998).

80. Ernst, *Sundance*, 163, citing Longabaugh family records.

81. Kirby, *Rise and Fall*, 88. Although Kirby does not say so, his source was probably the Pinkerton files.

82. Ernst, *Sundance*, 163, citing Pinkerton files.

83. Ernst, *Sundance*, 163, citing the Pinkerton files; Kirby, *Saga of Butch*, 48.

84. Kirby, *Rise and Fall*, 90–91.

85. *New York Times*, Feb. 1, 1901.

86. Kelly, *Outlaw Trail*, 288; Kirby, *Rise and Fall*, 88; Ernst, *Sundance*, 163; Kirby, *Saga of Butch*, 49.

87. Ernst, *Sundance*, 163. According to Harry's family, the photo was to be a wedding memento. It also became a valuable part of the Pinkerton agency's files and was used on many Wanted posters.

88. Ernst, "Sundance Kid: My Uncle," 8.

89. *New York Times*, Feb. 1, 10, 1901.

90. *New York Times*, Feb. 14, 1901.

91. The fact that Harry and Etta left for Buenos Aires on a ship comes from the Pinkerton files. See Pointer, *In Search of Cassidy*, 196. The fact that they sailed on the SS *Herminius* comes from Kirby, *Rise and Fall*, 93, and *Saga of Butch*, 64, 65. Kirby's evidence that they sailed on the *Herminius* is not too strong, since it is based on a process of elimination. Kirby studied the New York Maritime Register for the date Longabaugh and Etta were supposed to have left New York (February 20, according to the Pinkertons), and concluded that they most likely took the *Herminius* because it took the most direct route to Buenos Aires. The *Herminius* did not leave on the 20th, however; it was scheduled to, but was delayed and left the following day (Kirby, *Saga of Butch*, 64).

92. Buck, personal communication, August 30, 1997. Buck bases his opinion that Butch was with Longabaugh and Etta when they sailed to Argentina together upon evidence in the possession of an Argentine journalist, Francisco Juárez. Juárez, however, refuses to reveal this evidence. Meadows, *Digging Up Butch*, 49.

Wagner

1. *The Denver Republican*, July 4, 1901.

2. Kennan, *Harriman*, 173, citing Park, "Recollections of E. H. Harriman." Park was division superintendent at North Platte, Nebraska, and later general superintendent of the line.

3. Harriman, like Butch, had also raced horses. As a young man, upon becoming wealthy, one of Harriman's first purchases was a nondescript trotting horse that went on to become one of the fastest trotters in the East (Kennan, *Harriman*, 20).

4. Kennan, *Harriman*. 173, quoting from Park's "Recollections."

5. Carlson, " Tipton Robbery," 12.

6. Patterson, *Train Robbery Era*, 238. Following the Tipton, Wyoming, robbery on August 29, 1900, Wanted posters offering rewards of $2,000 for each robber dead or alive were issued by the Union Pacific Railroad and its subsidiary, the Pacific Express Company. The posters were signed by F. C. Gantsch, general superintendent of both companies.

7. Reedstrom," Bandit Hunter Train," 23.

8. *The Denver Republican*, July 4, 1901.

9. *The Denver Republican*, July 4, 1901; Dullenty, "He Saw 'Kid Curry,'" 9.

10. Early reports placed the number of robbers at three; a few say five, but eyewitnesses and most sources say four. *The Denver Republican*, July 4, 1901; Dullenty, "He Saw 'Kid Curry,'" 10; Greene, "Cassidy in Fremont," 10.

11. Pinkerton, *Train Robberies*, 74; Kelly, *Outlaw Trail*, 282; Dullenty, "Wagner Train Robbery," 41; Dullenty, "He Saw 'Kid Curry,'" 8; Kirby, *Saga of Butch*, 61.

12. Pointer, *In Search of Cassidy*, 181.

13. Pointer, *In Search of Cassidy*, 270; Kirby, *Saga of Butch*, 62.

14. Dullenty, "Wagner Train Robbery," 40–41.

15. The fact that Harvey Logan may have led the gang that day lends support to the theory that Butch was already in South America. Francisco Juárez is adamant that Butch arrived in Buenos Aires the same time as Longabaugh and Etta Place. Juárez insists that he has a document signed by Butch in Argentina the very day of the Wagner robbery. Meadows, *Digging Up Butch*, 49. Dan Buck believes that Juárez probably has the proof. Says Buck, "I have no reason to doubt Juárez, with whom we have had numerous dealings. He enjoys catching other historians in errors. He refuses to show the document, but then he won't show any of the many others he has, although I have seen the cartons of material in his den. He told us he's saving them for his book" (personal communication, August 30, 1997).

Buck believes that the story that Longabaugh and Etta sailed to Argentina without Butch in February 1901 is based perhaps on reading too much (or too little) into the Pinkerton records. A Pinkerton memo dated July 29, 1902, says: "On February 20, 1901, Place and his wife sailed for Buenos Aires." Later, it says that these two returned to the States on the *Soldier Prince*, and added "We have no record of [Butch's] having returned from South America by steamers entering New York." Buck suggests that it is quite possible that the Pinkerton clerks simply failed to mention Butch being on the outgoing vessel (personal communiation, August 30, 1997).

16. Kelly, *Outlaw Trail*, 283; Kirby, *Saga of Butch*, 61; Dullenty, "He Saw 'Kid Curry,'" 9.

17. Dullenty, "Wagner Train Robbery," 40.

18. Kirby, *Saga of Butch*, 61; Dullenty, "He Saw 'Kid Curry,'" 9. Charles Kelly,

unaware when he wrote his account of the robbery that Harry Longabaugh had left for South America, mistakenly reported that it was Harry who boarded the train at Malta (Kelly, *Outlaw Trail*, 283).

19. *The Denver Republican*, July 4, 1901. Some writers insist on calling the robbery site Exeter. See for example Pointer, *In Search of Cassidy*, 172; and Heck, *Pass Patrol*, 71. Most writers, however, refer to it as the Wagner robbery. A good account of the robbery and its aftermath can be found in the *Great Falls Tribune*, July 4 through July 12, 1901.

20. *The Denver Republican*, July 4, 1901; Kelly, *Outlaw Trail*, 283.

21. Dullenty, "He Saw 'Kid Curry,' " 9.

22. Dullenty, "Wagner Train Robbery," 41–42.

23. Dullenty, "He Saw 'Kid Curry,' " 9. Ira Merritt's account of the robbery was made available to Dullenty by Mr. and Mrs. Cash Merritt of Republic, Washington; Richard Bard Jr., of Colville, Washington; and William S. Twogood, Missoula, Montana.

24. Dullenty, "He Saw 'Kid Curry,' " 9.

25. Greene, "Cassidy in Fremont," 10.

26. Hatch, *American Express*, 93–95.

27. Pointer, *In Search of Cassidy*, 182; Dullenty, "He Saw 'Kid Curry,' " 10.

28. Dullenty, "He Saw 'Kid Curry,' " 10.

29. Kelly, *Outlaw Trail*, 284.

30. Greene, "Cassidy in Fremont," 10.

31. Pointer, *In Search of Cassidy*, 182–83, citing newspaper accounts.

32. Greene, "Cassidy in Fremont," 10. For a retracing of what is believed to be the gang's escape route, see Heck, *Pass Patrol*, 71–84.

Cholila

1. Meadows, *Digging Up Butch*, 49. Ed Kirby also refers to some "sources" that suggest that Cassidy accompanied the couple to Argentina, but he does not identify them (Kirby, *Saga of Butch* , 66).

2. Passports were not required by law in 1901. They were available, and had been since 1791, but their use was optional. Greenwood, *The Researcher's Guide to American Genealogy*, 413. Considering the background information required for a passport, it's a good bet that neither Harry nor Etta applied for one.

3. Pinkerton, *Train Robberies*, 74. It isn't known just how strong this evidence was; the Pinkertons may have come to this conclusion simply because Butch fit one or more of the witnesses' descriptions of one of the Wagner robbers.

4. Greene, "Cassidy in Fremont," in Dullenty, *Cassidy Collection*, 10; Kirby, *Saga of Butch*, 62. Neither Greene nor Kirby give sources for their information.

5. Kirby, *Saga of Butch*, 65. Kirby's source is apparently Lloyd's of London's shipping records.

6. Pointer, *In Search of Cassidy*, 196–97; Ernst, *Sundance*, 167, citing Pinkerton files.

7. Kirby, *Rise and Fall*, 94. The author does not give his source.

8. Ernst, *Sundance*, 167; Kirby, *Rise and Fall*, 94.

9. Meadows, *Digging Up Butch*, 41.

10. Pointer, *In Search of Cassidy*, 197, citing the Pinkerton files.

11. Martínez-Estrada, *X-Ray of Pampa*, 159.

12. According to a Buenos Aires newspaper, which for years had campaigned against lawlessness in the interior, the area was rank with "bands of outlaws [and] cattle thieves, who are ready to shoot, stab and pillage, if resisted. The police appear to be in collusion with the robbers. Complaints are made in vain for the official who listens, and takes notes, and smiles sympathetic assurances of prompt and severe castigation and restitution, laughs loud and long when the complainant has withdrawn, assured of active police measures in his behalf." *Buenos Aires Herald*, Mar. 15, 1906, quoted in Buck and Meadows, "Escape from Mercedes," 21.

13. Burns (Dullenty), "A Secret Hoard," 27–28.

14. *The Marine Engineer*, Dec. 1, 1901, as quoted in Kirby, *Saga of Butch*, 67.

15. Pointer, *In Search of Cassidy*, 197; Kirby, *Rise and Fall*, 97.

16. The Pinkerton operative's report was vague and unprofessional. Because of the way it was written—with physical descriptions of Harry and Etta given in a form that purported to be information obtained from the unidentified hospital—some writers have interpreted it to mean that Etta was also hospitalized. See Kirby, *Saga of Butch*, 69. If this is true it could mean that the couple did share a common disease, perhaps tuberculosis or a venereal infection. However, the fact that the Pinkerton operative did not identify the hospital suggests that he may have obtained his information from a third party, possibly Harry and Etta's landlady at the rooming house on 14th Street.

17. Pointer, *In Search of Cassidy*, 197, citing the Pinkerton files.

18. Meadows, *Digging Up Butch*, 41, 63.

19. Ernst, *Sundance*, 168.

20. Accounts of this robbery may be found in the Chicago newspapers of the day, particularly *The Chicago Tribune*, July 5 through July 7, 1902. See also Ernst, *Sundance*, 169.

21. Over the years Harry Longabaugh had occasionally been described as bow-legged. A Pinkerton report dated April , 1902, stated that he "was erect, bowlegged and walked with his feet far apart." Kirby, *Rise and Fall*, 97.

22. It would have been possible: both the New York Central and Pennsylvania Railroads were making Chicago-to–New York City runs in twenty hours. Sullivan, *Our Times*, 640.

23. Ernst, *Sundance*, 173.

24. Butch Cassidy to Mathilda Davis, August 10, 1902, reprinted in Dullenty, *Cassidy Collection*, 39. The original letter is on file at the Utah Historical Society, Salt Lake City.

25. *Nation*, Mar. 5, 1903 (book review), quoting from Prichard, *Heart of Patagonia*. Dan Buck believes that the Cholila Valley was more populated than Prichard suggests. According to Buck, Hesketh Prichard spent most of his time in the more desolate territory of Santa Cruz, which is south of where our trio had their ranch. Says Buck, "The Cholila Valley, near the Welsh-founded 16 de Octubre colony, was relatively populated (considering we are in the frontier). Settlers were coming west up the Chubut Valley from the Atlantic Coast, south down the foothills from the Neuquén and Río Territories, and east across the Andes from Chile. The Welsh first began settling in the foothills—called the *cordillera* by the locals—in the mid-1880s, and by the time our heroes arrived, mid-to-late 1901, they had plenty of neighbors." Buck, personal communication, August 30, 1997.

26. Meadows, *Digging Up Butch*, 6; Piernes, " Cassidy in Patagonia," in Pointer, *In Search of Cassidy*, 198.

27. He apparently did, since he came down with what he called, "a dose of the Town Disease." Buck and Meadows, "Leaving Cholila," 22.

28. Scott, "An American's Views," 683; Simpson, *Attending Marvels*, xv. The eastern slopes of the Andes Mountains, however, near where Butch and Longabaugh had their ranch, has been likened by some visitors to Appalachia, especially during the Argentine autumns (Scott, 684).

29. Perry, *Patagonia*, 67–68; Simpson, *Attending Marvels*, 278–79.

30. While the first major road was just then being built through the Andes and soon would connect western Chubut Territory to the Pacific Ocean, for years Patagonian bandits had been making use of little-known mountain passes to elude Argentinian authorities and to transport contraband to Chilean cities along the coast. Martínez Estrada, *X-Ray of Pampa*, 91. Over one such pass, 3,800-foot Paso Leon (also called Paso Cochamo) winds an ancient cattle trail first used by Jesuit missionaies in the early eighteenth century. Today, hardy tourists can book a two-week horseback ride on the Chile side of the mountains and follow "The Butch and Sundance Trail" over the pass and down into Cholila Valley. The ride terminates at Butch and Longabaugh's old ranch house where the current occupant, Aladin Sepulveda, now well past seventy, entertains with stories about the outlaw pair (Buck, *Saddle Up*, 3).

31. Pointer, *In Search of Cassidy*, 198, citing Justo Piernes, "Cassidy in Patagonia," *Clarín*, May 2, 1970. Dan Buck disagrees. Buck writes: "I have never seen any evidence that our trio used their real names in Argentina. All the documents signed by them in Argentina that have come to light bear the signatures of Ryan or

Place. As best I can tell, after rereading Piernes, he is quoting from a Chubut police report prepared [circa] 1949–50 that, in turn, borrows liberally from Pinkerton data given to the Buenos Aires police in 1903." Buck believes that Larry Pointer's translator misinterpreted some of Piernes's quotes from the police report, and in doing so gave the impression that the duo were using their real names. Buck adds that, although Pointer describes Justo Piernes as an "authoritative source," he was in fact nothing more than an ordinary newspaper reporter "with no particular knowledge of the bandits' story and must be read with extreme caution." Buck, personal communication, August 30, 1997.

32. Shaw-Lefevre, "Visit to the Argentine," 835.

33. Buck and Meadows to John Joerschke, reprinted in *True West*, November 1992: 6.

34. Buck and Meadows to John Joerschke, reprinted in *True West*, November 1992: 6.

35. George Newbery's family was from England by way of New York City. He was a dentist by profession and came to Buenos Aires in 1877. He also speculated in land and was a cattle trader. Daniel Buck and Anne Meadows, "The Wild Bunch in South America: A Maze of Entanglements," 19. According to Dan Buck, Newbery was attempting to organize a major North American colony in the Cholila area, and it was probably Newbery who first suggested that Butch, Longabaugh, and Etta settle in Cholila Valley. Buck, personal communication, August 30, 1997.

36. Meadows, *Digging Up Butch*, 40. In his report to his superiors in New York, Dimaio said that Newbery told him that to reach the outlaws ranch he would have to "travel by horseback for about 15 days through the jungle." Meadows, who is familiar with this area of Patagonia and knows that it is not jungle, found this statement perplexing. She wonders if Newbery was intentionally misleading Dimaio, or if Dimaio misled his superiors because he thought the trip too dangerous. As to the latter, Operative Frank Dimaio was not the sort to avoid danger. His prior record with the Pinkertons, which included undercover work against the Mafia, attested to his courage. If anything, Dimaio was a risk-taker. Horan, *The Pinkertons*, 418–41.

37. Meadows, *Digging Up Butch*, 40. A description of the plan to trick Butch and Longabaugh into showing up in Buenos Aires is in the Pinkerton files, in a memorandum written by Frank Dimaio on April 1903. Buck, personal communication, August 30, 1997.

38. Ernst, *Sundance*, 179.

39. Meadows, *Digging Up Butch*, 42–43. Buck and Meadows to John Joerschke, *True West*, November 1992:6.

40. Pinkerton, *Train Robberies*, 79.

41. Morn, *Eye That Never Sleeps*, 156.

42. Brown, *American West*, 344–45; *Denver Times*, Nov. 20, 1903.

43. Piernes, "Cassidy in Patagonia," in Pointer, *In Search of Cassidy*, 198; Buck and Meadows, "Leaving Cholila," 25; Buck, personal communication, August 30, 1997.

44. Meadows, *Digging Up Butch*, 2, 3. Meadows visited the site and was allowed to inspect the cabin and the grounds. Additional information was supplied by the niece of the present owner. See also Drago, *Etta Place*, 184.

45. Meadows, *Digging Up Butch*, 5, 6. On Meadows's visit to the cabin she was informed by a neighbor, Don Raúl, that he was told that Etta set a table "with a certain etiquette," which included "napkins [and] china plates."

46. Burns, "A Secret Hoard," 29.

47. Meadows, *Digging Up Butch*, 7. For the previous decade, wealthy Englishmen had been sending their university-trained sons to the Argentine interior to manage ranches in which their fathers had invested. Many of these young men were ill-suited for the task and were often the butt of jokes among the local ranchers. Shaw-Lefevre, "A Visit to the Argentine," 840.

48. Piernes, "Cassidy in Patagonia," in Pointer, *In Search of Cassidy*, 198.

49. Burns, "A Secret Hoard," 29. In Patagonia the *comisario* was equivalent to a local police inspector or sheriff. The author refers to the *comisario* as David Humphries; however, in Meadows's book, the name is given as Eduardo Humphreys. Meadows, *Digging Up Butch*, 63.

50. Slatta, *Cowboys of the Americas*, 33. When they had no work, many gauchos hunted ostriches for their feathers, which were prized by exporters. The ranchers hated the ostrich hunters, however, who often travelled in gangs, scattering livestock and sometimes starting fires to drive the birds into open pens.

51. Meadows, *Digging Up Butch*, 7; Buck and Meadows, "Leaving Cholila," 24. Solís was a Chilean who at the time was living in Río Pico, Argentina. It is believed that he worked for Butch and Harry for about eight months (Buck and Meadows, "Wild Bunch in South America," 7; Buck, personal communication, August 30, 1997).

52. Buffin, "A Gaucho's Day's Work," 1744. Dan Buck, who is quite familiar with the area, does not dispute Buffin's description of the gauchos, but he points out that in the early 1900s the ranchhands in Patagonia tended to be mostly Chilean (mainly "Chilotes" from the island of Chiloé) plus a few Scots and Welsh. Buck, personal communication, August 30, 1997.

53. Slatta, *Cowboys of the Americas*, 134–35.

54. As to Butch's lack of skill at gambling, see Greene, "Cassidy in Fremont," 2.

55. Slatta, *Cowboys of the Americas*, 154. As to Butch and learning Spanish, see Butch Cassidy to Mathilda Davis, August 10, 1902.

56. Slatta, *Cowboys of the Americas*, 156.

57. Slatta, *Cowboys of the Americas*, 156.

58. Slatta, *Cowboys of the Americas*, 157–58.

59. Webb, "Elton Cunningham," 14. Dan Buck wonders about Cunningham's "saddle story." Says Buck, "[M]aybe he misunderstood Butch's letter. Butch could have said 'I don't like the saddles down here,' [and] Cunningham, who probably didn't know Argentina from Mexico . . . translated that into Mexican saddle. The Argentina saddle is the *recado*, a layering of wool blankets and cow hides topped off with a sheepskin, totally unlike the elaborate, tooled leather Mexican saddles, which, in any event, were not used in Argentina. Moreover, American saddles were sold in Argentina at the better tack shops—as were the most recent models of American and European weaponry." Buck, personal communication, August 30, 1997.

60. Slatta, *Cowboys of the Americas*, 88–89. Slatta says the gauchos often rode barefooted or wore open-toed soft boots.

61. Slatta, *Cowboys of the Americas*, 129–30.

62. Ernst, *Sundance*, 175. The fact that they visited Fort Worth has led some Wild Bunch researchers, including Ernst, to speculate that Etta may have had friends or relatives there.

63. Ernst, *Sundance*, 175. According to Samanna, Harry sent a postcard from St. Louis to his other sister, Emma (Ernst, *Sundance*, 178).

64. J. P. Ryan to Dan Gibbon, Feb. 26, 1904, reprinted in Buck and Meadows, "Leaving Cholila," 22.

65. Buck and Meadows, "Wild Bunch in South America," 6, citing *La Prensa*, Jan. 18, 1906.

Moving On

1. Buck and Meadows, "Leaving Cholila," 24.

2. Buck and Meadows, "Leaving Cholila," 25, 27. The land company was probably the Cochamó Company, which was expanding into Argentina at the time. The land on which the ranch stood could not be sold, because Butch and Harry had not yet acquired title to it. The buildings, equipment, and livestock brought the pair 18,000 pesos, about $200,000 in today's dollars (Buck and Meadows, "Wild Bunch in South America," 9).

3. Meadows, *Digging Up Butch*, 7.

4. Piernes, "Cassidy in Patagonia," in Pointer, *In Search of Cassidy*, 200; Burns "A Secret Hoard," 29.

5. Burns, "A Secret Hoard," 29. For a while it was thought that Logan, if he did join Butch and Longabaugh in South America, used the alias Andrew Duffy, but this was disproved by outlaw historian Barbara Hegne. Hegne discovered that Andrew Duffy was a Montana saloonkeeper turned rustler who came to Argentina in

1907 (Buck and Meadows, "Neighbors on the Hot Seat," 8, citing letter from Hegne to authors, December 8, 1995, and Argentine police records).

6. *The New York Herald*, Sept. 23, 1906. Although it is now believed that Harvey Logan was killed in June 1904 following a train robbery near Parachute, Colorado, at the time the authorities had yet to firmly identify the robber's body. Pointer, *In Search of Cassidy*, 200–201, citing memos from William Pinkerton to Robert Pinkerton, dated July 9, 1904, and from Robert Pinkerton to agency files, dated January 15, 1907.

7. Meadows, *Digging Up Butch*, 67.

8. Meadows, *Digging Up Butch*, 67–68.

9. Meadows, *Digging Up Butch*, 69–70.

10. Buck, "Outlaw Symposium in Argentina," 3.

11. Buck and Meadows, "Leaving Cholila," 24.

12. Buck and Meadows, "Neighbors on the Hot Seat," 15.

13. If they did go to San Francisco, Donna Ernst believes they may have stayed with Harry's brother, Elwood Longabaugh. Ernst, *Sundance*, 182, citing private Longabaugh family records. According to Ed Kirby, in 1919 Elwood Longabaugh was living at 125 Arch Street and working as an innkeeper (Kirby, *Rise and Fall*, 113). Whether Elwood was in San Francisco as early as 1905, however, Kirby does not say.

14. Meadows, *Digging Up Butch*, 79.

15. Buck and Meadows, "Wild Bunch in South America," 28–29.

16. Meadows and Buck, "Showdown at San Vicente," 17.

17. Buck and Meadows, "Escape from Mercedes," 3–5, citing the *Buenos Aires Herald*, Dec. 20, 1905; Meadows, *Digging Up Butch*, 79–81.

18. Buck and Meadows, "What the Wild Bunch Did," 3–4; Meadows, *Digging Up Butch*, 81–83. For the local residents the rains may have been a blessing. According to one of the posse leaders, Cipriano Sosa, to slow down their pursuers the outlaws set the heavy brush and grass on fire. Had it not been for the rains, said Sosa, the fire would have done terrible damage (Buck and Meadows, "A Maze of Entanglements," 19, citing *La Prensa*).

19. Meadows, *Digging Up Butch*, 83, citing articles in *La Prensa*.

20. Buck and Meadows, "A Maze of Entanglements," 19, citing *La Prensa*.

21. Meadows, *Digging Up Butch*, 87.

22. Buck and Meadows, "Escape from Mercedes," 6, 21.

23. Meadows, *Digging Up Butch*, 93–94, 250, citing a letter from Roy Letson to Charles Kelly, probably written in the 1930s.

24. Meadows, *Digging Up Butch*, 97.

25. Chapman, "'Butch' Cassidy," 60. According to Larry Pointer, Percy Seibert was associated with a Bolivian supply company, which assigned him to work closely with the Concordia mine. Originally, Seibert had come to Bolivia in 1905 as a railroad engineer to survey proposed routes for the Bolivian Railway, but he was

involved in a controversy of some sort with his superiors and was dismissed. He stayed on in Bolivia, and the following year became associated with the supply company and its customer, Concordia (Pointer, *In Search of Cassidy*, 206, citing correspondence of the American Legation in Bolivia for the years 1904–1906, on file at the Federal Archive and Record Center, Denver, Colorado).

26. Chapman, "'Butch' Cassidy," 60.

27. Meadows, *Digging Up Butch*, 93.

28. Percy Seibert to "Elizabeth," January 15, 1964, reprinted in Pointer, *In Search of Cassidy*, 206–7. At the time, the original letter was in the possession of Mrs. Robert W. Cline of Williamsport, Maryland.

29. Meadows, *Digging Up Butch*, 95.

30. *The New York Herald*, Sept. 23, 1906.

31. Buck and Meadows, "Neighbors on the Hot Seat," 9, 10; Buck, personal communication, August 30, 1997.

32. J. P. Maxwell (aka Butch Cassidy) to "The Boys at Concordia," November 12, 1907, reprinted in Pointer, *In Search of Cassidy*, 208–9. When the letter was reprinted in Pointer's book (1977), the original was in the possession of Mrs. Robert W. Cline of Williamsport, Maryland.

33. J. P. Maxwell (aka Butch Cassidy) to "The Boys at Concordia," November 12, 1907.

34. Chapman, "'Butch' Cassidy," 61.

35. Chapman, "'Butch' Cassidy," 60.

36. Meadows, *Digging Up Butch*, 94–95.

37. Percy Seibert to "Elizabeth," January 15, 1964.

38. Chapman, "'Butch' Cassidy," 60.

39. Percy Seibert to "Elizabeth," January 15, 1964.

40. Meadows, *Digging Up Butch*, 96.

41. Chapman, "'Butch' Cassidy," 60.

42. Meadows, *Digging Up Butch*, 96.

43. Chapman, "'Butch' Cassidy," 61. The messenger Butch was referring to was probably Ernest C. Woodcock, the messenger in charge of the express car when the gang struck the Union Pacific at Wilcox, Wyoming, in June 1899. In another version of the incident, when Butch ordered the messenger to come out of the car, Woodcock answered "Come and get me." When Woodcock was finally forced out by a blast of dynamite, Harvey Logan was ready to kill him because of his stubbornness, but Butch interceded, saying "A man with his nerve deserves not to be shot." Horan and Sann, *Pictorial History*, 212.

San Vicente

1. Chapman, "'Butch' Cassidy," 60.

2. Meadows, *Digging Up Butch*, 101.

3. Chapman, "'Butch' Cassidy," 60. There is no source other than Percy Seibert that attributes the Santo Domingo payroll robbery to Butch and Longabaugh. Dan Buck suggests Seibert was simply recalling various mining camp holdups in the region, and Arthur Chapman decided to add them to the duo's list of accomplishments. Buck, personal communcation August 30, 1997.

4. Meadows, *Digging Up Butch*, 100.

5. Chapman, "'Butch' Cassidy," 60.

6. Meadows, *Digging Up Butch*, 100.

7. In this report of the robbery, Peró describes the robbers as "Yankees." However, at times other sources mention a North American and a Chilean. Meadows, *Digging Up Butch*, 134–35, 164–65, 182.

8. Carlos Peró to Aramayo officials at Tupiza, Bolivia, November 4, 1908, reprinted in Meadows, *Digging Up Butch*, 230–33. Percy Seibert also mentioned this robbery, but gave the date as 1909 (Chapman, "'Butch' Cassidy," 62). For additional documentation on the robbery, see Meadows, *Digging Up Butch*, 163–65.

9. Carlos Peró to Aramayo officials at Tupiza, Bolivia, November 4, 1908. The accounting records of the Aramayo company showed that an 80,000 *boliviano* payroll was shipped by the same route the previous week, suggesting the robbers did have inside information (Meadows, *Digging Up Butch*, 237).

10. Carlos Peró to Aramayo officials at Tupiza, Bolivia, November 4, 1908.

11. Malcom Roberts to Capt. Justo P. Concha, November 7, 1908, reprinted in Meadows, *Digging Up Butch*, 234–35. In this letter Roberts acknowledges Captain Concha's message and congratulates him on a job well done. On the shootout, see also Meadows, *Digging Up Butch*, 166–67.

12. Chapman, "'Butch' Cassidy," 62.

13. Meadows, *Digging Up Butch*, 135–36.

14. Meadows, *Digging Up Butch*, 135, 268; Buck, personal communication, August 30, 1997.

15. Meadows, *Digging Up Butch*, 266–67.

16. Meadows, *Digging Up Butch*, 264–65, 267. Another witness, Remigio Sánchez, a local miner, described the death scene this way: "The captain entered with a soldier, and then all of us entered and found the smaller gringo stretched out on the floor, dead, with one bullet wound in the temple and another in the arm. The taller one was hugging a large ceramic jug that was in the room. He was dead, also, with a bullet wound in the forehead and several in his arm."

17. Chapman, "'Butch' Cassidy," 62. In remote villages in Bolivia, and perhaps elsewhere in South America, it may not have been unusual for the only hotel or whatever served as a hotel to be in close proximity to the police station or constable's office. The practice was probably for the benefit of the guests, to assure them that they and their

possessions would be safe during the night. However, Dan Buck says there were no such lodgings in San Vicente in 1908 and that the scene was probably a Seibert-via-Chapman invention. Buck, personal communication, August 30, 1997.

18. Chapman, "'Butch' Cassidy," 62.

19. Chapman, "'Butch' Cassidy," 62. According to eyewitness Remigio Sánchez, once the soldiers, (led by Victor Torres) were about four steps from the door of the room, "one of the gringos—the smaller one—appeared and fired one shot and then another from his revolver at the soldier, who ran screaming to the house of Julian Saínz, where he died in moments." Meadows, *Digging Up Butch*, 264. If the bandits were Butch and Longabaugh, Butch was considered the shorter of the two. This could mean that Butch did not end his outlaw career without a killing to his credit.

20. Chapman, "'Butch' Cassidy," 62.

21. Chapman, "'Butch' Cassidy," 63.

22. Meadows, *Digging Up Butch*, 107. According to Meadows, Hampton later passed this information on to writer James D. Horan.

23. Kelly, *Outlaw Trail*, 314.

24. *The Steamboat Pilot* (Steamboat Springs, Colorado), Feb. 23, 1910, quoted in Burroughs, *Where West Stayed Young*, 133.

25. Unlabeled Pinkerton file. A Pinkerton agency file card on Lowe is reprinted in Horan and Sann, *Pictorial History*, 195.

26. Meadows, *Digging Up Butch*, 88, citing the Pinkerton files.

27. Warner, *Last of Bandit Riders*, 322.

28. Warner, *Last of Bandit Riders*, 323.

29. Kelly, *Outlaw Trail*, 314–16.

30. Buck, personal communication, August 30, 1997.

31. Warner, *Last of Bandit Riders*, 323.

32. Will Simpson to Charles Kelly, May 5, 1939, reprinted in Dullenty, *Cassidy Collection*, 31.

33. According to Senator Alan Simpson (R. Wyo.), his grandfather (Will) told the Senator's father that Butch died in South America. Alan Simpson to Dan Buck and Anne Meadows, October 12, 1988, cited in Buck, personal communication, August 30, 1997.

34. Meadows, *Digging Up Butch*, 127–28.

35. Horan and Sann, *Pictorial History*, 230, citing personal correspondence from Percy Seibert; Meadows, *Digging Up Butch*, 79, 93.

36. Ernst, *Sundance*, 187, citing the Bolivian Foreign Office Files for 1910, National Archives Records, Washington DC; Meadows, *Digging Up Butch*, 129.

37. Anne Meadows and Dan Buck made two trips to Antofagasta, searching for some trace of the report, but found nothing. Meadows, *Digging Up Butch*, 178–99.

38. Meadows, *Digging Up Butch*, 263.

39. Meadows, *Digging Up Butch*, 264–65.

40. Meadows, *Digging Up Butch*, 268–71. Dan Buck suggests one should not read too much into the fact that the dictionary was described as an *English* dictionary. He reminds us that the men doing the inventory were perhaps "a soldier and a smalltown *comisario*, not forensic scientists." Says Buck, "The dictionary could have been an English dictionary (I carried one on a year-long trip around South America) or it could have been a Spanish-English dictionary (one of the several pocket bilingual dictionaries I own says in English on one side, 'English-Spanish Dictionary' and in Spanish on the other, 'Dicionario Inglés-Español'). A soldier helping with the hurried inventory could have easily seen the word 'English' or 'Inglés' and yelled out, 'One English dictionary.'" Buck, personal communication, August 30, 1997.

41. Buck, personal communication, August 30, 1997. Yes, his name turned up, but did Enrique?

42. Buck, personal communication, August 30, 1997. Buck does have a point; however, James Hutcheon was a reputable businessman—the owner of a transportation company that hauled passengers and freight throughout southern Bolivia. As such, he and his company were entrusted with many lives and much property. It is possible that he did not want it to be known that his half-brother was a thief and a murderer.

43. Meadows, *Digging Up Butch*, 214. Presumably Enrique was half Scot and half Latin American, although that isn't known for sure.

44. Meadows, *Digging Up Butch*, 134–35, 164–65, 182.

45. Buck, personal communication, August 30, 1997. However, we cannot rule out the possibility that eyewitnesses to the robberies, including Carlos Peró, might have mistaken a masked half-Chilean, half-Scot man for a Yankee.

46. Daniel Buck and Anne Meadows, letter to the editor, *True West*, April 1994: 8.

47. Meadows, *Digging Up Butch*, 207.

48. Buck and Meadows, "Skulduggery," 39.

49. Meadows, *Digging Up Butch*, 210–12, 217, 275–78.

50. There were in fact more than the two corpses in the grave, but one was a baby whose mother still lived in the village, and she would not permit the body to be disturbed. This prevented the diggers from examining additional bodies that appeared to be buried further down. Meadows, *Digging Up Butch*, 293.

51. Meadows, *Digging Up Butch*, 291–93, 309.

52. Meadows, *Digging Up Butch*, 302–5.

53. Buck and Meadows, "Skulduggery," 39.

54. Meadows, *Digging Up Butch*, 309, 322–23.

55. Daniel Buck and Anne Meadows, letter to the editor, *True West*, April 1994: 8.

56. Buck and Meadows, "Skulduggery," 39.

57. Dan Buck, panel member of symposium "What Ever Happened to Butch and Sundance," Craig, Colorado, July 20, 1996.

58. Meadows and Buck, "Showdown at San Vicente," 16.

59. Daniel Buck and Anne Meadows, letter to the editor of *True West*, April 1994: 8.

60. *Salt Lake City Tribune*, Oct. 14, 1993; Stewart, "Butch and Sundance Revisited," 43.

61. *Los Angeles Times*, May 24, 1992.

62. *The Seattle Times*, Mar. 22, 1992.

63. *Los Angeles Times*, May 24, 1992.

64. *The Seattle Times*, Mar. 22, 1992.

Horizons

1. Meadows and Buck, "Showdown at San Vicente," 15.

2. Betenson and Flack, *Butch Cassidy*, 172.

3. Betenson and Flack, *Butch Cassidy*, 177.

4. Betenson and Flack, *Butch Cassidy*, 177.

5. Betenson and Flack, *Butch Cassidy*, 177–81.

6. Betenson and Flack, *Butch Cassidy*, 181–83.

7. Betenson and Flack, *Butch Cassidy*, 181–83. According to Cassidy biographer Ed Kirby, Lula told him during an interview at Circleville in the summer of 1970 that Butch answered, "Would I be dumb enough after all those years to steal a white, clearly branded mule and ride him into an area where the police and Bolivian Army were in evidence?" (Kirby, *Saga of Butch*, 88). Dan Buck, who is fairly certain that Lula's conversation with Butch never took place, points out that according to the report of the Aramayo payroll robbery, the mule in question was not white and that the area (the village of San Vicente) where the shootout occurred was not infested with Bolivian soldiers when Butch and Longabaugh were said to have ridden in (Buck, personal communication, August 30, 1997).

8. This statement bothers Anne Meadows. Says Anne, "Her [Lula's] claim that Butch told her Percy Seibert had deliberately misidentified the bodies so that his pals could come home without worrying about the Pinkertons proves that she made the whole thing up. . . . Seibert never saw the bodies, nobody identified them, and nobody spread the story here until the 1930s, when the statute of limitations had long since run out." Meadows, *Digging Up Butch*, 255. It would be difficult not to agree with Anne, except that Lula says only that Butch "heard" that Percy misidentified the bodies. Lula does not state this as a fact. Furthermore, there is no evidence that Seibert did identify the bodies.

9. Betenson and Flack, *Butch Cassidy*, 186–87, 192–93.

10. Betenson and Flack, *Butch Cassidy*, 192–93.

11. Lula Parker Betenson to Jim Dullenty, July 11, 1973. Dullenty, *Cassidy Collection*, 72.

12. *The National Enquirer*, June 10, 1973.

13. Lula Parker Betenson to Mrs. [Deleted], June 2, 1970, Dullenty, *Cassidy Collection*, 67–68.

14. Lula Parker Betenson to Jim Dullenty, Jan. 14, 1974, reprinted in Dullenty, *Cassidy Collection*, 73; Jim Dullenty to Lula Parker Betenson, Jan. 18, 1974, *Cassidy Collection*, 74.

15. Dullenty, *Cassidy Collection*, 52. Dullenty does not hold back when asked about Lula's book. In addressing the Chicago Corral of The Westerners in 1983, he told his audience "It would have been better if she had not written it. Except for the first four chapters dealing with early Parker family history, the book is worthless." Dullenty, "Phillips Really Cassidy?" 39.

16. Pointer, *In Search of Cassidy*, 19, citing interviews with Ellnor Parker by Jim Dullenty on June 30 and July 12, 1975, and his own interview with Max Parker on September 12, 1975, plus correspondence from Ellnor to Dullenty dated July 20 and August 11, 1975. See also Dullenty's "Interview with Max Parker, Kent, Washington, January 2, 1975," in Dullenty, *Cassidy Collection*, 77–82.

17. Betenson, "Lula Parker Betenson," 6.

18. Betenson, symposium panel member, "What Ever Happened to Butch and Sundance," Craig, Colorado, July 20, 1996.

19. Betenson, "Lula Parker Betenson," 9. According to Bill Betenson, Mark Betenson's statement that he saw Butch in Circleville in 1925 has in turn been confirmed by Mark's widow, Vivian Betenson, and by Mark's brother, Scott Betenson (Bill's grandfather).

20. DeJournette and DeJournette, *One Hundred Years*, 223–24. According to Daun DeJournette, this information came directly from Josie during an interview in the late 1950s.

21. DeJournette and DeJournette, *One Hundred Years*, 224.

22. Betenson and Flack, *Butch Cassidy*, 249, citing Flack's interview with Harv Murdock in Salt Lake City on April 11, 1972.

23. Burroughs, *Where West Stayed Young*, 135.

24. Pointer, *In Search of Cassidy*, 241, citing an interview with George Reynolds, in Riverton, Wyoming, on May 7, 1974. The connection between Welch and Reynolds was not given.

25. Burroughs, *Where West Stayed Young*, 135, citing a personal interview with Vernon.

26. Pointer, *In Search of Cassidy*, 240. Pointer's source was an interview with Boyd Charter in Billings, Montana, on December 1, 1973. According to Dan Buck,

Simpson did not believe that William Phillips was Butch Cassidy. Buck says that Simpson once said that he offered $100 to "a friend of Phillips" [Buck believes that it was Boyd Charter's father] to bring Phillips around the next time he was in town. Phillips was never brought to meet Simpson (Buck, personal communication, August 30, 1997).

27. DeJournette and DeJournette, *One Hundred Years*, 331, citing an interview with Edith MacKnight Jensen in 1973.

28. McClure, *Bassett Women*, 65.

29. Florin, *Ghost Towns*, 557–58.

30. Florin, *Ghost Towns*, 557–58.

31. Callan, "Cassidy in Southern Nevada," 5.

32. Baker, *Wild Bunch at Robbers Roost*, 201; Kirby, "Cassidy and Sundance Kid," 30; Meadows, *Digging Up Butch*, 203, citing an interview with Ed Kirby.

33. Meadows, *Digging Up Butch*, 203, citing an interview of Barbara Ekker by Ed Kirby.

34. Meadows, *Digging Up Butch*, 203 citing an interview with Ed Kirby.

35. Kirby, "Cassidy and Sundance Kid," 30.

36. Meadows, *Digging Up Butch*, 204, citing an interview with Ray Merrick, San Jose, California, in July 1988.

37. Betenson and Flack, Butch Cassidy, 194–95.

38. Betenson, "Lula Parker Betenson," 7–8.

39. Warner, *Last of Bandit Riders*, 323. In December 1937, Warner wrote Charles Kelly, "Forget all the reports on Butch Cassidy they are fake. . . . [H]e was killed in South America. He and a man by the name of Long—[unreadable] [were] killed in a soldier post their [sic] in a gun fight. This is straight" (Warner to Kelly, Kelly Collection, Dec. 22, 1937).

40. Warner and Lacy, "Warner's Daughter," 17.

41. Warner and Lacy, "Warner's Daughter," 17.

42. In September 1969, during an interview with Lula Parker Betenson, Ed Kirby said that Lula told him that while Butch was a fine person and everyone in Utah liked him, he really did hurt the Parker family. "What I really hold against him is that he broke my blessed little mother's heart. She prayed every night for his return." Kirby, *Saga of Butch*, 84. In 1975, while in the East to promote her book, Lula repeated this to a reporter from Waterbury, Connecticut (*Waterbury Republican*, May 25, 1975, quoted in Kirby, *Saga of Butch*, 97).

43. Warner and Lacy, "Warner's Daughter," 17. Copies of the letters do exist. They were viewed by members of the Western Outlaw-Lawman History Association during the association's 1994 conference in Craig, Colorado. Dan Buck, however, while calling the letters "one of the few tangible clues we have" related to the

possibility that Butch survived his South American adventure, is suspicious of their authenticity. Says Buck, "I can only speak for myself, but the handwriting bore absolute zero resemblance to Butch's—or to [William] Phillips's for that matter" (Buck, personal communication, August 30, 1997).

44. Steve Lacy, symposium panel member, "What Ever Happened to Butch and Sundance," a symposium held at Craig, Colorado, July 20, 1996.

45. Callan, "Cassidy in Southern Nevada," 5.

46. Barkdull, "Noisy, Sinful Goldfield," 13; Florin, *Ghost Towns*, 542.

47. Zanjani, *Goldfield*, 204. Pearl Baker devotes a short chapter to Maxwell in her *The Wild Bunch at Robbers Roost* (46–54). See also Kelly, *Outlaw Trail*, 180–86. Gunplay Maxwell, however, remains an enigma; Wild Bunch writers can't seem to agree on his real name or how and when he met his end.

48. Adams, "Rawhide Robbery," 13.

49. Zanjani, *Goldfield*, 21; Berk, "Cassidy Didn't Do It," 64.

50. Meadows, *Digging Up Butch*, 121. Meadows discounts this rumor because Rickard's wife, Edith Mae, was with him during his years in South America. As to Rickard in Goldfield, see Zanjani, *Goldfield*, 131–33.

51. Kirby, *Saga of Butch*, 106.

52. *Salt Lake City Tribune*, Oct. 10, 1993, reprinted in *The Outlaw Trail Journal*, Summer 1994: 33–34.

53. *Salt Lake City Tribune*, Oct. 14, 1993; Stewart, "Butch and Sundance Revisited," 42.

54. Buchanan, "Sometimes Cassidy," 41–42. If Davidson's story stopped here he might have gathered a few listeners, but he goes on. He says that uncle Bob Parker mined uranium ore in Utah, which he sold to Madame Curie, resulting in her discovery of radium. In 1901, he says that two Parkers reunited and joined the United States Navy. They both jumped ship in South America and uncle Bob Parker worked in the mines in Peru, while Robert LeRoy ranched in Patagonia, Argentina. They later rejoined the Navy and returned to the States. Uncle Bob Parker stayed in the service and was discharged in 1913. Later he became a prizefighter and defeated Jack Dempsey while Dempsey was the world's heavyweight champion. (If this is so, Parker would have had to have been at least forty-four years of age at the time.) After Robert LeRoy left the Navy he went to Mexico. When he returned he settled in Johnnie, Nevada, where he died in the late 1930s or early 1940s.

In a variant of the Davidson story uncovered by Anne Meadows, Robert LeRoy went to Goldfield, Nevada, and "made one of the greatest gold strikes on the continent." Later, near St. George, Utah, he amassed another fortune from silver and used the money to pay off everybody he had robbed. He then gave ten percent of his remaining wealth to the Mormon Church (Meadows, *Digging Up Butch*, 111–12). Davidson claims Bob Parker died in 1956 and is buried in the same grave as Robert LeRoy in Johnnie, Nevada (Buchanan, "Sometimes Cassidy," 41).

55. Buchanan, "Sometimes Cassidy," 44. Probably the only justification for repeating this tale is that somehow Davidson's story has managed to get published in book form: Arthur Davidson (assisted by James A. Aston), *"Sometimes" Cassidy: The Real Butch Cassidy Story,* 1994.

Phillips

1. The book was privately published in 1938 under the title *Outlaw Trail, A History of Butch Cassidy and His Wild Bunch, Hole-in-the-Wall, Brown's Hole, Robber's Roost.*

2. Mart Christensen to Charles Kelly, December 1, 1936, reprinted in Dullenty, *Cassidy Collection,* 60. The original letter is in the possession of the Utah State Historical Society, Salt Lake City, Utah.

3. Mart Christensen to Charles Kelly, December 1, 1936.

4. Tacetta B. Walker to Mart Christensen, August 8, 1936, reprinted in Dullenty, *Cassidy Collection,* 59. The original letter is in the possession of the Utah State Historical Society, Salt Lake City, Utah.

5. Tacetta B. Walker to Charles Kelly, August 1 1936, reprinted in Dullenty, *Cassidy Collection,* 58. The original letter is in the possession of the Utah State Historical Society, Salt Lake City, Utah.

6. Mart Christensen to Charles Kelly, June 19, 1936, reprinted in Dullenty, *Cassidy Collection,* 61. The original letter is in the possession of the Utah State Historical Society, Salt Lake City, Utah.

7. Pointer, *In Search of Cassidy,* ii.

8. Christensen to Kelly, June 19, 1936, citing an article Kelly had written for the January 1934 issue of the *Pony Express Courier.*

9. F. M. Carroll, M.D., to Charles Kelly, Dec. 2, 1937, reprinted in Dullenty, *Cassidy Collection,* 63. The original letter is in the possession of the Utah State Historical Society, Salt Lake City, Utah. See also Pointer, *In Search of Cassidy,* ii.

10. Mrs. Wm. T. Phillips to Charles Kelly, Oct. 4, 1938, reprinted in Dullenty, *Cassidy Collection,* 63.

11. Mrs. Wm. T. Phillips to Charles Kelly, Oct. 4, 1938.

12. Kelly, *Outlaw Trail,* 318.

13. Dullenty, "Regan Know Cassidy?" 5–6. Regan seemed sincere in his belief that the two men were not one and the same, but he weakened his evidence by saying too much. When he began recalling details about Cassidy's career, he made so many errors that he raised doubts as to whether he knew Butch at all.

14. Ernst, *Sundance,* 194.

15. Telephone interview with Jim Dullenty, Mar. 8, 1997.

16. Telephone interview with Jim Dullenty, Mar. 8, 1997.

17. Pointer, *In Search of Cassidy,* vii.

18. Pointer, *In Search of Cassidy*, 20–24, 242–43.

19. Mary Boyd Rhodes to W. Fields, August 19, 1937, reprinted in Pointer, *In Search of Cassidy*, 23. The original letter was last in the possession of Blanche Glasgow of Medical Lake, Washington. The letters from Phillips to Mary Boyd were last in the possession of Boyd's granddaughter, Mrs. Carl Manning of Casper, Wyoming. There is, however, some evidence that Mary Boyd was in on a scheme devised by Phillips to pass himself off as Cassidy. According to a Wyoming writer, Blanche Shroer, Mary confided as much to a close friend. Meadows, *Digging Up Butch*, 123.

20. Jeannine Zimmerman to Larry Pointer, November 19, 1973, reprinted in Pointer, *In Search of Cassidy*, 25.

21. Pointer, *In Search of Cassidy*, 25.

22. Buck, personal communication, August 30, 1997.

23. Buck, personal communication, August 30, 1997.

24. Telephone interview with Jim Dullenty, March 11, 1997.

25. Pointer, *In Search of Cassidy*, 35–36.

26. "Conclusion," in Phillips, *Bandit Invincible*, 59; Pointer, *In Search of Cassidy*, 35–36, citing an interview with Blanche Glasgow, Aug. 16, 1974.

27. Pointer, *In Search of Cassidy*, 260–61.

28. "Conclusion," in Phillips, *Bandit Invincible*, 59

29. Phillips, *Bandit Invincible*, 6.

30. Will Simpson to Harry Logue, February 4, 1937. Reprinted in Dullenty, *Cassidy Collection*, 29. Willow Creek is about eight miles south of Lander, just southeast of Table Mountain.

31. Pointer, *In Search of Cassidy*, 35, citing a letter from Ben Fitzharris in July 1973.

32. Pointer, *In Search of Cassidy*, 36.

33. Tanner, *Far Country*, 168.

34. Pearl Baker to Faun McCorkie Tanner, June 14, 1973. See Tanner, *Far Country*, 168–69. However, Baker may have later changed her mind. Pearl's letter to Tanner was written several months before the publication of Jim Dullenty's articles on Phillips in the Spokane *Daily Chronicle*. During an interview of Baker the following summer, Ed Kirby says that she told him that the Siebert article and the Dullenty papers proved that Phillips was Cassidy (Kirby, *Saga of Butch*, 89).

35. Dullenty, "Outlaw or Imposter?" 23.

36. Kyle, "Phillips Photo Fails," 28.

37. Dullenty, "Outlaw or Imposter?" 22–23.

38. Telephone interview with Dullenty, Mar. 8, 1997.

39. Dullenty, "Outlaw or Imposter?" 23–24.

40. Buck and Meadows, "Where Lies Butch?" 31.

41. Dan Buck and Anne Meadows, symposium panel members, "What Ever Happened to Butch and Sundance," Craig, Colorado, July 20, 1996.

42. Meadows, *Digging Up Butch*, 124–25. Dan Buck dismisses the Graham-Phillips-Seibert connection as mere coincidence. Says Buck, "Wayne Graham's marrying Percy Seibert's daughter proves only that concidences are sometimes both baffling and ultimately irrelevant." Buck points out that at the time Graham met Phillips, Graham had never been to South America and had never met the Seibert family. Graham met Seibert's daughter years later, while working in Chile. Also, Graham never saw Phillips again after their encounter in Spokane. (Buck, personal communication, August 30, 1997).

43. Meadows, *Digging Up Butch*, 124–25.

44. According to Dan Buck and Anne Meadows, even Larry Pointer himself has backed off somewhat from his original premise that Phillips was Cassidy. Buck and Meadows say Pointer believes that there were possibly three Butch Cassidys, one of whom was Phillips. Buck and Meadows, "Many Deaths," 54.

45. Meadows, *Digging Up Butch*, 202, citing an interview with Dullenty.

46. Dullenty, "Phillips Really Cassidy?" 40.

47. Pointer, *In Search of Cassidy*, 240.

48. Pearl Baker to Faun McCorkie Tanner, June 14, 1973; Tanner, *Far Country*, 168–69.

Afterthoughts

1. Harden, "Wanted," 21.

2. Patterson, *Birth, Flowering*, 188–89. For the most complete account of the Harvey Logan controversy, see Buck, "New Revelations," 6–13.

3. Pinkerton, *Train Robberies*, 79.

4. Buck, "New Revelations," 13.

5. Brock, "A Timely Arrival," 66. According to George Currie's niece, by the time Currie's father had an opportunity to identify the body it was in such bad condition that identification was almost impossible. But to put George's mother's mind to rest, the niece said that her grandfather said it was George. Pointer, *In Search of Cassidy*, 268, citing a letter from Evelyne Currie Marcinck to Jim Dullenty, October 28, 1974. See also *Denver Evening Post*, Mar. 1, 1900; *Denver Times*, May 2, 1900.

6. Kirby, *Rise and Fall*, 75.

7. Kirby, *Rise and Fall*, 113–16.

8. Kirby, *Rise and Fall*, 116–31.

9. There seems to be some facial resemblance—both men had rather prominent noses—but it is difficult to tell for certain because of the age difference in the available photographs of the two. Dan Buck thinks the idea is ridiculous. "Sundance was a handsome man pushing six feet in height," says Dan. "Beebee was an ugly,

gnomish-looking character, 5' 3" in lifts." Buck, personal communication, August 30, 1997.

10. Jim Dullenty, symposium panel member, "What Ever Happened to Butch and Sundance," Craig, Colorado, July 20, 1996.

11. Symposium, Western Outlaw-Lawman History Association, "What Ever Happened to Butch and Sundance," Craig, Colorado, July 20, 1996. The sole dissenter was Steve Lacy, who plans to publish his own book in which he claims to have startling new evidence on both Butch and Longabaugh.

12. The body was seized almost immediately by the authorities and persons who knew Jesse were called in to identify it. The body was then autopsied, propped up on a board, and shown off to hundreds of people in St. Joseph, Missouri. Photos of the body reveal scars that matched Jesse's two known chest wounds, and the autopsy record noted the missing tip of the middle finger of the left hand, a disfigurement said to have occurred when, as a youth, Jesse accidentally shot himself. Harden, "Wanted," 24; Settle Jr., *Jesse James Was His Name*, 118.

13. Harden, "Wanted," 26.

14. Buck and Meadows, "Where Lies Butch," 30.

15. In American criminal law, to obtain a conviction the evidence of guilt must be more than a preponderance, it must be "beyond a reasonable doubt."

16. Meadows, *Digging Up Butch*, 127–28.

17. If the Chilean judge was able to close the book on Boyd/Brown, he did not get much help from the Bolivian officials, who simply sent Aller copies of "John Doe" death certificates of the two men killed at San Vicente. Buck, personal communication, August 30, 1997.

18. Meadows, *Digging Up Butch*, 134–35, 164–65, 182.

19. Meadows, *Digging Up Butch*, 214.

20. Meadows, *Digging Up Butch*, 269.

21. Warner and Lacy, "Warner's Daughter," 17.

22. Baker, *Wild Bunch at Robbers Roost*, 83–86.

23. Kelly, *Outlaw Trail*, 261.

24. Baker, *Wild Bunch at Robbers Roost*, 84–85.

25. Baker, *Wild Bunch at Robbers Roost*, 86.

26. Tanner, *Far Country*, 164.

27. A contemporary account of the killing can be found in the *Grand Valley Times*, June 1, 1900. (The *Grand Valley Times* later became the *Moab Times-Independent*.) A reprint of the *Times* article appears in Baker, *Wild Bunch at Robbers Roost*, 87–88.

28. Kelly, *Outlaw Trail*, 264–65.

29. Baker, *Wild Bunch at Robbers Roost*, 89. Some believe Harvey Logan killed Tyler and Jenkins. The question has never been resolved. Firmage, *Grand County*, 160–61.

30. Baker, *Wild Bunch at Robbers Roost*, 93; Burroughs, *Where West Stayed Young*, 135, citing personal communication with Avvon Chew Hughel, whose family knew Dilly. According to Baker, when Dilly learned that a posse was after him for the killing of Tyler and Jenkins in May 1900, he hid out at Jack Chew's cow camp. (Baker, *Wild Bunch at Robbers Roost*, 89; Skovlin, "McCarty Names NOLA," 2.

31. Kelly, *Outlaw Trail*, 316. Other members of the group behind the expedition, supposedly Matt Warner, Elzy Lay, Bert Charter, and Charley Gibbons, apparently believed at the time that it was Butch. The photo, however, has never been found and, according to Anne Meadows, no one has ever turned up any solid evidence that there even was such an expedition (Meadows, *Digging Up Butch*, 112).

32. Kelly, *Outlaw Trail*, 289.

33. Hughel, *Chew Bunch*, 47–49.

34. Baker, *Wild Bunch at Robbers Roost*, 84; Hughel, *Chew Bunch*, 47.

35. Baker, *Wild Bunch at Robbers Roost*, 93.

36. Buck, personal communication, August 30, 1997. As to Dan Parker apparently being fooled by William Phillips, see Pointer, *In Search of Cassidy*, 19, citing interviews with Ellnor Parker by Jim Dullenty on June 30 and July 12, 1975, and Pointer's interview with Max Parker on September 12, 1975, plus correspondence from Ellnor to Dullenty dated July 20 and August 11, 1975. See also Dullenty's "Interview with Max Parker, Kent, Washington, January 2, 1975," in Dullenty, *Cassidy Collection*, 77–82. To be fair, however, it should be pointed out that some members of Lula's family do believe her account of Butch's return. According to Lula's great-grandson, Bill Betenson, Lula's son Mark was at the ranch when Butch showed up and said that he saw him. Bill Betenson, the grandson of Mark's brother, Scott, adds that this was recently confirmed to him by Mark's widow, Vivian. Betenson, "Lula Parker Betenson," 9.

37. Dullenty, *Cassidy Collection*, 52.

38. Buck, personal communication, August 30, 1997.

39. Kirby, *Saga of Butch*, 100.

40. Buck, personal communication, August 30, 1997.

Bibliography

Ackerman, William G., and Shane T. Johnson. "Outlaws of the Past: A Western Perspective on Prescription and Adverse Possession." *Land and Water Law Review* 31 (1996):79–112.

Adams, Frank. "The Rawhide Stage Coach Robbery, 1980. The Nevada State Police vs. Butch Cassidy's Understudy: C. L. 'Gunplay' Maxwell." *Quarterly of the National Association and Center for Outlaw and Lawmen History* (Jan.–Mar. 1996).

Allison, Mary. *Dubois Area History*. Dubois WY: Mary Allison, 1991.

"Armored Trains." *Scientific American*, Jan. 13, 1900.

Armstrong, Erma. "Aunt Ada and the Outlaws: The Story of C. L. Maxwell." *The Outlaw Trail Journal* (winter 1997).

Baars, Donald L. *Canyonlands Country*. Salt Lake City: University of Utah Press, 1993.

Baker, Pearl. *The Wild Bunch at Robbers Roost*. New York: Abelard-Schuman, 1971. Reprint, Lincoln: University of Nebraska Press, 1989.

Barkdull, Tom. "Noisy, Sinful Goldfield." *Frontier Times*, Nov. 1969.

Behymer, Bruce. "You Don't Chase the Wild Bunch on a Bicycle!" *Frontier Times*, Sept. 1970.

Bell, Mike. "Interview with the Sundance Kid." *The Journal of the Western Outlaw-Lawman History Association*, summer 1995.

———. "The Killing of Lonny Logan." *The English Westerners' Tally Sheet*, spring 1990.

Beman-Puechner, Barbara. "Bucking the Tiger." *The West That Was*. Thomas W. Knowles and Joe R. Lansdale, eds. New York: Wings Books, 1993.

Berk, Lee. "Butch Cassidy Didn't Do It." *Old West*, fall 1983.

Betenson, Bill (William). "Lula Parker Betenson." *The Outlaw Trail Journal*, winter 1995.

Betenson, William. "Alias 'Tom Ricketts,' The True Story of Butch Cassidy's Brother, Dan Parker." *The Outlaw Trail Journal*, winter 1996.

Betenson, Lula, and Dora Flack. *Butch Cassidy, My Brother*. Provo UT: Brigham Young University Press, 1975.

Boren, Kerry Ross. "Badges and Badmen." *The Outlaw Trail Journal*, winter 1993.

———. "Grandpa Knew Butch Cassidy." *Frontier Times*, Feb.–Mar. 1966.

———. "The Mysterious Pinkerton." *True West*, Aug. 1977.

Boren, Kerry Ross, and Lisa Lee Boren. "Anna Marie Thayne: Mrs. Sundance." *The Outlaw Trail Journal*, summer–fall 1993.

———. "Tom Vernon: 'Butch Cassidy Came Back,'" *The Outlaw Trail Journal*, summer–fall 1993.

Bristow, Allen P. "A Rude Awakening." *True West*, June 1996.

Brock, J. Elmer. "A Timely Arrival." *Annals of Wyoming*, Jan. 1943.

Brown, Dee. *The American West*. New York: Charles Scribner's Sons, 1994.

Buchanan, Bill. "Sometimes Cassidy." Book review. *The Outlaw Trail Journal*, winter 1995.

Buck, Daniel. "New Revelations about Harvey Logan Following the Parachute Train Robbery." *The Journal of the Western Outlaw-Lawman History Association*, spring 1997.

———."Saddle-Up for the Southern Andes: Horseback and Hiking Excursions in Patagonian Andes." *Americas*, Nov. 21, 1997.

———. "Surprising Development: The Sundance Kid's Unusual—and Unknown—Life in Canada." *The Journal of the Western Outlaw-Lawman History Association*, winter 1993.

Buck, Daniel, and Anne Meadows. "Escape from Mercedes: What the Wild Bunch Did in South America." *The Journal of the Western Outlaw-Lawman History Association*, spring–summer 1991.

———. "Etta Place: A Most Wanted Woman." *The Journal of the Western Outlaw-Lawman History Association*, spring–summer 1993.

———. "Leaving Cholila: Butch and Sundance Documents Surface in Argentina." *True West*, Jan. 1996.

———. "The Many Deaths of Butch Cassidy." *Pacific Northwest*, July 1987.

———. "Outlaw Symposium in Argentina: Butch and Sundance Found Innocent of Holdup." *Newsletter of the Western Outlaw-Lawman History Association*, spring 1997.

———. "Where Lies Butch Cassidy?" *Old West*, fall 1991.

———. "The Wild Bunch in South America: A Maze of Entanglements." *The Journal of the Western Outlaw-Lawman History Association*, fall 1992.

———. "The Wild Bunch in South America: Closing in on the Bank Robbers." *The Journal of the Western Outlaw-Lawman History Association*, fall–winter 1991.

————. "Wild Bunch in South America: Merry Christmas from the Pinkertons." *The Journal of the Western Outlaw-Lawman History Association*, spring 1992.

————. "Wild Bunch in South America: Neighbors on the Hot Seat: Revelations from the Long-Lost Argentine Police File." *The Journal of the Western Outlaw-Lawman History Association*, spring–summer 1996.

Buffin, William. "A Gaucho's Day's Work." *World's Work*, Feb. 1902.

Burns, James W. (Jim Dullenty). "A Secret Hoard in Argentina." *True West*, May 1983.

Burroughs, John Rolfe. *Where the Old West Stayed Young*. New York: William Morrow and Company, 1962.

Burton, Doris Karren. "Charley Crouse's Robbers' Roost." *The Outlaw Trail* Journal, winter 1993.

————. *History of Uintah County*. Salt Lake City: Utah State Historical Society/ Uintah County Commission, 1996.

————. *Queen Ann Bassett: Alias Etta Place*. Vernal UT: Burton Enterprises, 1992.

————. "Sheriff John Theodore Pope." *The Outlaw Trail Journal*, summer 1991.

Burton, Jeff. *Dynamite and Six-Shooter*. Santa Fe NM: Palomino Press, 1970.

Callan, Dan. "Butch Cassidy in Southern Nevada." *Newsletter of the Western Outlaw-Lawman History Association*, summer 1991.

Candee, Helen Churchill. "Oklahoma." *Atlantic Monthly*, Nov. 1900.

Carlson, Chip. "The Tipton Train Robbery." *The Journal of the Western Outlaw-Lawman History Association*, summer 1995.

Casebier, Caleb. "The Last of the Horseback Bandits." *Historian*, July 1997.

Chapman, Arthur. "'Butch' Cassidy." *Elks Magazine*, Apr. 1930.

Clay, John. *My Life on the Range*. Norman: University of Oklahoma Press, 1962.

Collins, James L. "Butch and the Wild Bunch." in *The West That Was*, Thomas W. Knowles and Joe R. Lansdale, eds. New York: Wings Books, 1993.

Condit, Thelma Gatchell. "The Hole-in-the-Wall." *Annals of Wyoming*, April 1958.

————. "The Hole-in-the-Wall." *Annals of Wyoming*, April 1959.

Cress, Cy. "Match Race that Broke Saguache." *Old West*, fall 1992.

DeJournette, Dick, and Daun DeJournette. *One Hundred Years of Brown's Park and Diamond Mountain*. Vernal UT: DeJournette Enterprises, 1996.

Dexter, Edwin G. "Influence of the Weather Upon Crime." *Appleton's Popular Science Monthly*, Sept. 1899.

Drago, Gail. *Etta Place: Her Life and Times with Butch Cassidy and the Sundance Kid*. Plano TX: Republic of Texas Press, 1996.

Dullenty, Jim. *The Butch Cassidy Collection*. Hamilton MT: Rocky Mountain House Press, 1986.

————. "Did Regan Know Phillips and Cassidy?" *The Journal of the Western Outlaw-Lawman History Association*, spring 1992.

———. "The Family Photo Album of 'Gentleman Outlaw' Elzy Lay." *The Journal of the Western Outlaw-Lawman History Association*, winter–spring 1995.

———. "The Farm Boy Who Became a Member of Butch Cassidy's Wild Bunch." *Quarterly of the National Association and Center for Outlaw and Lawman History*, winter 1986.

———. "From the Editor." *True West*, Sep. 1983.

———. "George Currie and the Curry Boys." *Quarterly of the National Association and Center for Outlaw and Lawman History*, Oct. 1979.

———. *Harry Tracy, The Last Desperado*. Dubuque IA: Kendall/Hunt Publishing, 1996.

———. "He Saw 'Kid Curry' Rob Great Northern Train." *Quarterly of the National Association and Center for Outlaw and Lawman History*, winter 1985.

———. "Historic Outlaw Sites." *Quarterly of the National Association and Center for Outlaw and Lawman History*, summer 1982.

———. "Houses that Butch Built." *The Journal of the Western Outlaw-Lawman History Association*, spring–summer 1992.

———. "Outlaw Hangouts You Can Visit." *True West*, Mar. 1983.

———. "Wagner Train Robbery." *Old West*, spring 1983.

———. "Was William T. Phillips Really Butch Cassidy?" *The Westerners Brand Book* (Chicago Corral), Nov.–Dec. 1982.

———. "Who Really Was William T. Phillips of Spokane: Outlaw or Imposter?" *The Journal of the Western Outlaw-Lawman History Association*, fall–winter 1991.

Edgar, Bob, and Jack Turnell. *Brand of a Legend*. Cody WY: Stockade Publishing, 1978.

Ernst, Donna B. "Blackened Gold and the Wild Bunch." *Quarterly of the National Association and Center for Outlaw and Lawman History*, Jan.–Mar. 1994.

———. "Friends of the Pinkertons." *Quarterly of the National Association and Center for Outlaw and Lawman History*, Apr.–June 1995.

———. *From Cowboy to Outlaw: The True Story of Will Carver*. Sonora TX: Sutton County Historical Society, 1995.

———. "Identifying Etta Place: Was She Just a Bad Girl from Texas?" *The Journal of the Western Outlaw-Lawman History Association*, spring–summer 1993.

———. "Powder Springs: Outlaw Hideout." *True West*, May 1997.

———. "The Sundance Kid: My Uncle. Researching the Memories of Snake River Residents." *Frontier Magazine*, Aug. 1997.

———. "The Sundance Kid: Wyoming Cowboy." *The Journal of the Western Outlaw-Lawman History Association*, spring 1992.

———. *Sundance, My Uncle*. College Station TX: Creative Publishing, 1992.

———. "Sundance: The Missing Years." *Old West*, spring 1994.

———. *The True Story of Will Carver*. Sonora TX: Sutton County Historical Society, 1995.

———. "Wanted: Friends of the Wild Bunch." *True West*, Dec. 1994.

Fetter, Richard L., and Suzanne Fetter. *Telluride, from Pick to Powder*. Caldwell ID: Caxton Printers, 1979.

Firmage, Richard A. *A History of Grand County*. Salt Lake City: Utah State Historical Society/Grand County Commission, 1996.

Flack, Dora. "Butch Cassidy: The Living Dead." *Frontier Times*, Jan. 1981.

Florin, Lambert. *Ghost Towns of the West*. Seattle: Superior Publishing, 1970.

French, William. *Some Recollections of a Western Ranchman: New Mexico, 1883–1899*. New York: Argosy-Antiquarian Ltd., 1965.

———. *Further Recollections of a Western Ranchman: New Mexico, 1883–1899*. New York: Argosy-Antiquarian Ltd., 1965.

Frye, Elnora L. *Atlas of Wyoming Outlaws at the Territorial Penitentiary*. Laramie WY: Jelm Mountain Press, 1990.

Geary, Edward A. *A History of Emery County*. Salt Lake City: Utah State Historical Society/Emery County Commission, 1996.

Greene, A. F. C. "'Butch' Cassidy in Fremont County." In *The Butch Cassidy Collection* (Jim Dullenty, ed.). Hamilton MT: Rocky Mountain House Press, 1986.

Greenwood, Val D. *The Researcher's Guide to American Genealogy*. Baltimore: Genealogical Publishing, 1975.

Griffith, Elizabeth. "Sundance Kid: The Man in the Attic." *The Journal of the Western Outlaw-Lawman History Association*, spring–summer 1996.

Hadley, Mary, and Jim Dullenty. "Cokeville, a Rough Town in the Old West." *Quarterly of the National Association and Center for Outlaw and Lawman History*, spring 1982.

Hampton, Wade. "Brigandage on Our Railroads." *The North American Review*, Dec. 1893.

Harden, Blaine. "Wanted." *The Washington Post Magazine*, Nov. 19, 1995.

Harlow, Alvin F. *Old Waybills*. New York: Appleton-Century, 1937.

Hatch, Alden. *American Express: A Century of Service*. Garden City NY: Doubleday, 1950.

Hawthorne, Roger. "Johnson County 'War' Part of Larger Event." *Quarterly of the National Association and Center for Outlaw and Lawman History*, fall 1987.

Hayden, Willard C. "Butch Cassidy and the Great Montpelier Bank Robbery." *Idaho Yesterdays*, spring 1971.

Heck, Larry E. *Pass Patrol: In Search of the Outlaw Trail*. Vol. 1. Aurora CO: Pass Patrol Outback Publications, 1996.

Heidt, Ray. "The Night Butch Cassidy Came to Coonville." *The Outlaw Trail Journal*, winter 1996.

Heslip, John R. "Graveyard of Violence: A Place of Fat Lizards and Bleached Bones." *True West*, Aug. 1981.

Horan, James D. *Desperate Men*. New York: Doubleday, 1949.

———. *The Pinkertons: The Detective Dynasty that Made History*. New York: Crown Publishers, 1967.

Horan, James D., and Paul Sann. *Pictorial History of the Wild West*. New York: Bonanza Books, 1954.

Huett, Wil. "Locked Up in Laramie." *True West*, Feb. 1991.

Hughel, Avvon Chew. *The Chew Bunch in Brown's Park*. San Francisco: The Scrimshaw Press, 1970.

Jarman, Rufus. "The Pinkerton Story." *Saturday Evening Post*, May 15, 22, 29, June 5, 1948.

Jessen, Kenneth. *Colorado Gunsmoke: True Stories of Outlaws and Lawmen on the Colorado Frontier*. Boulder CO: Pruett Publishing, 1986.

Kelly, Charles. *The Outlaw Trail: A History of Butch Cassidy and His Wild Bunch*. 2nd ed. New York: Bonanza Books, 1959.

Kelsey, Michael R. *Hiking and Exploring Utah's Henry Mountains and Robbers Roost*, Provo UT: Kelsey Publishing, 1990.

Kennan, George. *E. H. Harriman: A Biography*. Vol. 1. Boston: Houghton Mifflin, 1922.

Kildare, Maurice. "Bear River Loot." *Real West*, Sept. 1968.

Kirby, Edward M. "Butch Cassidy and the Sundance Kid: An Historical Essay." *The Outlaw Trail Journal*, summer 1991.

———. *The Rise and Fall of the Sundance Kid*. Iola WI: Western Publications, 1983.

———. *The Saga of Butch Cassidy and the Wild Bunch*. Palmer Lake CO: The Filter Press, 1977.

Kouris, Diana Allen. "The Lynching Calamity in Brown's Park." *True West*, Sept. 1995.

———. *The Romantic and Notorious History of Brown's Park*. Basin WY: Wolverine Gallery, 1988.

Kyle, Thomas G. "Did Butch Cassidy Die in Spokane? Phillips Photo Fails." *Old West*, fall 1991.

Lacy, Steve, and Jim Dullenty. "Revealing Letters of Outlaw Butch Cassidy." *Old West*, Winter 1984.

Lamb, F. Bruce. *The Wild Bunch: A Selected Critical Annotated Bibliography of the Literature*. Worland WY: High Plains Publishing, 1993.

Larson, T. A. *History of Wyoming*. Lincoln: University of Nebraska Press, 1978.

Lavender, David. *The Telluride Story*. Ridgeway CO: Wayfinder Press, 1987.

Longabaugh, William D. "The Sundance Kid: View from the Family." *True West*, July 1984.

Marion, W. L. "He Bit the Hand That Fed Him." *True West*, Apr. 1967.

Martin, R. I. "A Lively Day at Belle Fourche." *True West*, Apr. 1962.

Martínez Estrada, Ezequiel. *X-Ray of the Pampa*. Austin: University of Texas Press, 1971.

Mathisen, Jean A., "Rocky Mountain Riders: Wyoming's Volunteer Cavalry." *True West*, Nov. 1991.

McCarty, Tom. *Tom McCarty's Own Story*. Hamilton MT: Rocky Moutain House Press, 1986.

McClure, Grace. *The Bassett Women*. Athens OH: Swallow Press/Ohio University Press, 1985.

McPhee, John. "Annals of the Former World Rising from the Plain." *The New Yorker*, Feb. 24, Mar. 6, 1986.

McPherson, Robert S., *A History of San Juan County: In the Palm of Time*. Salt Lake City: Utah State Historical Society/San Juan County Commission, 1995.

Meadows, Anne. *Digging Up Butch and Sundance*. New York: St. Martin's Press, 1994.

Meadows, Anne, and Daniel Buck. "Showdown at San Vicente: The Case that Butch and Sundance Died in Bolivia." *True West*, Feb. 1993.

Michelson, Charles. "The Trade of Train Robbery." *Munsey's Magazine*, Feb. 1902.

Morn, Frank. *The Eye That Never Sleeps: A History of the Pinkerton National Detective Agency*. Bloomington: Indiana University Press, 1982.

Moss, Kathleen. "The Diary of Bertha Picard, 1895–97." *True West*, July 1986, Aug. 1986.

Moulton, Candy. *Roadside History of Wyoming*. Missoula MT: Mountain Press Publishing, 1995.

Parsons, Chuck. "Burial Plot." *True West*, Oct. 1996.

Patterson, Richard. "Butch Cassidy's First Bank Robbery." *Old West*, summer 1995.

———. "Butch Cassidy's 'Peaceful Years'—1889–1894." *True West*, Oct. 1996.

———. "Did the Sundance Kid Take Part in Telluride Robbery?" *The Journal of the Western Outlaw-Lawman History Association*, summer–fall 1994.

———. "The Fine Art of Robbing Trains." *True West*, Apr. 1986.

———. *Historical Atlas of the Outlaw West*. Boulder: Johnson Books, 1985.

———. "How They Railroaded Butch Cassidy into the Wyoming Prison for a $5 Horse." *The Journal of the Western Outlaw-Lawman History Association*, fall–winter 1995.

———. "The Pinkertons and the Train Robbers." *True West*, Aug. 1992.

———. "Splitting Up After Telluride." *The Outlaw Trail Journal*, summer 1996.

———. "Train Robbery." *The American West*, Mar.–Apr. 1977.

———. *Train Robbery: The Birth, Flowering and Decline of a Notorious Western Enterprise*. Boulder: Johnson Books, 1981.

———. *The Train Robbery Era: An Encyclopedic History*. Boulder: Pruett Publishing, 1991.

———. *Wyoming's Outlaw Days*. Boulder: Johnson Books, 1982.

Perkins, Kenneth. "Colorado's Historic Triangle." *True West*, June 1990.

Perkins, Rollin M. *Criminal Law*, 2nd ed. Mineola NY: The Foundation Press, 1960.

Perry, Roger. *Patagonia: Windswept Land of the South*. New York: Dodd, Mead, 1974.

Phillips, William T. *The Bandit Invincible: The Story of the Outlaw Butch Cassidy*. Hamilton MT: Rocky Mountain House Press, 1986.

Pinkerton, William A. *Train Robberies, Train Robbers, and The "Holdup" Men*. Chicago: William A. Pinkerton and Robert A. Pinkerton, 1907. Reprint, New York: Arno Press, 1974.

Pointer, Larry. *In Search of Butch Cassidy*. Norman: University of Oklahoma Press, 1977.

Poll, Richard D., ed. *Utah's History*. Provo UT: Brigham Young University Press, 1978.

Prichard, H. Hesketh. *Through the Heart of Patagonia*. New York: D. Appleton, 1902; (review) *Nation*, Mar. 5, 1903.

Rambler. "The Telluride Bank Holdup." *Shenandoah Tribune* (no date).

Rasch, Philip J. "Death Comes to Saint Johns." *Quarterly of the National Association and Center for Outlaw and Lawman History*, autumn 1982.

Reedstrom, E. Lisle. "The Bandit-Hunter Train." *True West*, Dec. 1990.

Reust, Francis William, and Daniel Davidson. "Daniel Sinclair Parker: Little Known Brother of Butch Cassidy and Friend Rob Southern Wyoming State in December of 1889." *The Frontier Magazine*, Dec. 1995–Jan. 1996.

Reynolds, Franklin. "Winnemucca Bank Robbery." *Frontier Times*, July 1978.

Robinson, James M. "Hay Gatherers on the High Plains." *True West*, Mar. 1982.

Rosa, Joseph G. "Agnes Wright Spring." *The English Westerners' Tally Sheet*, summer 1988.

Sandoval, Judith Hancock. *Historic Ranches of Wyoming*. Lincoln: University of Nebraska Press, 1986.

Scott, William B. "An American's Views of Patagonia." *Review of Reviews*, June 1903.

Selcer, Richard F. *Hell's Half Acre: The Life and Legend of a Red-Light District*. Fort Worth: Texas Christian University Press, 1991.

Settle, William A. Jr. *Jesse James Was His Name*. Columbia: University of Missouri Press, 1966.

Shaw-Lefevre, G. "A Visit to the Argentine Republic." *Nineteenth Century and After*, Nov. 1901.

Silvey, Frank. *History and Settlement of Northern San Juan County*. Moab UT: The Times-Independent, 1990.

Simpson, George Gaylord. *Attending Marvels: A Patagonian Journal*. New York: Time, 1965.

Siringo, Charles A. *A Cowboy Detective: A True Story of Twenty-Two Years with a World-Famous Detective Agency*. Chicago: W. B. Conkey, 1912. Reprint, Lincoln: University of Nebraska Press, 1988.

———. *Riata and Spurs: the Story of a Lifetime Spent in the Saddle as Cowboy and Detective*. Boston: Houghton Mifflin, 1927.

Skovlin, Jon. M. "Old Tom McCarty Names NOLA." *Newsletter of the National Outlaw and Lawman Association*, June 1, 1992.

Slatta, Richard W. *Cowboys of the Americas*. New Haven CT: Yale University Press, 1990.

Smith, Helena Huntington. *The War on Powder River*. New York: McGraw-Hill, 1966.

Spafford, Debbie. "Ann Bassett: 'Queen of the Cattle Rustlers,'" *The Outlaw Trail Journal*, winter–spring, 1992.

Spahr, C. B. "Industrial America: The Ranches of Wyoming." *Outlook*, Oct. 7, 1893.

Spring, Agnes Wright. *Near the Greats*. Frederick CO: Platte'N Press, 1981.

Stegner, Wallace. *Mormon Country*. New York: Buell, Sloan, Pearce, 1942.

Stewart, Arden. "Dad Nearly Rode with Butch." *The Outlaw Trail Journal*, summer 1991.

Stewart, John. "Butch and Sundance Revisited." *Quarterly of the National Association and Center for Outlaw and Lawman History*, Oct.–Dec. 1994.

Stoner, Mary E. "My Father was a Train Robber." *True West*, Aug. 1993.

Sullivan, Mark. *Our Times: The United States 1900–1925*. Vol. 2. New York: Charles Scribner's Sons, 1929.

Sweet, Richard D. "Gramps, Butch Cassidy, and the Black Cat Cafe." *Frontier Times*, Aug.–Sep. 1979.

Tanner, Faun McConkie. *The Far Country: A Regional History of Moab and La Sal, Utah*. 2nd ed. Salt Lake City: Olympus Publishing, 1976.

Taylor, Paul. "Silver Reef: Bastion of Hell in Mormon Utah." *True West*, Jan. 1985.

Van Cott, John W. *Utah Place Names: A Comprehensive Guide to the Origins of Geographic Names*. Salt Lake City: University of Utah Press, 1990.

Vrooman, Harry C. "Crime and the Enforcement of Law." *The Arena*, Apr. 1895.

Walker, Don D. "The Carlisles: Cattle Barons of the Upper Basin." *Utah Historical Quarterly*, summer 1964.

Walker, Gary Lee. "Recollections of the Duchesne Strip." *The Outlaw Trail Journal*, winter–spring 1993.

Walker, Tacetta B. *Stories of Early Days in Wyoming: Big Horn Basin*. Casper: Prairie Publishing, 1936.

Warner, Joyce, and Steve Lacy. "Matt Warner's Daughter Meets Butch Cassidy." *Quarterly of the National Association and Center for Outlaw and Lawman History*, spring 1982.

Warner, Matt (as told to Murray E. King). *The Last of the Bandit Riders*. New York: Bonanza Books, 1938. Reprint 1950.

Webb, William E. "Elton A. Cunningham: A Member of the Wild Bunch." *The Outlaw Trail Journal*, summer 1994.

———. "The Outlaw Trail: The Trail That Never Was." *The Outlaw Trail Journal*, summer–fall 1992.

Wilde, Pat. *Treasured Tidbits of Time*. Vol. 1. Montpelier ID: Wilde, 1977.

Woods, Lawrence M. *British Gentlemen in the Wild West: The Era of the Intensely English Cowboy*. New York: The Free Press, 1989.

Yochelson, Samuel, and Stanton Samenow. *The Criminal Personality*. New York: J. Aronson, 1976.

Zanjani, Sally. *Goldfield: The Last Gold Rush on the Western Frontier*. Athens, OH: Swallow Press/Ohio University Press, 1992.

INDEX